Reflections on Religious Individuality

Religionsgeschichtliche Versuche und Vorarbeiten

Herausgegeben von
Jörg Rüpke und Christoph Uehlinger

Band 62

De Gruyter

Reflections on Religious Individuality

Greco-Roman and Judaeo-Christian Texts and Practices

Edited by
Jörg Rüpke and Wolfgang Spickermann

De Gruyter

ISBN 978-3-11-048797-8
e-ISBN 978-3-11-028678-6
ISSN 0939-2580

Library of Congress Cataloging-in-Publication Data

A CIP catalog record for this book has been applied for at the Library of Congress.

Bibliografische Information der Deutschen Nationalbibliothek

Die Deutsche Nationalbibliothek verzeichnet diese Publikation in der Deutschen Nationalbibliografie; detaillierte bibliografische Daten sind im Internet über http://dnb.dnb.de abrufbar.

© 2012 Walter de Gruyter GmbH & Co. KG, Berlin/Boston

Druck: Hubert & Co. GmbH & Co. KG, Göttingen
∞ Gedruckt auf säurefreiem Papier

Printed in Germany

www.degruyter.com

Contents

Jörg Rüpke, Wolfgang Spickermann
Introduction   1

Individuals and Personhood

Annette Hupfloher
Kultgründungen durch Individuen im klassischen Griechenland   11

Ian H. Henderson, McGill University
'... Hidden with Christ in God' (Colossians 3:3): Modes of
Personhood in Deutero-Pauline Tradition   43

Representative and Charismatic Individuality

Richard Gordon
Representative Individuality in Iamblichus' *De vita pythagorica*   71

Sarah Iles Johnston
Sosipatra and the Theurgic Life: Eunapius *Vitae Sophistorum*
6.6.5–6.9.24   99

Blossom Stefaniw
Gregory Taught, Gregory Written: The effacement and
definition of individualization in the Address to Origen and the
Life of Gregory the Wonderworker   119

Ron Naiweld
The Father of Man: Abraham as the rabbinic Jesus   145

Contents

Reading and Writing

Guy G. Stroumsa
Reading Practices in Early Christianity and the Individualisation
Process 175

Greg Woolf
Reading and Religion in Rome 193

Ulrike Egelhaaf-Gaiser
„Einer jeden Gottheit ihren eigenen Kult": Verbriefte
Individualreligion am *Clitumnus fons* (Plinius *epist.* 8,8) 209

Veit Rosenberger
Four Letter-writers: Religion in Pliny, Trajan, Libanius, and
Julian 247

Index (compiled by Elisa Groff) 261

Introduction

Jörg Rüpke, Wolfgang Spickermann

The research group "Religious individualization in a historical perspective" at the Max Weber Centre (University of Erfurt)[1] intends to investigate *cases of individualization within the medium of religion and their consequences for religious change*, that is, in terms of their religious historical dynamics. In particular, it focuses on the presence and extent of the individual scope for religious action, the resulting forms of religious traditions, and religious reflections on individuality prior, and external to, occidental modernity and during the period of modern theory formation.

"Religious individualization" is an ambiguous term. On the one hand, it refers to the role of religion in the process of individuation. Ancient religions offered ritual forms addressing the individual's status of health problems, they offered support for a variety of existing social bonds and offered new alternatives, they offered concepts and generic forms to reflect about one's self. In many cases, these institutions were part of a primary and secondary socialization, which is at the same time individuation. Consequently, one might ask about the degree of de-traditionalization and of differentiation involved in these processes and offered by these forms. On the other hand, one can ask about the role of individuality in the shaping of religions. Do religious institutions – that is, organisations, rituals, texts, beliefs – accommodate, value or favour individuality? If that is the case, and effects are observable with an eye to the role of religion in individuation processes that value individuality, one can speak of religious individualization. This would not be a statement about religion in general, but about a specific historical, temporal and spatial constellation, a development that can leave permanent traces – in texts, institutions, or historical memory –, but is subject to change and easily open to processes of de-individualization.

---

1   Initiated by Hans Joas and Jörg Rüpke and funded by the German Science Foundation (DFG, KFOR 1013) since 2008 (http://www.uni-erfurt.de/fileadmin/user-docs/Kollegforschergruppe/Proposal_kfg_engl.pdf).

Chronologically, the research group started by analyzing the history of Mediterranean antiquity, concentrating on notions of individuation and religious deviance. Both terms indicate the range of possible questions. To talk about the individual is to focus on actors within a society. In an individual biographical process people learn about their duties and their options, different according to individual capacities, social position, gender, and age. The changing frameworks of such a process, the demands on conformity or individual decision, form important elements in any history of individuality.[2] Individuation is inseparably bound up with socialization, the development of a social persona with individuality. The concept of individuation, the development of personal self-identity, would hardly be separable from social functionality in integration for ancient thinkers. However, it can be used for historical analysis to map the possible fields of developing different types and degrees of individuality in religion, to look for opportunities offered by religions for increasing individual differences and spaces of action not defined by traditions, and to subsequently ask for the consequences of religious institutions and practices for the persons involved.[3]

If de-traditionalization is an important indicator of individuality, cases of deviant behaviour might help to identify the boundaries set against de-traditionalized behaviour as well as identify behaviour, which is not simply the ignoring or transgressing of norms, but is the developing of new ways of honouring the gods, for instance. In considering deviance, infringements on the norm, we can identify actual variations of religious behavior. How much room was there for religious individuality in antiquity? Must we question the common assumption of the collective character of pre-modern religions? But the individual is only one end of this journey, since regarding deviance also raises normative debates which try to limit or enable variations: Who established these positions? How were they enforced? Whatever there may have been in terms of individual religiosity, it happened within a communal, sometimes even rigorous framework. And yet, the ancient sources, especially normative texts, rendering judgments in any way, do not only shed light on this normative framework, granting access only to intellectual and upper class deferral and polemic. These texts also allow for a view of a – to speak with Michel de Certeau – wholly different, con-

---

2   See e.g. GIARDINA 1989.
3   RÜPKE 2013 (forthcoming).

torted, overreaching acquisition of norms by individuals, even if these remain anonymous.[4]

The present volume will concentrate its search for religious individuality on texts and practices related to texts. The creation of texts offers opportunities to express one's own religious experience and shape one's own religious personality – within the boundaries of what is acceptable in specific situations and genres. Inscriptions in public or at least easily accessible spaces might substantially differ in their range of expressions and topics from letters within a sectarian religious group (which, at the same time, might put enormous pressure of conformity on its members, regarded as deviant by a majority of contemporaries). Furthermore, texts might offer and advocate new practices in reading, meditating on, remembering, or repeating these very texts. Such practices might contribute to the development of religious individuality, experienced or expressed in factual isolation, responsibility, competition, and finally in philosophical or theological reflections about "personhood" or "self". It is for the latter, that the central role of what we term "religion" is evident.[5] The words of Patricia Cox Miller, referring to late antiquity, could easily be generalized: "Orienting the self in relation to the divine remained a constant. Rather, the shift involved a change in view of the soul's ability to make contact with god or gods."[6]

What is "individuality"? First of all, we are talking of differences between and distinctiveness of persons. Such terms imply that individuality is not a purely descriptive term but has to be related to discourse and practical constraints. As such, it would not be fruitful to analyze whether "religious individuality" is given in a specific situation or person. Many phenomena – ritual innovations, unusual combinations of gods addressed in prayers, spectacular buildings or tombs – might indicate individuality and are results of local or trans-regional traditions at the same time. Thus, it is preferable to regard individuality as a heuristic method to analyze the relationship between structures, norms, and opportunities on the one hand, and the individual agent on the other. For heuristic purposes, however, it is adequate to identify *different types* of individuality,[7] rather than measure different phenomena on a *unified scale* of "individuality". Jörg Rüpke has proposed to differentiate five types of in-

4   RÜPKE 2011.
5   BRAKKE, SATLOW, WEITZMAN 2005, 3.
6   MILLER 2005, 31.
7   Cf. the "dimensions" listed by KIPPELE 1997, ch. 9.

dividuality, which are not necessarily co-related and which he termed practical, moral, competitive, representative, and reflexive individuality. Such a typology enables us to distinguish consequences of the rupture of family bonds by death, travelling, or temporary social displacements ("pragmatic") from the ascription and acceptance of responsibility for one's own deeds ("moral"). Elite competition in its manifold facets ("competitive") could be taken into account as the formulation of biographies and yard sticks of individual performances that are regarded as "representative", put into practice in different degrees by different individuals. Finally it seemed important not to make the identification of such types of individuality dependent on accompanying reflections about individuality in literary and philosophical discourse.[8] This idea is taken up and further developed by some contributors of this volume, first proposed at a conference held at the Max Weber Centre in March 2010.

The volume begins with two chapters which map the wide range of "texts and practices". First, an analysis of individual cult foundations by private persons from the fifth century BC to the first century AD. Starting with a glance on Xenophon's sanctuary for Ephesian Artemis at Skillous, Annette Hupfloher describes several cases of individuals introducing new gods, for instance the establishment and embellishment of a sanctuary for the Nymphs and Pan at Vari by a certain Archedamos. As told by inscriptions, it is individual religious experience which led to the foundation, the forms of which are rather traditional. Artemidoros' sanctuary on the island of Thera is another famous case of a former immigrant establishing step by step a highly complex and highly individual religious cult location (thus interesting himself in local security). In a diachronic analysis religious innovation and its textual elements are shown to be an instrument open to local citizens, women, and immigrants. It opens considerable space for individual action and expression and is as important for the classical period as it is for the Hellenistic.

Ian Henderson's analysis of the Pseudo-Paulinian letter to the Colossians remains in the Greek world of the Eastern Mediterranean, but addresses a text that cannot be analyzed in terms of the author's social position. Using the concept of a "reflective ideology of individuality", Henderson identifies a particular economy of pseudepigraphy that is used to develop the anthropological argument about individuality and modifies Pauline eschatology. The collective character of the church

---

8   Rüpke 2013, introduction.

and the ethical dimension of social life are inseparably bound up with the believer's embodied individuality. It is the text and the relationship to Christ promoted by the text which constructs a central Christian concept of personhood.

Representative and charismatic individuality are concepts employed in the second group of chapters. Richard Gordon analyzes representative individuality in a text from the turn of the third to the fourth century AD, Iamblichus' *De vita pythagorica*. He argues that Pythagoras is viewed as a model for a certain type of individuality, an optional alternative to traditional forms of competitive individuality, to the effect that the acquisition of symbolic capital by a part of the educated élite of the Roman Empire could be extended from external prestige, institutionalized power and modes of display to include forms of moral distinction, with an emphasis on hard labour and constant effort.

Sarah Iles Johnston employs the fourth century philosopher Sosipatra and her Theurgic Life based on the description of her life in Eunapius' *Vitae Sophistorum* 6.6.5–6.9.24. She shows that Sosipatra is intended to serve as model for the individual private and religious life to Eunapius' readers, an ideal to which the average person might aspire, but is seldom achieved. That is why Eunapius has awarded her a prominent place in his narrative. She is the ideal Iamblichean theurgist, her passivity of both body and soul actually being a *desideratum*. In this regard, Sosipatra is interpreted as the most highly accomplished theurgist about whom we read in the *Lives* of Eunapius and, indeed, in any ancient source.

The contribution of Blossom Stefaniw: "Working Wonders with Gregory and Gregory: Effacement and definition of individualization from the third to the fourth century" compares the panegyric farewell address of Gregory Thaumaturgus to Origen around AD 242 and Gregory of Nyssa's panegyrical biography from AD 380 to trace religious change from the early third to the late fourth century by examining shifts in the scope for, and form of, individualization, or its opposite, concentrating on the religious activities of one person. Stefaniw observes that Gregory of Nyssa is able to force religious change (at least in the rhetorical realm) in a way that was unthinkable for the young Gregory of Thaumaturgus and proves a massive increase in scope for individualization, a "continuity of the wonder-working sleight of hand involved in effacing and defining individualization at the same time, but also a displacement of the realm in which such projects can take effect".

Ron Naiweld analyzes the use of the figure of Abraham as a model for the individual moral life of a holy man by Palestinian rabbis in the context of Jewish-Christian polemic in the turn of the sixth century. Abraham's fighting against personal desires in order to accomplish God's Law and to fulfill God's divine program by taking onto himself the sins of past and future generations, paints him as a counterpart to Jesus Christ. Just like Christ, Abraham radically modifies the relationship between God and the world; and just like Christ, Abraham is regarded as the person whose life should serve as a model for everyone who wishes to lead a moral life.

The third group of contributions is entitled "Reading and Writing" and includes the individual reception and composition of texts. The article of Guy Stroumsa "Reading practices in late antique Christianity and the individualization process" argues that eastern monks were responsible for a new attitude to books that had much to do with the individualization process, and which would eventually permit and even embody the late antique cultural and religious transformation. Stroumsa points out that the Christian ascetic movement, culminating in the birth and rapid growth of monasticism in the Near East and from there to other parts of the Empire, represents one of the most striking aspects of a religious revolution, which finds its epitome in the end of sacrifice in the fourth century AD. The reading of Scripture in monastic communities had a purpose entirely different from the one ordinarily attributed to reading: the transmission of knowledge. The aim of the constant repetition of a text known by heart was not the production of any new wisdom. This activity was rather soteriological in essence: it was meant as a technical method for the concentration of the mind of the individual, a way of praying Scripture, so that the Word of God may directly find a way into heart and mind.

Additionally, Greg Woolf asks why reading figures so little as a ritualized form of self-fashioning in Roman religious practices of earlier ages. He argues that the reading practices of Roman Christians in late antiquity developed out of the reading cultures of the early empire. When Christianity began to be attractive to members of those very select social classes which practiced reading during the early empire, that inheritance increased in importance, as self-fashioning through reflective reading had been a prominent part of Roman imperial intellectual life.

Ulrike Egelhaaf-Gaiser examines the description of the source of Clitumnus in Umbria in the eighth letter of Pliny (8,8), and interpretes it as a pattern for individual religion. Although Pliny's description mentions many small sanctuaries of local gods, Clitumnus is described as the main deity and his old traditional temple represents the center of the site. With his mention of numerous inscriptions upon pillars and walls by different persons, celebrating the virtues of the fountain, and the divinity that presides over it, Pliny ascribes to the graffiti as communication media an even greater virtue for the literate reader. What the graffiti are lacking in formal aesthetics, they gain in individual authenticity: Their minimal material value is compensated for by a significant ideal and individual statement.

Veit Rosenberger (Erfurt) presents letters of Pliny, Trajan, Libanius and Julian as a helpful medium in the search for traces of religious 'individualization' or 'individuation' in antiquity. While Pliny, Trajan and Libanius do not offer insight into their religious experience, Julian is different: he talks about how the gods ordered him to act and about his religious practices; he gives information about his concept of religion on the discursive level. His philosophical influences, e.g. Iamblichus and Libanius, do not show such decided individualization, because they lack the ambitious plans and motives of the emperor. Rosenberger emphasizes that we have strong reasons to believe that individualization gained immensely in momentum with the rise of Christianity.

Finally we would like to thank Marcus Hellwing and Ulrike Frenzel for their support in the editing of this volume, Diana Püschel, who had had the organizational burder of the conference, for continuous help.

Bibliography

BRAKKE, DAVID et al. (ed.) 2005. *Religion and the self in antiquity*. Bloomington, Ind.: Indiana Univ. Press.

GIARDINA, ANDREA (ed.) 1989. *L'uomo romano*. Roma: Laterza.

KIPPELE, FLAVIA 1997. *Was heißt Individualisierung? Die Antworten der soziologischen Klassiker*. Opladen: Westdeutscher Verlag.

MILLER, PATRICIA COX 2005. "Shifting Selves in Late Antiquity." In: D. Brakke, M. L. Satlow and S. Weitzman (eds.), *Religion and the self in antiquity*. Bloomington, Ind.: Indiana Univ. Press: 15–39.

RÜPKE, JÖRG 2011. *Aberglauben oder Individualität? Religiöse Abweichung im römischen Reich*. Tübingen: Mohr Siebeck.

RÜPKE, JÖRG (ed.) 2013 (forthcoming). *The Individual in the Religions of the Ancient Mediterranean* Oxford: Oxford Univ. Press.

Individuals and Personhood

Kultgründungen durch Individuen im klassischen Griechenland

Annette Hupfloher

1 Xenophon

Als Xenophon, der bekannte Schriftsteller, Zeitgenosse des Sokrates und Platon, in den 390er Jahren mit reicher Beute vom Kriegszug der „Zehntausend" zurückkam und, aus Athen verbannt, sich in der Nähe von Olympia niederließ, gründete er eine Kultstätte für die Göttin Artemis von Ephesos.[1] Er kaufte in Skillous ein großes Grundstück, das Agrarflächen und ein Jagdrevier umfasste; er ließ Tempel, Altar und Kultbild für diese Artemis errichten und versuchte, mit dem so entstandenen Kultbezirk den größeren und berühmteren in Ephesos im kleinen nachzubilden; mit Geld aus der Kriegsbeute richtete er eine Vermögensstiftung ein, deren Erträge zu zehn Prozent für das jährliche Opferfest für die Göttin und zur Erhaltung des Tempels bestimmt waren. Die ansässige Bevölkerung wurde zur Teilnahme am Jahresfest geladen und wird wohl freudig teilgenommen haben, da frisches Wildbret, Fleisch vom Schlachtopfer, Gerstenkuchen, Brot, Wein und Süßigkeiten dabei kostenlos verteilt wurden. Diese Zustimmung vorausgesetzt, ist dennoch zu fragen, wie es möglich war, dass ein reicher Ausländer aus Athen in der kleinen Ortschaft Skillous im Hinterland von Olympia auf der Peloponnes Grund erwarb und eine neue Kultstätte für eine bislang dort wohl nicht verehrte Göttin[2] einrichtete.

Die übliche Forschungsmeinung deckt diesen Fall nicht ab: sie rechnet damit, dass zum Landerwerb von Nichtbürgern auch in kleinen Städten des antiken Griechenland eine Genehmigung der örtlichen Be-

---

1 Xen. *an.* 5,3,5–13 mit LENDLE 1995, 321–322.
2 Repliken des ‚vielbrüstigen' Bildes der Artemis von Ephesos streuen weit: vgl. generell FLEISCHER 1973; auf der Peloponnes gab es Statuen und Kultstätten dieser Göttin in der römischen Kaiserzeit in Megalopolis (Paus. 8,30,3), Alea (Paus. 8,23,1) und Korinth (Paus. 2,2,6).

hörden erteilt werden musste,[3] dass neue Götter und Kulte nur auf kollektiven Beschluss der Bürger hin eingeführt werden durften,[4] dass das Bürgerrecht antiker Poleis ein streng gehütetes Gut war, das selten nur und als Gegenleistung für große Verdienste an Ortsfremde vergeben wurde.[5] Diese legalistische Sichtweise basiert auf umfangreichen Quellenbeständen aus dem klassischen Athen einerseits und auf Inschriften hellenistischer Zeit andererseits, wo in Bürgerrechtsverleihungen und Isopolitieverträgen solche Rechte oft zugesprochen wurden.[6] Generalisierungen auf der Basis von Einzelfällen tragen in diesem Punkte jedoch nicht, da die antiken Poleis autonom waren und dementsprechend die Aktionsmöglichkeiten des Einzelnen je nach Ort, Umständen und sozialem Kontext stark variieren konnten.

Ob Xenophon, der Athener in Skillous, aufgrund seiner ökonomischen Lage und seines Sozialprestige das Bürgerrecht der Kleinstadt erhalten hat oder nur das Recht, Land zu erwerben, ob er die Volksversammlung vom Nutzen und Vorteil eines neuen Tempelbezirkes überzeugen konnte – all dies ist möglich und denkbar; er drückt es in dem Text, der die Situation überliefert, nicht aus. Dieser autobiographische Text[7] ist für die Einschätzung der Handlungsspielräume und Erlebniswelten von Individuen dennoch höchst interessant. Er ist autobiographisch, obwohl in der dritten Person verfasst, denn der Autor hat den Rahmentext, die Anabasis, unter einem Pseudonym[8] veröffentlicht, das bereits in der Antike aufgedeckt wurde. Wie jeder Text ist auch dieser interessengeleitet, und so wird gerade auch dem Abschnitt, der die Kulteinrichtung in Skillous schildert, von der Literaturwissenschaft apologetische Tendenz zugeschrieben:[9] Der Autor wolle dem Vorwurf entgegenarbeiten, er sei mit seinem Anteil aus der Kriegsbeute nicht den Regeln entsprechend umgegangen. Dies könnte erklären, warum die Schilderung der Kulteinrichtung so ausführlich und detailreich ist. Für uns bietet Xenophons Text gerade durch seinen Detailreichtum die Gelegenheit, Anlass, Motivation und Vorgehen bei einer Kultgründung

---

3   THALHEIM 1905; GAWANDKA 1976.
4   So etwa GARLAND 1992, 18–20; AUFFARTH 1995, 348. Dagegen KRAUTER 2004, 239.
5   PATTERSON 1981; OSBORNE 1981–1983; BLOK 2007.
6   Vgl. auch KRAUTER 2004, 53–54.
7   Hg. und Kommentar von W. MÜRI 1990.
8   Nach MÜRI 1990, 493: Xen. *an.* 3,1,2; Plut. *mor* 345 e.
9   MÜRI 1990, 494–495.

auf Einzelinitiative bemerkenswert genau zu sehen und intensiv studieren zu können.

Das Geld für die Vermögensstiftung stammt aus Kriegsbeute (Xen. *an.* 5,3,4): Zehn Prozent des Erlöses aus dem Verkauf von Kriegsgefangenen, die man nach dem ‚Zug der Zehntausend' in Kleinasien gemacht hatte, legten die Feldherren als Geld für Votive beiseite. Der Anteil des Xenophon ging zum einen nach Delphi, wo er ein namentlich beschriftetes Weihgeschenk für Apollon aufstellen ließ (5,3,5), zum anderen nach Skillous, wo er, mittlerweile aus Athen geflüchtet und von den Gegnern der Athener, den Lakedaimoniern (Spartanern), offenbar mit einem Landgut ausgestattet, die Kultstätte für Artemis von Ephesos gründete. Dass diese bewusst als eine kleine Replik des großen und berühmten Artemisheiligtums in Ephesos gestaltet wurde, geht wohl darauf zurück, dass Xenophon bei dem Kriegszug in Kleinasien das Vorbild besucht und das Geld aus der Kriegsbeute dort vorübergehend eingelagert hatte.[10] Als der Kultgründer konnte er die Gottheit der neuen Kultstätte bestimmen. Auch die Festlegung der Regeln für die Bewirtschaftung des offenbar großen Kultbezirkes lag bei ihm: jährlich sollten wiederum zehn Prozent der Erträge aus Obstgarten und Landwirtschaft für das Opferfest verwendet werden und Überschüsse daraus zur Erhaltung des Tempels bestimmt sein. Die Regeln wurden inschriftlich fixiert und ergeben so eine *lex sacra* − hier literarisch überliefert, später von einem antiken Xenophon-Fan auf Ithaka auf Stein repliziert.[11]

Gut sichtbar ist das religiös gebundene Vorgehen des Stifters: wer eine Kultstätte errichten will, lässt den Gott durch Los oder Orakelauskunft eine geeignete Stelle aussuchen;[12] die so gefundene Lokation stimmt dann in einigen Elementen überein mit dem kleinasiatischen Vorbild (5,3,7−8); so werden überregionale Zusammenhänge konstruiert. Weitere Übereinstimmungen werden bewusst geschaffen, indem das Bild der Gottheit und die Form des Tempels ähnlich wie in Ephesos gestaltet werden (5,3,12). Deutlich ist das Bemühen, das Vorbild nachzuahmen, ausgesprochen wird aber auch das Bewusstsein, dass eine vollständige Replik in ländlicher, abgelegener Lage und mit begrenzten finanziellen Mitteln nicht möglich ist (5,3,13). Die Ritualpraxis in Skillous wirkt denn auch einigermaßen konventionell und reflektiert einen eher allgemeinen

---

10   Zur Bankfunktion von Heiligtümern: vgl. Rosenberger 2002, 128.

11   IG 9,654 aus dem 2. Jh. v. Chr. Zu *leges sacrae* vgl. Parker 2004.

12   5,3,7 : theos − die maskuline Form weist auf Apollon von Delphi, in dessen Heiligtum ein anderer Teil der Kriegsbeute geweiht worden war.

Begriff von der Göttin Artemis als Göttin der Jagd und des Waldes als einen spezifisch ephesischen. Das jährliche Opferfest vereinte die Gründerfamilie, in Skillous Ansässige und Nachbarn (5,3,9) zu einem Festmahl, das allenfalls durch seinen Wildbretanteil aus dem sonst Üblichen herausragt. Der neugegründete Kult wurde den lokalen Verhältnissen wie auch den Familienverhältnissen (5,3,10) des Gründers angepasst. Dass die Jahresfeste öffentliche Bankette enthielten, dürfte die Bürger, die Rat- oder Volksversammlung von Skillous motiviert haben, nicht gegen den neuen Kult zu opponieren.

2 Forschungslage, Überlieferung und Methodik

Kultgründungen sind von den Altertumswissenschaften bisher nur selten und ausschnittweise thematisiert worden; Büchertitel wie „Introducing New Gods"[13] focusieren auf der kollektiven Ebene der antiken Polisgesellschaften, sie untersuchen Erweiterungen des *städtischen* Götter- und Kultspektrums[14] und fahnden ebenda nach den Ursachen. Aufgrund der Quellenlage konzentrieren sich solche Arbeiten oft auf weithin bekannte, gut dokumentierte Verhältnisse wie Athen, wo im fünften Jahrhundert v. Chr. etwa Pan, Bendis und Asklepios eingeführt wurden, oder Rom, wo man zu Beginn des dritten Jahrhunderts v. Chr. Aesculapius kommen ließ, um 200 v. Chr. dann Magna Mater und Venus Erycina. Andererseits hat das Phänomen in Form der Frage nach Kultübertragungen[15] und Reliquientranslationen mit nachfolgender Gründung von Kultstätten in der vorchristlichen Antike eine gewisse Aufmerksamkeit erregt; auf diese Weise können Diffusionsprozesse studiert werden: die Ausbreitung des Asklepioskultes seit dem fünften Jahrhundert v. Chr. oder des Isis- und Sarapiskultes seit dem dritten Jahrhundert v. Chr.[16] Fragt man hingegen nach den Agenten solcher Prozesse und nach den konkreten Abläufen bei der Verbreitung der Kulte, so zeigt sich schnell, dass Individuen als Kultgründer oft und deutlich fassbar sind, besser sogar als soziale oder politisch verfasste Gruppen. Vor allem durch epigraphisches und ar-

13 GARLAND 1992, vgl. auch AUFFARTH 1995.
14 PIRENNE-DELFORGE 2000.
15 SCHMIDT 1909.
16 Asklepios: WACHT 1998; RIETHMÜLLER 2005 (mit Focusierung auf die Frühzeit des Asklepioskultes in Griechenland); MELFI 2007; Isis- und Serapis: VIDMAN 1970; BOMMAS 2004.

chäologisches Material sind etliche Fälle bekannt, in denen einzelne Personen als Gründer und Gestalter von Kultstätten wirkten. Oft sind es die inscribierten Texte von Votiven, die einen Hinweis darauf geben, dass der Errichter des Votives zugleich der Initiator des Kultes war und diejenige Person ist, die ein Interesse an der Perpetuierung desselben hatte.

Ich habe eine Liste solcher Fälle zusammengestellt und versuche nun, diese im Zusammenhang zu untersuchen und systematisch organisierte Fragen anzulegen: Welche Personen waren in der Lage, selbständig Kultstätten zu gründen und auszustatten, welcher Statusgruppe und Gesellschaftsschicht gehörten sie an? Welche Umstände der Kultgründung sind in diesen Texten zu erkennen, und welcher Bezug bestand zur Polisebene? Solche Untersuchungen wurde bisher nur unter anderer Focusierung unternommen: B. LAUM[17] hat schon zu Beginn des zwanzigsten Jahrhunderts die inschriftlich überlieferten Stiftungstexte zusammengestellt und systematisch analysiert; dabei ging es um Vermögensstiftungen verschiedenen Zweckes, wobei die religiösen Stiftungen generell nur einen sehr kleinen Teil einnehmen[18] und Kultgründungen abseits des Grabbrauches nur am Rande vorkommen. Die testamentarisch verfügte Errichtung von Grabkulten zur Heroisierung von Privatpersonen ist ab der hellenistischen Zeit häufig überliefert, aber für die hier verfolgte Fragestellung nur insofern interessant, als sie ebenfalls religiöse Aktionsmöglichkeiten von Individuen und Familien[19] aufzeigen. Eine neuere Arbeit von B. DIGNAS[20] focusiert mit dem Titel „How to found a cult? Epigraphical manifestations" in einem verwandten Untersuchungsgebiet und verzeichnet gegenüber Laum zahlreiche Neufunde von einschlägigen Inschriften, zeigt aber auch, dass gerade bei den Stiftungsinschriften hellenistischer Zeit oft nicht festzustellen ist, ob es sich um die Neugründung einer Kultstätte handelt oder um eine Vermögensstiftung zugunsten eines bereits bestehenden Kultes. Beides, die testamentarische Stiftung wie auch die finanzielle Dauerförderung einer bestehenden Kultstätte mittels einer Vermögensstifung zu Lebzeiten, ist hier nicht das Ziel der Untersuchung, denn die Focusierung auf solche Fälle führt dazu, hauptsächlich die Aktivitäten vermögender Familien hellenistischer Zeit in den Blick zu nehmen; vielmehr gilt es gezielt auch

---

17 LAUM 1914.
18 LAUM 1914, 60–87; zu den rechtlichen Aspekten vgl. MANNZMANN 1962; zu drei Gründungen klassischer Zeit vgl. PURVIS 2003.
19 Vgl. GRAF 1995, 112: „eine neue Form des Geschlechterkultes".
20 DIGNAS (2007), Hinweis von W. Spickermann.

danach zu fragen, ob abseits des oberschichtlichen Stiftungsbrauches, der in hellenistischer Zeit so häufig überliefert ist, und der sich bei Xenophon schon in klassischer Zeit feststellen lässt, Kultgründungen durch Individuen der Mittel- und Unterschichten nachweisbar sind.

3 Archedamos in Vari, Pantalkes bei Pharsalos

Das folgende Beispiel überliefert einen solchen Fall aus dem südlichen Attika: Dort, in der Karstlandschaft des Hymettosgebirges, wurde ab der Mitte des fünften Jahrhunderts v. Chr. eine natürliche Höhle und ihre Umgebung von einem Mann namens Archedamos zu einer Kultstätte für die Nymphen, für den Hirtengott Pan, für Apollon und einige andere Gottheiten ausgebaut. In der Höhle[21] wurden Götterbilder und Altäre teils aus dem anstehenden Fels herausgearbeitet, teils mittels Verzapfungen auf Stufen und Simsen befestigt. An den Wänden sind Reliefs und Inschriften zu erkennen, die dem Gestalter und Ausstatter der Kultstätte zuzurechnen sind, der hier über längere Zeit, wohl einige Jahrzehnte lang tätig war: *Archedamos ho Theraios*[22] steht auch neben einer Figur, die ungelenk einen Bildhauer mit erhobenem Werkzeug wiedergibt und die daher wohl als ein Selbstporträt des Archedamos einzuordnen ist.

Archedamos ist, das zeigt seine Namensform (Absenz von Patronymikon und Demotikon) deutlich, kein attischer Bürger, sondern stammt aus Thera (der Kykladeninsel Santorini) oder aus einer Ortschaft namens Therai auf der Peloponnes.[23] Die Inschriften verraten aber noch mehr über die Person des Gestalters und die Ausstattung der Kultstätte – er stattete in der zweiten Hälfte des fünften Jahrhunderts nicht nur die Höhle mit Kulteinrichtungen aus, sondern legte „für die Nymphen" auch einen Garten an,[24] der wohl außerhalb der Höhle lag und von einer Quelle gespeist wurde, die heute nicht mehr zu lokalisieren ist.[25] Einer der spätesten Texte des Ensembles[26] bezeichnet Archedamos als *nympholep-*

---

21 WICKENS 1986, II 90–110; 169; SCHÖRNER / GOETTE 2004; BAUMER 2004, 18–
    20; 108–109.
22 IG I³ 978; 977 Z.1.
23 Vgl. LARSON 2001, 243.
24 IG I³ 977.
25 Letzter Hinweis auf Wasser in der Höhle: KÄSTNER 1953 (1974), 91.
26 IG I³ 980; die Datierung dieser Texte ist schwierig und beruht ausschließlich auf
    den Buchstabenformen: HALLOF 2004, 42–59.

tos[27] – als von den Nymphen Hingerissenen oder Begeisterten – und sagt, er habe auf Geheiß der Nymphen die Höhle gestaltet. Wir entnehmen daraus, dass ein religiöses Erlebnis der Anlass für die Aktivitäten des Archedamos war, und dass es dabei primär um die Nymphen ging.[28] Ein Immigrant ohne attisches Bürgerrecht schuf sich so eine Kultstätte, die er selbst über längere Zeit nutzen konnte. Archedamos war nicht der einzige Nutzer, auch dies zeigt das archäologische Material deutlich, und er war vielleicht nicht der erste Nutzer oder gar der Entdecker der Höhle, denn eine Inschrift auf einem losen Stein, der in der Höhle gefunden wurde, ist zeitlich früher anzusetzen: ein Votivtext, der von einem „Ziegenhirten des Skyron für die Nymphen"[29] selbst angefertigt (Nagelritzung) und aufgestellt wurde. Dies dürfte ein Abhängiger, wohl ein Sklave, eines Mannes namens Skyron gewesen sein. Eine Forschungskontroverse dreht sich um die Frage, ob aufgrund dieses Textes Archedamos überhaupt als der Gründer (*ktistes*) des Nymphenheiligtums anzusprechen ist[30] und ob er dort vielleicht auch einen Gründerkult nach dem Vorbild der Koloniegründer erhalten haben könnte (heroisiert worden sei). Letzteres ist unwahrscheinlich und jedenfalls aufgrund der Zeugnisse in Vari nicht zu erhärten. Die Nutzungsgeschichte[31] der von Archedamos ausgestatteten Höhle ist lang und von Unterbrechungen gekennzeichnet. Auch wenn dieser von den Nymphen begeisterte Mann nicht der erste Nutzer gewesen sein sollte, so war er doch der maßgebliche Gestalter[32] des Kultbezirkes in klassischer Zeit. Anders sind die Texte und Bilder an den Höhlenwänden nicht zu erklären. Die Nymphenhöhle von Vari zog zur Zeit des Archedamos und danach weitere Besucher und Kultteilnehmer an: dies ist deutlich abzulesen an den vielen Fragmenten von Tonvotiven

---

27 Zur Nympholepsie vgl. HIMMELMANN-WILDSCHÜTZ 1957; CONNOR 1988; LARSON 2001, 13–18.

28 Die Kultanlage trägt in der Forschung die Bezeichnung „Pangrotte", was die Behandlung historisch-genetischer Aspekte oft auf eine Diskussion der Einführung des Pankultes in Attika (Hdt. 6,105) verengt: vgl. etwa WICKENS 1986, I 169; BAUMER 2004, 20.

29 IG I³ 974. HALLOF 2004, 55.

30 HIMMELMANN-WILDSCHÜTZ 1957, 10 „eine Art *ktistes*"; SCHÖRNER / GOETTE 2004, 118 (contra Himmelmann).

31 Es gibt Spuren profaner Nutzung in helladischer Zeit, Streufunde aus der Archaik, fundlose Zeitabschnitte in Hellenismus und Kaiserzeit, ein Wiedereinsetzen religiöser Nutzungsspuren in der hohen Kaiserzeit und in der Spätantike (Münzen, Öllampen): vgl. SCHÖRNER / GOETTE 2004, 107–110; BAUMER 2004, 18.

32 So auch SCHÖRNER / GOETTE 2004, 118; BAUMER 2004, 20.

und Keramikgefäßen, die in der Höhle gefunden wurden, und auch an
einer inschriftlich fixierten Vorschrift für das Verhalten der Kultteilnehmer, die festlegt, dass „die Eingeweide draußen ausgespült"[33] werden
sollten: Fleischopfer konnten also in der Höhle präsentiert, verteilt, ab-
gelegt oder verzehrt (?) werden, während die mit der Schlachtung verbundenen, Unrat produzierenden Tätigkeiten im Freien stattfinden
sollten. Die Raumorganisation bei der Höhle folgt also dem in antiken
griechischen Kultstätten üblichen Muster. Über die Riten in solchen
ländlichen Heiligtümern von Nymphen und Pan ist einiges bekannt:
Schlachtopfer sind dabei nicht durchgehend üblich, sondern eher die
Ausnahme, zumindest im Nymphenkult.[34] Für die Feste bei Pan und den
Nymphen in Attika sind Tänze und ausgelassenes Treiben mit Gesang
und Klatschen per Analogie zu erschließen,[35] während über den Besuch
von ‚Individualpilgern', die außerhalb der Festzeiten kamen, wenig
Spezifisches zu erfahren ist, das etwa über die Gangrichtung in der
Höhle[36] hinausgeht; diese ist einerseits durch ihre natürliche Form, andererseits durch die künstlich geschaffenen Zurichtungen festgelegt. Die
Details der Votiverrichtung, die damit verbundenen Handlungen (Gebete, performative Akte etc.), sind für uns hier unsichtbar. Über die
Personen hingegen, die beschriftete Votive hinterließen, ist vergleichs-
weise viel zu erfahren: bei den durch Graffiti namentlich gekennzeich-
neten Tongefäßen sind Frauen und Männer klassischer Zeit fassbar[37] und
im vierten Jahrhundert (nach der für Archedamos erschlossenen Lebenszeit) wurden etliche wertvolle Votivreliefs von männlichen[38] Kult-
teilnehmern aufgestellt; sie zeigen die für solche Höhlen einschlägige
Thematik, was die Bilderwelt angeht (Nymphen, Hermes, Pan) und
wurden von attischen Bürgern und von Sklaven, teils auch von Stifter-
gemeinschaften errichtet.[39] G. SCHÖRNER bemerkt in einer zusammenfassenden Analyse dieser Votive, dass die qualitätvollsten Stücke von
Einzelpersonen errichtet wurden, während die zwei von Personen-

---

33 IG I³ 982 mit HALLOF 2004, 44–45.
34 Vgl. VAN STRATEN 1995, 90; SCHÖRNER / GOETTE 2004, 113 A. 560.
35 Siehe etwa die Texte aus Pharsalos, SEG 1, 247–248; LARSON 2001, 17;
    SCHÖRNER / GOETTE 2004, 113.
36 SCHÖRNER / GOETTE 2004, 112–113.
37 SCHÖRNER / GOETTE 2004, 113; 96–97 (Frauennamen).
38 Ein Personenname der Liste, Soteris, konnte für Männer und für Frauen ver-
    wendet werden. SCHÖRNER / GOETTE 2004, 65 R 3 (Ath. NM inv. 2009); 67
    Anm. 380; 76.
39 SCHÖRNER / GOETTE 2004, 60–77.

gruppen gestifteten Exemplare von geringerer handwerklicher Qualität, also wohl preisgünstiger zu bekommen waren.[40] Dies ist vor allem hinsichtlich eines Votivreliefs (jetzt im Athener Nationalmuseum, inv. 2009)[41] von Interesse, das mindestens dreizehn Personen gemeinsam aufstellen ließen, die nach Ausweis ihrer Namen (Herkunftsbezeichnungen wie Thrax und Phryx) wahrscheinlich Sklaven[42] waren. Dies schlägt einen Bogen zurück zu dem Ziegenhirten des Skyron, den seine soziale Position als Abhängiger dazu brachte, sich in seinem Votivtext über die Person seines Herrn zu definieren.

Wo aber ist Archedamos sozial zu situieren? Er war sicherlich nicht sehr vermögend, verfügte zwar über eine grundlegende Bildung und Literalität, nicht aber über eine handwerkliche Ausbildung als Bildhauer – dazu sind die Ausarbeitungen im Fels einschließlich des Selbstporträts zu laienhaft ausgeführt. Er war kein attischer Bürger, wohnte abseits des politischen Geschäftes, das sich in den Unterabteilungen der attischen Bürgerschaft (Phylen, Demen, auch Phratrien) und in den Rats- und Volksversammlungen Athens abspielte, und dürfte in der Landwirtschaft oder im Handwerk tätig gewesen sein; dabei blieb offenbar genügend Zeit für religiöse Imagination und für die Ausgestaltung der Höhle als eine Kultstätte. Sein rechtlicher Status könnte der eines Metöken gewesen sein, doch ist unklar, ob im fünften Jahrhundert dies bereits eine fest definierte Statuskategorie war, die auf Registrierung der ansässigen Fremden in Athen beruhte und die Steuerpflicht einschloss.[43] So ist hinsichtlich der Person des Archedamos wenig mehr als „soziale Marginalität" festzustellen, die eventuell durch seine individuell konstruierte Rolle im religiösen Bereich als Nymphenbegeisterter (*nympholeptos*) und als Gestalter eines umfangreichen Kultbezirkes kompensiert wurde.

Persönliche Präferenzen und biographische Bezüge sind dabei für uns aufgrund der Besonderheit der archäologischen Überlieferung weniger gut zu erkennen als bei Xenophon in Skillous, wo der autobiographische Text die Motivation des Autors, die zur Auswahl der Göttin Artemis von Ephesos führte, zu rekonstruieren erlaubt. Bei Archedamos in Vari war persönliches religiöses Erleben der Ausgangspunkt für die Ausarbeitung und Nutzung der Kulthöhle, ihre Ausstattung, soweit sie überdauert hat, unterscheidet sich aber kaum von anderen Kultstätten: Götterbilder,

---

40 SCHÖRNER / GOETTE 2004, 76.
41 SCHÖRNER / GOETTE 2004, 64 R 3.
42 SCHÖRNER / GOETTE 2004, 67.
43 WHITEHEAD 1977, 141–147.

Altäre, Votive. Auch die Götterkombination (Nymphen und Chariten, Pan, Hermes, Apollon,[44] wohl auch Kybele) entspricht ungefähr der, die in anderen Nymphenhöhlen verehrt wurde. Wir kennen weitere gut erhaltene antike Beispiele von Nymphenkult in Höhlen[45] und mindestens zwei, die ebenfalls durch Individuen ausgestattet und betrieben wurden: die Höhle bei Kafizin auf Zypern mit ihren Tausenden von beschrifteten Tongefäßen, und eine Höhle bei Pharsalos in Thessalien. Antike Kultstätten in Höhlen sind in der Kultstättenstatistik generell überrepräsentiert, weil ihre natürliche Form die Erhaltung von Artefakten und Ausstattung begünstigt.[46]

Aufschlussreich ist ein Vergleich mit der Höhle am Berg Karapla bei Pharsalos;[47] hier ist an der Felswand nahe beim Eingang eine Inschrift erhalten, die aus der Perspektive des Gründers verfasst ist und Besucher der Kultstätte anspricht:[48]

> *Gott zum Glück. Willkommen, ihr Männer und Frauen, Jungen und Mädchen, im Heiligtum der Nymphen und des Pan, des Hermes, Apollons des Herrschers, des Herakles und (seiner) Genossinnen, in der Höhle des Chiron und des Asklepios und der Hygieia. Diesen gehört der Platz und alle heiligen Dinge dort, die Pflanzen und Bildtafeln, die Götterbilder und alle Geschenke. Die Nymphen, die sich hier aufhalten, haben den Pantalkes zu einem tüchtigen Mann gemacht und zum Aufseher eingesetzt. Er hat die Pflanzen gehegt und mit den (eigenen) Händen die Anlage gestaltet, wofür als Gegengabe sie ihm allzeit ein unbelastetes Leben schenkten. Herakles verlieh ihm Kraft, Tüchtigkeit und Stärke, so dass er die Felsen bearbeiten und den Weg anlegen konnte; Apollon und sein Sohn Hermes geben Gesundheit und für immer ein glückliches Leben, Pan gibt Lachen, Frohsinn und rechten Übermut, Chiron machte ihn weise und lehrte ihn dichten. Doch kommt mit gutem Glück herauf, bringt alle Opfer dar, betet, vergnügt euch! Hier vergisst man alles Unglück, das Gute findet man … und Sieg im Kampf (?).*

Wir erfahren in diesem Gedicht viel über die rituelle Praxis – dass diese Kultstätte Besuchern offenstand, dass nicht nach Geschlecht oder Altersgruppen segregiert gefeiert wurde, dass Opfer und Gebet in fröhlicher Stimmung verrichtet werden sollten und der Entspannung dienten. Dabei sind die Machtverhältnisse klar herausgestellt: der Gründer und Gestalter

---

44 vgl. aber: IG I³ 981: Apollonos: Herso, letzteres ein Beiname des Apollon oder ein Heros namens Hersos?
45 Zusammengestellt und analysiert von LARSON 2001; vgl. auch WICKENS 1986.
46 PEEK 1938; LARSON 2001, 15; PARKER 1996, XXVIII map II.
47 Zur Höhle: LARSON 2001, 16–18; RIETHMÜLLER 2005, 293–295.
48 SEG 1, 248; Übersetzung nach der Edition von PEEK 1938, 23–24 mit Kommentar zur Lesung und Interpretation von Z. 6.

des Sakralbezirkes, Pantalkes, führt die Aufsicht[49] und überwacht ihn, er sichert seine und der Gottheiten Eigentumsrechte, indem er darauf hinweist, dass auch die mobile Ausstattung (Bildtafeln, Götterbilder, Geschenke = Votive) den Göttern gehört. Anders als in Vari gibt es hier jedoch keine schriftlich fixierten Verhaltensregeln zur Opferpraxis, was durchaus auf die gewählte literarische Form des Gedichtes zurückgehen kann; *leges sacrae* sind selten nur metrisch gefasst.[50] Jede der Gottheiten des Bezirkes ist auf Pantalkes bezogen: Er sieht sich selbst in einer wechselseitigen Beziehung zu den Nymphen, denen er den Kultbezirk anlegte, wofür sie ihm ein glückliches Leben schenkten.[51] Auch die Auswahl der anderen Gottheiten des Bezirkes ist ganz auf den Gründer ausgerichtet: ein persönliches Pantheon, dessen Elemente in dem Gedicht einzeln erläutert werden. Im Vorgehen finden wir weitgehende Ähnlichkeiten zur Situation in Vari: wie Archedamos legte Pantalkes einen Nymphengarten an[52] und arbeitete die Kultstätte eigenhändig aus,[53] wie Archedamos schuf er sich ein eigenes religiöses Aktionsgebiet außerhalb[54] der Polisgrenzen. Auch die Zeitstellung ist ähnlich,[55] doch gibt es in der Kultanlage bei Pharsalos keinen Hinweis auf den rechtlichen Status des Kultgründers und auf seine Heimatstadt.

4 Artemidoros auf Thera

Der in den Altertumswissenschaften am häufigsten behandelte Fall[56] einer Kultgründung durch eine einzelne Person spielt in der Epoche des Hellenismus auf der Kykladeninsel Thera. Artemidoros, Sohn des Apollonios aus Perge in Kleinasien, richtete am Rande der Stadt Thera um 250 v. Chr. einen Kultbezirk unter freiem Himmel ein. Dieser offene

---

49 SEG 1, 248, Z. 10.
50 Sokolowski 1957; 1962; 1969. Lupu 2003; Parker 2004.
51 SEG 1,248, Z. 12.
52 Wortgleich zu IG I³ 977: SEG 1, 248, Z. 12.
53 Ebd. Z. 11.
54 Die antike Stadt Pharsalos lag ca. 5 km nördlich der Höhle des Pantalkes am Berg Karapla, beim heutigen Farsala: vgl. Peek 1938, 18; Riethmüller 2005, 293.
55 SEG 1, 247 gehört noch in das 5. Jh., 248 eventuell in das 4. Jh.; Datierung wiederum lediglich anhand der Buchstabenformen möglich.
56 Wilamowitz-Moellendorff 1955 2. Aufl., 382–385; Nilsson 1950, 189–190; Palagia 1992; Graf 1995, 107–112.

Bezirk zog sich als eine mehrteilige Anlage entlang einer Straße[57] hin, die
zum Marktplatz der Stadt führte. Was heute noch erkennbar ist (Abb.
1–7), besteht in einer auffälligen, schwarzen Pflasterung des Weges und in
umfangreichen Felsabarbeitungen, die eine Art Schaufassade bilden aus
Altären, Reliefs und einer Stufenanlage mit Bettungen für Stelen und
Statuen, die durch Inschriften bezeichnet und kommentiert werden. Aus
diesen Texten geht hervor, dass Artemidoros aufgrund einer Traumvision
handelte, als er den zentralen Altar der Homonoia, der „Eintracht"
(concordia), errichtete.[58] Zu beiden Seiten dieses Altares sind weitere
Opferplätze angebracht, links Tierbilder in den anstehenden Fels in
Relieftechnik eingearbeitet und Epigramme hinzugesetzt: ein Adler und
ein Epigramm an Zeus Olympios, ein Löwe und eines an Apollon Ste-
phanephoros, ein Delphin und eines an Poseidon.[59] Auch ein Reliefporträt des Artemidoros samt Epigramm findet sich beim Delphin, und in
der Nähe des Adlers die Zeilen „Unvergänglich, unsterblich, nicht al-
ternd und ewig sind die Altäre, mit denen als Priester ein Temenos ge-
gründet hat Artemidoros."[60] Rechts des zentralen Altares befindet sich ein
weiterer für die Dioskuren und die erwähnte Stufenanlage, auf der die
inscribierten Texte Hekate und Priapos nennen und zwei Mal wiederum
den Namen des Artemidoros aufführen. Man wird annehmen dürfen, dass
hier Statuetten dieser Götter und womöglich auch weitere Stifterporträts
standen.

    F. GRAF hat dieses Ensemble 1995 im Ganzen analysiert und über-
zeugend als das Ergebnis einer grundsätzlich zweipoligen Konzeption
interpretiert:[61] zum einen sind hier Götter versammelt, die als Schutz-
götter der Menschen und als Helfer in privaten Notlagen bekannt sind
und in den Epigrammen auch *explicite* als solche bezeichnet werden
(Dioskuren, Samothrakische Götter), zum anderen solche, die als Götter
der Polis Thera eingeordnet werden können (Zeus, Apollon, Poseidon).
Auch die Zentralgottheit der Anlage, Homonoia, ist wohl eher auf die
Lösung eines Konfliktes auf der öffentlichen Ebene zu beziehen denn auf
der privaten. Homonoia gab dem Artemidoros als Dank für die Altar-

---

57 Vgl. HILLER VON GAERTRINGEN 1904, 90–91 mit Fig. 73.
58 IG 12,3 Suppl. 1342.
59 IG 12,3 Suppl. 1345–1347.
60 IG 12,3 Suppl. 1345; Übersetzung nach H. v. GAERTRINGEN 1904, 97.
61 GRAF 1995, 107–112. Die konkurrierende, biographisch sequenzierende
    Deutung von O. Palagia vernachlässigt die Aussagen der inscribierten Texte zu
    Priapos, Hekate und Pan, die eindeutig auf die Polis der Theräer bezogen sind,
    vgl. GRAF 1995, 109 mit A. 44.

Abb. 1: Der Aufweg zur antiken Stadt Thera, Photo A. Hupfloher.

Abb. 2: Überblick über die Ruinen des hellenistischen Thera, Photo A. Hupfloher.

Abb. 3: Der Bezirk des Artemidoros, Zentralbereich, Photo A. Hupfloher.

Abb. 4: Der Bezirk des Artemidoros, Stufenanlage, Photo A. Hupfloher.

Abb. 5: Der Bezirk des Artemidoros, Pflasterung und Reliefbilder, Photo A. Hupfloher.

Abb. 6: Detail: das archaisierende Reliefporträt des Artemidoros, Photo A. Hupfloher.

Abb. 7: Die Exedra des Artemidoros, Photo A. Hupfloher.

stiftung den großen Kranz der Stadt, besagt ein später hinzugesetztes Epigramm oberhalb dieses Altares, und an anderer Stelle zeigt sich, dass der Kultgründer nicht nur den Ehrenkranz, sondern auch das Bürgerrecht der Stadt erhalten hat.[62]

Die hier rekonstruierbare Situation ist die eines Mannes, der im Laufe des 3. Jahrhunderts von Perge in Kleinasien nach Thera auswanderte. Er ist nicht, wie man früher meinte, zusätzlich in einem epigraphischen Text in Ägypten fassbar und somit als ein Söldner im Dienst der Ptolemäer nachgewiesen.[63] In der Stadt Thera hingegen treffen wir an zwei weiteren Stellen wiederum auf denselben Artemidoros: Einerseits war er an der Errichtung der Tempel für die ptolemäischen Herrscher wohl finanziell beteiligt,[64] andererseits ließ er am Aufweg zur Stadt eine Exedra errichten (Abb. 7) und einen kleinen Altar für die Göttin seiner Heimatstadt, Artemis Pergaia. Sie wirkte ihm, so der Text, als Retterin und habe ihm 90 Lebensjahre vorhergesagt, denen Pronoia, die Vorsehung, noch drei

---

62 IG 12,3 Suppl. 1341 mit GRAF 1995,108 A.41; IG 12,3 Suppl. 1344.
63 GRAF 1995, 107 A. 36; WITSCHEL 1997, 23 A. 45.
64 IG 12,3,464 mit GRAF 1995, 111 A. 63; WITSCHEL 1997, 43.

weitere hinzugesetzt habe.[65] Dies klingt retrospektiv und lässt an eine Grabanlage im Zusammenhang mit der Exedra denken, wofür auch das dort angebrachte Epigramm spricht, das von der Heroisation des Artemidor, beglaubigt durch Delphi, handelt.[66]

Religiöse und soziale Aktivität als Mittel der Integration in die Bürgerschaft einer Kleinstadt sind hier recht gut zu fassen.[67] In Anbetracht des hohen Lebensalters des Artemidor kann diese Integration jahrzehntelang gedauert haben, was die bisher noch ausstehende Analyse der Chronologie der Monumente im Bezirk und außerhalb als ein Desiderat erscheinen lässt.[68] Bürgerrechtsverleihungen sind oft die Antwort der Städte auf Wohltaten in Form von Geldspenden direkter oder indirekter Art. Der Kultgründer Artemidor wird wohl nicht nur die Anlagen für den Herrscherkult, sondern auch die Feste der zum Bezirk gehörenden Götter finanziert haben, deren Priester er war. Dieser euergetische Kontext macht klar, dass er ein vermögender Mann war oder auf Thera geworden ist. Sicherlich gehörte er zur Oberschicht[69] dieser Kleinstadt. Von seinem selbstbewussten Agieren im öffentlichen Raum dieser Stadt zeugen die von ihm errichteten Monumente.

5 Vergleichsfälle

Die bisher ausführlich dargestellten, gut dokumentierten Fälle von Kultgründungen zeigen bereits eine beträchtliche Spannbreite an Situationen, in denen Einzelne religiös eigenständig agieren konnten. Eine Erweiterung des Spektrums der untersuchten Fälle erhöht diese Spannbreite und erlaubt darüber hinaus noch weitere Differenzierungen im Bereich des Sozialstatus' der Gründer und der zeitlichen Einordnung des Phänomens. Die großen Familienstiftungen hellenistischer Zeit im Grabkontext oder zugunsten bereits bestehender Kultstätten werden in der folgenden Tabelle nicht aufgeführt.

---

65 IG 12,3 Suppl. 1350; Hiller von Gaertringen 1904, 101 mit Abb. 84; Graf 1995, 110.

66 IG 12,3 Suppl. 1349. Hiller von Gaertringen 1904, 102; Graf 1995, 109 mit A. 51.

67 Explicite auch in den Epigrammen für die Dioskuren und die anderen göttlichen Helfer, deren Kultplätze allen offen stehen (IG 12,3 Suppl. 1333) und immer wieder auf die Theräer bezogen werden: 1335 b–c, 1342–1344.

68 Einige Beobachtungen zur Chronologie: Graf 1995, 108 A. 41; 109.

69 So auch Graf 1995, 111.

Tabelle: Auswahl an Kultgründungen durch Individuen im antiken Griechenland

Zeit	Gründer	Herkunft	Kultort	Typus/Beleg	Gottheiten
480–471/0 v. Chr. (Exil)	Themistokles[70]	Athen	Athen, Melite	Kultbezirk mit Tempel und Stifterporträt (?)	Artemis Aristobule
420/19 v. Chr.	Telemachos[71]	Athen?[72]	Athen, Südhang Akropolis	Kultbezirk mit Tempel und Incubationshalle	Asklepios und Hygieia
2. Hälfte 5. Jh. v. Chr.	**Archedamos**[73]	Thera/i	Vari, Südattika	Kultbezirk in Höhle, *lex sacra*	Nymphen, Pan u. a.
5. Jh. v. Chr.	Pantalkes[74]	?	bei Pharsalos, Thessalien	Kultbezirk in Höhle, *Einladung*	Nymphen, Pan u. a.
1. H. 4. Jh. v. Chr.	Xenokrateia[75]	Athen	Athen, Phaleron	Kultstätte mit Weihrelief und Altar, *lex sacra*	Fluss Kephisos u.v.m.
390/380 v. Chr.	**Xenophon**[76]	Athen	Skillous bei Olympia	Tempelbezirk mit Vermögensstiftung	Artemis von Ephesos
ca. 300 v. Chr.	Apollonios[77]	Memphis Ägypten	Delos	Kultstätte in Miethaus	Sarapis und Isis

70 Plut. *Them.* 22,2; *mor.* 869 C-D; GARLAND 1992, 64–81.
71 IG II² 4960 a-b; 4961; SEG 25,226; vgl. ALESHIRE 1989; GARLAND 1992, 118–121; AUFFARTH 1995; WULFMEIER 2005, 37–39.
72 PARKER 1996, 179 vermutet in Telemachos einen in Athen wohnenden Epidaurie; anders GARLAND 1992,128 „probably an Athenian". IG II² 4960 nennt keine weiteren Namensbestandteile des Telemachos.
73 SCHÖRNER / GOETTE 2004.
74 SEG 1, 247–248; PEEK 1938, 18–26 mit Taf. 1–2; LARSON 2001, 16–18; RIETHMÜLLER 2005, 293–296.
75 IG II² 4547–4548 = LSS 17; Abb. des Votivreliefs u. a. bei LARSON 2001, 123 fig. 4.3–4; PARKER 2005, 429 fig. 30; KALTSAS 2001, 133.
76 Xen. *an.* 5,3,4–13.
77 IG 11,4, 1299 mit VIDMAN 1970, 34–35; BOMMAS 2004, 55–59; DIGNAS 2008, 77.

Tabelle: Auswahl an Kultgründungen durch Individuen im antiken Griechenland
(Fortsetzung)

Zeit	Gründer	Herkunft	Kultort	Typus/Beleg	Gottheiten
3. Jh. v. Chr.	**Artemi- doros**[78]	Perge	Thera	Kultbezirk unter freiem Himmel, *Einladung*	Homonoia, Dioskuren, u. v. m.
2. H. 3. Jh. v. Chr.	Onesa- goras[79]	?	bei Kafizin, Zypern	Kultbezirk in Höhle	Nymphe, Zeus, Apollon u. a.
1. Jh. n. Chr.	Xanthos, Sklave des Gaios Orbios[80]	Lykien	Attika, Nähe Sounion	Kultstätte mit *lex sacra*	Men Tyrannos
1. Jh. n. Chr.	Anony- mos[81]	Attika	Attika	Kultstätte mit *lex sacra*	Asklepios u. a.

Ein Überblick über die hier zusammengestellten Fälle erweist zunächst, dass ein primärer Zusammenhang zwischen Migration und
Kultgründung – etwa über eine vermutete Exklusivität der öffentlichen
Kulte in der klassischen Polis,[82] die Migranten wie Xenophon, Archedamos und Artemidoros, aber auch Apollonios auf Delos und Xanthos im
südlichen Attika in private Aktionsweisen gedrängt hätte – nicht zu erhärten ist. Vielmehr sind bei Themistokles und Xenokrateia zwei
ebenfalls relativ gut dokumentierte Situationen erkennbar, in denen
Einheimische neue Kultstätten errichteten; bei Telemachos, Pantalkes
und einigen anderen dieser Liste ist einigermaßen wahrscheinlich, dass sie
ebenfalls in heimischem Kontext agierten, wenn die Quellenlage hier
auch keine gesicherten Aussagen über das Bürgerrecht der Gründer zu-
lässt. Vielmehr ist bei den für uns als Immigranten kenntlichen Personen
auffällig, dass sie diesen Status – und zwar, indem sie eine Aussage über

78 IG 12,3, 421–422; 12,3 Suppl. 1333–1350; Hiller von Gaertringen 1904,
    89–102.
79 SEG 30, 1608; Mitford 1980.
80 IG II² 1365–66; 4856; LSCG 55; Lauffer 1979, 181–185.
81 IG II² 1364 = LSCG 54.
82 Vgl. die Diskussion dieser weitverbreiteten Annahme bei Krauter 2004, 53–
    113.

ihre Herkunft in selbstfabrizierte Texte aufnahmen – deklarierten und nicht etwa zu verschweigen suchten.

Die einzige Frau in dieser Zusammenstellung,[83] Xenokrateia, agierte in heimischem Umfeld. Ob man bei Frauen im Kontext der antiken Polisgesellschaften von Bürgerrecht sprechen kann, ist zwar strittig,[84] doch ist hier aufgrund des Votivtextes klar, dass Xenokrateia aus einer attischen Bürgerfamilie stammte: sie wird als Mutter und Tochter eines Xeniades aus dem Demos Cholleidai bezeichnet.[85] Die von Xenokrateia errichtete Kultstätte ist durch zwei Ausstattungselemente bekannt, die sich erhalten haben – ein beschrifteter Altar und ein qualitätvolles Votivrelief, das die Stifterin, ihren kleinen Sohn und die zehn Gottheiten darstellt, denen die Anlage gewidmet war. Flussgötter (Kephisos, Acheloos) und Gottheiten mit Bezug zu Geburt und Haushalt (Hestia, Eileithyia, Artemis Lecho, Nymphai genethliai) dominieren das Ensemble, dessen Zusammenstellung ebenso spezifisch und individuell ist wie etwa jene des Pantalkes in Thessalien und des Artemidor auf Thera. Der Anlass der Kulteinrichtung war im weitesten Sinne das erfolgreiche Aufziehen[86] des Sohnes der Stifterin. Die Beschriftung der Reliefbasis enthält zuletzt die Bestimmung, hier dürfe opfern, wer immer guten Willens sei; dies hat zur Einordnung dieses Textes als *lex sacra* geführt, zeigt aber nur, dass der Kultstifterin wichtig war, andere als Familienmitglieder als Opfernde zuzulassen. Diese Kultstätte dürfte privat in dem Sinne gewesen sein, dass weder der Demos Cholleidai noch der Demos der Athener mit dieser Sache jemals beschäftigt waren,[87] öffentlich war sie hinsichtlich der Zulassung anderer Nutzer.

---

83 In hellenistischer Zeit finden wir etliche Frauen als agierende Personen in den Familienstiftungen, so etwa in der Stiftung der Epikteta auf Thera (IG 12, 3, 436 = LAUM 1914, no.42 mit WITTENBURG 1990), der Agasigratis in Kalaureia: IG 4, 840 = LAUM 1914, no.57 und der Areta in Aigosthena: IG 7, 43 = LAUM 1914, no.21. Noch in das 4. Jh. v. Chr. gehört die Stifung von Tempel und Statue für Demeter und Kore durch Chrysina auf Knidos: London British Museum 1859.12–2636 (CEG II 860) mit KRON 1996, 153; DILLON 2002, 24; CONNELLY 2007, 134–135.

84 Diskussion u.a. bei PATTERSON 1986; WHITEHEAD 1986, 79; 176.

85 LSS 17 = IG II² 4547–8; IG I³ 986–7: Votivrelief, Reliefunterstatz und wohl Altar oder Markierung eines Altares. Cholleidai: IG I³ 987, Z. 6; zur Fundsituation der Objekte: WALTER 1937, 97–119.

86 IG I³ 987, Z. 3–4: didaskalias, ein absoluter Genitiv? Vgl. WALTER 1937, 99– 100.

87 So auch GARLAND 1992, 20.

Kultgründungen konnten also sowohl von Bürgern als auch von Nicht-Bürgern und Frauen vorgenommen werden. Der einzige Sklave der Liste agierte im ersten Jahrhundert n. Chr. und ist wohl durchaus als eine Ausnahme anzusehen. Hinsichtlich des rechtlichen Status der Kultgründer überwiegen die freien Personen, hinsichtlich des Geschlechtes die Männer.

Die Schichtzugehörigkeit dieser Personen festzustellen, ist aufgrund der defizitären Dokumentationslage nicht überall auf sicherer Grundlage möglich: Attische Schriftsteller und Politiker wie Xenophon und Themistokles – es ist der Sohn des Neokles, der gefeierte „Sieger von Salamis", dessen Kultgründung bei Plutarch überliefert ist – sind der Oberschicht zuzurechnen, Xenokrateia aufgrund ihrer aufwendigen Gründung mit einem hochwertig ausgeführten und großen Weihrelief[88] wohl ebenfalls. Auch Artemidoros auf Thera war, dies zeigt der euergetische Kontext seiner Aktivitäten, ein Angehöriger der Oberschicht. Den Onesagoras auf Zypern hält man für einen erfolgreichen Steuereinnehmer oder Geschäftsmann,[89] was auch für den Sklaven Xanthos gelten könnte, der im Süden Attikas im Umfeld der Silberminen von Laureion[90] lebte und der es offensichtlich dort, wo viele Sklaven arbeiteten, zu einigem Wohlstand gebracht hat. So konnte er seine Kultstätte mit mehreren beschrifteten Monumenten aus Stein ausstatten lassen, die detailliert die Vorschriften im Kult des Men Tyrannos darstellen, eines ursprünglich kleinasiatischen Gottes, der mit lykischen Arbeitern[91] nach Attika gekommen war und als dessen Priester Xanthos offenbar fungierte. Einfache ländliche Verhältnisse sind bei dem anonymen Kultgründer aus dem Attika der römischen Kaiserzeit greifbar, dessen Aktivität aus einem kurzen epigraphischen Text hervorgeht,[92] bei Archedamos in Vari, und Attika, und eventuell auch bei Pantalkes in Thessalien. Demnach war die Möglichkeit, Kultstätten einzurichten, auch nicht an Schichtzugehörigkeit und Vermögensverhältnisse gebunden. Eine relevante Bedingung dieser Möglichkeit dürfte aber die konkrete räumliche, die soziale und auch die politische Situation gewesen sein, im besonderen die Nähe oder

---

88 Athen, Nationalmuseum inv. 4019; Abb. des Reliefs etwa bei PARKER 2005, 429 fig. 3, der 430 A.49 Xenokrateia nicht als Gründerin des Bezirkes und Heiligtums gelten lassen möchte; anders zurecht LINFERT 1967 und nun MYLONOPOULOS 2008, 66.
89 MITFORD 1980, 251–256; 261–262.
90 LAUFFER 1979, 178–185.
91 IG II² 1366 Z.21 nimmt die Gründung eines Kultvereines in Aussicht.
92 IG II² 1364.

die Ferne zu einem politischen Zentrum, wo der Normierungs- und
Reglementierungsgrad wahrscheinlich höher war als auf dem Lande. In
Fällen, die außerhalb Attikas situiert sind (Skillous, Pharsalos, Thera,
Delos), ist darüber generell wenig bekannt, so dass – zirkulär – allenfalls
aus der Existenz der Kultstätten selbst erschlossen werden kann, dass ihre
Errichtung den örtlichen Regelungen und Erwartungshaltungen ent-
sprach. Nur selten ist eine Konfliktsituation fassbar, und wo dies der Fall
ist, ging es offenbar um Baugenehmigungen (Delos)[93] und räumliche
Abgrenzungsprobleme (Telemachos, Athen[94]), die freilich auch An-
feindungen sozialer Art reflektieren können, von denen in den Texten
nicht die Rede ist. Die komplexe Situation in Athen und Attika, wozu
wir am besten informiert sind, verlangt eine gesonderte Betrachtung.

6 Die Situation in Athen und Attika

Bei der Lektüre der Forschungsliteratur zu Athen und Attika gewinnt
man leicht den Eindruck, gerade hier sei der Regulierungs- und Nor-
mierungsgrad hinsichtlich religiöser Initiative und Aktivität sehr hoch
gewesen.[95] R. GARLAND etwa rechnet damit, dass ab circa 460 v. Chr. Rat
und Volksversammlung von Athen über das Pantheon der Stadt wachten
und die Einführung neuer Gottheiten, damit auch die Gründung neuer
Kultstätten, genehmigen mussten.[96] Diese Sichtweise basiert auf der
herausragend dichten Überlieferungslage zu Athen, aufgrund derer zu
beobachten ist, wie etwa seit dem Beginn des fünften Jahrhunderts generell die öffentliche Aktivität zunimmt und dann ab der Mitte des
Jahrhunderts auch häufiger in nun ausführlicher werdenden Steinin-
schriften dargestellt wird. Nachrichten über Kultaktivitäten – zum Beispiel über die Einführung des Pan-Kultes[97] nach der Schlacht bei
Marathon – kommen zunächst aus dem neuen Genre der Geschichts-
schreibung, später dann aus inschriftlichen Verfahrensvorschriften, die
per Volksbeschluss festgelegt und publiziert wurden. Von Themistokles
und Kimon, die als Protagonisten in der ersten Hälfte des fünften Jahrhunderts bekannt sind, erfahren wir hingegen in einiger Ausführlichkeit

93 Im narrativen Vorspann der sog. Sarapisaretalogie, IG 11,4, 1299, Z. 24–29.
94 Vgl. GARLAND 1992, 126.
95 GARLAND 1992, 18–20; 115; PARKER 1996, 215–217; SCHOLZ 2000, 169–170.
96 GARLAND 1992, 19.
97 Hdt. 6,105 zu Pan, 7,189 zu Boreas.

erst aus dem wesentlich späteren essayistischen und biographischen Werk des Plutarch, der zu Beginn des zweiten Jahrhunderts n. Chr. schrieb. Unnötig zu erwähnen, dass sowohl diese große zeitliche Distanz als auch die divergierenden Erkenntnisinteressen von antiken Verfassern und modernen Lesern solcher Texte der Untersuchung der Umstände von Kultgründungen im Athen des fünften Jahrhunderts nicht günstig sind. Bei Themistokles erfahren wir in einem Zuge mit der Nachricht, er habe eine Kultstätte für Artemis Aristobule in der Nähe seines Wohnortes in Melite eingerichtet, die Haltung der attischen Öffentlichkeit gegenüber dieser Neugründung: er habe die Menge der Athener auch damit gegen sich aufgebracht.[98] Worum es genau dabei ging, ist unklar. Plutarch wusste von einem möglicherweise als anstößig geltenden (weil herosähnlichem) Themistokles-Porträt im Artemistempel,[99] aber auch der Beiname Aristobule („vom besten Rat") der Artemis kann Anstoß erregt haben, da sich der „Sieger von Salamis" viel auf seine Fähigkeit als Ratgeber in öffentlichen Angelegenheiten zugute hielt und von anderen auch dementsprechend gepriesen wurde. Er stand in den Jahren nach Salamis in Konkurrenz zu den anderen Akteuren des politischen Lebens in Athen und unterlag ihnen schließlich 471/70 im Verfahren der Ostrakophoria. Ein kausaler Zusammenhang zwischen der Kultgründung und seiner Ostrakisierung ist sicherlich auszuschließen, wenn auch die Einrichtung der neuen Kultstätte kaum von öffentlichen Behörden autorisiert worden war. Die historiographischen und essayistischen Quellen zum fünften Jahrhundert thematisieren die Möglichkeit einer solchen Autorisierung generell nicht, sie sprechen entweder kollektiv von den Athenern als Akteuren oder sie beschreiben die Aktionen Einzelner. Ist vom Kollektiv die Rede,[100] so erscheint die Annahme eines Volksbeschlusses recht na-

---

98 Plut. *Them.* 22,1; *mor.* 869 cd mit GARLAND 1990, 64−81, im bes. 73−75.

99 Das bekannte Themistokles-Porträt aus Ostia aus dem 2. Jh. n. Chr. wird oft mit dem Heiligtum in Melite in Verbindung gebracht, wo sein griechisches Vorbild gestanden haben könnte: vgl. TRAVLOS 1970, 211; GARLAND 1992, Abb. 13. Ob die von Plutarch erwähnte Statue im Artemistempel von Melite zur Lebenszeit des Themistokles entstand, ist aber unklar.

100 So etwa beim Aition für die Einführung des Pankultes in Athen: Hdt. 6,105 beschreibt das Erlebnis des Langstreckenläufers Pheidippides und als Reaktion die Kulteinführung durch die Athener. Im Plutarchtext zu den Umständen der Translation der Gebeine des Theseus nach Athen (Plut. *Thes.* 36; *Kim.* 8,6) erhalten die Athener ein Orakel und richten dem Theseus dann ein Heroon im Zentrum der Stadt ein. Kimon hingegen, bei dem durchaus die Initiative zur Eroberung von Skyros, wo die Gebeine gesucht und gefunden wurden, gelegen haben kann, wird nur als der Ausführende dargestellt.

heliegend, aber auch bei den Aktivitäten einzelner Personen wird häufig angenommen, dahinter stehe eine Autorisierung durch Rat und Volksversammlung.[101] Dies kann in einigen Fällen wohl durchaus zutreffen, wie etwa die Überlieferungssituation zu Athena Hygieia auf der Akropolis nahezulegen scheint, wo Plutarch ganz auf die Person des Perikles focusiert, der aufgrund einer Traumvision die Folgen eines Arbeitsunfalles beim Bau der mnesikleischen Propyläen zum Besseren wenden konnte und zum Dank dafür Statue und Altar der Athena Hygieia errichten ließ, während die erhaltene Inschrift pauschal „die Athener" als Akteure ausweist.[102] Hingegen ist eine Kulteinführung in Athen durch öffentliche Beschlussfassung in den epigraphischen Texten nicht erhalten und allenfalls indirekt zu fassen; die meisten der in diesem Zusammenhang in der Forschung diskutierten Texte betreffen finanzielle und organisatorische Details der Kultverwaltung, nicht die Einführung neuer Kulte oder die erstmalige Festsetzung von rituellen Abläufen und organisatorischen Details: bei Athena Nike auf der Akropolis wurde die Kultverwaltung in den 440er Jahren neu organisiert[103] und in den Vorschriften zum Bendiskult im Piräus ging es detailliert um Zuständigkeiten, um die Opferpraxis und die Festorganisation.[104] In beiden Fällen war die Kultgründung vorausgegangen – bei Athena Nike führen die archäologischen Funde unter dem Niketempel bis mindestens in archaische Zeit zurück,[105] bei Bendis liefert womöglich eine Zeile in den Listen der Tamiai der „anderen Götter" zum Jahre 429/8 einen *terminus ante quem* für die öffentliche Trägerschaft des Festes.[106] Auch hat sich in der Eingangsszene zur Politeia des Platon (327 a; 328 a; 354 a) die Erinnerung an das erste öffentliche Fest mit Fackelreiten und Pannychis für Bendis erhalten. In dem fiktiven Setting dieses Dialogs ist von zwei Abteilungen des Festzuges die Rede, einer einheimischen und einer thrakischen (327 a), was ein ähnliches Bild ergeben haben dürfte wie die Aufzüge bei den Dionysien, Panathenäen und Eleusinien zur Zeit des Ersten Attischen Seebundes, als man die Bündner und Kleruchen zur Mitwirkung an

---

101 GARLAND 1992, 111–115 zu Bendis; AUFFARTH 1995, 342–347 zu Asklepios.
102 Plut. 13,13; IG I³ 506.
103 IG I³ 35: Z. 5 die Bestimmung der Priesterin durch Los; Z. 10 die Einkünfte der Priesterin, Z. 11 ff. wird ein Neubauprojekt für Tempel und Altar (aus Marmor) skizziert; diese Aktivitäten finden statt im Zuge der großen Um- und Neubauten auf der Akropolis in perikleischer Zeit.
104 IG I³ 136 mit GARLAND 1992, 111–112.
105 Vgl. MARK 1993.
106 IG I³ 383 Z. 143; GARLAND 1992, 111–114.

diesen Festen teils einlud, teils verpflichtete.[107] Wenn irgendwo, dann lassen sich bei der Einführung des Bendiskultes öffentliche Verfahrensweisen und im modernen Sinne politische Motive bei der Kultgründung wahrscheinlich machen.[108] Alle anderen Fälle von Kultgründungen in Athen, von denen wir aus epigraphischen Zeugnissen wissen, zeigen die Initiative und Aktivität von Individuen abseits des politischen Geschäftes, in privatem Kontext und offenbar ohne Autorisierung durch zentrale Polisorgane.

Zwei Zeugnisse aus Athen sind in diesem Zusammenhang wichtig, da sie die bestehenden Verhältnisse beschreiben: Das erste stammt wohl aus den 420er Jahren und ist ein Zusatzantrag zu dem Volksbeschluss der Athener über die Erstlingsfrüchte von Eleusis;[109] der Seher Lampon ergriff die Gelegenheit der Beschlussfassung um anzufügen, der Archon Basileus solle sich auch um die Abgrenzung der Kultstätten im Pelargikon kümmern, wo viele Altäre offenbar ohne Plan und System errichtet worden waren. „Künftig soll man innerhalb des Pelargikon keine Altäre mehr errichten ohne Einwilligung des Rates und des Volkes und keine Steine mehr aus dem Pelargikon herausbrechen …"[110] Der Beschluss ist nicht genereller Art, sondern richtet sich auf eine zentralgelegene, ummauerte Sakralzone am westlichen Abhang der Akropolis, die wahrscheinlich aus historischen Gründen schützenswert erschien;[111] auch achtete man darauf, die vorhandenen Kultstätten nun nicht etwa abzubauen, sondern wollte sie in ein neues Ordnungskonzept integrieren. Ob die Reglementierung in diesem Falle griff, wissen wir nicht.

Das zweite Zeugnis stammt aus Platons Idealstaatsentwurf in seinem Spätwerk, den Nomoi; es enthält neben anderen Reglementierungsvorschlägen auch ein Verbot für Privatleute, in ihrem Haus eine Kultstätte zu besitzen (Plat. *leg.* 909 e). Ausschließlich in öffentlichen Kultstätten solle geopfert werden, da Kultstätten einzurichten keine leichte Aufgabe sei und die Personen, die sie üblicherweise durchführten, wenig dafür

---

107 Dekret zu den Aparchai von Eleusis: IG I³ 78, Z. 31–40, zu Brea IG I³ 46, Z. 16–19, zu Erythrai IG I³ 14, Z. 2–4.

108 So auch schon die ältere Literatur vgl. GARLAND 1992, 112; Thuk. 2,29,4 überliefert die Interessenlage der Athener in Thrakien in der Anfangsphase des Peloponnesischen Krieges. Einen luziden Überblick über die komplexe Überlieferungslage zum Bendiskult in Athen im 5. und im 4. Jh. gibt PARKER 1996, 170–175.

109 Das sog. Aparchai-Dekret IG I³ 78, Z. 47 ff.

110 Übersetzung nach HGIÜ 1 no.123.

111 Vgl. BESCHI 1967/8, 391–394.

geeignet: Frauen und Kranke oder generell Menschen in Krisensituationen oder aber in außerordentlichen Glücksmomenten neigten dazu, ohne weitere Überlegungen oder aufgrund von Träumen oder Visionen Opfer und Votive zu versprechen oder gar die Errichtung von Kultstätten. Sie füllten so mit Altären und anderen Kultstätten die Häuser und die Siedlungen übermäßig an. Platons Text, der aus der Mitte des vierten Jahrhunderts stammt, überliefert eine stark negativ besetzte Schilderung der Verhältnisse seiner Zeit:[112] Wer immer es will, kann Kultstätten errichten und tut es. Er trifft auf ein weitgehend unreglementiertes[113] Feld.

Gerade weil dies so war, konnte ein solches Handeln durchaus auch gefährlich werden. Das juristische System Athens, das keinen Staatsanwalt, wohl aber die Möglichkeit der Popularklage kannte,[114] gestattete damit generell die Instrumentalisierung von populären, mehrheitsfähigen Bedrohungsvorstellungen, die sich durchaus auch auf den religiösen Bereich richten konnten; dies zeigt etwa die Rede des Lykurgos gegen Leokrates, dem man vorwarf, beim Verlassen seiner Heimatstadt seine Familiengötter (*ta hiera ta patroa*) mitgenommen zu haben (Lyk. *Leokr.* 25–26). Hier griff das Kollektiv der Polisbürger, verkörpert in dem konservativen Ankläger und Staatsmann Lykurgos, weit in den aus unserer Sicht privaten Bereich der Religion ein, was zeigt, dass in Athen grundsätzlich jegliches Verhalten vor Gericht gebracht werden konnte, wenn sich nur ein Ankläger fand. Wer hat in diesem Zusammenhang nicht längst an Sokrates[115] gedacht? Sowohl bei diesem prominentesten Fall als auch bei den Asebieprozessen des fünften und vierten Jahrhunderts,[116] in denen der Anklagepunkt des Einführens neuer Götter regelmäßig auftaucht, ist unwahrscheinlich, dass es um die Gründung neuer Kultstätten im oben verhandelten Sinne ging. Vielmehr entsteht hier der Eindruck, dass latente Bedrohungsvorstellungen auf sozial marginale Personen projiziert worden sind. Der Sokratesprozess prägt und formt die Forschungsdiskussion zu den Kultgründungen im antiken Griechenland schon seit langer Zeit; die daraus entwickelten Fragen nach „neuen und fremden" Göttern führten zu einer Konzentration auf die athenischen

---

112 Eine Zunahme von Kultgründungen möchte ich anders als GRAF 1995, 112 aus dieser Stelle nicht ableiten; vgl. auch PARKER 1996, 216.

113 So auch PARKER 1996, 215–216.

114 BLEICKEN 1986, 225–6; 306; COHEN 1991, 201–210.

115 Zur Quellenlage und zum Stand der historischen Forschung zum Sokratesprozess: vgl. u. a. GARLAND 1992, 136–151; HANSEN 1995; PARKER 1996, 199–217; SCHOLZ 2000; PARKER 2005, 81–82.

116 Vgl. COHEN 1991, 203–217; TRAMPEDACH 2003; KRAUTER 2004, 231–240.

Verhältnisse und zu einer Vernachlässigung der außerattischen, wo
manches Mal deutlicher erkennbar ist, unter welchen Umständen es zur
Neugründung von Kultstätten kam.

7 Diachronische Perspektiven: Tradition und Innovation in hellenistischer Zeit

Der Hellenismus gilt als eine höchst dynamische Epoche; die räumliche
und die soziale Mobilität großer Bevölkerungsgruppen im Laufe und im
Gefolge des Alexanderzuges nahm stark zu, damit weiteten sich auch die
Erfahrungshorizonte und die individuellen Handlungsspielräume.[117]
Kultgründungen durch Individuen gelten als ein typisches und neuartiges
Phänomen dieser Zeit, als ein Ausdruck zunehmender ‚Individualisie-
rung' im religiösen Bereich, und oft wird in solchen Szenarien auf das
Beispiel des Artemidoros verwiesen, der um 250 v. Chr. auf Thera einen
Kultbezirk individueller Prägung gründete. Die oben zusammengestell-
ten Vergleichsfälle zeigen jedoch, dass die Praxis der Kultgründung durch
Individuen bereits in klassischer Zeit gut bezeugt ist und dass individuelle
Entscheidungen und persönliche Erlebnisse dabei auch in dieser Epoche
eine Rolle spielten. Wieweit dies für uns erkennbar ist, hängt von der
Überlieferungslage ab. Dies kann auch gegen das statistische Argument
verwendet werden, das darauf abhebt, die Anzahl privater Kultgründungen habe in hellenistischer Zeit stark zugenommen. Hiergegen muss
man einerseits darauf verweisen, dass eine von Zufällen der Überlieferung
abgekoppelte Statistik antiker Verhältnisse nicht zu gewinnen ist, und dass
andererseits sich im Laufe des vierten und dritten Jahrhunderts v. Chr. der
Repräsentationsbrauch stark verändert hat: die Anzahl der erhaltenen
Stein-Inschriften insgesamt nimmt dramatisch zu, was zu der Einschätzung führt, dass eine Zunahme in absoluten Zahlen wohl keine Veränderung von Verhaltensweisen bezeugt, sondern lediglich eine Zunahme
des Diskurses darüber in diesem Medium. Eine Gesamtstatistik von
Kultgründungen durch Individuen erbrächte daher keine neuen Ge-
sichtspunkte.

Die hier behandelten Fälle von Kultgründungen ergeben ein anderes
Bild als es die bisherige Forschung zeichnet: Wir sehen nicht nur die
Oberschicht agieren, nicht nur Bürger, sondern auch Immigranten in-

---

117 GEHRKE 1990, 71–72.

nerhalb und außerhalb der antiken Städte. Es zeigen sich generell große Handlungsspielräume von Individuen im Bereich der religiösen Initiative und Aktivität, und dies schon in klassischer Zeit. Von hier aus verlaufen klar erkennbare Traditionslinien in die hellenistische Zeit, die sich damit in diesem Bereich der Religion als wesentlich weniger innovativ erweist als gemeinhin angenommen wird. Die Ergebnisse der Analyse des Phänomens ‚Kultgründungen' unterstützen daher die Sichtweise von J. MIKALSON und anderen[118] Wissenschaftlern, die – im Gegensatz beispielsweise zu H. VERSNEL und P. GREEN[119] – die Religion der klassischen und hellenistischen Zeit als von gemeinsamen, eben konservativen Tendenzen charakterisiert betrachten. Dieser Perspektive nach ist eine Zone historischen Wandels in diesem Bereich erst zwischen Hellenismus und Kaiserzeit zu erkennen.

Bibliographie

AAA = *Archaiologika analekta ex Athenon.*
AM = *Mitteilungen des Deutschen Archäologischen Instituts, Athenische Abteilung.*
ASAA = *Annuario della Scuola Archeologica di Atene.*
ALESHIRE, SARA B. 1991 (ed.). *Asklepios at Athens. Epigraphic and Prosopographical Essays.* Amsterdam.
—1989. *The Athenian Asklepieion: The People, Their Dedications, and the Inventories.* Amsterdam.
AUFFARTH, CHRISTOPH 1995. „Aufnahme und Zurückweisung „neuer Götter" im spätklassischen Athen: Religion gegen die Krise, Religion in der Krise?", in: EDER, WALTER (Hg.). *Athenische Demokratie im 4. Jh. v. Chr.* Stuttgart. 337–365.
BAUMER, LORENZ E. 2004. *Kult im Kleinen: Ländliche Heiligtümer spätarchaischer bis hellenistischer Zeit. Attika-Arkadien-Argolis-Kynouria.* Rahden.
BESCHI, LUIGI 1967/68. „Il monumento di Telemachos, fondatore dell'Asklepieion Ateniese", *ASAA 29/30.* 381–436.
—1983. „Il rilievo di Telemachos ricomletato", *AAA 15.* 31–43.
BLEICKEN, JOCHEN 1986. *Die athenische Demokratie.* Paderborn u. a.
BLOK, JOSINE H. 2007. „Fremde, Bürger und Baupolitik im klassischen Athen", *Historische Anthropologie 15.* 309–326.
BÖMER, FRANZ 1990. *Untersuchungen über die Religion der Sklaven in Griechenland und Rom,* Bd. 3. Stuttgart 2. Aufl.

---

118 STEWART 1977, 517–519; GRAF 1995, 114; MIKALSON 1998, 315–320; KRAUTER 2004, 46.
119 VERSNEL 1990, 189–205; GREEN 1990, 396–399. GEHRKE 1990, 75–76 betont beides, Traditionen und Innovationen.

BOMMAS, MARTIN 2005. *Heiligtum und Mysterium: Griechenland und seine ägyptischen Gottheiten*. Mainz.

COHEN, DAVID J. 1991. *Law, Sexuality, and Society: The Enforcement of Morals in Classical Athens*. Cambridge.

CONNELLY, JOAN B. 2007. *Portrait of a Priestess. Women and Ritual in Ancient Greece*. Princeton and Oxford.

CONNOR, WALTER R. 1988. „Seized by the Nymphs", *ClAnt* 7. 179–189.

DIGNAS, BEATE 2008. „"Greek" Priests of Sarapis?", in: DIGNAS, BEATE; TRAMPEDACH, Kai (edd.). *Practitioners of the Divine*. Cambridge-Ma., London. 73–88.

—2007. „How to found a cult: epigraphical manifestations", in: *Acts of the 13th international congress of Greek and Latin epigraphy*. (in Druck).

DILLON, MATTHEW 2002. *Girls and Women in Classical Greek Religion*. London.

DUNAND, FRANÇOISE 1973. *Le culte d'Isis dans le bassin oriental de la Méditerranée*. Leiden.

FLEISCHER, ROBERT 1973. *Artemis von Ephesos und verwandte Kultstatuen aus Anatolien und Syrien*. Leiden.

GAERTRINGEN, FRIEDRICH FRH. HILLER VON 1899. *Thera I*. Berlin.

—1904. *Thera III. Stadtgeschichte von Thera*. Berlin.

GARLAND, ROBERT 1992. *Introducing New Gods: The Politics of Athenian Religion*. New York.

GAWANDKA, WILFRIED 1975. *Isopolitie: Ein Beitrag zur Geschichte der zwischenstaatlichen Beziehungen in der griechischen Antike*. München.

GEHRKE, HANS-JOACHIM 1990. *Geschichte des Hellenismus*. Grundriß der Geschichte. München.

GRAF, FRITZ 1995. „Bemerkungen zur bürgerlichen Religiosität im Zeitalter des Hellenismus", in: WÖRRLE, MICHAEL; ZANKER, PAUL (Hg.). *Stadtbild und Bürgerbild im Hellenismus*. München. 103–114.

GREEN, PETER 1990. *Alexander to Actium: The Historical Evolution of the Hellenistic Age*. Berkeley.

HALLOF, KLAUS 2004. „Die Inschriften", in: SCHÖRNER, GÜNTHER; GOETTE, HANS R. 2004. *Die Pan-Grotte von Vari*. Mainz. 42–59.

HANSEN, MOGENS H. 1995. *The Trial of Socrates from the Athenian Point of View*. Kopenhagen.

HGIÜ = BRODERSEN, KAI; GÜNTHER, WOLFGANG; SCHMITT, HATTO H. 1992–1999. *Historische Griechische Inschriften in Übersetzung*, Bd. I–III. Darmstadt.

HIMMELMANN-WILDSCHÜTZ, Nikolaus 1957. *Theoleptos*. Marburg.

HOEPFNER, WOLFRAM (HG.) 1997. *Das dorische Thera V: Stadtgeschichte und Kultstätten am nördlichen Stadtrand*. Berlin.

IG = *Inscriptiones Graecae*.

KÄSTNER, ERHART 1953 (1974). *Ölberge, Weinberge: Ein Griechenland-Buch*. Frankfurt / M. und Leipzig.

KALTSAS, NIKOLAOS 2001. *Ethniko archaiologiko mouseio. Ta glypta*: Athenai.

KRAUTER, STEFAN 2004. *Bürgerrecht und Kultteilnahme: Politische und kultische Rechte und Pflichten in griechischen Poleis, Rom und antikem Judentum*. Berlin; New York.

LARSON, JENNIFER 2001. *Greek Nymphs: Myth, Cult, Lore*. Oxford.

40 Annette Hupfloher

LAUFFER, SIEGFRIED 1979. *Die Bergwerksklaven von Laureion.* Wiesbaden. 2. Aufl.
LAUM, BERNHARD 1914. *Stiftungen in der griechischen und römischen Antik: Ein Beitrag zur antiken Kulturgeschichte.* Aalen. ND Stuttgart 1964.
LENDLE, OTTO 1995. *Kommentar zu Xenophons Anabasis.* Darmstadt.
LINFERT, ANDREAS 1967. „Die Deutung des Xenokrateiareliefs", *AM 82.* 149–157.
LSAM = Sokolowski, FRANCISZEK 1955. *Lois sacrées de l'Asie mineure.* Paris.
LSCG = Sokolowski, FRANCISZEK 1969. *Lois sacrées des cités grecques.* Paris.
LSS = Sokolowski, FRANCISZEK 1962. *Lois sacrées des cités grecques,* Supplement. Paris.
LUPU, ERAN 2005. *Greek Sacred Laws: A Collection of New Documents.* Leiden.
MANNZMANN, ANNELIESE 1962. *Griechische Stiftungsurkunden: Studie zu Inhalt und Rechtsform.* Münster.
MARK, IRA S. 1993. *The Sanctuary of Athena Nike in Athens: Architectural Stages and Chronology.* Princeton.
MELFI, MILENA 2007. *I santuari di Asclepio in Grecia.* Roma.
MIKALSON, JON D. 1998. *Religion in Hellenistic Athens.* Berkeley; Los Angeles; London.
MITFORD, TERENCE B. 1980. *The Nymphaeum of Kafizin: The Inscribed Pottery.* Berlin.
MÜRI, WALTER 1990. *Xenophon, Anabasis. Der Zug der Zehntausend.* Griechisch und Deutsch. München; Zürich.
MYLONOPOULOS, IOANNIS 2008. „Natur als Heiligtum – Natur im Heiligtum", *ARG 10.* 51–83.
NILSSON, MARTIN P. 1950². *Geschichte der griechischen Religion,* Bd. 2. München.
PALAGIA, OLGA 1992. „Cult and Allegory: The Life Story of Artemidoros of Perge", in: SANDERS, JAN M. (ed.). *Philolakon: Lakonian Studies in honour of Hector Catling.* London. 171–178.
PARKER, ROBERT 1990. *Miasma: Pollution and Purification in Early Greek Religion.* Oxford.
—1996. *Athenian Religion: A History.* Oxford.
—2004. „What are Sacred Laws?", in: HARRIS, EDWARD M.; RUBINSTEIN, Lene (ed.). *The Law and the Courts in Ancient Greece.* London. 57–70.
—2005. *Polytheism and Society at Athens.* Oxford.
PATTERSON, CYNTHIA B. 1981. *Pericles' Citizenship Law of 451/50.* New York.
—1986. „Hai Attikai: The Other Athenians", in: SKINNER, MARYLIN (ed.). *Rescuing Creusa: New Methodological Approaches to Women in Antiquity.* Austin. 49–68.
PEEK, WERNER 1938. „Metrische Inschriften", in: CROME, JOHANN F.; GUNDERT, HERMANN et al. (Hg.). *Mnemosynon. Festschrift für Th. Wiegand.* München.
PFISTER, FRIEDRICH 1909. *Der Reliquienkult im Altertum.* Gießen.
PIRENNE-DELFORGE, VINCIANE (ed.) 1998. *Panthéons des cités des origines à la Periégèse de Pausanias,* Kernos Suppl. 8. Liège.
PURVIS, ANDREA 2003. Singular Dedications. Founders and Innovators of Private Cults in Classical Greece, New York and London.
RIETHMÜLLER, JÜRGEN W. 2005. *Asklepios: Heiligtümer und Kulte I-II.* Heidelberg.

ROSENBERGER, VEIT 2002. „Tempelwirtschaft. II. Klassische Antike", *DNP 12.* 127–129.

SCHMIDT, ERNST 1909. „Kultübertragungen", *RVV 7,2.* Gießen.

SCHÖRNER, GÜNTHER; GOETTE, HANS R. 2004. *Die Pan-Grotte von Vari, mit epigraphischen Anmerkungen von K. Hallof.* Mainz.

SCHOLZ, PETER 2000. „Der Prozeß gegen Sokrates. Ein der athenischen Demokratie?", in: BURCKHARDT, LEONHARD; UNGERN-STERNBERG, Jürgen (Hg.). *Große Prozesse im antiken Athen.* München. 157–173.

SEG = *Supplementum Epigraphicum Graecum.*

SOURVINOU-INWOOD, CHRISTIANE 1988. „Further Aspects of *Polis* Religion", in: BUXTON, RICHARD (ed.) 2000. *Oxford Readings in Greek Religion.* Oxford. 38–55.

—1990. „What is *Polis* Religion?", in: MURRAY, OSWYN; PRICE, SIMON (edd.). *The Greek City: From Homer to Alexander.* Oxford. 295–322.

STEWART, ZEPH 1977. „La religione", in: BIANCHI BANDINELLI, RANUCCIO (Hg.). *Storia e civiltá dei Greci, Bd. 8: La societá ellenistica. Economia, diritto, religione.* 503–616.

THALHEIM, THEODOR 1905. *RE 5,2.* 2584–2585 „s.v. enktesis".

TRAMPEDACH, KAI 2001. „Gefährliche Frauen. Zu athenischen Asebieprozessen im 4. Jhd. v. Chr.", in: VON DEN HOFF, RALF; SCHMIDT, STEFAN (Hg.). *Konstruktionen von Wirklichkeit: Bilder im Griechenland des 5. und 4. Jahrhunderts v. Chr.* Stuttgart. 137–155.

VERSNEL, HENK S. 1990. *Ter unus.* Leiden.

VIDMAN, LADISLAV 1970. *Isis und Sarapis bei den Griechen und Römern: Epigraphische Studien zur Verbreitung und zu den Trägern des ägyptischen Kultes.* Berlin.

WACHT, MANFRED 1998. *RAC 18.* 179–265 „s.v. Inkubation".

WALTER, OTTO 1937. „Die Reliefs aus dem Heiligtum der Echeliden in Neu-Phaleron", *Archaiologike Ephemeris* 1937. 97–119.

WHITEHEAD, DAVID 1977. *The Ideology of the Athenian Metic.* Cambridge.

—1986. *The Demes of Attica: A Political and Social Study, 508/7–250 BC.* Princeton.

WICKENS, JERE M. 1986. *The Archaeology and History of Cave Use in Attica,* PhD Indiana University. Ann Arbor.

WILAMOWITZ-MOELLENDORFF, ULRICH VON 1955². *Der Glaube der Hellenen II.* Bern.

WITSCHEL, CHRISTIAN 1997. „Beobachtungen zur Stadtentwicklung in hellenistischer und römischer Zeit", in: HOEPFNER, WOLFRAM (Hg.) 1997. *Das dorische Thera V: Stadtgeschichte und Kultstätten am nördlichen Stadtrand.* Berlin. 17–46.

WITTENBURG, ANDREAS 1990. *Il testamento di Epikteta.* Roma.

WOOLF, GREG 1997. „Polis-religion and its Alternatives", in: CANCIK, HUBERT / RÜPKE, JÖRG (Hrsg.). *Römische Reichsreligion und Provinzialreligion.* Tübingen. 71–84.

WULFMEIER, JOHANN-CHRISTOPH 2005. *Griechische Doppelreliefs.* Münster.

'... Hidden with Christ in God' (Colossians 3:3): Modes of Personhood in Deutero-Pauline Tradition

Ian H. Henderson, McGill University

The putative letter of the 'apostle Paul' to his 'holy and faithful brothers who are in Colossae' (Col 1:1) may seem to be a wilfully arbitrary choice as the focus for a discussion of individualization and religious experience. Nowadays Colossians is usually read in terms of a transition from early Pauline faith- and Spirit-centred charisma toward the ecclesial and Christological world-view of *Frühkatholizismus*. In particular, scholarly readings of Colossians seem to turn on history-of-religion analysis of the Christological hymnic passage (1:14−20), of the apparently conservative table of household duties (3:18−4:1), and of the text's projected 'opponents' (2:8−23).[1] The choice here of Colossians as a case-study of religious individuality will, however, be justified by reference to this text's quite specific economy of pseudepigraphy and to its − ultimately analogous − interest in the simultaneous glorification and hiddenness of the emerging Christian subject. I do not know whether to regard the particular act of pseudepigraphy encoded in Colossians as cause or effect of a more broadly self-reflective individuality. In either case, the repeated moments in Colossians which undercut the letter's dominant impression of salvation as collective and cosmic are interesting data for enquiry into individuality and experience in Greco-Roman religion.

1 The earliest Christian pseudepigraphy and reflective individuality

What I will try to illustrate here is that Colossians, at the same time that it expresses an important movement toward ecclesial and moral institutionalization, also insistently validates movements toward intensified individuality. In the rhetoric of Colossians such movements do not seem

---

1   PERVO 2010, 11, 64−71.

to me to be contradictory. On this reading, the production of Colossians quite intentionally combined the representative individuality of Paul and his associates with the strangely reflective individuality implied in the act of devout pseudepigraphic deception. Little can be inferred about the real historic author of Colossians, but we can be sure that our pseudepigrapher was unusually familiar with Paul's thought and that our pseudo-Paul knew that 'he' was not Paul, knew this clearly enough to go to unusual lengths literarily to conceal this non-identity from the book's audience. Indeed, the writer to the Colossians – or, as we shall see, to their neighbours – knows that 'he' is not really Paul and that the Colossians are not really the Colossians, with greater deceptive determination than other pseudo-Pauline writers afterward. As JOHN MARSHALL writes in a study of the Pastoral letter to Titus,

> behind every letter is a story, but behind a forged letter there are at least two – and one is a lie. The technique of the pseudonymous letter is to bridge surreptitiously the gap between the fiction it tells and the historical situation in which it seeks to have an effect.[2]

The underlying socio-linguistic hypothesis of the present essay is that lying of the careful and nuanced kind represented by Colossians is likely to constitute a discourse of reflective individuality even or especially where, as in Colossians, the content of the lie is ambiguously both individualising and collectivizing. I want to claim that the complexity and precision of the Colossian pseudepigraphy – and especially its interest in individual cognition and individual embodiment within the collective identity of the Body of Christ – makes it implausible to gloss over its particular duplicity as an unselfconscious act of pious impersonation.[3] Without attributing anachronistic sensibilities about intellectual property to pseudo-Paul or to his audience, the writer calculated correctly that pretending to be Paul would enhance the persuasiveness of his argument. The writer would also know that detection of this device would discredit the letter, especially if the pseudepigraphy were detected on the basis of an excessively realised eschatology (2 Thess 2:2). Thus pseudo-Paul to the Colossians understood himself clearly enough to be not-Paul to be able to modify in highly selective ways central Pauline theological formulae, while maintaining a satisfyingly deceptive Pauline matrix.

---

2   MARSHALL 2008, 781.
3   MARSHALL 2008, 782; see HEIL 2010, esp. 5–6, defending a more-or-less authentic Pauline authorship.

Moreover, the points of the pseudepigrapher's boldest interventions into Pauline theological tradition have to do precisely with the eschatological character of the individual and the relationships among individual, collective and cosmic embodiment. ANGELA STANDHARTINGER has proposed at least experimentally imagining a 'group of authors' behind Colossians especially because of the letter's extensive use of an authorial first person plural (1:3–21, 28; 4:3, 10–14) and because the text 'implies a system of imitation of Paul'.[4] From the point of view I am taking here, however, such phenomena in the text suggest rather the reflective individuality of an author or authors who are conscious of the Paul whose voice they are projecting and modifying. Colossians represents to an exceptional degree of refinement the subjectivity and reflective individuality of an impostor.

2 The Letter to the Colossians as the first Christian pseudepigraphon

Colossians has a special place in the complicated history of Pauline, Christian, indeed, religious pseudepigraphy: Colossians seems to be the oldest extant attempt to imitate and appropriate the name, voice and character of Paul as apostolic letter-writer. It is also among the most convincing pseudepigrapha in early Christian literature. In what follows here I do not propose to reconsider Colossian pseudepigraphy, which I regard as long since proven, nor will I offer any especially original reading of Colossians itself. Instead I will highlight some of the self-conscious, non-routine choices, literary but also deeply religious, which the act of pseudepigraphy in this pioneering case apparently involved.

2.1 Relation to the authentic Pauline letters

Colossians depends for its circumstantial references especially on the little letter to Philemon and seems particularly dependant also on Paul's other authentic 'prison' letter, that to the Philippians.[5] Nevertheless, as NICOLE FRANK's intertextual study has shown, the author of Colossians draws creatively and imaginatively on vocabulary, imagery and

---

4   STANDHARTINGER 2004, 573 n. 4.
5   KILEY 1986.

thought documented to us in the whole range of the authentic Pauline corpus, however those influences were mediated to our pseudo-Pauline writer.[6] The initial decision to imitate and supplement Paul may thus have taken place in a context and for an audience in which Paul was known as authoritative, apostolic letter-writer, but in which a corpus of authenticated Pauline letters was by no means as yet universally accessible or normative. The act of pseudepigraphy seems to me even more interesting as a reflective act of imagined individuality if the writer and audience know Paul, as STANDHARTINGER insists, overwhelmingly by oral tradition, including an oral tradition that Paul had been a letter-writer.[7]

2.2 The style of 'Paul'

Stylistically, as E. P. SANDERS has shown, Colossians is almost too Pauline: heavy use in Colossians of Pauline phrases suggests deliberate pastiche, at least up to 3:11, especially as the recognizable paulinisms are embedded in a copious, pleonastic, elaborated stylistic decorum.[8] Greco-Roman rhetorical culture highly valued the ability to imitate personal style, as well as the ability to match style to content and projected audience.[9] The author to the Colossians made the choice – the rhetorically deliberate choice – to imitate Paul's voice selectively while modulating it into a noticeably more sophistic register. One recent apologetic defence of Pauline authorship makes the interesting but over-valued suggestion that the stylistic register of Colossians may have been partly determined by the concern to address the presumed rhetorical tastes of a projected Asiatic audience 'in the Lycus valley'.[10] Stylistic modulation might indeed be determined by audience considerations, though in my view it was more likely a pseudepigraphic tactic serving to mask potentially serious differences in basic thought between the Paul of Colossians and the Paul of, say, Philippians. Thus W. BUJARD has pointed to quite profound differences in 'thought-structure' and modes of argument between Paul and Colossian pseudo-Paul.[11]

---

6 FRANK 2009.
7 STANDHARTINGER 1999, 91–152.
8 SANDERS 1966.
9 HENDERSON 2003, 23–4.
10 WITHERINGTON 2007, 102.
11 BUJARD 1973.

More noticeable to an actual audience to some extent familiar with Pauline discourse would be the absence or theological marginality of many key Pauline terms: *pneuma* and cognates (only 1:8; 2:5 and *pneumatikos* in 1:9; 3:16); *nomos*; *dikaiosunē* and cognates (only *dikaios* in 4:1); *pisteuein* (though *pistis* five times). I hope to return to the remarkable development in Colossians of authentic Pauline imagery of the collective embodiment of the believing community (Col 1:18; 2:19); Colossian language of embodiment seems to me to have some interest for our themes.

2.3 Colossians without the Pauline eschatological reservation

Finally, and for me decisively, the eschatology of Colossians, though generally Pauline, is specifically quite different from that of the authentic Paulines: in the authentic Paulines the resurrection is always carefully expected in the future, though anticipated in the present by the experience of the Spirit; famously in Colossians the Jesus-devotee is already raised with him from death (2:12–13; 3:1), while charismatic phenomena are, if anything, associated with the ritual abuses attacked in chapter 2 (8–23, 18). The use of realized resurrection language to describe the present, especially post-baptismal, condition of Jesus-devotees is not only something that Paul carefully, scrupulously avoids (compare Col 2:12; 3:1; Rom 6:4–5; 8:11; 1 Cor 6:14; Phlp 3:11), it comes close to formulations which 1 Corinthians 15 was written to exclude and resembles also the only doctrinal positions explicitly condemned in the later pseudo-Pauline Pastoral Letters (2 Tim 2:11, 18; compare 2 Thess 2:2).[12] Colossians calmly and systematically violates the '*eschatologische Vorbehalt, auf dem Paulus immer insistiert habe*'.[13] Reference to an already actualized resurrection of Jesus-devotees is thus an aspect of Colossians – and later of Ephesians – which I think the author of Romans and 1 Corinthians would actually have repudiated. 'Over against the more conservative tradition of the Pastorals', Colossians and, then, Ephesians constitute at least 'a more speculative, adventurous stream' especially in regard to the relation between baptism and resurrection in Christian personal experience.[14] Perhaps especially if the author to the

---

12 See WEDDERBURN 1993, 63.
13 WOLTER 2010, 28.
14 WEDDERBURN 1993, 63.

Colossians and/or his audience have received much of their knowledge
of Paul from oral tradition rather than from intense, direct familiarity
with complex texts, the marked contrast must be reflectively deliberate,
between the Colossian symmetrical formula ('buried in baptism ... also
raised' 2:12) and the carefully deferred modality/futurity of the authentic Pauline parallel formula in Paul's own writing ('buried through baptism ... in order that we may walk in newness of life' Rom 6:4) and in
the tradition received by the Pastorals ('If we have died ... we shall live'
2 Tim 2:11). Surely also such precisely contrasting formulae have implications for the reflective individuality of those who receive them.

3 Traces of individuality in Colossians

3.1 Local specificity without polemical confrontation

Unlike the literary executors who in various obscure stages collected
and edited Paul's authentic correspondence and eventually embraced
also Colossians, Ephesians and the Pastorals, the author to the Colossians
decided to assume the identity and authority of the imprisoned, presumably already dead apostle; at the same time the writer decided to address
his work putatively to a Jesus-community at Colossae, an unimportant
polis (even without imagining the effects of an earthquake in AD 62)
conveniently close to the centres of Hierapolis and especially Laodicea
(2:1; 4:13–16).[15] References to these nearby centres are really the only
local colour in Colossians, reinforced by personal references largely elaborated and varied from those in Philemon 23 (Col 4:7–17) – and a
personal signature by 'Paul' himself (4:18; compare Phlm 19; 1 Cor
16:21; 2 Thess 3:17). The putative author does not project himself as
founder of the addressee community, but emphasizes especially his association with Epaphras as vicarious representative of 'Paul' to the regional
community and of the community to the distant 'Paul' (1:7–8; 4:12–
13). The writer's instruction to his putative audience to obtain the letter
sent to Laodicea (4:16) may have suggested to another pseudepigrapher
the idea of writing in turn the derivative text received predominantly as
the Letter to the Ephesians, but containing only one, textually doubtful
reference to the locality of the audience. The whole of Colossians 4 at
any rate constitutes an elaborately plausible and un-falsifiable picture of

---

15 PERVO 2010, 66; TSUJI 2010, 260.

the sort of trans-regional social network within which letters by an apostle might circulate to readers not in the textually represented primary address community.[16]

The post-Colossian pseudepigraphon of Ephesians shows an almost complete lack of localisation and social networking (the address 'in Ephesus' itself is textually problematic [1:1]; Tychicus is barely named [6:21–2]). By contrast, Colossians' only partially deceptive evocation of a particular regional network that *could* have received apostolic letters is not merely a cunning way for the latter to be 'really addressed universally to all the Pauline churches'.[17] Rather the regional reference, however colourless, suggests an author who actually wanted his Paul to be read in the target region. The impression of regional particularity is also reinforced in the sections referring to 'opponents'. 'Opponents' is not quite the right word here: several authentic Pauline texts explicitly portray Paul and his authority as opposed by enemies and rivals within the Jesus-movement, occasioning more or less speculative scholarly reconstructions of the historic conflicts, slogans and opponents behind Paul's reports.[18] Colossians actually forebears from most of the characteristics of authentic Pauline polemics, especially from *ad hominem* attacks. In Colossians, 'Paul', though himself engaged from afar in a hard *agōn* on behalf of his correspondents and others who had never met him in the flesh (2:1; 1:24), warns them in their own setting of potential threats from uncharacterized tempters rather than of actual attacks from false teachers. Once again, in emphasizing the fictionality of Colossians, STANDHARTINGER stresses this schematic and potential feel of the abuses against which 'Paul' warns: 'the author of Colossians does not argue but rather compiles warnings addressed to unspecified persons (τὶς, μηδείς) (2.4, 8, 16, 18.) The few descriptions hardly permit the identification of a particular religio-historical group.'[19] Instead, on her view, Colossians was designed to encourage endurance in perceived situations of generalised distress among proto-Christian communities. Similarly, MORNA HOOKER long ago noted the 'calm' with which the text points toward potential threats, without really stooping to engage and refute; Colossians does not take a polemical tone.[20]

---

16 TSUJI 2010, 260.
17 STANDHARTINGER 2004, 586.
18 BERGER 1980.
19 STANDHARTINGER 2004, 585.
20 HOOKER 1973.

Against STANDHARTINGER and HOOKER, however, and in limited defence of all those who have variously reconstructed particular history-of-religion situations behind the perceived 'Colossian heresy' or heresies, the text does seem to become unnecessarily specific in its un-combative evocation of potential problems.[21] On one side the text warns vaguely enough against anyone who might delude by cunning speech (ἐν πιθανολογίᾳ, Col 2:4) or anyone who tries 'kidnapping you through philosophy and empty deceit' (2:8), surely universal and non-local enough possibilities. On the other hand, as FRED WISSE puts it,

> more specific warnings are found in 2:14–23. It is clear that the author's concern here is not so much false doctrine as self-imposed ascetic practices that went well beyond what was expected from, or would be appropriate for, believers. The brief description[s] of these practices sound similar to certain Jewish dietary, purity, and holy-day observances, but are not presented as motivated by submission to the laws of Moses, as is the case in the undisputed letters of Paul. Rather they appear to be motivated by a desire to achieve superior humility through the mortification of the flesh, and to engage in a form of worship like that of the angels in heaven.[22]

The authorial voice in Colossians thus refrains from clarifying its discomfort with *philosophia*, but is significantly less coy about practices which seem to me more compatible with some sort of convergence of Jewish and Phrygian devotional behaviour than with an abstract interaction with Pauline tradition intended for a universal audience. That is, the 'Colossian heresy' is not represented in Colossians as a heresy, that is, as a doctrinal deviation or as adherence to a particular deviant leader in competition with the author, yet it is also not merely a literary device imitatively projecting the conflict which readers might expect from a Pauline letter.

STANDHARTINGER and HOOKER suggest that the calmness of our letter's warnings against unwise practices arises from the supposedly very limited rhetorical function of conflictual language, namely of lending verisimilitude to the pseudepigraphic fiction. In part, I am impressed by the particularity of the rituals pseudo-Paul warns against and even more by the coolness of the warnings which is in marked contrast to the authentic Paul's approach. If the Colossian pseudo-Paul had wished to use conflictual language merely to add verisimilitude to the pseudepi-

---

21 Listing possible heresies see KILEY 1986, 61–2; STANDHARTINGER 1999, 16–27, 181–194; FRANCIS 1975.
22 WISSE 2006, 274.

graphic fiction, a closer imitation of authentic Pauline models could easily have been offered and harmlessly exploited (for example in the *pseudapostoloi* of Gal 1:6–9; 2:4; 2 Cor 11:1–14). More fundamentally, I want to suggest a different rhetorical function for Colossians' un-polemical warnings against unnamed persons hardly portrayed as opponents.

Pseudepigrapha, especially when composed, like Colossians, within living memory of the transmission of authentic literary models by the putative author, must embody a relatively definite attitude to those authentic models and their author: crudely, affirmative, neutral or critical/corrective.[23] In fact, I suppose, the author of Colossians was typical of most religious pseudepigraphers in combining a basic attitude of affirmation, admiration, perhaps continuation and elaboration of the pseudonymous author whose authority is being appropriated, along with a more-or-less subliminal or pronounced element of critique, correction, clarification or supplement. Rhetorically, the persuasive success of the element of critique or correction rests upon the credibility of the pseudepigraphic ethos established by the text as a whole. The greater the readers' access to authentic texts or tradition from the putative author, the greater attention the pseudepigrapher must give to the ethopoetic effect of the whole.

In Colossians, I suspect, the polemical, often *ad hominem*, element in authentic Pauline discourse has been represented, yet deliberately softened and directed at real practices which the projected real-life readers are expected to agree are abuses, but which are not strongly associated with personal 'opponents' of Paul. The purpose of this subdued, but real polemical component is not just to bolster verisimilitude, but more particularly to distract the audience from the more seriously critical and corrective relation between pseudo-Paul and authentic Paul with respect to personal eschatology and the realisation or futurity of the believer's participation in the resurrection of Christ.

3.2 Letters from heaven

In a comparatively unnoticed essay, HANS DIETER BETZ proposed a reading of the Colossian pseudepigraphon which is in two respects especially helpful for what I am trying to do here: first, in that BETZ at-

---

23 SCHULTE-MIDDELICH cited in FRANK 2009a, 21.

tempts seriously to imagine the self-conscious individuality of the pseudepigrapher over against the projected individuality of Paul the authentic letter-writer; and, second, in that BETZ stresses the material argumentative link between the pseudepigrapher's implied, though carefully
hidden, individuality and the reflective, programmatic individuality of
the letter's highly selective correction and supplementation of Paul's
personal eschatology.[24] BETZ reads Colossians as a particularly intense in-
tersection of two sub-genres of ancient letter, the 'magical letter' intended in ritual reading to give effect to a speech-act of enchantment;
and the 'heavenly letter' intended to actualise the 'second presence' of
a putative author who is not merely distant geographically, but who is
absent in heavenly occultation, a god or divine hero.[25] On this view,
Colossians would be an outstanding instance of the type of inspired 'religious pseudepigraphy' which WOLFGANG SPEYER tried to define over
against philosophical and literary-rhetorical imitation.[26]

BETZ' reading begins from the variation in Colossians of the familiar
Greco-Roman *topos* of presence in absence through epistolary self-representation (Isocrates *Ep.* 1.1).[27] In the authentic Paulines the *apōn-parōn*
topos is intensified by the spiritual charisma of the apostle and his addressees: in 1 Corinthians Paul, though absent in the body, is present in the
Spirit and has passed divine judgement on an errant brother (1 Cor
5:3–4); elsewhere Paul, under attack from opponents among his addressees reinforces the *topos* of expressly epistolary presence in bodily absence with the threat of his imminent *parousia* (2 Cor 10:1–13:10,
esp. 10:8–11); in the letter to the Philippians the *topos* is again varied,
this time by Paul's gathering sense that his imprisonment may result
in the permanent deferral of his personal *parousia* (Phil 1:27–30;
2:12). In Colossians, then, BETZ detects a further, decisive, variation
of the Pauline *topos*:

> Paul's absence is now one of his σάρξ, not one of his σῶμα, as in Paul's au-
> thentic letters. The reason is that the σάρξ passes away at death, while the
> σῶμα is transformed.[28]

On BETZ's reading, then, in 'a passage extremely difficult to interpret'
the writer of Colossians 'indicates' that 'Paul is dead' (Col 1:24).

---

24   BETZ 1995.
25   See further STANDHARTINGER 2004, 583; STÜBE 1918; KLAUCK 2006, 352–353.
26   SPEYER 1956/66; see KLAUCK 2006, 403.
27   BETZ 1995, 510.
28   BETZ 1995, 513.

Paul's bodily absence from those of his addressees who have never seen his πρόσωπόν ... ἐν σαρκί (2:1), is now permanent, although the deceased apostle is able both to see (2:5) and to hear (1:4). For Betz,

> it should be evident that for the author Paul is in heaven; for him the promise of the gospel (1:5, 23) has come true.[29]

It is, I think, quite helpful to describe Colossians as a sort of epistolary apocalypse in this way, as completing revelation about the resurrection of the dead, on which Paul himself had expressed the provisional incompleteness of his experience (Phil 4:11–16).[30] Writing about 1 Thessalonians 1–3, Jane Heath has much more recently argued that the *apōn-parōn topos* is much more than a motif from letters of friendship: Paul presents himself not as "an 'empathetic friend'..., but a bearer of the presence of God, whose presence was again made vivid through rhetorical *enargeia*".[31] Betz persuades me that 'Paul's pseudepigraphic presence-in-absence is even more transcendent as it is represented in Colossians where Paul's absence 'in the flesh' is compensated not only by presence 'in the spirit', but also above all by concrete incorporation with the readers in the Body of Christ.

Neither in Betz' article nor in Colossians itself, however, is it obvious to me to whom it 'should be evident' that Paul was already dead at the time of writing. Is the audience of Colossians expected to discern that the 'heavenly letter' has a revelatory status different from that of Paul's previous writings? Or is this 'intended effect' as a 'heavenly letter' meant, like so much other Greco-Roman magic, to work secretly, without the subjects' knowledge? Was, for example, the author of the letter to the Ephesians aware that the Colossian letter which he so heavily used was like his own production, pseudepigraphic? Surely Colossians is designed to persuade its innocent audience that it was written by the real Paul, before his death, so that when 'Paul' says, 'Now I rejoice in the sufferings for you ... in my flesh for the Body [of Christ], which is the Church' (1:24) the audience hear premonitions fulfilled in the meantime, rather than the heavenly reminiscences of the now exalted saint. It is thus finally only the unknown, historical, pseudo-Pauline author of Colossians who could ever have been fully conscious of the lay-

---

29 Betz 1995, 514.
30 Berger 1984, 302–3; compare Rev 2–3.
31 Heath 2009, 30.

ers of paradox in Paul's epistolary and eschatological, corporeal presence
to the readers of Colossians.

BETZ at any rate asks, 'What did the *author* of this letter ... have in
mind ...?'[32] BETZ' categories of 'magical' and 'heavenly' letter in this
case help us perceive the difference in under-lying ethos between the
production of the letter to the Colossians and the significant body
and tradition of positive theory and socially acceptable practice of imi-
tative and fictional letter-writing in Greco-Roman antiquity. Even on a
reading less insistent than that proposed by BETZ, the writer to the Colossians implies a self-conscious religious experience of mediating the
revelatory voice of the dead Paul. I do not expect to understand the
subjective and psychological aspects of the authorial experience presup-
posed by the composition of Colossians, but it seems to me inescapably
an experience of moral, to some extent consciously alienated individuality. Yet that self-conscious, apocalyptic, religious experience was deliberately concealed in order to facilitate literary transmission of Paul's
mysterion to the pseudepigrapher's real audience (Col 1:24–2:5). Instrumental to the relative success of the pseudepigraphic concealment were
the literary-rhetorical conventions of stylistic imitation and ethopoetic
fiction taught in the progymnasmatic school-exercises with, indeed,
special emphasis on fictive letter-writing.[33] On the progymnasmatic distinction between *ēthopoiia* proper and *eidōlopoiia*, GEORGE KENNEDY
notes,

> the status of the speaker at the time the speech is imagined as being given is
> what determines whether it is ethopoeia or eidolopoeia. A speech Heracles
> might have given while alive is an example of ethopoeia, a speech he might
> have given after death is an eidolopoeia.[34]

On this distinction, Colossians is actually an ethopoetic text encoding,
however, an essentially non-fictive and eidolopoetic consciousness on
the part of the dead apostle's real-time ghost-writer.

BETZ supposes the writer of Colossians was 'one of Paul's former
close collaborators' and that the highly distinctive literary 'self-portrait'
of Paul in Colossians 1:23–2:5 is informed substantially by the writer's
'personal memory of the apostle during his lifetime'.[35] Thus the compo-

---

32 BETZ 1995, 512 my emphasis.
33 Theon, *Prog.* 10 (SPENGEL 1854, 115) (8 in the order of KENNEDY 2003, 47);
    Nicolaus, *Prog.* 10 (SPENGEL 1856, 490–91).
34 KENNEDY 2003, 115, n. 79.
35 BETZ 1995, 512, 516.

sition of the pseudonymous letter is not only an intense act of religious ethopoeia, but also a real, personal gesture of epistolary friendship and, we might wish to add, philosophical school-succession. I do not see positive evidence that the writer had known Paul or was in any social sense a school-disciple of Paul's. The very common scholarly attribution of Colossians to a 'School of Paul' is, I think, almost always misleadingly unclear, except in the sense that for Colossians Paul seems to be imagined as the unique guarantor of apostolic authority: he has associates, but no peers – and no successor.[36] Perhaps there is an element of cunning self-concealment in the letter's central warning, against anyone who tries 'kidnapping you through philosophy and empty deceit according to the tradition of humans' (2:8), rather like the disingenuous warnings in the pseudepigraphal 2 Thessalonians against accepting forged letters (2 Thess 2:2; 3:17). At any rate, even if the author of Colossians was personally connected with Paul or a Pauline milieu, the distinctive character of Colossians within the Pauline corpus suggests a model of more intense inspiration in the writer's self-understanding, an intensity which I want also to relate to the theology of personhood in the letter.

I agree, moreover, with BETZ 'that it is not likely that the portrait [of Paul in Colossians 1:23–2:5] is simply derived from one or more of the authentic letters of Paul'.[37] Instead, the projected *Selbstcharakterisierung* of Paul has a basic function in the overall argument of the letter, an overall argument which, I will now try to show, however sketchily, is centrally concerned with a post-Pauline ideology of reflective individuality in which the individual is both hidden and revealed and in which resurrection embodiment is the link between earthly and heavenly existence. The purpose of this extended introduction has been to show that the reflective individuality of Colossians is grounded in the real religious and imaginative experience of the individual pseudepigrapher forging a continuity and development between the pre- and post-mortem authority of the apostle.

---

36 STANDHARTINGER 2004, 572–3.
37 BETZ 1995, 516; compare FRANK 2009a, 89–90.

3.3 Christology, cosmology, ecclesiology

ANGELA STANDHARTINGER begins her own abbreviated analysis of the theological argument of Colossians by noting that a 'main characteristic of the letter is a transformation of eschatological ideas and language into spatial thought'.[38] Epistolary convention focuses on the partial overcoming of the discontinuities of time and location by the written word, and 'Paul' uses the opening address and thanksgiving to emphasize the transfer of the gospel and of news of its reception across space and time, connecting 'Paul' and the Colossian saints with others throughout the kosmos and with a hope stored up in heaven (1:1–6). Yet 'Paul' also specifies here for the first time Epaphras as individually substantiating ἐν πνεύματι the link between Paul and his letter's audience (7–8). The two occurrences of the central Pauline lexeme pneuma refer not to invasive, proleptically eschatological divine power (Rom 8:23), but to a mode of individual personal presence, in 1:8 of Epaphras, in 2:5 of Paul himself. This personal communication across space and time leads in 'Paul's' prayer to a remarkable insistence on the cognitive (epignosis, sophia, sunesis [1:9, 10; compare 2:2; 3:10]) and affective (areskeia, hupomone, makrothumia [1:10–11]) processes which lead to assimilation to God's holy ones (1:12). This distinctive language of cognition and affection is everywhere in Colossians and is the base-line in what I take to be its reflective discourse of individuation.

This brings us to the famous Christological 'hymn' of Colossians 1:15–20. I do not see that there is much at stake for my present argument (that there is a deep homology between the revelatory hiddenness of the pseudepigrapher in 'Paul' and the transforming, re-embodying hiddenness of the believing self in Christ) in the question whether indeed to regard this section as 'hymnic' or 'credal', that is, as a pre-existent text more-or-less adapted from a Hellenistic and/or Jewish Sapiential matrix. Perhaps such hymnic language was in cultic use by the author and/or audience (Col 3:16). The question is a general one, as poetised passages in elevated style appropriate to especially exalted, Christological content are a feature of the authentic letter to the Philippians and of several pseudo-Pauline letters.[39] Recent research has tended to recognise rather the encomiastic rhetorical functions of such formally marked

---

38 STANDHARTINGER 2004, 588.
39 Phil 2:6–11; Eph 1:3–14; 5:14, see Clement Protr. 9.84; 1 Tim 3:16; 6:14b–16; 2 Tim 2:11–13.

passages in their existing argumentative contexts rather than in their possibly autonomous prior existence.[40] Such passages are not presented in their epistolary contexts as quotations of familiar texts, nor does their argumentative use seem to depend on their recognition by the reader as expressing an authoritative *lex orandi*. The Colossian purple passage may well be adapting and formally concentrating prevenient tradition.[41] For the present, it matters only that this stylistically emphasized passage is sufficiently marked within Colossians as to be certainly a function of the conscious compositional work of the author, whether it was selected, included and adapted by him or composed by him expressly for its present context.[42] Whatever its compositional process, the hymn-encomion is present in the text as a deliberate shift in the authorial voice, a kind of self-transcendence in speech.

At first, the passage's cosmological, Christological and ecclesiological content would seem to militate against its interest for a discourse about individuality. One hymnic feature which the passage lacks is any direct address to the honouree: the passage is evocative rather than invocatory.[43] In context, the passage is introduced to set the redemption of the author and readers (1:13–14, 21–23) in the universal horizon of Christ's cosmic Headship.[44] The internal structure of the impressively poetised passage as it actually appears is to move from an acclamation of the εἰκὼν τοῦ θεοῦ as agent of both heavenly and earthly creation and Head of the Body (1:15–18) to a second strophe closely parallel in form specifying the subject as 'first-born of the dead' who is active again, both 'in heaven and on earth' and who has 'made peace through the blood of his cross' (18b-20): a reference to the Cross which is usually regarded as a somewhat clumsy addition to an older resurrection-centred text.[45] The argumentative point is the intimate association of Cross and resurrection in relation to the corporeal and corporate status of the readers. The hinge between the two strophes is the surprising phrase identifying 'the Body' with 'the Church' (18a). Virtually all who think that pseudo-Paul here was using an existing poem regard this phrase as an authorial addition, since the first strophe

40 VOLLENWEIDER 2010, 225–227; ALETTI 2009; OSBORNE 2009; BRUCKER 1997; BERGER 1984, 240, 345, 372.
41 WEDDERBURN 1993, 12–20.
42 PIZZUTO 2006.
43 VOLLENWEIDER 2010, 226.
44 ALETTI 2009, 261.
45 WEDDERBURN 1993, 16.

up to that moment is about the creation of 'all things' and the second
strophe which follows is about the reconciliation of 'all things'.[46]
Only the equation of Body and Church suggests that the rest of the letter is, after all about groups of human persons. Moreover, the association
of 'Body' and 'Church', ambiguously, with death establishes a basis for
subsequent references to embodiment, mortality and resurrection.

3.4 Eschatological embodiment and the individual

STANDHARTINGER emphasizes quite rightly the collective character of
the soteriology implied so far; I want to insist that the writer now
works quite hard to establish a complementary individuality.[47] Thus
in a first application of the poem's heightened language to the actual existence of the community, the writer re-emphasizes reconciliation 'in
the body of his flesh through death' (1:22). Several rhetorical critics
agree with JEAN-NOËL ALETTI in identifying 1:21–23 as 'the basic thesis
statement of Colossians', re-orienting the impersonal language of the
poem back toward the addressees of 1:3–14 and toward the individual
specificity of the Cross.[48] Characteristically for Colossians the obstacle
which is removed by the Cross is a cognitive disposition (*dianoia*) against
the gospel. One of the most marked features of this section, then, is the
contrast between the impersonality of the so-called hymn and the functional individuation of the one who died on the cross, the ones who
have changed their hostile attitude into hope and, most explicitly of
τοῦ εὐαγγελίου, … οὗ ἐγενόμην ἐγὼ Παῦλος διάκονος (1:23).

Notwithstanding that this Pauline ἐγώ is, for us, pseudepigraphic, it
is for the projected readers of Colossians an intensely individualized mir-
ror-image of the impersonality of the poem.[49] BETZ recalls the epistolary
theorist's idealization of a letter as εἰκὼν τῆς ψυχῆς.[50] For us, the awareness of pseudepigraphy should, I surmise, evidence an intensely paradoxical individuality of authorial self-consciousness in the *Selbstcharakterisierung* section (1:24–2:5). Here 'Paul' quite astonishingly identifies his

---

46 WEDDERBURN 1993, 14–16.
47 STANDHARTINGER 2004, 590.
48 SUMNEY 2002, 343; WITHERINGTON 2007, 137; DETTWILER 2009, 330–334;
    ALETTI1993, 39, 52.
49 BETZ 1995, 516.
50 BETZ 1995, 515; ps.-Demetrius *Eloc.* 4.227.

own sufferings with those of Christ ἐν τῇ σαρκί μου ὑπὲρ τοῦ σώματος αὐτοῦ, ὅ ἐστιν ἡ ἐκκλησία (1:24). I mentioned above that the distinction between *sarx* and *sōma* in Colossians is subtly different from the authentic Paul's usage. To quote BENJAMIN WHITE's summary,

> the self, or to use a Pauline term, 'the inner person' (2 Cor 4.16; Rom 7.22; ὁ ἔσω ἄνθρωπος), is housed within a body that has σάρξ as its primary quality. This fleshly body is 'the outer person' (2 Cor 4.16; ὁ ἔξω ἡμῶν ἄνθρωπος) or 'earthly tent' (2 Cor 5.1; ἡ ἐπίγειος ἡμῶν οἰκία) that will perish. It is characterized by 'mortality' (2 Cor 4.11; θνητός) and 'weakness' (Rom 6.19, 8.3; Gal 4.13; ἀσθένεια) and will face 'destruction' (1 Cor 15.15; Gal 6.8; φθορά). This is not to say that the flesh, as a creation of God, is inherently evil. Rather, through its mortality and weakness the flesh becomes the house of Sin (see Rom 7.17, 7.18, 8.3), viewed as a hostile power ruling over humanity.
>
> ... the 'age to come' is the age of the Spirit and is in a strange way already present among those who are 'in Christ' (2 Cor 5.17).[45] Those who 'walk in the Spirit' will no longer find themselves being controlled by the Sin in their flesh (Gal 5.16). Σάρξ, which typifies the age that is passing away, has no place in the New Age, the kingdom of God. Paul firmly states, 'Flesh and blood (σὰρξ καὶ αἷμα) cannot inherit the kingdom of God' (1 Cor 15.50). Σάρξ, however, should not be confused with σῶμα. Concerning the resurrection he says, 'It is sown as a physical body [σῶμα ψυχικόν], but it is raised as a spiritual body [σῶμα πνευματικόν]' (1 Cor 15.44). Paul cannot escape the idea of embodiment.[51]

White notes that in the pseudo-Pauline letter he is studying, 3 Corinthians, a shift has taken place toward the un-Pauline idea that it might, after all, be the *sarx* which is resurrected. Colossians, by contrast, had moved in a nearly opposite direction, if anything, intensifying the transformation of the *sōma* away from the *sarx* not only in death, but also in the life experience of the Colossian believers (compare the Valentinian *Treatise on the Resurrection* 45.23–27).[52] I cited BETZ earlier to the effect that Colossians has transformed the older authentically Pauline epistolary *topos* of bodily absence into an absence now 'of his σάρξ, not one of his σῶμα. ... The reason is that the σάρξ passes away at death, while the σῶμα is transformed'.[53] Paul's *sarx* is now, in fact dead, his *sōma* is absent, but alive and conscious of the addressees, as the author momentarily lifts the veil of pseudepigraphy (Col 2:5). At the same

---

51 WHITE 2009, 510–511.
52 PERVO 2010, 216.
53 BETZ 1995, 513.

time, however, Christ's σῶμα, ὅ ἐστιν ἡ ἐκκλησία (Col 1:18, 24) is emphatically present to the addressees as, indeed, they participate in it.

Famously, the authentic Pauline image of the Church as the Body of Christ (1 Cor 6:15; 12:12) has changed in Colossians to specify Christ as the Head (1:18; 2:19). One function of this is to coordinate cosmic and ecclesial headship, primacy in creation and in the resurrection at a level of discourse which hardly calls individualization to mind (1:15–20; 2:19); at another level, however, the resurrection embodiment of Christ means that the readers' present somatic existence is already conditioned concretely 'in the stripping of the body of the flesh in the circumcision of Christ' (2:11). This is especially evident in what DETTWILER calls the 'deuxième reprise' of the hymnic passage, applying it very concretely to the existence of the target audience (Col 2:9–15).[54] The author of Colossians is able not only to transform the Pauline eschatological scruple against undermining the corporeal futurity of the resurrection into the unreserved declaration that those who have been buried with Christ in baptism have already been raised with him; the Colossian 'Paul' can also speak affirmatively about circumcision. Circumcision, anticipating baptism, is a rite which really points to the corporeal separation of *sarx* and *soma* in the individual even prior to biological death. Notwithstanding the strongly cosmic and corporate, collective character of Christ's Headship and embodiment, Christ's embodiment of the divine (2:9) and the resurrection embodiment of the Colossian believer are also both irreducibly individual as well as present in time and space. Consequently, Colossians shows unusual sympathy for Torah-observance at the same time that releases its audience from regulation. Indeed Torah-prescribed rites of food and time are all really about the embodiment of Christ in the whole existence of all of the baptized organically connected, yet differentiated 'joints and sinews', through the Head (Col 2:19). I find it striking, then, that, in Colossians 2:21, a verse which C.F.D. MOULE says is 'by common consent regarded as hopelessly obscure', one concern is against religious practice which expresses itself in an improper attitude of strictness toward the *sōma*, understood here as the naturally embodied individual.[55]

This intensification of the resurrection embodiment of Christ in his Colossian limbs may suggest a modest insight into the 'nailing' to the Cross of the 'writ against us' (τὸ καθ'ἡμῶν χειρόγραφον [2:14]). Ephe-

---

54 DETTWILER 2009, 335–339.
55 MOULE 1957, 108.

sians 2:15 seems to gloss the *cheirographon* as the Torah itself with its commandments and rules and Christian readers understandably often elide this with the *titulus* which in the Gospels is attached to Jesus' Cross (John 19:19; Mark 15:26). I doubt that the author of Colossians intended the *cheirographon* to be the Torah, rather than its abuse, but, more concretely, the only thing that is plausibly 'nailed' to the Cross is, as Ephesians suggests (2:14), the *sarx* of Jesus (20:25), that is, Christ himself in his individual mortality.

3.5 Revelation and self-hiddenness

Among the authentic letters of Paul are, as, again, BETZ has noted, the oldest extant texts employing the language of ὁ ἔξω and ὁ ἔσω ἄνθρωπος (2 Cor 4:16; Rom 7:22).[56] The distinction reappears in the post-Colossian Ephesians 3:16, but not in Colossians itself. Since the distinction is by no means ubiquitous in authentic Paul, its absence from our text may require no special explanation. Something like the authentic Paul's few direct expressions of personal inwardness may, however, be found in yet another modulation of a Pauline schema in Colossians. 1 Corinthians 2:7–10 and Colossians 1:26–28 are usually the defining cases of the so-called *Revelationsschema*.[57] We may wish to add Romans 16:25–27 (widely regarded as post-Pauline) and Ephesians 3:4–5.[58] Each of these passages refers to a *mysterion* which has been hidden through the ages and has only now been revealed (compare 4 Ezra 7:26–28). 1 Corinthians 2:7–10 may be related to the language of inner and outer person as in the next sentence Paul refers rather cryptically to the 'spirit of a person which is in the person' (2:11). I agree with STANDHARTINGER that the 'theological accent' of the pattern is different in Colossians than in the Corinthian instance especially because of the relationship between Colossians 1:26–28 and 3:3–4 and, I would add, 2:2–3.[59]

Thus in Colossians we read that the mystery of God has indeed been hidden but is now revealed to his holy ones so that they have access to wisdom and knowledge – and to Christ himself, 'the hope of glory' still to come (Col 1:26–2:3). As SUMNEY notes, 'Seek the things above'

---

56 BETZ 2000.
57 STANDHARTINGER 1999, 148–152.
58 BERGER 1984, 269; FRANK 2009a, 101.
59 STANDHARTINGER 1999, 151.

(Col 3:1), must have come as a shock to the initial readers of Colossians, who have just been warned against seeking visionary experiences (2:18).[60] In Colossians 3:1–4, however, this performance of the traditional Pauline Revelation-scheme is boldly combined with the separate Pauline motif of the eschatological revelation of Christ (1 Cor 1:7; Gal 1:12; 1 Thess 1:7) and of 'sons of God' (Rom 8:19). The latter motif, of the revelation in and of the believers themselves, acquires new meaning in the context of the Colossian letter's insistence that the death of the *sarx* and the Resurrection of the *soma* have already happened not only in the experience of Christ, and in the (imagined) experience of the (fictionally) alive yet (actually) dead 'Paul', but also in the cognitive and affective experience and embodied behaviour of the audience (Col 3:1–2). So in Colossians 3:3–4 – as my title suggests, the climax of my reading of this letter – notwithstanding that the Colossian saints have already been raised up in the resurrection of Jesus' Body, their present life, the bodily life of their own resurrection is now 'hidden with Christ in God' (Col 3:3). Colossians thus speaks more emphatically than any earlier proto-Christian text about the present existence of devotees in their eschatological embodiment collectively and as individuals. The text nevertheless at a key moment reinstates the ultimate futurity not only of Christ's revelation, but also of the Colossians' self-revelation.

This expression of glorious self-hiddenness of the Colossian Jesus-devotee marks the turning-point in the letter toward moral instruction and personal epistolary news. The actual morals enjoined in Colossians 3 and 4 are fairly conventional, but the theological basis of the paraenetic advice which Colossian 'Paul' now gives is emphatically the proleptic, but concretely embodied presence of Christ (3:11), 'the peace of Christ' (15), 'the word of Christ' (16). How is it possible or necessary for people who have died and been raised with/as the *sōma* of Christ, to put to death their earthly body-parts (Νεκρώσατε οὖν τὰ μέλη τὰ ἐπὶ τῆς γῆς [3:5])? Christ, though still ultimately to be revealed, is experienced directly in the *sōma* as the guide to correct behaviour, and without the mediation of any intrusive, inspiring *pneuma*. Colossian 'Paul' therefore returns to earlier imagery both in Colossians and in authentic Paul of eschatological clothing/unclothing (Col 3:10–12; 2:11–15; Rom 13:14; 1 Cor 15:53–54; Gal 3:27) and of the image of the unseen re-

---

60 SUMNEY 2002, 350.

vealed in the firstborn and his devotees (Col 3:10; 1:15; Rom 8:29; 2 Cor 3:18).

Perhaps this intense orientation of the Jesus-devotee's actual bodily existence to the resurrected and corporate Body of Christ lies behind Colossian 'Paul's' transformation of authentic Pauline kinship language. Colossians almost abolishes and certainly marginalizes Pauline language of fictive kinship (1:1, 2; 4:7, 9,15); in addition, Colossians, far more than authentic Paul, inserts conventional Greco-Roman household relationships into the devotees' relationships with one another and with 'the Lord' in the (in)famous *Haustafel* (3:18–4:1). PERVO assumes that the absence of fictive kinship language from Colossians 'portrays a distance between the author and the recipients', but in fact it does the opposite: Paul and the Colossians are not especially fraternal or domestic together, because they are embodied together in Christ: kinship language and household language (2:6) is a vestigial metaphor compared with the participatory (synecdochic) language of Body.[61] In the *Haustafel* conventional – quite un-metaphorical – familial relationships and roles are asserted, but also lose symbolic authority in a Jesus-community which does not think of itself as a household, since it is a Body, and the Resurrected Body of Christ, at that. The resurrected self who lives hidden with Christ in God exists here and now in familial relationships which are outwardly almost hyper-normal, though inwardly directed toward the Lord.

All this is intimately related, in characteristic Colossian fashion, to Paul's once-off reference to the 'old person' (Rom 6:6–8):

... ὁ παλαιὸς ἡμῶν ἄνθρωπος συνεσταυρώθη, ἵνα καταργηθῇ τὸ σῶμα τῆς ἁμαρτίας, τοῦ μηκέτι δουλεύειν ἡμᾶς τῇ ἁμαρτίᾳ, ὁ γὰρ ἀποθανὼν δεδικαίωται ἀπὸ τῆς ἁμαρτίας. εἰδὲ ἀπεθάνομεν σὺν Χριστῷ, πιστεύομεν ὅτι καὶ συζήσομεν αὐτῷ·

Whereas in the authentic Paul the old person has been crucified with Christ and therefore also transformed in relation to sin, in Colossians the 'new person' has been activated cognitively in something which at least involves the reflective self-understanding of the individual subject reconstituted in the image of God and relativizing a surprising range of social-cultural identities (Col 3:9–11):

...ἀπεκδυσάμενοι τὸν παλαιὸν ἄνθρωπον σὺν ταῖς πράξεσιν αὐτοῦ, καὶ ἐνδυσάμενοι τὸν νέον τὸν ἀνακαινούμενον εἰς ἐπίγνωσιν κατ'εἰκόνα τοῦ κτί-

---

61 PERVO 2010, 65; compare FRANK 2009, 426–8.

σαντος αὐτόν, ὅπου οὐκ ἔνι Ἕλλην καὶ Ἰουδαῖος, περιτομὴ καὶ ἀκροβυστία,
βάρβαρος, Σκύθης, δοῦλος, ἐλεύθερος, ἀλλὰτὰ πάντα καὶ ἐν πᾶσιν Χριστός.

Perhaps because of the experience of writing in the still apostolic epistolary voice of the dead Paul, the author to the Colossians has pushed
Pauline personal eschatology simultaneously in the directions of cosmic
universality and of intensified personal embodiment here and now.

4 Conclusion

I am not sure exactly what should be meant by a discourse of reflective
individuality: a central goal of the present essay has been to explore
what such a discourse might be like if it occurred in the context of
early Jesus-devotion. Notwithstanding my uncertainties, it seems to
me useful to describe Colossians as an intentionally reflective ideology
of individuality. Colossians both in its quite particular economy of pseudepigraphy and in its development of Pauline eschatology, and notwithstanding its intensely corporate ecclesiology, seems to offer a relatively
self-conscious argument in favour of an embodied individuality which
is consciously both hidden with Christ (and Paul!) and also renewed
in ethical behaviour and in the characteristically active Colossian ἐπί-
γνωσις τοῦ μυστηρίου (Col 2:2). Such a description seems to me potentially useful especially in relation to wider study of Pauline anthropology
and pseudepigraphy.

Bibliography

ALETTI, JEAN-NOËL 2009. "Les passages néotestamentaires en prose rythmée.
    Propositions sur leurs fonction multiples", in: GERBER, DANIEL; KEITH,
    PIERRE (edd.). *Les hymnes du Nouveau Testament et leurs fonctions*. Lectio
    divina 225. Paris. 239–263.
—1993. *Saint Paul, Épitre aux Colossiens: introduction, traduction et commentaire.*
    Études bibliques, nouv. sér. 20. Paris.
BAUMGARTEN, ALBERT I.1998. *Self, soul, and body in religious experience*. Studies in
    the history of religions 78. Leiden; Boston.
BERGER, KLAUS 1980. "Die impliziten Gegner. Zur Methode des Erschliessens
    von 'Gegner' in neutestamentlichen Texten", in: LÜHRMANN, DIETER;
    STRECKER, GEORG (edd.). *Kirche. Festschrift G. Bornkamm*. Tübingen. 373–
    400.
—1984. *Formgeschichte des Neuen Testaments*. Heidelberg.

BETZ, HANS DIETER 2000. "The Concept of the 'Inner Human Being' (ὁ ἔσω ἄνθρωπος) in the Anthropology of Paul", *New Testament Studies 46*. 315–41.

—1995. "Paul's 'Second Presence' in Colossians", in: FORNBERG, TORD; HELLHOLM, DAVID (edd.). *Texts and contexts: Biblical texts in their textual and situational contexts: essays in honor of Lars Hartman*. Oslo; Boston. 507–518.

BROX, NORBERT 1976. "Pseudo-Paulus und Pseudo-Ignatius: Einige Topoi Altchristlicher Pseudepigraphie", *Vigiliae Christianae 30*. 181–188.

—1977. *Pseudepigraphie in der heidnischen und jüdisch-christlichen Antike*. Wege der Forschung 484. Darmstadt.

BRUCKER, RALPH 1997. *'Christushymnen' oder 'epideiktische Passagen' : Studien zum Stilwechsel im Neuen Testament und seiner Umwelt*. Forschungen zur Religion und Literatur des Alten und Neuen Testaments 176. Göttingen.

BUJARD, WALTER 1973. *Stilanalytische Untersuchungen zum Kolosserbrief als Beitrag zur Methodik von Sprachvergleichen*. Studien zur Umwelt des Neuen Testaments 11. Götingen.

DETTWILER, ANDREAS 2009. "Démystification céleste. La fonction argumentative de l'hymne ay Christ (Col 1,15–20) dans la lettre aux Colossiens", in: GERBER, DANIEL; KEITH, PIERRE (edd.). *Les hymnes du Nouveau Testament et leurs fonctions*. Lectio divina 225. Paris. 325–340.

DUFF, PAUL B. 2008. "Transformed 'from Glory to Glory': Paul's Appeal to the Experience of His Readers in 2 Corinthians 3:18", *JBL 127*. 759–780.

ENGBERG-PEDERSEN, TROELS 2009. "The Material Spirit: Cosmology and Ethics in Paul", *New Testament Studies 55*. 179–197.

FRANCIS, F. O. 1975. *Conflict at Colossae: A Problem in the Interpretation of Early Christianity Illustrated by Selected Modern Studies*. Sources for Biblical Study 4. Missoula, Montana.

FRANK, NICOLE 2009a. *Der Kolosserbrief im Kontext des paulinischen Erbes : eine intertextuelle Studie zur Auslegung und Fortschreibung der Paulustradition*. Wissenschaftliche Untersuchungen zum Neuen Testament 2.271. Tübingen.

—2009b. "Der Kolosserbrief und die 'Philosophia': Pseudepigraphie als Spiegel frühchristlicher Auseinandersetzungen um die Auslegung des paulinischen Erbes", in: JÖRG FREY, et al. *Pseudepigraphie und Verfasserfiktion in frühchristlichen Briefen = Pseudepigraphy and Author Fiction in Early Christian Letters*. Wissenschaftliche Untersuchungen zum Neuen Testament 2.246. Tübingen. 411–432.

VON GEMÜNDEN, PETRA 2009. *Affekt und Glaube Studien zur historischen Psychologie des Frühjudentums und Urchristentums*. Novum testamentum et orbis antiquus. Studien zur Umwelt des Neuen Testaments 73. Göttingen.

—2006. "Der Affekt der epithumia und der nomos: Affektkontrolle und soziale Identitätsbildung im 4. Makkabäerbuch mit einem Ausblick auf den Römerbrief", in: SÄNGER, DIETER; Konradt, Matthias (edd.). *Das Gesetz im frühen Judentum und im Neuen Testament: Festschrift für Christoph Burchard zum 75. Geburtstag*. Novum Testamentum et orbis antiquus. Studien zur Umwelt des Neuen Testaments 57. Göttingen; Fribourg. 55–74.

—1999. "Die urchristliche Taufe und der Umgang mit den Affekten", in: Ass-
MANN, JAN; STROUMSA, GUY G. (edd.). *Transformations of the innerself in ancient religions*. Studies in the history of religions 83. Leiden. 115–136.

HEATH, JANE M. F. 2009. "Absent Presences of Paul and Christ: *Enargeia* in 1
Thessalonians 1–3", *JSNT 32*. 3–38.

HEIL, JOHN PAUL 2010. *Colossians: Encouragement to Walk in All Wisdom as Holy
Ones in Christ*. Early Christianity and its Literature 4. Atlanta.

HENDERSON, IAN H. 2003. "Speech representation and religious rhetorics in
Philostratus' *Vita Apollonii*". *Studies in Religion, Sciences Religieuses 32*.
19–37.

HOOKER, MORNA D. 1973. "Were there false teachers in Colossae?", in: LIN-
DARS, BARNABAS; SMALLEY, STEPHEN S. (edd.). *Christ and Spirit in the
New Testament*. Cambridge.

HÜNEBURG, MARTIN 2009. "Paulus versus Paulus: der Epheserbrief als Korrektur des Kolosserbriefes", in: FREY, JÖRG et al. Pseudepigraphie und Verfasserfiktion in frühchristlichen Briefen = Pseudepigraphy and Author Fiction
in Early Christian Letters. Wissenschaftliche Untersuchungen zum Neuen
Testament 2.246. Tübingen. 387–409.

KENNEDY, GEORGE A. 2003. *Progymnasmata: Greek Textbooks of Prose Composition and Rhetoric*. Writings from the Greco-Roman World 10. Atlanta.

KILEY, MARK. 1986. *Colossians as Pseudepigraphy*. Bible Seminar 4. Sheffield.

KLAUCK, HANS-JOSEF 2006. *Antike Briefliteratur und das Neue Testament: Ein
Lehr- und Arbeitsbuch*. Paderborn. 1998; English translation by Daniel P
Bailey. *Ancient letters and the New Testament: a guide to context and exegesis*.
Waco, Texas.

MARSHALL, JOHN W. 2008. "'I Left You in Crete': Narrative Deception and
Social Hierarchy in the Letter to Titus", *JBL 127*. 781–803.

Moule, C. F. D. 1957. *The Epistles of Paul the Apostle to the Colossians and to Philemon: an introduction and commentary*. Cambridge Greek testament
commentary. Cambridge.

OSBORNE, THOMAS P. 2009. "'Récitez entre vous des psaumes, des hymnes et
des cantiques inspirés' (Ep 5,19). Un état de la question sur l'étude des 'hymnes' du Nouveau Testament", in: GERBER, DANIEL; KEITH, PIERRE (edd.).
Les hymnes du Nouveau Testament et leurs fonctions. Lectio divina 225.
Paris. 57–80.

PERVO, RICHARD I. 2010. *The making of Paul: constructions of the Apostle in early
Christianity*. Minneapolis.

PIZZUTO, VINCENT A. 2006. *A cosmic leap of faith: an authorial, structural, and theological investigation of the cosmic Christology in Col. 1:15–20*. Contributions to
biblical exegesis and theology, 41. Leuven; Dudley, MA.

SANDERS, ED PARISH 1966. "Literary Dependence in Colossians", *Journal of Biblical Literature 85*. 28–45.

SEIM, TURID K.; ØKLAND, JORUNN 2009 (edd.) *Metamorphoses: resurrection, body
and transformative practices in early Christianity*. Ekstasis 1. Berlin; New York.

SPEYER, WOLFGANG 1965/66. "Religiöse Pseudepigraphie und literarische Fäl-
schung im Altertum", *JACh 8/9*. 88–125; repr. in BROX 1977, 195–263.

SPENGEL, LEONHARD VON 1854. *Rhetores Graeci*. Vol. 2. Leipzig.

—1856. *Rhetores Graeci.* Vol. 3. Leipzig.
STANDHARTINGER, ANGELA 1999. *Studien zur Entstehungsgeschichte und Intention des Kolosserbriefs.* Supplements to Novum Testamentum 94. Leiden; Boston.
—2004. "Colossians and the Pauline School", *New Testament Studies 50.* 572–593.
STENDAHL, KRISTER 1963. "The Apostle Paul and the Introspective Conscience of the West", First published in English in *Harvard Theological Review 56.* 199–215. Rpr. in *Paul Among Jews and Gentiles.* Philadelphia: 1976. 78–96.
STÜBE, RUDOLF 1918. *Der Himmelsbrief: ein Beitrag zur allgemeinen Religionsgeschichte.* Tübingen.
SUMNEY, JERRY L. 2002. "The Argument of Colossians", in: ERIKSSON, ANDERS; OLBRICHT, THOMAS H.; ÜBELACKER, WALTER G. (edd.). *Rhetorical argumentation in biblical text: essays from the Lund 2000 conference.* Emory studies in early Christianity. Harrisburg, PA. 339–352.
TSUJI, MANABU 2010. "Persönliche Korrespondenz des Paulus: Zur Strategie der Pastoralbriefe als Pseudepigrapha", *NTS 56.* 253–272.
VOLLENWEIDER, SAMUEL 2010. "Hymnus, Enkomion oder Psalm? Schattengefechte in der neutestamentlichen Wissenschaft", *NTS 56.* 208–231.
WEDDERBURN, ALEXANDER J. M. 1993. "The Theology of Colossians", in: LINCOLN, ANDREW T.; WEDDERBURN, ALEXANDER J. M. (edd.). *The theology of the later Pauline letters.* New Testament theology. Cambridge, England; New York. 3–71.
WHITE, BENJAMIN L. 2009. "Reclaiming Paul? Reconfiguration as Reclamation in 3 Corinthians", *Journal of Early Christian Studies 17.* 497–523.
WISSE, FREDERIK 2006. "Heterodidaskalia: Accounting for Diversity in Early Christian Texts", in: HENDERSON, IAN H.; OEGEMA, GERBERN S. (edd.). *The Changing Face of Judaism, Christianity, and Other Greco-Roman Religions in Antiquity.* Studien zu den Jüdischen Schriften aus hellenistich-römischer Zeit 2. Gütersloh. 265–279.
WITHERINGTON, BEN 2007. *The letters to Philemon, the Colossians, and the Ephesians: a socio-rhetorical commentary on the captivity Epistles.* Grand Rapids, MI.
WOLTER, MICHAEL 2010. "Die Entwicklung des paulinischen Christentums von einer Bekehrungsreligion zu einer Traditionsreligion", *Early Christianity 1.*15–40.

Representative and Charismatic Individuality

Representative Individuality in Iamblichus' *De vita pythagorica*

Richard Gordon

As an initial set of heuristic distinctions, the Erfurt Research Group on 'Religious Individualisation in historical Perspective' has found it useful to differentiate between individuation, individualisation, and individuality.[1] Individuation is the development of personal identity in the course of socialisation, and therefore universal; individualisation denotes an objective, generalised, long-term process of change in the relation between individuals and the wider society, in the direction of emancipation from traditional ties; individuality is a measure of differences, permitted, tolerated, or fostered, between socialised individuals – values of individuality are used to legitimate individualisation-processes, while individualist doctrines mediate between such values and broader conceptions of society and humankind.[2] The notion of individuality is thus inextricably bound up with explicit or implicit values and beliefs within a given social order.[3]

Both individualisation and individuality in this sense are historically-variable phenomena. There is good reason to assume that, from the Hellenistic period, if not already in the later Classical period, and to an even greater extent in the Roman Empire, at least the central and provincial socio-political élites were subjected to pressures towards individualisa-

---

1   Musschenga in VAN HARSKAMP AND MUSSCHENGA 2001, 5; cf. Rüpke 2013b.
2   KIPPELE 1998, 20–21, who rightly complains of the lack of clarity in modern sociological work in this area, offers a similar set of distinctions, of which I provide a selection here: the empirical individual = person; individuation = a psychological term denoting personal development into an adult individual, eventuating as one's 'identity'; individualisation = a long-term process of change in the relation between individual and society; individuality = the sum total of qualities that differentiates each individual from others.
3   'Individualität und Gesellschaftsbezogenheit eines Menschen stehen nicht nur nicht im Gegensatz zueinander, sondern die einzigartige Ziselierung und Differenzierung der psychischen Funktionen eines Menschen, der wir durch das Wort "Individualität" Ausdruck geben, ... ist ... nur dadurch möglich, daß ein Mensch in ... einer Gesellschaft aufwächst': ELIAS 1987, 41.

tion. To appreciate this, we need simply list some of the relevant sociological criteria.[4] They include: increasing scale of urbanisation, increasing numbers of differentiated social relationships, relationships conducted over greater geographical distance, and through larger numbers of in-
termediaries, greater interdependence of social relations, increase in but
also specialisation of available roles, greater objectification of social relations (anonymity, rationalisation and instrumentalisation). The rele-
vance of such shifts to the experience of Roman élites, particularly in
Italy and in the eastern Empire, will be apparent from a brief summary
of recent work on economic history.

As a large 'agrarian empire',[5] the Roman Empire transferred the no-
tional surplus product of the vast agrarian sector — that is tax- and rent-
paying peasants or peasant-equivalents — to the land-owning élites, who
thus generated considerable secondary demand (craft-production, mer-
chant-shipping, services) and thereby supported a relatively large non-
agrarian population.[6] The increasing prosperity of the élites — the annual
income of Pliny the Younger, a middling senator in wealth terms, was
perhaps 10,000 times minimum subsistence (= 250 kg wheat-equivalent
per person per year), that of middling aristocrats in the western Empire
in the fourth century CE between 1333–2000 Roman pounds of gold,
roughly 52,000–78,000 times minimum subsistence[7] — attests to the rel-

---

4   KIPPELE 1998, 201–204. Since she draws upon the classic sociological literature,
     which was concerned with modern processes of individualisation, she includes a
     number of criteria that relate solely to modern industrial societies. These I have
     omitted.

5   I prefer this neutral term, which aligns the Roman Empire with other historical
     empires and the issue of 'archaic globalisation' (cf. BAYLY 2004, 27), to Wrig-
     ley's 'advanced organic economy' adopted by JONGMAN 2007, 596.

6   The major function of the politico-legal system, headed by the emperor, and
     implemented in the census, was to enforce these two types of extraction, of
     which tax, at around 6–10 % of actual GDP, was the smaller element, cf. LO
     CASCIO 1997; 2000; 2007, 622–625; HOPKINS 2002, 204–208. I here ignore
     the armed forces (costing c. 450 million HS per year), which in Hopkins'
     first model of the economy (HOPKINS 1980) play a significant part in the circu-
     lation of tax-receipts, in specie and in kind. For an estimate of the non-agrarian
     population (between 10 and 20 % of the total of c. 60 million), see HOPKINS
     2002, 200 and 203.

7   HOPKINS converts the figure of 1333–2000 Roman lbs (Olympiodorus
     frg. 41.2 Blockley) into 6–9 million HS at the rate of 1 lb gold = 45 aurei
     equivalent to 100 HS (2000, 207 n.37). I give the multipliers on the basis of
     JONGMAN's figure of 115 HS as the minimum value of average annual subsis-
     tence (2007, 599–600). This is misleading for the late empire, but no one

ative, indeed growing, efficiency of the system of extraction. Though low by modern standards, agrarian (grains, oil, wine, animal products) and industrial production, at any rate until the contraction in the late second century, achieved levels not equalled until the Early Modern period.[8] Urban landscapes altered: 'within a few centuries, the Romans quarried more marble than has been quarried in all centuries since'.[9] In the eastern Mediterranean there is evidence of a continuous expansion of site-numbers, including villages, a corresponding increase in agricultural activity, including new irrigation projects, and higher consumption of an increasing variety of goods from non-local production, implying broader exchange-networks.[10] The range and scale of élite benefactions in Asia Minor reached a peak in second century CE; the Princeton excavations at Antioch on the Orontes between 1932–39, which revealed the famous mosaic-floors and innumerable small finds – appliqués for furniture, locks and keys, jewelry, toilet articles and so on – , attest to a high level of consumption among the several strata of élite-families there, which can be generalised to several other cities of the region.[11] Indeed, consumption levels all over the eastern Mediterranean seem to have increased; it has been argued that 'with a wider availability and range of goods, circulating at greater speed, selective consumption and consumer choice became a more pervasive and powerful phenomenon in the Roman world'.[12] The archaeological remains that provide evidence for increased urbanisation, greater choice among

---

doubts that at that period 'citizens lost their power to withstand elite pressure and ... could be exploited more easily' (ibid, 602; cf. 617). Briefly on the *colonatus*, GIARDINA 2007, 749–753.

8 The Greenland ice-cores show copper/aluminium ratios from ancient (precious-metal) mining peaking in I-II[P]; confirmed by lake-sediment results from Sweden and Switzerland (WILSON 2002, 26–27, cf. KEHOE 2007, 547). Evidence for mining activities in southern Spain ceases after c. 170 CE, and in northern Spain from c. 200, numbers of workings dropping to just 12 % of the II[P] figure (DUNCAN-JONES 2004, 50).

9 JONGMAN 2002, 44. On the Italian (Ostian) brick-making industry, see briefly KEHOE 2007, 561–562.

10 ALCOCK 2007, 679–692.

11 Asia Minor: PARRISH 2001; Antioch: ELDERKIN 1934–1941; KONDOLEON 2000; on the Diocletianic city after the Sassanid destruction, see POCCARDI 2001. Generalised: one thinks of the extraordinary finds at Zeugma in Commagene (EARLY ET AL. 2003), granted that it was the HQ of *leg. IV Scythica* and located on an important crossing of the Euphrates.

12 ALCOCK 2007, 694, cf. KEHOE 2007, 559–566; JONGMAN 2007, 615–617.

available goods, extended social networks, and specialisation of roles thus also have important implications for the process of élite individual-isation understood not as 'privatisation' but as opening up the range of possibilities both for distinctive action within a wider set of mainly in-formal (but slowly shifting) rules or norms, and for self-consciousness about such action.[13]

Against this background, we can turn to the values implied by dif-ferent notions of individuality. JÖRG RÜPKE outlined five types of indi-viduality in this sense:[14]

o   pragmatic: mainly the result of extended travel, or other temporary social displacements,
o   moral: the individual's behaviour as measured by capacity to live up to (usually) consensual ethical rules,
o   competitive: élite competition for status within recognised parame-ters,
o   representative: the emergence of exemplary individuals within a given tradition of achievement (social, literary, philosophical, reli-gious ...),
o   reflexive: individuality based on a specific legitimating (philosoph-ical) discourse.

The aim of such a typology is to minimise the influence of modern con-notations of the term individuality by delimiting and specifying the forms that seem appropriate in the case of the ancient world. Compet-itive, representative and reflexive forms tend to be historically linked, exemplary individuals often emerge within competitive élites, reflexive individuality as a real-world achievement is generally oriented towards, or modelled on, a representative exemplar or model. Exemplary indi-viduals are significant in studying historical individuality in that they at-tract a more or less dense figurative discourse, whose elements reflect aspirations and embody emergent ideals that cannot yet be turned into any sort of habitus, but may do so once associated with the exem-plary figure in a continuing tradition.

---

13   The Erfurt Research Group thus begins from the Weberian emphasis upon 'Handlungsmöglichkeiten and Abwägungsprozesse' within a pre-existent framework of social values, cf. KIPPELE 1998, 191–192, 208–210. Freedom, however, which for Weber was central to individualisation, is not a significant criterion for us.
14   See introduction.

De vita pythagorica and the Pythagorean Tradition

The fictional persona of Pythagoras lends itself to an enquiry into representative individuality precisely because of its long-term accretion of elements which could be adapted to different agendas and re-assembled more or less at will by interested parties.[15] Pythagoras rapidly became 'Pythagoras', a cypher that could be filled with virtually any content. Whereas the Pre-socratics had been concerned with Pythagoras for his religious beliefs (i. e. the theory of metempsychosis), he became from fourth century BC the emblem of a particular, ethically-coherent life-style. Democritus already may have written a book on his ethical teaching;[16] Plato, who mentions his name only once, cites him as the revered model for the Πυθαγόρειον τρόπον ... τοῦ βίου, the Pythagorean way of life, that enjoys such renown;[17] Aristotle, who lists five central themes of his teaching, *dikaiosyne, psyche, nous, kairos* and *harmonia*, knew enough to write (at least) two exoteric volumes on the Pythagorean teachings, mainly, it seems, on number-theory in relation to the ethics and religious teachings.[18] The extinction of Pythagorean communities in the late Classical period encouraged the further elaboration of the fictional figure through the literary tradition, most importantly in the *Life of Pythagoras* by Aristoxenus of Tarentum, who contrasted Pythagoras positively with Socrates, and the similar works by Heracleides Ponticus and Dicaearchus – many of the wonders associated with Pythagoras in the later tradition, from the exact estimate of the fish-catch to the biting of a poisonous snake, probably originated in these fourth-century accounts.[19] The intensive re-working of these themes in the epi-

---

15   In the notes I use the following acronyms: IVP = Iamblichus, *De vita pythagorica*; PVP = Porphyry, *Vita Pythagorae*; PVPlot = Porphyry, *Vita Plotini*; DLVP = Diogenes Laertius, Pythagoras (= *Vit. phil.* 8.1–50).

16   Diog. Laert. 9.38 = *D-K* 68 A1.20–22, but perhaps [Democritus].

17   Plato, *Rep.* 600ab, cf. 530d 6–10 on the Pythagoreans' teaching of the sister disciplines of astronomy and harmony. The forged *Epist.* XIII (360b7) refers to the *Timaeus* as τὰ Πυθαγόρεια.

18   *Met.* 1.5, 985b 23 ff.; Diog. Laert. 5.25; cf. for the figure, O. Gigon, *Aristotelis opera, 3: Librorum deperditorum fragmenta* (Berlin, 1987) 408–419. Aristotle of course also criticises Plato for his excessive pythagoreanising: ibid. 987a 29–30.

19   On Heracleides, Aristoxenus and Dicaearchus, see Lévy 1926, 22–36; 44–52; for the biographical tradition as a whole, see Cuccioli Melloni 1969. For the significance of the Pseudo-pythagorean literary tradition (§ 198–99) for Iamblichus (for all that he inveighs against some of it, § 2) see Burkert 1972, 97–105; Macris 2002. No doubt influenced by Kingsley 1995, Riedweg

deictic oratory of the second century CE in Greece and Asia Minor (i. e. the Second Sophistic) must have lent them a canonical status, which meant that no self-respecting treatment of the Life could afford to dispense with them.[20]

Iamblichus' *De vita pythagorica* is an appropriate text in this context,[21] since it formed part of an extensive set of lectures, the (probably) ten volumes of the '*Pythagorean Compendium*',[22] delivered by Iamblichus at his neo-Platonist academy in Apamea, the metropolis of Syria Secunda, in the years after he left Athens, i. e. some little time before the accession of Constantine (say 300 CE).[23] Eunapius' *Life* suggests that he enjoyed an easy life-style, including ownership of at least two suburban villas, and that the 'school' will have been composed of well-off young men who lived in his house, or nearby, and spent their days in his company, sometimes over several years.[24] This accommodation to the requirements of élite-status helps to explain the sharp differences between

---

2002, 138 f., 157 f., 161 f. discerns a continuity from the Classical period through to the neo-Platonists; I continue to prefer Burkert's view that the institutional tradition was interrupted in the Hellenistic period and that the highly imaginative pseudo-Pythagorica supplied such continuity as there was (BURKERT, 1961; 1972, 109–120); PVP § 53 seems reasonably conclusive. I am also very much inclined to doubt Thom's argument in favour of an early date for the *Carmen aureum* (not later than 300–250 BC), which relies entirely on the fact that l.54 is cited by Chrysippus ap. Gellius, *NA* 7.2.12 = *SVF* 2: 1000 = 62D § 5 Long and Sedley (THOM 1995, 35–58). No other line is cited in an apposite context by any author earlier than Plutarch; the older view, that the text is mainly a cento from the Ionic ʿΙερὸς Λόγος with lower-quality connecting verses, is surely correct (VAN DER WAERDEN 1965, 851–52).

20 Cf. Lucian, *Pseudolog.* 5 f. (on a sophist at Olympia).

21 I cite Jackson Hershbell's translation of IVP, where necessary with corrections/ amendments (DILLON/HERSHBELL 1991); as a rule, however, von Albrecht's is better (VON ALBRECHT 1963).

22 The Greek title seems to have been περὶ τῆς Πυθαγορικῆς αἱρέσεως: LURJE 2002a, 27; DALSGAARD LARSEN 1972, 66–67 calls it 'Synagoge Pythagorica'. Only four of the (probably) ten volumes survive; the subjects of the remainder have to be deduced from the fragments and secondary accounts, cf. DALSGAARD LARSEN 1972, 66–147; O'MEARA 1989, 30–105; STAAB 2002, 193–202.

23 Apamea: DILLON 1973, 11–13; idem 2002a, 6; idem 2002b, 11–21. On the basis of Malalas, *Chron.* XII p. 312.11–12, DALSGAARD LARSEN 1972, 40 prefers to locate the school in Daphne by Antioch.

24 Eunapius, *Vit Soph.* 5.1.11–15, p.12 f. Giangrande; on his pupils' devotion, ibid. 5.1.4–7, p. 11 Giangr. PENELLA 1990, 44 thinks the villas may have been in Chalcis, Iamblichus' native city (whichever Chalcis that was, *ad Belum* or *ad Libanum*), though this seems to me implausible.

the Pythagorean life-style described in *De vita pythagorica*, for all its hostility to luxury and its emphasis upon self-restraint and ethical behaviour, and, say, Christian asceticism as presented in early coenobitic literature – the horror of a Malchus at the idea of having sexual relations with a woman, even after being enslaved by barbarians,[25] is quite foreign to the *De vita pythagorica*, where we learn only of attempts to limit men's extra-marital sexual relations – indeed, by enjoining wives to sacrifice on the same day as they have enjoyed sexual relations with their husbands, the text treats the notion of purity within marriage more positively than such rules in the world outside.[26] As so often, ancient ideas about individuality presume a relatively high degree of financial security and the casual perpetuation of the grossly asymmetric power- and property-relations that such security implied. I return below to the question of the social role of a work such as the *De vita pythagorica*.

In the heyday of Quellenforschung and the fetishism of origins, it used to be thought that Iamblichus' work was a wretched cento of borrowings, a 'konzeptionloses Konglomerat' useful only for playing guessing-games about which texts he had copied from.[27] Indeed, some still incline to this low view.[28] It was MICHAEL VON ALBRECHT, a good generation ago, who first argued that it is important not for what it fails to tell us about the 'real' Pythagoras but for its account of the priorities and perspectives of later neo-Platonists and Pythagoreans, traceable through Plotinus, Porphyry and Iamblichus, and for its presentation of 'the' late-antique view of the person ('Menschenbild').[29] Iamblichus' aim was to ground an entire educational theory in a story about psychological maturation as measured by the acquisition, step by step, of a succession of virtues. First came the exoteric teaching, the social-political virtues, and then the esoteric ones, which involved the acquisition of knowledge

---

25 Jerome, *Vit. Malchi* ap. *PL* 23: 55–62.

26 IVP § 132; cf. also the emphasis on marital fidelity in § 57, with no mention of asceticism; the ban on divorce (§ 84); and the injunction in the same section not to sleep with a superstitious woman (?). Note also the insistence on having children in § 83 and 86 (ostensibly not in order to perpetuate the family but to continue the worship of the gods). Some of these views recur in Iamblichus' περὶ γάμου χρήσεως.

27 E.G. ROHDE 1871/1901; DEUBNER 1935. Note that both authors wrongly took the work to be an inept *biography* rather than an account of the Pythagorean *way of life*.

28 RIEDWEG 2002, 52.

29 VON ALBRECHT 1966/2002.

about one's own soul through the practice of the 'cathartic virtues'. For a few adepts, a higher level of virtue involved strict self-control and complete psychic catharsis. The true test was the ability to display these virtues in practical life (134), and ultimately the understanding and practice of *philia*, friendship. Comparable judgements are now routine.[30]

If we ask why Iamblichus began his grand course of lectures with the *De vita pythagorica*, the answer must lie in its pedagogical purpose, namely to set up the figure of Pythagoras as a vivid ideal exemplar of the philosophical life, 'authenticated' by the concrete, striking details accumulated in the literary tradition, and emotionally validated for the target-group by the continual insistence in the biographical section on Pythagoras' aura (θαυμαστὸς ἐφαίνετο, 10), and the extravagant admiration he enjoyed (θαυμαστέον, § 28; ὑπερφυῶς ἐθαύμαζον, § 32), while at the same time representing his own (Iamblichus') version of neo-Pythagoreanism as the legitimate modern form of this teaching. This latter insinuation is evident, for example, in the adroit, and twice emphasized, shift between the older Pythagorean distinction between two different but equally valid orientations, the Acousmatics and the Mathematics, and the later neo-Pythagorean one, based on the hierarchical distinction usual in neo-Platonic contexts, between θιλοσοφοῦντες/ὁμιληταί/ ζηλωταί and ἀκροαταί.[31] Here Iamblichus set himself against Porphyry's negative position with regard to the possible revival of Pythagoreanism within neo-Platonism (for Porphyry, Pythagoras' antiquity meant merely that he was close to the aboriginal ἀληθὴς λόγος, but had been superseded by the succession Plato → Plotinus and his successors), inclining rather to Numenius' enthusiasm for Pythagoras as the origin of all Platonism.[32] One major aim of *De vita pythagorica*, in the aftermath of Plotinus' doctrine of the acquisition of virtue, was to induce reflection on *paideia*, its aims and methods, and even its psychology, before embarking on the properly philosophical material contained in the remaining books

---

30 Clark 1989; Dillon and Hershbell 1991; Brisson and Segonds 1996.

31 IVP § 30 – § 89, also § 80–81; cf. Staab 2002, 267.

32 PVP, which enjoyed far wider circulation and influence than IVP, occupied the first of four books on the history of philosophy in narrative succession: Beutler 1994, 287 f.; Burkert 1972, 98 n. 3; des Places 1982, 10 f. Pythagoras' school at Croton is not seen as a model for the present, simply as a forerunner of Platonic education; cf. Edwards 1993. For his part, Plotinus mentions Pythagoras just twice (Enn. 4.8.1.21 and 5.1.9.28): Waszink 1996 n. 2. On Numenius' position, see Frede 1987; for his influence upon Porphyry, Waszink 1966.

of the *Compendium*.[33] The study of the 'mathematical' subjects explored in these books, arithmetic, geometry, astronomy and music, was supposed to realise the ethical disposition figured in the image of Pythagoras.[34] At the same time, in emphasizing the philosophical qualifications required of the good teacher (implicitly: Iamblichus himself) it proposed itself as an example of a true *praeparatio philosophica*.[35] The work thus offers analogies to the Hermetic tracts discussed by GIULIA SFAMENI GASPARRO and the Gnostic literature studied by GIOVANNI FILORAMO, but also significant differences, particularly with regard to the absence of ecstatic experience as an ideal and the stress laid on social action and social responsibility.[36]

There have been numerous attempts at analysing the structure of *De vita pythagorica* in the hope of laying bare its implicit line of argument. VON ALBRECHT discerned four major sections, one divided into two sub-sections: Chap. 1: Introduction; Chaps. 2–6: Pythagoras' childhood, youth and travels; Chaps. 7–11: Exoteric accomplishments; Chaps. 12–27: Esoteric teaching: (a) Assumptions (Chaps. 14–17); (b) The doctrines (Chaps. 18–27); Chaps. 28–33: Pythagoras as guide to the major virtues; Chaps. 33–36: Appendix.[37] DILLON and HIRSCHBELL, on the other hand, found six major sections: Chaps. 2–5: Early Life; 6–8: Beginning of public mission; 8–11: the four speeches at Croton (a prelininary compendium of the teaching); 12–27: Pythagorean philosophy and way of life; 28–33: The Pythagorean

---

33 LURJE 2002b. It is relevant to add that Iamblichus elsewhere criticizes 'many Platonists and Pythagoreans' for believing that all souls undergo judgement (*De anima* 44 [456], p. 70 FINAMORE AND DILLON), for in his view, as in the view of 'the ancients', the souls of the pure (including theurgists) 'follow the gods' (ibid. 46 [457]).

34 Here IVP differes sharply from pre-Plotinian versions of Pythagoreanism, for example Nicomachus of Gerasa, for whom what counted was the *mathematika*.

35 Cf. § 59: 'Noble is this care bestowed on education (παιδείας ἐπιμέλεια) which is directed to the improvement of human beings' (also § 63 ad init.). Note also the use in § 29 (funding of the school in Croton) of the expression κεκινημένους εἰς τὴν φιλοσοφίαν, 'stimulated' or 'encouraged' to study philosophy. On the value of mathematics to Iamblichus and later Syrianus, see BECHTLE 2006, 15–41, 61–90.

36 In RÜPKE 2013. See also the earlier synthetic discussion in FILORAMO 1999.

37 VON ALBRECHT 1966, 61–63 (omitted from the repr. in VON ALBRECHT [2002]). These 36 'chapters' (each of which carries an ancient *kephalaion*) are to be distinguished from the shorter sections (§), of which there are 267 in Deubner's ed.

virtues; 34–36: Conclusion.[38] Simpler still is KYTZLER's divison into three main blocks with a finale: Chaps. 1–13: Legendary biography; 14–33: Basics of Pythagorean teaching and life-style; 34–36: A brief account of the School.[39] GREGOR STAAB, whose detailed breakdown is the most thorough so far, largely adopts KYTZLER's scheme, while sub-dividing the large section II into two parts: Chaps. 2–12: Biography of Pythagoras; 12–27: Pythagorean *paideia*; 28–33: Pythagoras as an ideal for the philosophical life; 34–36: Finale.[40] Despite their differences, all these analyses serve to emphasize the minor role of the biographical element in Iamblichus' conception, especially when we consider that almost half the work (Chaps. 28–33 = §§ 134–240) consists of the account of the six major virtues *eusebeia, sophia, dikaiosyne, sophrosyne, andreia and philia* (in that order).

The typical antique mode of conceptualising individuality was in terms of a discourse about the soul. Insofar as the soul was conceptualised as composed of competing elements, this discourse was happier dealing in metaphors of restraint, containment and domination than of growth and development. At the same time, however, particularly in (later) Stoicism, it developed a sophisticated language of introspection and self-examination. In the Pythagorean tradition, the *Carmen aureum* recommends examination of one's conscience every morning and evening.[41] For Iamblichus too the acquisition of an ethical foundation of life, including practical life, summarized in the notions of *sophrosyne* and *philia*, is the aim of philosophical training.[42] It is this capacity that separates human beings from animals, Greeks from barbarians, free persons from slaves, philosophers from ordinary people (οἱ τυχόντες).[43]

---

38 DILLON AND HIRSCHBELL 1991, 26–28. BRISSON AND SEGONDS 1996, xvii also find six main sections (one subdivided), but they are different – three occur in the last three chapters.

39 B. KYTZLER in: ENGELS AND HOFMANN 1997, 483–484.

40 See the detailed analysis in STAAB 2002, 478–487.

41 *Carmen* 40–44, with THOM 1995, 38–43, 163–167. By contrast with other contemporary movements, notably Christianity (STROUMSA 1999), no mention is made of penitence or confession; those whose moral character is unacceptable are simply excluded ab initio: IVP 94–95.

42 For Iamblichus, as for other neo-Platonists, happiness could only be achieved through the realisation and practice of the virtues with the help of religion, cf. STAAB 2002, 169–182. Compare the Jewish position that the sacred writings confer a moral capacity on individuals, on which see Tessa Rajak in RÜPKE 2013.

43 IVP 44 (speech to the ephebes of Croton).

Every individual has the power to make a choice (κατὰ τὴν ἰδίαν προαίρεσιν) of this kind,[44] just as every individual can only absorb the modicum of 'wisdom' appropriate to his nature and his abilities.[45] The project is presented in terms of *discipline* (κατάρτυσις τῶν ψύχων), to be achieved by understanding theory but also by πόνοι, self-restraint and -denial, even punishment 'by fire and sword', and ending with the purification of one's thoughts and understanding (*dianoia*).[46] By means of such purification, the spiritual 'eye' is marvellously (δαιμονίως) clarified and enabled to grasp *to noêton*, the intelligible, the truth about reality.[47] In this strenuous ambition, the model, as in much ancient moral philosophy including Christianity, is Heracles, who

> being himself a god, yet obedient to someone older than himself, struggled through his labors and established for his father (Zeus) the triumphal contest at Olympia in commemoration of his achievements (40).[48]

We may see this aim of encouraging an individual 'otherness', mainly but not entirely restricted to themes quite compatible with wider moral values,[49] as an attempt to protect the school from the accusation that it encouraged alienation from the wider society or constituted a critique of dominant social values – moral heroism can make others decidedly uncomfortable. A similar strategy seems to be implicit in the repeated insistence upon Pythagoras' divine or semi-divine or daemonic nature (his precise identity is happily fudged, as commonly in the genre of the encomium, to which Iamblichus is heavily indebted for

---

44   ibid. On *prohairesis* as a term in the philosophical discourse of Iamblichus' time, see RIST 1975.

45   IVP 90: κατὰ τὴν οἰκείαν φύσιν ἑκάστου καὶ δύναμιν.

46   IVP 68, 101. This comparable to PVP's scheme: purification from external influences, then the purification of thoughts, finally the purification of the soul as a whole.

47   IVP 70, referring to Plato, *Rep.* 527d-e; cf. DILLON 1982.

48   On Heracles as a Pythagorean hero, see PVP § 14 and 35, cf. DETIENNE 1960; MALHERBE 1988; GRAF 1998.

49   E.g. the emphasis on the favourable reaction (§ 45) of the Crotoniate ephebes' fathers to P.'s speech in the gymnasium, which started with the injunction 'Respect your elders' (§ 37); the list of kinds of lawless behaviour prompted by greed in § 78: rape, robbery, parricide, sacrilege, magic/poisoning; and the injunction to die in battle with wounds to the front (§ 85). Even recollection exercises (§§ 164–165) were thoroughly familiar to the rhetorical classes.

his topoi).[50] Whereas Iamblichus rejects the story that Pythagoras' mother Parthenis was made pregnant by Apollo, he does allow that his soul was 'sent down' by the god, a view legitimated by a detailed oracular response to his father Mnesarchus by the Pythia,[51] and by the fact that the mass of the Samian people considered him to be θεοῦ παῖδα, on account of his prepossessing appearance (ὑπὸ τῆς φυσικῆς θεοειδείας) and way of life.[52] Later, arrived in Croton, he is counted a god, or a *daimon*; a peppering of more specific 'reports' follows, that he is Delphic Apollo, or Hyperborean Apollo,[53] or Paian, or one of the *daimones* who dwell in or round the moon, or even an Olympian sent to benefit human beings through the gift of philosophy.[54] Aristotle is cited to confirm this uncertainty: of rational beings there are gods, humans, and people such as Pythagoras.[55] All this uncertainty was thematised in the literature by an *akousmaton*: τίς εἶ, Πυθαγόρα; § 140), which, by assuming the irrelevance of the correct answer: 'an ancient philosopher, the son of Mnemarchus/Mnesarchus', underwrote the continuous production of pseudo-answers; but at the same time, by removing Pythagoras from the human world, suggested the impossibility of carrying desirable imitation too far.[56] Such a reading is confirmed by the later recital of wonders in

---

50 Cf. DELATTE 1915/1974, 279–280; DILLON AND HERSHBELL 1991, 11–12. Compare the ambiguity about Sosipatra's teachers stressed by Sarah Johnston elsewhere in this volume (p.000).

51 The earliest evidence for the form Mne*s*archus is Heracleitus frg.129 D-K. Iamblichus himself calls the father Mne*m*archus, apparently to highlight the derivation from μνήμη, even though μνησ- has exactly the same semantic value. DLVP § 1 mentions a counter-tradition emanating from Phlious according to which his father's name was Marmacus, cf. DELATTE 1922/1979, 148.

52 IVP § 5–7; note also the expressions κατεπέμφθαι εἰς ἀνθρώπους § 8; and ὡς δαίμων τις ἀγαθός § 10. These are of course typical features of the theios anêr: BIELER 1935–1936/1967, 34–36.

53 Repeated at § 91 (recognition as such, 'and not just a mortal resembling him', by Abaris the Hyperborean), at § 135 and emphatically at § 140, cf. 143. The identification is elsewhere given as a citation from Aristotle's *On the Pythagoreans* (frg. 191 Rose); cf. DLVP § 11 with DELATTE 1922/1979, 170.

54 IVP § 30.The account, which also appears in PVP § 20, is evidently derived from Nicomachus. The detail of the lunar *daimones* must be Iamblichus' own, however, since it fits his daemonology only too well (Joh. Lydus, *De mens.* 4.25 and 149).

55 τὸ δὲ οἷον Πυθαγόρας: IVP § 31 = Arist. frg. 192 Rose.

56 The implied answer seems to be 'a god'; see also the riddle at § 143–144. At 172 Pythagoras is listed with Charondas, Zaleucus and other legislators, who are granted *isotheoi timai*, like the Roman emperor.

connection with Abaris, predictions of earthquakes, stilling of storms and rough waters, zooming about on an arrow.[57] This is of course not the 'meaning' of the claim to quasi-divinity, but one of its implicit effects. At the same time, we find an interesting shift in the significance of the word θεῖος, which, when applied to a philosopher (such as Iamblichus himself), comes in neo-platonic contexts to indicate the clarity of teaching and the conduct of life that manifest a special affinity to the divine world.[58]

Religious Practice and the Construction of Individuality

At this point we may turn to the more specific question of the contribution of religious practice to the representative individuality envisaged by Iamblichus. When Pythagoras met Abaris, the aged barbarian priest of Hyperborean Apollo, he excused him from the usual lengthy admission procedures into his group, and rapidly taught him the contents of his two books, *Peri physeôs* and *Peri theôn*.[59] The fiction neatly indicates the dual self-representation of Iamblichan neo-Pythagoreanism, as religious praxis combined with an arduous philosophical programme of natural and 'mathematical' enquiry, which had already been intimated through the narrative mode in the account of Pythagoras' visits to the Greek pre-Socratic sages, and his lengthy journeys to the wise nations to learn astronomy, geometry, arithmetic and music but also religious lore.[60] Elsewhere, the religious rationale (*logos*) for this philosophy is formulated as ἀκολοθεῖν τοῦ θεοῦ, 'following the deity'.[61] In this passage, the world is represented as a version of the Roman Empire (perhaps originally the Achaemenid Empire), ruled by a *basileus*. In such a world, it makes no sense to address all one's political efforts to a satrap

---

57 IVP 135–136.
58 Cf. Staab 2002, 286.
59 IVP 90. On the supposed books of Pythagoras, cf. DLVP 6–9 with Delatte 1922/1979, 159–168; van der Waerden 1965, 847–856 (his group A).
60 IVP 11–19. § 59 provides the justification for astronomy, as the contemplation of 'very beautiful' objects (*ta kallista*) and their order, which provide concrete instances of *to prôton* and *to noêton*, the proper teachers of wisdom, cf. Staab 2002, 288–291 on the grounds that the magi forbid the pollution of fire by a corpse.
61 IVP 86–87, repeated for emphasis at 137.

or provincial governor (*hyparchos*) and ignore the *basileus*.[62] The political metaphor provides a reassuring sense of the approachability and accessibility of the deity, a sense that is promptly undone by the reprise of a synthesis between philosophy (τὴν θείαν φιλοσοφίαν) and religion (θεραπείαν) at § 151, where Pythagoras' religious praxis turns out to be an eclectic mixture of themes taken from the Orphics, the wise foreign nations, the established mysteries at Eleusis, Imbros, Samothrace and Lemnos, other religious associations (*ta koina*), and even the Celts and Iberians. Such a list at once recalls Pythagoras' 'Wanderjahre' as described in the biographical section: after stops in Miletus, Priene and elsewhere along the coast of Asia Minor, he visits Sidon, Byblos and Tyre in Phoenicia and has himself initiated in all the mysteries there, not from superstition (οὐχὶ δεισιδαιμονίας ἕνεκα) but from a desire for *theôria*.[63] These however all turned out to be derived from Egypt, where he spent twenty-two years visiting all the temples and sacred sites, talking to priests and προφῆται, ignoring no rite that was somewhere held in honour (οὔτε τελετὴν τῶν ὅπου δήποτε τιμωμένων ... § 18). Captured by Cambyses' troops and taken to Babylon, where he spent twelve years, he encountered the magi, who taught him the perfect worship of the gods (θεῶν θρησκείαν ἐντελεστάτην, § 19).

These spurious details have two functions. On the one hand, the idea that Pythagoras was an universal initiate into mysteries Greek and foreign made him the perfect (and unsurpassable) model for a neo-Pythagorean, and tendentially justified the apparently irrational, or at least under-determined, specific rules for religious behaviour that are so marked a feature of the *De vita pythagorica* (although only one, namely the injunction against cremation of the dead, is justified in appropriate terms).[64] Secondly, they serve to associate Pythagoras, Empedocles, Democritus, Plato, and so the neo-Pythagoreans, with the religious practice of earliest mankind, which was held to be especially authentic and to be as nearly reflected as possible in the religions of the wise nations.[65] The detail that Pythagoras acted in Phoenicia not from un-

---

62   The image occurs already at Philo, *Decal.* 61; on Philo's somewhat unstable monotheism, see RADICE 2009, 128–129.

63   For *theôria*, see also IVP 59, with STAAB 2002, 290.

64   IVP 154. The reason given is that the divine shall not come into contact with the mortal, evidently a version of the magian rule that (divine) fire should not be polluted by a corpse. The magi of course went further, and forbade interment as well, on the grounds that the earth is also divine.

65   DÖRRIE 1966, 22; BOYS-STONE 2001, 99–122; SCHOTT 2008, 19.

grounded fear of the gods but from a desire to learn by seeing is intended not merely to deflect the accusation that so much enthusiasm implies lack of discrimination but to suggest that the sheer variety of human encounters with the divine leave plenty of space for Pythagorean rules, which by implication derive their legitimacy from their consonance with the 'Urreligion' of primitive mankind. If they make no sense, they at least make that much sense.[66]

The formal aim of neo-Pythagorean training in a religious context was to provide the mental peace proper to an encounter with the divine. The aim of the highest virtue of all, Pythagorean *philia*, the attempt to create harmony within oneself and with others, in the nuclear and extended family, and one's community, all the way down to one's treatment of animals, was to enable the soul to have more direct and immediate contact with the other world, both in religious praxis and when asleep (i. e. to encourage communicative dreams).[67] This drive to detach communication with the divine world from the routines of festival and civic cult, to say nothing of the implicit instrumentality of votive religion, is again perceptible in the observation, evidently in one of the Pseudo-pythagorica, that the Olympian gods take note of the intentions of sacrificants, not the sheer quantity of animals sacrificed.[68] A similar point is made about simplicity at funerals: the more extravagant the display, the sooner Hades will summon one.[69] Simplicity and self-denial prolong one's life because they please the gods of the underworld too. This is not the only point at which virtue is given a twist in the direction of life-advantage.

The special status of the divine world, its sheer otherness and unpredictability, is repeatedly emphasised. 'Piety' (here *eusebeia*) is translated into the injunction that one ought not to doubt any report, however marvellous, about the doings of gods (περὶ θεῶν μηδὲν θαυμαστὸν ἀ πιστεῖν) or concerning the Pythagorean religious teachings (περὶ θείων

---

66 At IVP 138 it is suggested that many of the specific injunctions about religious behaviour are derived from the mysteries – which may even in some cases have been true.

67 IVP 70: τῆς ἐπιτηδειοτάτης πρὸς θεοὺς ὁμιλίας ὕπαρ τε καὶ κατὰ τοὺς ὕπνους. On the general aim, cf. ERLER 1999.

68 IVP 122: ταῖς τῶν θυόντων διαθέσεσιν, οὐ τῷ τῶν θυομένων πλήθει προσέχουσιν.

69 Funeral arrangements are referred to in general at IVP 85 and 155.

δογμάτων)– 'since the gods are able to do all things'.[70] The attempt to practice the catchword οὐκ ἐψευδοδόξηται, 'there is nothing false in the lore',[71] evidently produced (at least ideally) a tendency to what would normally in this social class have been considered 'superstition', a preparedness to take popular stories (such as those about Abaris and Aristeas of Proconnesus) and strange or uncanny experiences seriously – i. e. a disposition to 'holy silliness'.[72] The repeated emphasis elsewhere on the importance of divination, the 'sole means' of discovering (μόνη ... ἑρμήνεια) the gods' purpose, is consistent with this aim,[73] and is explicitly presented as being perceived by the worldly (and the 'atheist' – an everready spectral aid in such contexts) as simple-mindedness (euêtheia) or as fraud (alazoneia).[74] Given his interest in theurgy, such an emphasis is not unexpected in a text by Iamblichus,[75] but it is also consistent with a resolve to shift the individual out of a preoccupation with dominant social meanings, 'common-sense' and second-hand impressions.[76] In confirmation of this, we find Pythagoras' implied reason for concerning himself with prophecies, oracles and omens, indeed everything that happens by chance (φήμαις καὶ μαντείαις καὶ κληδόσιν, ὅλως πᾶσι τοῖς αὐτομάτοις) as the fact that they – and especially omens of the type at issue here, such as twitchings of the face or skin – have no apparent cause and must therefore be intended as messages from the other world.[77]

---

70 IVP 148 (partly repeating 138–139). As usual, such repetitions are to be read as rhetorical reinforcement within the genre of the lecture and not, as was formerly the case, as the result of clumsy ineptitude on Iamblichus' part.
71 This phrase is translated by VON ALBRECHT 2002 ad loc. p. 131: 'Das überlieferte Vertrauen in den Wahrheitsgehalt ihrer Lehren ...'; Hirschbell's 'there is no such thing as false belief' (p.165) seems definitely wrong.
72 IVP 138–139.
73 Here again, the explicit claim is anticipated in the biographical section, where, as an ephebe, Pythagoras visits all the oracle-sites in Greece (IVP § 25). For Pythagoras' epitaph on the tomb of Apollo at Delphi, see PVP § 16.
74 IVP 138, cf. STAAB 2002, 355–356.
75 Note, for example, Iamblichus' explanation of the truthfulness of the oracle of Clarian Apollo, De myst. 3.11; and the asssertion, against Porphyry, that the gods voluntarily descend to provide insight, ibid. 1.12; cf. in general WALLIS 1972, 120–124; SHAW 1985. Plotinus had resolutely rejected all such belief in revelation (PVPlot 16)
76 On the debt to theurgy of Iamblichus' concept of the soul and its 'vehicle', see FINAMORE 1985, 11–32; 125–164.
77 IVP 149; here again von Albrecht's translation (2002, 131) is more accurate than Hirschbell's 'in short, to all things without visible cause' (p. 167).

It is not necessary here to discuss in detail the numerous specific injunctions about ritual behaviour.[78] Although some, such as the rule against giving birth in a temple (§ 153), are certainly mere repetitions of convention, and others, such as not cutting one's nails during festivals (§ 154), could be seen as a matter of good form, most are deliberately 'unmotivated', and are designed by their arbitrariness and sheer number to generate a subjective sense of difference from the ordinary (local) rules for dealing with the divine current in ancient communities. Their importance within the group is underscored by the joint claims that they are 'directed towards the divine', and that they obey a basic Pythagorean principle.[79] Being induced by one's belief to behave in unorthodox ways (particularly in the sacrificial régime) is an obvious means of distancing the subject from an earlier mode of being-in-the-world.[80] While the very randomness of the new rules enhances their importance as actions, the process of enacting them produces over time a new physical habitus, a significant contribution to the construction of an imagined religious community through individual choice. The oddity of such unmotivated rules is thematised by Iamblichus, who remarks that while some of them come with grounds, most do not; and in the case of those for which reasons are alleged, many are spurious, since they were added after Pythagoras, and indeed outside the Pythagorean community, in order to rationalise the strange.[81] At the same time, the end-result of such super-fine attention to the divine will turns out banal, a mere reiteration of the traditional theodicy: to the good, the gods will give blessings, to the wicked, the opposite.[82] But the notion of 'good' has shifted, summarised as 'what pleases God', οἷς τυγχάνει ὁ θεὸς χαίρων (§ 137).

Another function of 'unmotivated' ritual action is that the self-doubt it induces leaves space for faith. A striking feature of *De vita pythagorica*, as I have already implied, is the insistence on *pistis*, as a motivating force

---

78 IVP 83–84, 152–154, 155–156.
79 IVP 86: ἅπαντα … ἐστόχασται πρὸς τὸ θεῖον , καὶ ἀρχὴ αὕτη ἐστί. At § 177 Pythagoras asks whether his interlocutor would expect Apollo at Delphi to give his reasons.
80 I do not here discuss the text's ambivalences about the Pythagorean attitude towards sacrifice, which are evidently designed to accommodate a Theophrastean-Porphyrian line within a conventional sacrificial régime.
81 IVP 86.
82 IVP 87, repeated almost word for word for emphasis at § 137. Note also § 174, on the gods' responsibility for régimes of justice.

in the search for 'knowledge' and 'wisdom', which is in turn the foundation of theoretical knowledge of God; and on the folly of those who
lack belief (οἱ ἀπιστοῦντες).[83] Elsewhere, in his definition of the injunction μὴ ἀπιστεῖν, Iamblichus suggests that there are some things that
cannot be doubted (because of their logical nature) and implies that
the neo-Pythagorean should learn to extend that faith to other aspects
of the lore.[84] This language seems itself to derive from Porphyry's late
position, which was that one must believe that we can only be saved
by turning to God (μόνη σωτηρία ἡ πρὸς τὸν θεὸν ἐπιστροφή), a commitment that involves discovering the truth about him, and loving that
truth, a love that will 'nourish the soul' all through one's life.[85]

One last point here concerns the possible relation between this view
of Pythagoras, as a representative individual particularly devoted to religious practice, and concurrent Christianity in the phase shortly before
the promulgation of Licinius' edict of toleration in the East (313 CE).[86]
Such a connection has been suspected from at least the time of le Père
Festugière.[87] In the nature of the case, such interplay is likely to be hard
to prove one way or the other. Nevertheless, there do seem to be one or
two passages where an allusion to, even a repudiation of, Christian (and
Jewish) claims appears plausible.[88] Whereas most recent editors, following DEUBNER, have bracketed the reference to the coenobitic life of the
philosophountes at Croton, who hold their goods in common, STAAB has
shown that Iamblichus' additions to the putative text of Nicomachus
here are all plausible.[89] If so, given the strong, albeit not exclusive, asso-

---

83 IVP 138, cf. n. 70 above.
84 *Protrept.* p. 111.14–16: 'The injunction 'do not doubt/disbelieve' means: fol-
    low up and assimilate what you will not doubt, i.e. the *mathêmata* and the ra-
    tional proofs'. Book 7 of the *Compendium* was devoted to an exploration of the
    way Pythagorean number-theory reinforced the theology: Syrianus, *In Metaph.*
    CAG VI.1 p. 140 Kroll.
85 Porphyry, *ad Marcellam* 24, cited by STAAB 2002, 357–358. These claims may
    themselves be derived from the Chaldaean Oracles, cf. des PLACES 1982, 160
    on *ad Marcellam* ad loc.
86 On the edict, see recently VAN DAM 2007, 169–171.
87 Cf. FESTUGIÈRE 1937/1971, 490–491 (490–491); FOWDEN 1977, cf. FAUTH
    1987; a judicious review of the wider issues in du TOIT 2002.
88 I incline to doubt whether ὁ τοῦ θεοῦ παῖς in IVP 10 is to be considered an
    allusion to Christian claims, as suggested by GORMAN 1985. It has far too
    long an ancestry in pagan θεῖος ἀνήρ discourse.
89 IVP 29–30, bracketed by e.g. von Albrecht and Dillon/Hirshbell (who admit
    in a note however [p.53 n.5] that it might be an insertion by Iamblichus hi-

ciation between the term κοινόβιος and emergent monachism, we might here have a trace of a claim to pagan priority.[90] JOHN DILLON has construed Thales' announcement that he could foretell nothing but good (ἐκ παντὸς εὐηγγελίζετο) if Pythagoras goes to converse with the priests in Egypt, as another such attempt at claiming historical priority.[91] Pythagoras' long solitary sojourn in a temple (ἐμόναζε ... κατὰ τὸ ἱερόν) on the coast below Mt. Carmel, may likewise be an anticipation of Elijah's residence there.[92] On the other hand, given its consonance with traditional pagan injunctions such as ἕπου 9εῷ 'follow god', Pythagoras' formulation of his basic rule of piety, 'to follow God' (πρὸς τὸ ἀκολουθεῖν τῷ 9εῷ), is more naturally to be understood in this context as a call to ὁμοίωσις 9εῷ rather than a reference to Christian claims about their goal.[93] We must conclude that 'correction of the record' cannot be taken as a major aim of the *De vita pythagorica*, no doubt because Christianity seems only to have penetrated the Apamene on any scale towards the very end of Constantine's reign, and so posed no locally-recognisable threat during Iamblichus' residence there.[94]

Teachers, Students and Representative Individuality

It is time to return to the *De vita pythagorica* as an introduction to a particular type of higher education. EDWARD WATTS has rightly insisted on the novelty for the students of the great rhetorical and philosophical schools – the ambivalent experience of freedom from home, the initiation rituals, the strictly-enforced academic hierarchy, money worries.[95]

melf); cf. STAAB 2002, 261–267. *Philosophountes* is, of course the neo-Pythagorean term.

90 The adj. κοινόβιος seems however to have been current as a technical term in astrology; cf. κοινοβίωσις in *PDura* 32.10 (254 CE), meaning 'cohabitation'.

91 IVP 12 with DILLON AND HIRSHBELL 1991, 39 n. 13. It is a Christian commonplace that Pythagoras' stay in Egypt proved that his teaching depended on Moses.

92 IVP 14 with STAAB 2002, 249–250. Hermippus already claimed that Pythagoras took his teaching from the Jews (Origen, *c. Celsum* 1.14).

93 IVP 137. STAAB here inclines to see yet another allusion to Christian claims (2002, 317–318).

94 TROMBLEY 1995, 2: 283–311. Antioch however had been the focus of persecutions by Galerius and Maximinus (SCHOTT 2008, 112). For the long-term threat to traditional euergetism from Christian charity, see GIARDINA 2007, 767.

95 WATTS 1999, 236–241.

From that point of view, although Apamea hardly counted among the leading schools, the image offered by the *De vita* of a functioning community guided by *sophrosyne* and *philia* constituted an ideal far removed from experiential reality and perhaps for that very reason attractive. On the other hand, as BLOSSOM STEFANIW suggests elsewhere in this volume (p. 129), insofar as religious change comes about through discourse, the teacher – or an analogue – needs to embody the ultimate goal of the educational project jointly engaged in by the members of the school. For Iamblichus, the figure of Pythagoras, thanks to endless pseudo-historical re-writing culminating in Porphyry's *Vita* (likewise the initial text in a larger compendium),[96] provided precisely such a model, capable of combining traditional social morality with more specific features of neo-Platonist psychology. Such a modernised figure from remote antiquity, analogous to Philostratus' Apollonius,[97] allowed Iamblichus to present his teaching as representative of an aspect of Hellenic culture hallowed by ages, an alternative to the Homeric hero so dominant in the rhetorical school.

The question of pay-off nevertheless remains. STEFANIW rightly invokes the relation between heavy intellectual and moral investment and the extraordinary status of the ideal teacher, whether Plotinus, Origen, Ammonius or another. As an autonomous discourse, philosophy was free to create its own heroes. And it is a truism that intelligent people tend to be good at the sort of tasks that are valued in their group or sub-group – whatever their 'objective' instrumental value.[98] Nevertheless, despite the privileges attached to senior status, only a few students were gripped with sufficient 'philosophic frenzy' to persevere to the end.[99] Most abandoned philosophy for law, or returned to rhetoric, the prerequisites for an administrative career. Their families' main interest lay in the status and contacts to be acquired through attendance at such a school. Despite the widespread destructions of the 250s in the steppe by Šapur I, and the renewed outbreaks of 'plague' in the years 250–270, the local élites of the eastern Empire had continued to extend their landholdings and develop social ambitions for their sons. As for Py-

---

96 PVP was part of Porphyry's φιλόσοφος ἱστορία in four books, now to be dated c.268–270 CE: BEUTLER 1954, 287–288 (no. 27a); SEGONDS 1982, 166.
97 Cf. FLINTERMANN 1995; FRANCIS 1995, 83–129.
98 Note the praise of 'mental culture' (*paideia*) for the young, rather than the cult of the body, at 42–44.
99 Synesius, *Ep.* 139 (tr. Fitzgerald), cited by WATTS 2005, 240.

thagoras viewed as a model for a certain type of individuality, we might say that he represents an optional alternative to traditional forms of competitive individuality, such that the acquisition of symbolic capital by a section of the élite could be extended from external prestige, institutionalised power and modes of display to include forms of moral distinction, complete with an emphasis upon hard labour and constant effort – an extension paralleled by the concurrent real-world shift of the élite's investment in display away from the city to the suburban and rural villa.

The very fact that this option was open only to privileged young men, and only for a limited part of their lives, suggests that the reflexive (or moral) individuality striven for, based in this case upon appetitive restraint and ethical scrupulousness, in the name of a supremely moralised heaven, functioned as a sort of alibi, or exemplary fiction, for the adult male élite as a whole, the actual possessors of power and property. Such a discourse was valid only within the academy, but we may suspect it had a certain status beyond. The forms of individuality, pragmatic and competitive, effective for the local élites had long since been acquired; but through their sons they stood proxy for another distinctive form of individuality, acquired through acknowledgement of the merit attributable to severe self-regulation, in Elias' terms, 'hypercivility'. It is that hypercivilty that 'Pythagoras' represented. The seriousness of the study, the sheer extent and technical detail of the other nine books of the *Pythagorean Compendium* (and its analogues in other such schools, such as the ten volumes on the Pythagorean theory of number by Anatolius, Iamblichus' teacher), served to veil this alibi function from the students and their sponsors. At the same time, it is not absurd to suggest that among the unintended consequences of this type of teaching, both as school-lecture and as copied text, was the emergent conviction that the gods indeed had no interest in the quantity of animals sacrificed but only in the attitude of heart, that, as in the Theophrastan-Porphyrian line of argument, vegetable sacrifices were more pleasing to them; and that, if one were forced by one's position to sacrifice (like the *acusmatici*), one would rather it were a cock or a lamb, not an ox.[100] GUY STROUMSA once argued that it was post-Temple Judaism, with its enforced abandonment of blood-sacrifice, its spiritualisation of the liturgy

---

100 IVP 122; 150; cf. the critique of Abaris' 'barbarian' sacrifices, 147. Iamblichus himself found nothing reprehensible in animal sacrifices to δαίμονες: *De myst. aeg.* 5.15.

and its democratisation of cult, that helped transform paganism.[101] The argument is not to be dismissed out of hand. But the presence of a 'Theophrastan' Pythagoras in the philosophical schools of the late third and early fourth century, as exemplified in the *De vita pythagorica*, surely made the issue of what and how to sacrifice inescapable for the sons of the local élites of the eastern Mediterranean. To that extent, even if long-standing forms of individuality within the élites remained dominant, the religious features of representative individuality may indeed have had implications for emergent moral individuality.

Bibliography

Selected texts and translations

VON ALBRECHT, MICHAEL (tr.). *Pythagoras: Legende, Lehre, Lebensgestaltung*. Zurich, Stuttgart 1963 = VON ALBRECHT et al. (eds.). 32–218.

VON ALBRECHT, MICHAEL et al. (eds.). *Jamblich, Περὶ τοῦ πυθαγορείου βίου*. SAPERE 4 Darmstadt 2002).

BRISSON, LUC; SEGONDS, ALAIN-PHILIPPE (tr., comm.). *Jamblique, Vie de Pythagore*. Paris 1996.

CLARKE, GILLIAN (tr., comm.). *Iamblichus. On the Pythagorean Life*. Translated Texts for Historians 8. Liverpool 1989.

DELATTE, ARMAND (ed., comm.). *La vie de Pythagore de Diogène Laërce*. Mémoires de l'Académie royale de Belgique, Classe des lettres et des sciences morales et politiques 17.2. Brussels 1922, repr. Westport CN.

DES PLACES, EDOUARD (ed., comm.). *Porphyre, Vie de Pythagore; Lettre à Marcella*. Paris 1982.

DEUBNER, LUDWIG. *Iamblichi De vita pythagorica liber²*, ed. U. [= H.] Klein. Stuttgart 1975.

DILLON, JOHN; HERSHBELL, JACKSON (eds., tr.). *Iamblichus. On the Pythagorean Way of Life*. SBL Texts and Translations 29. Atlanta 1991.

DUNCAN-JONES, RICHARD P. (2004). "Economic Change and the Transition to Late Antiquity", in: SWAIN, SIMON; EDWARDS, MARK (eds.). *Approaching Late Antiquity: The Transformation from Early to Late Empire*. Oxford. 20–52.

GIANGIULIO, MAURIZIO (ed., tr.). *Giamblico: La vita Pitagorica*. Classici della BUR L825. Milan 1991.

NAUCK, AUGUSTUS. *Iamblichi de vita pythagorica liber, cum de Pythagorae Aureo Carmine*. St. Petersburg 1884; repr. Amsterdam 1965. Useful for the excellent index vocabulorum, pp. 247–355.

PERIAGO LORENTE, MIGUEL (tr., comm.). *Vida pitagórica; Protreptico*. Biblioteca clásica Gredos 314. Madrid 2003.

---

101 STROUMSA 2005, 105–144.

PERIAGO LORENTE, MIGUEL (tr., comm.). *Vida de Pitágoras / Porfirio. Argonaúticas órficas. Himnos órficos.* Biblioteca clásica Gredos 104. Madrid 1987.

Literature cited

ALCOCK, SUSAN E. 2007. "The Eastern Mediterranean", in: Scheidel, Walter; Morris, Ian; Saller, Richard P. 671–697.

ASSMANN, JAN; STROUMSA, GUY G. (edd.) 1999. *Transformations of the Inner Self in Ancient Religions.* Studies in the History of Religions (Numen) 83. Leyden.

BAYLY, CHRISTOPHER A. 2004. *The Birth of the Modern World 1780–1914.* Malden, Oxford.

BECHTLE, GERALD 2002. "Pythagoras: Zwischen Wissenschaft und Lebensführung", in: Erler, Michael; Graeser, Andreas (edd.). 36–55.

—2006. *Iamblichus: Aspekte seiner Philosophie und Wissenschaftskonzeption.* St. Augustin.

BEUTLER, R. 1954. s.v. Porphyrios no.21, *RE* 22. 275–313.

BIELER, LUDWIG (1935–36/1967) Θεῖος ἀνήρ: *Das Bild des "göttlichen Menschen" in Spätantike und Frühchristentum*, Vienna, repr. Darmstadt.

BLUMENTHAL, HENRY J.; CLARK, GILLIAN E. (edd.) 1993. *The Divine Iamblichus. Philosopher and Man of Gods.* London, Bristol.

BOWIE, EWEN 1978. "Apollonius of Tyana: Tradition and Reality", *ANRW* II.16.2. 1652–1699.

BOYS-STONES, GEORG 2001. *Post-Hellenistic Philosophy: A Study in its Development from the Stoics to Origen.* Oxford.

BURKERT, WALTER 1961. "Pythagoreische Pseudopythagorica", *Philologus* 105. 16–43; 226–246.

—1972. *Lore and Science in Ancient Pythagoreanism* (corr. ed., tr. E.L.: Minar). Cambridge MA.

—1982. "Zur geistesgeschichtlichen Einordnung einiger Pseudopythagorica", in: von Fritz, Kurt (ed.). *Pseudepigrapha.* Entretiens Fondation Hardt 18. Vandoeuvres. 23–55.

CLARK, GILLIAN 2000. "Philosophic Lives and the Philosophic Life: Porphyry and Iamblichus", in: Hägg, Tomas; Rousseau, Philip. 29–51.

MELLONI, CUCCIOLI R. 1969. *Ricerche sul Pitagorismo, 1: Biografia di Pitagora.* Studi pubbl. dall'Istituto di Filol. Class., Univ. di Bologna 25. Bologna.

DALSGAARD LARSEN, BENT 1970. *Iamblique de Chalcis, exégète et philosophe* [Diss. Aarhus 1970]. Aarhus.

—1975. "Jamblique dans la philosophie antique tardive", in: idem (ed.). *De Jamblique à Proclus.* 1–26.

—(ed.) 1975. *De Jamblique à Proclus.* Entretiens Fondation Hardt 21. Vandoeuvres.

DELATTE, ARMAND 1915/1974. *Études sur la littérature pythagoricienne.* Bibliothèque de l'Ecole des hautes études, Sciences hist. et philol. 217. Paris, repr. Geneva.

DETIENNE, MARCEL 1960. "Héraclès, héros pythagoricien", *RHR* 158. 19–53.

DEUBNER, LUDWIG A. 1935. "Bemerkungen zum Text der Vita Pythagorae des Iamblichos", *SB preuss. Akad. Wiss., phil.-hist. Kl.* 1935.19. Berlin. 610–690; also as Separatum. 1–85.

DILLON, JOHN M. (ed., com.) 1973. *Iamblichi Chalcidensis in Platonis dialogos commentariorum fragmenta.* Philosophia Antiqua 23. Leyden.

—1982. "Self-definition in Later Platonism", in: Meyer, Ben F.; Sanders, Ed P. (edd.). *Jewish and Christian Self-definition, 3: Self-Definition in the Graeco-Roman World.* London. 60–75.

—1987. "Iamblichus of Chalkis (c.240–325 AD)", *ANRW* II.36.2. 862–987.

—2002a. "Introduction", in: Finamore, John F.; Dillon, John. 1–9.

—2002b. "Jamblich: Leben und Werke", in: von Albrecht, Michael et al. (edd.). 11–21.

Dörrie, Heinrich 1966. "Die Schultradition im Mittelplatonismus und Porphyrios", in: idem (ed.). 4–25.

—1975. "Die Religiosität des Platonismus im 4. und 5. Jhdt. n. Chr.", in: Dalsgaard Larsen, Bent (ed.). 257–281.

—(ed.) 1966. *Porphyre.* Entretiens Fondation Hardt 12. Vandoeuvres.

DU TOIT, DAVID S. 2002. "Heilsbringer im Vergleich: Soteriologische Aspekte im Lukasevangelium und Jamblichs De vita Pythagorica", in: von Albrecht, Michael et al. (edd.). 275–301.

EARLY, ROBERT ET AL. 2003. *Zeugma: Interim Reports.* Journal of Roman Archaeology Suppl. Series 51. Portsmouth RI.

EDWARDS, MARK J. 1993. "Two Images of Pythagoras: Iamblichus and Porphyry", in: Blumenthal, Henry J.; Clark, Gillian E. (edd.). 159–172.

ELDERKIN, GEORGE W. 1934–41. *Antioch on the Orontes. The Excavations of 1932/1933—36/1937–39.* 3 vols. Princeton.

ELIAS, NORBERT 1987. *Die Gesellschaft der Individuen* (M. Schröter, ed.). Frankfurt a.M.

ENGELS, LODEWIJK J.; HOFMANN, HEINZ (edd.) 1997. *Spätantike, mit einem Panorama der byzantinischen Literatur* = K. von See (ed.), *Neues Handbuch der Literaturwissenschaft* 4. Wiesbaden.

ERLER, MICHAEL 1999. "Philosophie als Therapie – Hellenistische Philosophie als 'Praeparatio platonica' im Platonismus der Spätantike", in: Fuhrer, Therese; Erler, Michael (edd.). 105–122.

ERLER, MICHAEL; GRAESER, ANDREAS (edd.) 2000. *Philosophen des Altertums, von der Frühzeit bis zur Klassik. Eine Einführung.* Darmstadt.

FAUTH, WOLFGANG 1987. "Pythagoras, Jesus von Nazareth und der Helios-Apollon des Julianos-Apostata. Zu einigen Eigentümlichkeiten der spätantiken Pythagoras-Aretalogie im Vergleich mit der thaumasiologen Tradition der Evangelien", *ZNTW* 28. 26–48.

FESTUGIÈRE, ANDRÉ-JEAN 1937/1971. "Sur une nouvelle édition du 'De vita Pythagorica' de Jamblique", in: idem. *Études de philosophie grecque.* Paris. 535–550.

FILORAMO, GIOVANNI 1999. "The Transformation of the Inner Self in Gnostic and Hermetic Texts", in: Assmann, Jan; Stroumsa, Guy G. (edd.). 137–149.

FINAMORE, JOHN F. 1985. *Iamblichus and the Theory of the Vehicle of the Soul.* American Classical Studies 14. Chicago CA.

FINAMORE, JOHN F.; DILLON, JOHN 2002. *Iamblichus, De Anima: Text, Translation and Commentary.* Philosophia Antiqua 92. Leyden.

FLINTERMANN, JAAP-JAN 1995. *Power, Paideia and Pythagoreanism: Greek identity, conceptions of the relationship between philosophers and monarchs, and political ideas in Philostratus' Life of Apollonius.* Amsterdam.

FOWDEN, GARTH 1977. "The Platonist Philosopher and his Circle in Late Antiquity", *Philosophia* 7. 359–383.

FRANCIS, JAMES A. 1995. *Subversive Virtue: Asceticism and Authority in the II^P Pagan World.* Univ. Park PA.

FREDE, MICHAEL 1987. "Numenius", *ANRW* II.36.2. 1034–1075.

FUHRER, THERESE; ERLER, MICHAEL (edd.) 1999. *Zur Rezeption der hellenistischen Philosophie in der Spätantike. Akten der 1. Tagung der Karl- u. Gertrud-Abel-Stiftung vom 22.–25. Sept. 1997 in Trier.* Philosophie der Antike 9. Stuttgart.

GIANGIULIO, MAURIZIO 1997. "Sapienza pitagorica e religiosità apollinea", in: Cassio, Albio C.; Pocetti, Paolo (edd.). *Forme di religiosità e tradizioni sapienzali in Magna Grecia. Atti del convegno, Napoli, 14–15 dic. 1993.* AION, sez. filologico-lettereria 16. Pisa. 9–27.

GIARDINA, ANDREA 2007. "The Transition to Late Antiquity", in: Scheidel, Walter; Morris, Ian; Saller, Richard (edd.). 743–768.

GORMAN, PETER 1985. "The 'Apollonios' of the neo-Platonic Biographies of Pythagoras", *Mnemosyne* 38. 130–144.

GRAF, FRITZ 1998. s.v. Herakles, *DNP* 4. 73–107.

HÄGG, TOMAS; ROUSSEAU, PHILIP 2000. *Greek Biography and Panegyric in Late Antiquity.* Berkeley.

HAHN, JOHANNES 1989. *Der Philosoph und die Gesellschaft: Selbstverständnis, öffentliches Auftreten und populäre Erwartungen in der hohen Kaiserzeit.* HABES 7. Stuttgart.

HOPKINS, KEITH 1980. "Taxes and Trade in the Roman Empire (200 BC – AD 400)", *Journal of Roman Studies* 70. 101–125.

—2002. "Rome, Taxes, Rent and Trade", in: Scheidel, Walter; von Reden, Sitta (edd.). *The Ancient Economy.* Edinburgh. 190–230. Orig. publ. in *Kodai* 6/7 (1995/96). 41–75.

KINGSLEY, PETER 1995. *Ancient Philosophy, Mystery and Magic: Empedocles and Pythagorean Tradition.* Oxford.

KIPPELE, FLAVIA 1997. *Was heisst Individualisierung? Die Antworten der soziologischen Klassiker.* Opladen.

JONGMAN, WILLEM M. 2002. "The Roman Economy: From Cities to Empire", in: de Blois, Lukas; Rich, John (edd.). *The Transformations of Economic Life under the Roman Empire. Proceedings of the Second Workshop of the International Network: Impact of Empire (Roman Empire, c.200 BC – AD 476), Nottingham July 4–7, 2001.* Amsterdam. 28–47.

—2007. "The Early Roman Empire: Consumption", in: Scheidel, Walter; Morris, Ian; Saller, Richard. 592–618.

KONDOLEON, CHRISTINE (ed.) 2000. *Antioch: The Lost Ancient City.* Princeton.

LÉVY, ISIDORE 1926. *Recherches sur les sources de la légende de Pythagore.* Bibliothè-que de l'École des hautes études. Sciences religieuses 42. Paris.

LO CASCIO, ELIO (ed.) 1997. *Terre, proprietari e contadini dell'impero romano. Dall' affitto agrario al colonato tardoantico.* Richerche 15: Storia. Rome.

—2000. "La struttura fiscale dell'Impero Romano", in: idem. *Il Princeps e il suo imperio: Studi di storia amministrativa e finanziaria romana.* Documenti e studi (Bari) 26. Bari, Edipuglia, 177–203. Orig. publ. in Crawford, Michael H. (ed.). *L'impero romano e le strutture economiche e soziali delle province.* Bibl. di Athenaeum 4 (British School at Rome), Como, New Press (1986). 29–59.

—2007. "The Early Roman Empire: The State and the Economy", in: Schei-del, Walter; Morris, Ian; Saller, Richard. 5619–5647.

LURJE, MICHAEL 2002 a. "Einführung in die Vita Pythagorica", in: von Albrecht et al. (edd.). 25–31.

—2002 b. "Die Vita Pythagorica als Manifest der neuplatonischen Paideia", in: von Albrecht et al. (edd.). 221–254.

MACRIS, CONSTANTINOS 2002. "Jamblique et la littérature pseudo-pythagorici-enne", in: Mimouni, Simon C. (dir.). *Apocryphité. Histoire d'un concept trans-versal aux religions du livre: en hommage à P. Geoltrain.* Bibliothèque de l'École des hautes études. Sciences religieuses 113. Turnhout. 77–129.

MALHERBE, ABRAHAM J. 1988. s.v. Herakles, *RAC* 14. 559–583.

O'MEARA, DOMINIC J. 1989. *Pythagoras Revived: Mathematics and Philosophy in Late Antiquity.* Oxford. (repr. 1997).

PARRISH, DAVID (ed.) 2001. *Urbanism in Western Asia Minor.* Journal of Roman Archaeology Suppl. Series 45. Portsmouth RI.

PENELLA, ROBERT J. 1990. *Greek Philosophers and Sophists in the Fourth Century AD: Studies in Eunapius of Sardis.* ARCA 28. Leeds.

POCCARDI, GRÉGOIRE 2003. "L'île d'Antioche à la fin de l'antiquité: histoire et problème de topographie urbaine", in: Lavan, Luke (ed.). *Recent Research in Late-Antique Urbanism.* JRA Suppl. Series 42. Portsmouth RI. 155–172.

RADICE, ROBERTO 2009. "Philo's Theology and Theory of Creation", in: Ka-mesar, Adam (ed.). *The Cambridge Companion to Philo.* Cambridge. 124–145.

RIEDWEG, CHRISTOPH 2002. *Pythagoras: Leben – Lehre – Nachwirkung.* Munich.

RIST, JOHN M. 1975. "Prohaeresis. Proclus, Plotinus et alii", in: Dalsgaard Lars-en (ed.). 103–122.

ROHDE, ERWIN 1871/1901. "Die Quellen des Iamblichos in seiner Biographie des Pythagoras", *RhMus* 26, 554–76 = *Kleine Schriften* [ed. F. Schöll] 2. Tübingen. 101–128.

RÜPKE, JÖRG (ed.) 2013. The Individual in Ancient Mediterranean Religions. Oxford: Oxford University Press (forthcoming).

SCHEIDEL, WALTER; MORRIS, IAN; SALLER, RICHARD (edd.) 2007. *The Cam-bridge Economic History of the Greco-Roman World.* Cambridge.

SCHOTT, JÉRÉMY M. 2008. *Christianity, Empire and the Making of Religion in Late Antiquity.* Philadelphia..

SEGONDS, ALAIN-PH. 1982. "Les fragments de l'Histoire de la philosophie", in: des Places, Édouard (éd., comm.). *Vie de Pythagore. Lettre à Marcella.* Paris. 163–197.

SHAW, GREGORY 1985. "Theurgy: Rituals of Unification in the Neoplatonism of Iamblichus", *Traditio* 41. 1–28.

STAAB, GREGOR 2002. *Pythagoras in der Spätantike: Studien zu De Vita Pythagorica des Iamblichos von Chalkis.* Beiträge zur Altertumskunde 165. Munich, Leipzig.

STROUMSA, GUY G. 1999. "From Repentance to Penance in Early Christianity", in: Assmann, Jan; Stroumsa, Guy G. (edd.). 167–178.

—2005. *La fin du sacrifice. Les mutations religieuses de l'Antiquité tardive.* Paris.

TAORMINA, DANIELA P. 1999. *Jamblique, critique de Plotin et de Porphyre. Quatre etudes.* Paris.

THESLEFF, HOLGER 1961. *An Introduction to the Pythagorean Writings of the Hellenistic Period.* Acta Academiae Aboensis, Humaniora 24.3. Åbo, Åbo akademi. 8–27.

THOM, JOHAN C. (ed., tr., comm.) 1995. *The Pythagorean Golden Verses.* RGRW 123. Leyden.

TROMBLEY, FRANK R. 1995. *Hellenic Religion and Christianization, c.370–529.*[2] 2 vols. RGRW 115.1–2. Leyden.

VAN DAM, RAYMOND 2007. *The Roman Revolution of Constantine.* Cambridge.

VAN DEN WAERDEN, BARTEL L. 1965. s.v. Pythagoras. Die Schriften und Fragmente, *RE Suppl.* 10. 843–864.

VAN HARSKAMP, ANTON; MUSSCHENGA, ALBERT W. (edd.) 2001. *The Many Faces of Individualism.* Morality and the Meaning of Life 12. Leuven.

VON ALBRECHT, MICHAEL 1966/2002. "Das Menschenbild in Iamblichs Darstellung der pythagoreischen Lebensform", *Antike & Abendland* 12. 51–63 = von Albrecht et al. (edd.). 255–274.

WALLIS, RICHARD T. 1972/1995. *Neoplatonism.* London, (ed. 2, by L.P. Gerson).

WASZINK, JAN H. 1966. "Porphyrios und Numenios", in: Dörrie, Heinrich (ed.). 33–78.

WATTS, EDWARD 2005. "The Student Self in Late Antiquity", in: Brakke, David; Satlow, Michael; Weitzman, Steven (edd.). *Religion and the Self in Antiquity.* Bloomington. 234–251.

WILSON, ANDREW 2002. "Machines, Power and the Ancient Economy", *Journal of Roman Studies* 92. 1–32.

Sosipatra and the Theurgic Life: Eunapius *Vitae Sophistorum* 6.6.5–6.9.24

Sarah Iles Johnston

The life of Sosipatra, as narrated by the late fourth-century biographer Eunapius,[1] exists in a twilight of superficial fame. The past few decades of renewed attention to women in antiquity has ensured that Eunapius' description of Sosipatra (the only description of her that we possess) is excerpted in many survey treatments of ancient women[2] and particularly in treatments of women in later antiquity.[3] It is sometimes also adduced as a partial parallel for Hypatia, a more famous, and better studied, philosophic woman of about the same time.[4]

But beyond re-narrating Sosipatra's story, as these brief treatments do,[5] no one has said much about her—or rather, about the character whom Eunapius presents under her name. This is odd, for (at least) two reasons. First, Sosipatra's story provides some of the richest glimpses we have into the private intellectual and religious lives of the neoplatonists, and how they developed as both philosophers and theurgists. In fact, we can take this observation even further: Sosipatra's story, which has sometimes been described by scholars as a 'fairy-tale' or as having a 'fairy-tale' feeling,[6] might be read as demonstrating what Eunapius

---

1   *VS* 6.6.5–6.9.24, §§ 466–471.
2   E.g. Lefkowitz and Fant 1982, 452.
3   E.g. Clark 1993, 130, 133. O'Meara 2003, 83 briefly discusses her among the 'philosopher queens' he treats.
4   E.g. Dzielska 1996, 62, 80. The article by Harich-Schwarzbauer 2009 and the forthcoming treatment by Lewis are welcome exceptions to the rule of adducing Sosipatra only to shed light on Hypatia. Harich-Schwarzbauer interprets Sosipatra's story as holding the key to Eunapius' implicit teachings about theurgy, and Lewis thoroughly contextualizes Sosipatra within the few other examples we have of female philosophers in late antiquity.
5   Not always correctly; one gets the impression that some scholars either read it so quickly that they fail master the details or attempt to recall it from earlier readings: e.g. Luck 1999, 151–52, who says that the Strangers take Sosipatra away for five years.
6   E.g. Luck 1999; Luck 1985, 156. Pack 1952 does not use the term 'fairy tale', but he calls it 'romantic' and contextualizes it within 'folk literature'.

and his audience understood to be the *ideal* traits and personal habits of such an individual—as an exercise in ideology, in other words. Although all of the *Lives* are meant to serve as guides for their readers to some degree, then, Sosipatra's could be understood, rather, more in the way that early Christian hagiographies are: that is, as a model for life to which the average person might aspire but seldom achieve. There is a question implicit in that formulation, however, to which I will return: *could* Eunapius' average reader do anything to imitate Sosipatra? Or was Eunapius providing an ideal model not for the sake of imitation, but rather for some other reason altogether?

Second, the story of Sosipatra interrupts what can be understood as Eunapius' overall narrative. That is, if we agree that one of Eunapius' central purposes in the *Lives* was to laud Iamblichus and trace the pedagogical chain by which his teachings were transmitted,[7] then the story of Sosipatra, who is connected to Iamblichus as neither a student nor a relative, presents a potential impediment. And yet word-for-word, Eunapius lavishes more attention on her than on any figure in his *Lives* other than Maximus (whose story is lengthy because it is closely entwined with that of the future Emperor Julian and several other figures). We will want to consider Eunapius' reasons for paying so much attention to Sosipatra—indeed, for perhaps inventing, at least in part, the character he calls by this name.[8]

My two sets of questions are interrelated, of course: once we understand the sense in which Sosipatra is intended to serve as a model for Eunapius' readers, then we may better understand why Eunapius has awarded her a prominent place in the narrative. And, once we attune ourselves better to the purposes of that narrative, we may better understand why her life is highlighted by Eunapius even if it cannot serve as a model in the practical sense of that word. I will first examine Sosipatra's story in some detail, attempting to clarify some of its puzzling aspects,

---

7   As expressed, for example, PENELLA 1990, e.g. 32–33.
8   The question of whether or not a 'real' Sosipatra ever existed cannot, of course, be settled. My own opinion is that she did. Her husband, Eustathius; her son, Antoninus; and her close friend Aedesius are entwined by Eunapius in so many incidents of the period that it is hard to believe they are fictional—and to have presented readers with a character who was so closely involved with their lives and yet completely fictional surely would have strained acceptance of his narrative. It is likelier that her story had a basis in fact but was much embroidered by Eunapius and perhaps his sources.

and then look at its position in the overall narrative. Finally, I will return to the question of Sosipatra as a model.

1 The Story

Sosipatra's story is introduced into the narrative by mention of her marriage to Eustathius, one of Iamblichus' most accomplished students.[9] In his own *Life*, Eustathius is described as having a 'most noble character' and as being 'gifted with eloquence' to such a degree that the Emperor Constantius sought his advice and sent him on important embassies. People all over the Greek world clamored to hear Eustathius, both for the value of what he said and for the elegance with which he said it.[10]

Yet in spite of Eustathius' impressive accomplishments, when we segue from his biography into that of Sosipatra, it is by way of the following phrase: 'After this [career], the renowned Eustathius married Sosipatra, who by her surpassing wisdom made her own husband seem inferior and insignificant'[11]—she's presented as quite a woman, then, from her very debut in the narrative. Immediately after this, we turn away from her marriage and travel back to her beginnings. Eunapius tells us that she was born near Ephesus, on an estate owned by her wealthy father, but Eunapius fails to offer any further information about her family—notably omitting even her father's name. This silence nicely underscores a characteristic that is important to Sosipatra's story: she will become the remarkable woman that she does without the help of human tutelage or nurture. In fact, signs of her preternatural character and abilities were already present nearly from birth: while still a very young child, she brought blessings on everything she encountered.[12]

The decisive turn in her life occurs when she is five years old. Two elderly men, one slightly older than the other, arrive at her father's estate, dressed in skins and carrying large wallets such as travelers use for their provisions. They persuade the steward to let them care for the vines, and produce a harvest beyond all expectations—indeed, everyone who sees it thinks that some gods must have been at work. The owner

---

9   *VS* 6.6.5, § 466.
10   *VS* 6.5.1 – 6.6.5, §§ 465 – 466.
11   *VS* 6.6.5 – 6, § 466.
12   *VS* 6.6.6; § 467.

'offers them Greek hospitality' at his table, where the old men are cap-
tivated by Sosipatra's beauty and charm. They say to her father,

> this abundant vintage that you praise is just child's play for us, just a small
> sample of what we can do—we keep our other [abilities] hidden and secret.
> If you want a worthy return for the *xenia* you show us at this table—not in
> money or perishable, corruptible benefits but one that is far above you and
> your mode of life, a gift that will be famous above the skies and stars—then
> hand over to us your daughter Sosipatra for the next five years (for we are
> her truer parents and guardians). You need not fear that she will suffer any
> disease or death during this time.
>   Be careful not to set foot on this soil until the five years are up; on its
> own, wealth will arise for you in this place, blossoming forth from the soil.
> Moreover, not only will your daughter exceed the nature of a woman or of
> a human being, but you yourself will also understand more fully what your
> child really is ...[13]

After hearing these words, the father summons his steward, tells him to
do whatever the old men command, and flees the estate as quickly as
possible. When he returns five years later, he hardly recognizes his
daughter, so tall and beautiful has she become.

In its basic framework, this story evokes other tales. We probably
think first of Baucis and Philemon, who were visited in their Phrygian
village by Jupiter and Mercury, disguised as humans. In return for Baucis
and Philemon's hospitality, the gods caused their wine jug to pour forth
unceasingly (a miracle echoed by the abundant grape harvest in Sosipatra's story) and then made the two mortals the priestly keepers of a new
temple, until, at the end of their lives, they became stately, intertwined
trees. We know this story only through Ovid's narration,[14] but it, or a
broader pattern of which Baucis and Philemon's tale is just one itera-
tion, seems to have been widely known in Asia Minor: Barnabas and
Paul are mistaken for Jupiter and Mercury when they visit the Phrygian
town of Lystra and cure a crippled man.[15] More generally, as Sosipatra's
father himself remarks at the end of the first part of her tale,[16] Homer
had already realized that:

> the gods, in the likenesses of strangers from distant countries, put on all
> kinds of shapes and wander through cities.[17]

---

13   *VS* 6.6.10–12, § 467.
14   *Met.* 8.629–725.
15   Acts 14:8–13. On this point, see PACK 1952.
16   *VS* 6.7.7, § 468.
17   *Od.* 17.485.

Sometimes the gods visit in order to judge and punish those whom they meet (as the young men who speak these lines in the *Odyssey* warn An-tinoos, who has been abusing the disguised Odysseus), sometimes they visit to offer counsel (as Athena does for Telemachus at several points in the *Odyssey*), and sometimes they visit to reward and help their favor-ites—even, as in the Homeric *Hymn to Demeter,* attempting to make them more than mortal creatures (an episode that also seems to be evoked by the story of Sosipatra, especially given that Sosipatra's father is forbidden to witness what the Strangers do to his daughter). Other an-cient authors tell similar tales: in fact, the visiting god is a frequent pres-ence in ancient myth. That we are meant to think along these lines when reading Eunapius is suggested not only by the father's quotation of Homer, but by several other remarks that Eunapius inserts: when the first harvest miracle is performed, men on the estate are said to 'sus-pect the intervention of the gods';[18] Eunapius himself describes the vis-iting Strangers as 'either heroes, or *daimones* or of yet some even more god-like race'.[19] And at the end of their visit, when the two Strangers depart, telling Sosipatra that they will travel to the 'Western Ocean' but then return again one day, Eunapius comments that 'this proved very clearly that [they] were *daimones*'.[20]

The divine, or semi-divine, nature of these Strangers is one of the things that lends Sosipatra's story the 'fairy-tale' quality that scholars have noted. But it serves other purposes, too. First, it is vital to some-thing that I have already mentioned: Eunapius wishes to emphasize that Sosipatra becomes what she does *without human tutelage.* The Strangers control her development between the ages of five and ten; after they depart, Sosipatra's father allows her to finish developing on her own (al-though her habit of remaining silent for long periods sometimes annoys him)[21]. During this later period, Eunapius tells us, she

> … had no other teachers, but ever on her lips were the works of the poets, philosophers and orators; and those works that others comprehend only in-completely and dimly, and then only by hard work and painful drudgery, she could expound with careless ease, serenely and painlessly, and her light swift touch made their meaning clear.[22]

---

18 *VS* 6.6.9, § 467.
19 *VS* 6.7.1, § 467.
20 *VS* 6.7.11, § 468.
21 *VS* 6.8.1–2, § 469.
22 *VS* 6.8.2, § 469.

Second, the divine or semi-divine nature of the Strangers hints at what, exactly, it is that Sosipatra is becoming. After her father leaves her in their care, the Strangers 'initiate Sosipatra into mysteries that no one knew about' and 'divinize her to some purpose—the nature of which was not revealed even to those most eager to learn'.[23] Later, we learn a little more. After her father returns home, he implores the Strangers to reveal who they are. 'Enigmatically, and with bent heads', they describe themselves as 'not uninitiated in the wisdom that is called Chaldean'.[24] This circumlocution probably means that they are adherents of the Chaldean Oracles i. e., theurgists.[25]

Another hint in the same direction lies in the Strangers' remarks as they depart, which I mentioned just above. Given that 'Western Ocean' had been, since Homer, a way of referring to the boundary between the world of the living and the world of the dead, it sounds as if the Strangers plan to 'die' and later 'return to the world of the living'. This probably alludes to a doctrine found in theurgic sources (and nowhere else during the first few centuries CE) according to which souls that have been perfected in the course of repeated bodily incarnations, 'enter the angelic ranks' and ascend beyond the earthly, material realm. Such perfection and ascent frees these souls from ever needing to be incarnated again, but many of them nonetheless volunteer to do so in order to improve the souls of other people through their teachings.[26] In other words, it sounds as if Sosipatra's teachers are theurgic angels, who, having spotted a promising soul, temporarily returned to earth in order to nurture her, and then returned to their own realm.

The same doctrine probably underlies the prophecy that Sosipatra makes to her new husband. She tells Eustathius that after death, his soul will rise to the orbit of the moon—which she describes as a 'fair and fitting abode'. This is true, theurgically speaking: anything above the realm of the earth is a step up. More specifically, some theurgic sources suggest that the lunar realm was home to *daimones* and heroes,

---

23 *VS* 6.7.1–2 § 467.
24 *VS* 6.7.5–6, § 468, nach 2.
25 Although the word 'Chaldean' did not exclusively refer to the Oracles and the doctrines they advocated (theurgic doctrines), this was the most common connotation at the time Eunapius was writing, and particularly within a context such as that of his *Lives*, which concerns people such as Maximus and Julian, who were known to practice the theurgy of the Oracles. Further Lewy 1978, 443–447, esp. 443.
26 See Johnston 2004.

who in the theurgic system are helpful creatures of higher orders than humans. Sosipatra claims that her own soul, however, will rise into a yet loftier realm—it is easiest to understand this as the realm of the sun, which in theurgic doctrine, and in some other philosophical and religious systems of the time, was the highest point that a human soul could reach, even after it had been completely purified. Echoing Socrates' *daimonion,* however, a god interrupts Sosipatra before she can give such details, forbidding her to say more about her postmortem fate.[27]

I have temporarily skipped ahead in the story as Eunapius tells it, in order to elucidate the nature of the Strangers and of Sosipatra; we need to return now to what the Strangers did to her. I already noted that they performed initiations and divinization rituals that they were hesitant to identify or reveal, although they eventually admitted that they had something to do with 'Chaldean wisdom'. After Sosipatra's father returns and realizes how wondrously his daughter has developed, he begs the Strangers to 'initiate her to a yet more perfected degree'.[28] They nod their assent; the father then falls asleep and the Strangers hand over to Sosipatra,

> ... in a very tender and scrupulous manner, the whole array (*stolên*) of clothing in which she had been initiated (*tetelesto*) and added certain implements (*organa*) and then put many books into Sosipatra's chest, commanding that she should then have it sealed up.[29]

Several things are notable. The first is the plurality of initiations and consecrations that Sosipatra undergoes, apparently both before and after her father returns to the estate. This has parallels in more familiar mystery cults—Apuleius' Lucius undergoes a series of initiations at the end of the *Golden Ass*, the mysteries of Mithras had at least seven different grades of initiation, and Eleusis had two. But the final stage of Sosipatra's initiations, during which special clothing, tools and certain books were handed over to her (we later learn that the Strangers told her to keep these things until they returned from the Western Ocean) suggests that she had reached a level at which she now was equal to those who initiated her—a trustworthy keeper of their secrets. She is, indeed, described as becoming *tetheiasmenê* at this point—perhaps we

---

27 *VS* 6.8.3–6, § 469.
28 *VS* 6.7.6, § 468.
29 *VS* 6.7.8, § 468.

should translate this as 'worthy to be considered divine'?[30]—and also as having been 'filled with divinity' (*enthousiôsê*),[31] a state prized by the theurgists, who viewed it as one of the few secure means of receiving information from the gods (they distrusted almost every other form of divination).

Another matter is what we can call Sosipatra's 'clairvoyance' or 'second-sight'—that is, the ability to see what is happening in another place, at the moment that it happens. As E.R. DODDS already noted,[32] this phenomenon does not appear in Greek or Roman sources before late antiquity; we find it first in connection with Apollonius of Tyana (one of Eunapius' avowed heroes) who 'sees' Domitian's murder even though he is thousands of miles away,[33] and then we find it, remarkably, three times in Eunapius' story of Sosipatra: first when she tells her father everything that has just happened on his journey home; then when she is able to tell Maximus exactly what he did in a ritual he has just performed; and finally when she sees a chariot accident involving her cousin Philometor even as it is occurring on a distant road, and describes the injuries he is receiving and how he is rescued.[34]

In each of these cases, the people around Sosipatra comment that she must be a god—one of them adding the remark that only gods can know everything that happens because only gods are omnipresent. This emphatic association between divine status and clairvoyance may be one reason that cases are so rare in antiquity, and also the reason that when they do finally show up, it is in connection with Apollonius of Tyana (whom Eunapius and others declared to have been a god)[35], and Sosipatra, who, as we have seen, Eunapius characterized as a divine, or semi-divine, creature as well.[36]

Be that as it may, the three episodes of clairvoyance further underscore Sosipatra's uniqueness amongst the figures whom Eunapius presents in his *Lives*. This is not to say that none of the others perform ex-

---

30 Cf. its use at Dam. *Isid.* 36 (of Plato and Pythagoras).
31 *VS* 6.8.1, § 469.
32 DODDS 1973, 159–76.
33 Philostr. *VA.* 8.25–26.
34 *VS* 6.7.3–5, § 468; 6.9.7–8 § 470; 6.9.12–15, § 470.
35 2.1.3, § 454.
36 The closest thing we can find to second-sight before Apollonius of Tyana involves the Herodotean episode in which Croesus tests the oracles; Delphic Apollo is able to tell Croesus' envoys what Croesus was doing far away at a designated time—but Apollo, of course, truly is a god.

traordinary feats: Iamblichus pulls two *erotes* out of springs, is rumored to levitate with a golden glow, and discerns the ghost of a dead gladiator masquerading as Apollo.[37] Sosipatra's son, Antoninus, predicts the fall of the Serapeum.[38] About the theurgic activities of Maximus I will have more to say below, but here we at least should note that Eunapius cites Eusebius as saying that he caused a statue of Hecate to smile and laugh, and that he made the torches in its hands blaze up—in other words, he performed theurgic statue animation. Maximus also performed a supernatural service for Sosipatra that she apparently was unable, or perhaps unwilling, to perform for herself: he discovered that the cause of odd feelings she had been having was a love charm worked against her by Philometor; he also figured out how to counteract it (it was his counter-active ritual that Sosipatra witnessed through clairvoyance).[39] In short, there is no dearth of remarkable talents amongst the men in Eunapius' *Lives;* in the next section of this paper we will need to consider how those talents differ from Sosipatra's, and what Eunapius intends the differences to mean.

But for now let us stay with Sosipatra. One part of her story that I have not touched on yet needs to be noted before we go further. After the death of Eustathius, Sosipatra moves to Pergamon, where Aedesius (Eustathius' kinsman and fellow student under Iamblichus) watches over her and her children, and the two of them share students:

> Sosipatra held a chair of philosophy that rivaled [Aedesius'], and after attending the lectures of Aedesius, the students would go to hear hers; and though there was none who did not greatly appreciate and admire the accurate learning of Aedesius, they positively adored and revered the woman's inspired (*enthousiasmon*) teaching.[40]

Whatever the origin of her gifts, then, Sosipatra promulgated her knowledge in the standard Platonic way: she taught students. If we take seriously the comment that Aedesius' students went from his lectures straight to hers, then we know the names of at least some of Sosipatra's students: Maximus, Chrysanthius (like Maximus, a future teacher of Julian, and also the teacher of Eunapius himself) and several others whose careers are also narrated by Eunapius, such as Priscus (another one of Julian's teachers) and Eusebius.

---

37 *VS* 5.1.7–9, § 458; 5.2.1–9, §§ 459–60; 6.11.11–12, § 473.
38 *VS* 6.9.15–17, §§ 470–71.
39 *VS* 7.2.6–12, § 475; 6.9.3–10, § 469–70.
40 *VS* 6.9.1–2, § 469.

2 The Story's Place in Eunapius' Narration

Let us return to the observation that one purpose of Eunapius' narration, overall, is to trace the chain of teacher-student relationships by which Iamblichus' ideas were transmitted to later generations of Neoplatonists, down to Eunapius himself. At this point, it may help to chart the relationships amongst some of the people whom we have discussed. (See chart on facing page.)

Everyone on this chart can trace themselves back, pedagogically, to Iamblichus, with the exception of Sosipatra herself. She is only an 'affine' of Iamblichus, so to speak—linked to him through marriage to his student Eustathius and through her friendship and collaboration with his student Aedesius.

Sosipatra, in fact, has been grafted onto the Iamblichean tree from a completely different place—specifically, if my interpretation is correct, from the ranks of the angels. This is the main reason that Eunapius avoids anything but the barest mention of her birth family; not only was it irrelevant to who and what she became, but it would have distracted from the point he wished to emphasize, namely that Sosipatra injected the Iamblichean line with divinity. This injection does not truncate the line, or even diminish it (Eunapius still boasts that he himself is pedagogically descended from Iamblichus), but it does have interesting implications, as I will show.

Yet perhaps it would be better to say that Sosipatra injects the line with a *renewed* divinity—after all, Iamblichus himself is portrayed by Eunapius as having divine qualities. So why does Eunapius need Sosipatra, anyway? One answer is that Iamblichus' own students excelled in philosophy and oratory but failed to carry on the master's theurgical tradition. Eunapius explicitly makes this point about Aedesius—although he also concedes that Aedesius may have hidden any theurgic talents he did have, due to the Constantinian laws against pagan practices, especially those that might be defined as magic.[41] Eustathius performs no feats of theurgic ritual, either—although ironically, his otherwise successful visit to the Persian court is thwarted when the *magi,* jealous of the king's admiration of Eustathius' philosophical and rhetorical powers, accuse Eustathius of using *goêteia* to enhance his eloquence.[42] A third student, Sopator, went to the imperial court to teach philosophy, but as in

41 *VS* 6.4–5, § 461.
42 *VS* 6.5.8–10, § 466.

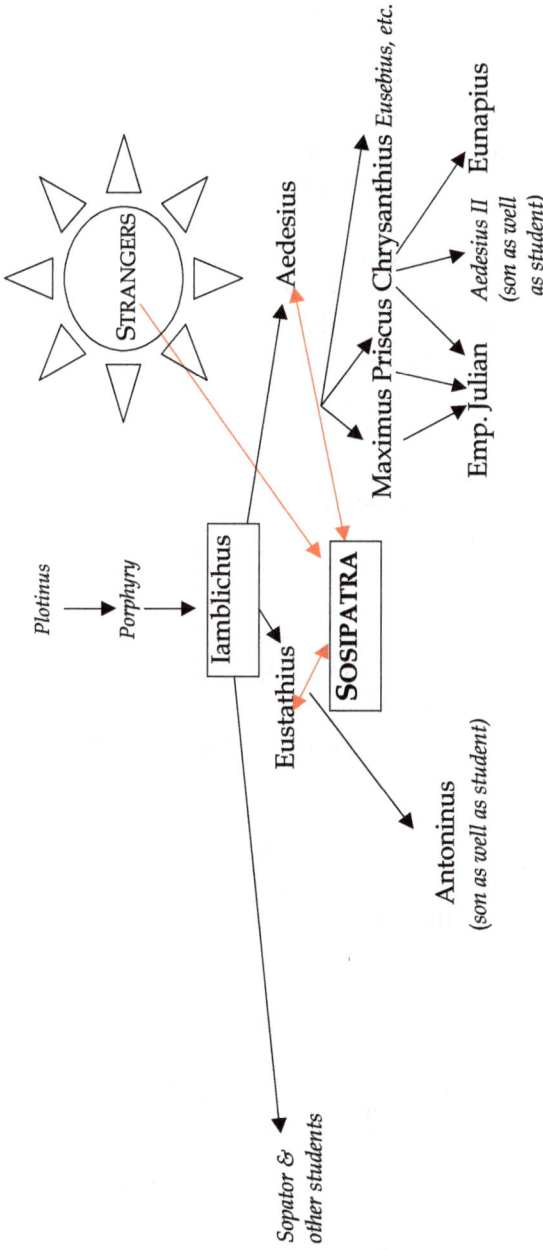

Relationships amongst Philosophers Pertaining to Sosipatra

• Single-ended arrows indicate a teacher-student relationship (and sometimes also a parent-child relationship). Double-ended arrows represent a marriage or a teaching partnership.
• Eustathius was the husband of Sosipatra, and by her the father of Antoninus. After the death of Eustathius, Aedesius watched over Sosipatra and they shared students.

the case of Eustathius, his success there brought envy, and then his downfall, orchestrated again through charges of magic. An envious fellow-philosopher, Ablabius, accused Sopator of using his wisdom to 'charm the winds' and thus to keep the grain ships land-locked. Ablabius persuaded Constantine to have Sopator beheaded.[43]

The stories of Aedesius, Eustathius and Sopator suggest a further reason that Eunapius may have found Sosipatra useful: if he wanted to reinforce the theurgic side of the pedagogical line from which he traced his own descent, it would have been awkward to do so by enhancing the theurgic reputation of either a figure who was known to have hidden such talents out of fear (Aedesius) or a figure who had been accused, however wrongly, of misusing such talents (Sopator or Eustathius).[44] But Eunapius takes this further, narrating Sosipatra's tale in such a way as to make it hard to draw her into such a pattern even if one wished to. Ritually speaking, she is portrayed as notably passive. Already in connection with her initiation by the Strangers, we hear nothing about Sosipatra *doing* anything. She presents the raw material, so to speak, and the two Strangers perfect it. Even the items that the Strangers leave with her—the array of clothing, the ritual implements and the books—are not, apparently, for her own use. After the Strangers have put them into her chest, they tell her to have the chest sealed, and to look after it until their return; there is no suggestion that she will open it in their absence to use the items. Her episodes of clairvoyance seem simply to have come upon her (as did the episode experienced by Apollonius of Tyana). She is several times described as *enthousiasmos* but this, again, is a quality that is understood to overtake those who experience it (the Pythia being the most famous example), even if they prepare themselves for the event by doing such things as bathing or dressing in a particular way.

---

43 *VS* 6.9–12, § 463.
44 The Strangers' reluctance (or rather Eunapius' reluctance) to cloak the more familiar name of their art with the phrase 'not uninitiated in the wisdom that is called Chaldean', is interesting in this respect. The word 'theurgy' is used three times in Eunapius: (1) he says that Antoninus stayed away from the art (at least publicly) for fear of imperial laws (6.10.7); (2) he says that Maximus, practicing it publicly with arrogance and lack of caution, comes to a bad end (7.6.2); (3) he says that Porphyry left 'natural philosophy' (physikon) and theurgy to the sacred rites and mysteries (*teletais* ... *mystêriois*); the implication is that he did not practice them, or did not practice them publicly, at least (4.2.3) (The passage is troublesome; for a possible interpretation, PENELLA 1990, 42–3).

Even more markedly, on the one occasion when Sosipatra would have found it particularly useful to perform a ritual, she asked Maximus to do so on her behalf instead. This brings us back to the tale of Philometor's love-charm:

> Philometor … was overcome by her beauty and eloquence, and recognizing the divinity of her nature, fell in love with her. And his passion possessed and completely overwhelmed him. Not only was *he* completely conquered by it, but *she* also felt its onslaught. So she said to Maximus … 'Pray find out what ailment (*pathos*) I have, that I may not be troubled by it … Do you exert yourself on my behalf and so show that you are pious (*theophiles*)'. When he had heard this, Maximus went away puffed up with pride as though he were now associating with the gods because so wonderful a woman had put such faith in him.
>
> Meanwhile, Philometor pursued his purpose, but Maximus, having discovered by sacrificial lore (*sophias thytikês*)[45] what Philometor was using, strove to counteract and nullify the weaker [spell] with whatever power and force he could. When Maximus had completed his rites, he hastened to Sosipatra and bade her to observe carefully whether she had the same sensations in the future. But she replied that she no longer had them, and then described to Maximus his own prayer and the whole ritual; she also told him the hour at which it took place, as though she had been present, and revealed to him the signs (*sêmeia*) that had appeared. Maximus then fell to the earth in amazement and proclaimed her visibly a goddess … (Wright's Loeb translation, modified).[46]

The incident evokes Porphyry's story of how Plotinus had to deal with magical attacks made against him by Olympius of Alexandria.[47] Eunapius' tale, however, is far longer and more dramatic (I have abbreviated it here), and in part because of this drama, it manages to demonstrate even better than the other incidents I have mentioned the fine line that Eunapius wanted Sosipatra to walk. On the one hand, Sosipatra is not allowed even such benign involvement in her defense against magical attack as Plotinus had chosen (Plotinus simply turned back the magic through the force of his soul, *psychês dynamis*). Her passivity is underscored through its contrast with the elaborate description of how Maximus counteracted the spell. But on the other hand, Sosipatra's detailed knowledge of the ritual that Maximus performed, obtained by her clairvoyance, emphatically reminds us that, even if she takes a pas-

---

45   That is, divination through the entrails of sacrificed animals; cf. Porph. *Abst.* 2.53.

46   *VS* 6.9.3–10, § 469–70.

47   *Vit. Plot.* 10.1–13.

sive role, her powers are superior to his in everything but the most quo-
tidian matters. Such ritual passivity is in marked contrast not only to
Maximus' behavior as we see it in this story, but also to ritual activity
as we see it more generally in Eunapius' *Lives*. In addition to turning
away Philometor's love spell, Maximus animates a statue of Hecate;
Maximus and Chrysanthius pursue both divinatory arts and 'miraculous
things' (*ta peri theiasmon*), and then train the future Emperor Julian accordingly.[48] Antoninus foretells the fall of the Serapeum and learns
the secret rites of the Egyptian gods. Iamblichus performs the feats I
mentioned earlier.

Eunapius' reaction to such activities is nuanced: he admires Antoninus for his ritual accomplishments but adds that 'he displayed no tendency to theurgy or that which contradicts the perceptions of the senses,
perhaps because he kept a wary eye on imperial views and policies that
were opposed to these practices'.[49] Maximus, of course, comes to a very
bad end indeed, which Eunapius narrates fully, suggesting that Maximus' fate was due in part to his arrogant and careless display of his theurgic talents, which led to others at court becoming envious, and thereby to the charge that Maximus was involved with the famous divinatory
episode in which the name of the next emperor was revealed. Although
he escaped the first purge of those who were charged, Maximus was
eventually hunted down and killed, most brutally, by the emperor's as-
sassin.[50] Ritual power, then, as Eunapius presents it, is one of the traits of
Iamblichus' pedagogical grandchildren, but it is a trait to be used spar-
ingly, with caution and humility.

Even in his discussion of Iamblichus' ritual powers, Eunapius is
careful to make it clear that these things are not to be undertaken lightly.
He characterizes Iamblichus as keeping to himself such rituals as he
thought were necessary for worshipping the divine. When he is cajoled
into demonstrating his theurgic powers to his students by drawing the
two *erotes* out of their springs, he precedes his performance with the remark that such a thing is not pious (*eusebes*), but that for their sakes he
shall nonetheless do it. Eunapius adds that he himself would not have
repeated the story were it not for its potential to convert the unbeliev-
ing; he refuses to repeat some other stories about Iamblichus' powers
that he can not verify. In describing Iamblichus' unmasking of the

---

48   *VS* 7.2.1, § 474.
49   *VS* 6.10.7, § 471.
50   *VS* 7.6.2–8, § 480.

false Apollo, Eunapius stresses that this is to be credited to the fact that Iamblichus had learned to look not with the eyes of the body, but with those of the mind (which echoes the advice that Iamblichus himself gives to aspiring theurgists in the *De mysteriis*).[51] Discernment of ghosts is not a 'magical' ability, in other words, but the result of having perfected one's *nous* and *psyche*.

Sosipatra's ritual passivity, then, is a safe way of re-introducing the theurgic element into the Iamblichean line after the dry-spell of the generation that immediately followed Iamblichus. Eunapius makes it clear that Sosipatra is closely linked to the divine—indeed, that she has been initiated into the highest theurgic mysteries by divine emissaries and expects to rise to the highest existential rank available to the human soul—and yet she is at no risk of being charged with illicit activities, or of abusing the lower forms of ritual power that ruined others. Her injection into the Iamblichean line from outside of its pedagogical chain, which means from outside of the politics and power-plays of the empire, means that her theurgic reputation can be exalted, free of any of the blemishes that marred the male descendents of Iamblichus' pedagogy.

Gender plays an interesting role here. On the one hand, her femininity makes it easier to portray Sosipatra as immune from the temptations and dangers that thwarted her male colleagues. As a woman, she was trained at home, she taught from home, and she therefore took no part in the power plays that enmeshed her theurgic brethren.[52] But on the other hand, her femininity presented an extra hurdle to anyone who wished to treat of her story, for she had to stand in contrast not only to the ritually active men of Eunapius' narration but also, implicitly, to a long list of ritually active—and concomitantly terrifying—women who had paraded through centuries of Greek and Roman literature. Male theurgists could take Pythagoras as a forerunner, but any woman who combined even a hint of magical powers with a proclivity to using them was at risk of being lumped together with Medea, Circe, the hags of Latin poetry, Lucan's super-witch Erictho and Heliodorus'

---

51 *VS* 5.1.6–5.2.8, §§ 458–60.
52 As PENELLA 1990, 61 and LEWIS forthcoming discuss, other women did occasionally belong to philosophic circles, and in two cases (Hypatia and Asclepigenia) seem to have taught men, but they nonetheless typically remained outside of public life—Hypatia being the exception that proved the rule with dire effects.

female necromancer. To present a woman as a theurgist, then, much less as the perfect theurgist, must have been a challenge for Eunapius. To succeed in doing so by emphasizing her ritual passivity was an authorial *tour de force* for him.

3 Sosipatra as Model

But the theme of this volume is religious individuality and how it may translate (or not) into group activities. It is easy to see how Sosipatra's story represents a case of individuality: even within the small, elite religious world of the theurgists, her experiences are laudably unusual. Can those experiences, as presented by Eunapius, become a model for others? The fact that some of their uniqueness is rooted in Sosipatra's passivity makes one wonder. Most of Eunapius' readers are likely to have been men; how would such passivity have been understood by them?

I would suggest that passivity made Sosipatra the *ideal* Iamblichean theurgist, beyond even Iamblichus' own attainments. In the *De mysteriis,* Iamblichus emphasizes that the theurgist should use rituals only to prepare himself to be worked upon by the gods, or for certain other tasks that he had to undertake at early stages. He insists that rituals are necessary for the soul's improvement and eventual ascent (*contra* Porphyry and Plotinus) but also insists that they belong primarily to the early preparatory part of the theurgist's progress—a stage that is represented, perhaps, in the case of Sosipatra by the secret ceremonies performed upon her by the two Strangers during her youth.

This point comes out particularly well in Iamblichus' defense of divination, in the third book of *De mysteriis*. Let us first observe that *enthousiasmos* (which, as I noted above, is a state that typically is understood, by both theurgists and non-theurgists, as coming upon a person at the will of a god) is the preferred method of divination.[53] It is described by Iamblichus as using energies that are 'no way human;' rather, 'that which is [usually] inaccessible becomes accessible due to divine possession'. The divine spirit (*pneuma*) is represented as descending upon the medium, who is obedient to it and directed by it; the medium is not able to exercise any activity of his own because no human activity could possibly

---

53 E.g., *DM* 3.4.

find its way into to such an operation when it is properly conducted.[54] In the next section of Book III, Iamblichus makes this point even more emphatically:

> Nor would one reasonably suppose that [divination] would occur [through human actions], for being transported by a god is neither a human accomplishment, nor does it base its power in human parts [of the body] or activities. But, on the one hand, these are otherwise subordinate, and the god uses them as his instruments; on the other hand, the entire activity of divination comes to its fulfillment through the god acting by himself, purely detached from other things, without the soul or body moving in any way. Hence the divination being done rightly, as I say, really and truly happens. But when the soul takes the initiative, or is disturbed during the divination, or the body interrupts and perverts the divine harmony, the divinations become turbulent and false, and the possession (*enthousiasmos*) is no longer true nor genuinely divine.[55]

To the extent that humanly-conducted ritual has any place in all of this, it is strictly preparatory, according to Iamblichus. Drinking water at the Oracle of Claros, inhaling fumes at Delphi or water vapor at Didyma— all of these help to purify the luminous spirit (*augoeidês pneuma*) that is within the prophet, and make that spirit ready to receive the god when the god chooses to come, but that is all—there is no power of divination within the substances themselves, within the human who ingests them, or inherent in the ritual actions *per se*.[56]

Much more could be said along these lines, drawing not only on other parts of the *De mysteriis,* but from the *Chaldean Oracles* and other ancient works that discuss theurgy as well. I trust, however, that my point has been demonstrated: for the Iamblichean theurgist, passivity of both the body and the soul was actually a *desideratum*. In this regard, Sosipatra was the most highly accomplished theurgist about whom we read in the *Lives*—indeed, about whom we read in any ancient source.[57] It perhaps tells us something about human nature that Maximus is the more familiar character, in spite of the fact that he fell far short of theurgic ideals: deliberate ritual actions that bring impressive effects and involvement with high imperial offices grab our attention—

---

54 *DM* 3.6.
55 *DM* 3.7; CLARKE, DILLON AND HERSHBELL's 2003 translation, slightly modified.
56 *DM* 3.11 and cf. 3.13–15.
57 Her name is enticing in this regard: 'savior of the paternal line'. It ideally represents what I have argued is one of her roles in the narrative—the figure who renewed the divine elements in Iamblichus' pedagogical legacy.

and apparently grabbed the attention of ancient authors as well, given that several ancient authors tell us about Maximus (Eunapius, Ammianus, Julian, Libanius) and only one tells us about Sosipatra.[58] But if one were to look deliberately for models in Eunapius, it is impossible to surpass Sosipatra for having lived an appropriately productive theurgic life.

Bibliography

CLARK, GILLIAN 1993. *Women in Late Antiquity: Pagan and Christian Lifestyles.* Oxford.

CLARKE, EMMA C.; DILLON, JOHN M.; HERSHBELL, JACKSON P. (Translation and commentary) 2003. *Iamblichus. On the Mysteries.* Writings from the Greco-Roman World 4. Atlanta.

DZIELSKA, MARIA 1996. *Hypatia of Alexandria.* Cambridge, MA.

DODDS, ERIC R. 1973. *The Ancient Concept of Progress and Other Essays on Greek Literature and Belief.* Oxford.

HARICH-SCHWARZBAUER, HENRIETTE 2009. "Das Seelengefährt in der Lehre der Theurgin Sosipatra (Eunapios *VPS* 466, 5, 1–471, 9, 17)." *Archaiognosia* Suppl. 8. 61–71.

JOHNSTON, SARAH ILES 2004. "Working Overtime in the Afterlife, or No Rest for the Virtuous", in: BOUSTAN, RA'ANAN S.; REED, ANNETTE Y. (edd.). *Heavenly Realms and Earthly Realities in Late Antique Religions.* Cambridge. 85–100.

LEFKOWITZ, MARY R.; FANT, MAUREEN B. 1982. *Women's Lives in Greece and Rome.* Baltimore.

LEWIS, NICOLA DENZEY Forthcoming. "Living Images of the Divine: Female Theurgists in Late Antiquity", in: KALLERES, DAYNA; STRATTON, KIMBERLY (edd.). *Daughters of Hecate.* Oxford.

LEWY, HANS 1978. *Chaldaean Oracles and Theurgy.* 2nd ed. Paris.

LUCK, GEORG 1999. "Witches and Sorcerers in Classical Literature", in: ANKERLOO, BENDT; CLARK, STUART (edd.). *Witchcraft and Magic in Europe: Ancient Greece and Rome.* Philadelphia. 91–158.

—1985. *Arcana Mundi. Magic and the Occult in the Greek and Roman Worlds.* Baltimore.

O'MEARA, DOMINIC J. 2003. *Platonopolis: Platonic Political Philosophy in Late Antiquity.* Oxford.

PACK, ROGER 1952. "A Romantic Narrative in Eunapius", *TAPA* 83. 198–204.

---

58 I note, however, that Gore Vidal makes something of her in his novel *Julian* (1964)—although not perhaps what she would have wished. There, Sosipatra appears as a sort of new-age flower-child, scattering vague pieces of psychic advice here and there, and always with a certain arrogance.

PENELLA, ROBERT J. 1990. *Greek Philosophers and Sophists in the Fourth Century A.D.* Classical and Medieval Texts, Papers and Monographs 28. Liverpool.

Gregory Taught, Gregory Written: The effacement and definition of individualization in the Address to Origen and the Life of Gregory the Wonderworker

Blossom Stefaniw

Every now and then, the fates are kind to historians of late antique religion. Sometimes, the fates are so kind that they allow for the preservation of texts in a constellation which facilitates tracing diachronic religious change with a reasonable degree of elegance and symmetry. In this particular case, the two sources so happily preserved directly connect to Gregory Thaumaturgus. One is his farewell address to his teacher Origen from around 242 and the other is Gregory of Nyssa's panegyrical biography of the Thaumaturg from 380. On the basis of this chronological distribution, it is possible to trace shifts in the scope for and form of individualisation from the early third to the late fourth century, in terms of the religious representation of one person. Hypothetically, two accounts which both portray laudable religious activity and both relate to the same person can be compared in order to find out whether and how the representation of religious individualisation changed over time. Even when taking differences of genre, authorship, and occasion into consideration, it seems possible to exploit the similarities of two texts in which the religious behaviour of a certain person is put forward for public recognition. Both will manifest what sort of scope for religious individualisation was taken as not only legitimate but also laudable, thus providing us with an ideal account of individualization in religious life. While it would be sheer recklessness to take this as the basis for conclusions about the third century or for the fourth century in general, surely it is fair to take these sources as illustrative of an area of religious life involving identification with and attachment to an exceptional individual.

Often, the fates seem kinder than they really are. Our two texts, which will be introduced in more detail below, cannot accurately be said to be concerned with one and the same person in the same way. In one case, Gregory is the author of the text, and in the other he is the subject. There are substantial and inescapable categorical differences between a person acting as an author and a person who is the subject of an account written by someone else. The latter Gregory, portrayed as a bishop, is on the other side of the discursive looking glass, so that the connection between the young Gregory authoring his farewell to his teacher and the mature Gregory being remembered as working wonders in Cappadocia is not a simple chronological continuity, but rather reflective of a disruption of narrative space. The true complexity of what, at first glance, seemed so satisfactorily symmetrical and manageable does not stop there. While comparing Gregory-the-student (author) with Gregory-the-bishop (subject) maintains the connection to one name, if not one person, crossing the discursive line from author to subject is a violation which can only be resolved, or at least balanced, by making a more thorough comparison of the two texts on two additional analytical levels.

Due to these considerations, this essay will not only compare Gregory-the-author with Gregory-the-subject, but must also compare the religious agency of the subjects of each text and that of the authors of each text. That is, in the following, the Origen of the farewell address is compared with the Gregory of the Nyssan's panegyric, and the authorial activity of the Nyssan is compared with that of Gregory Thaumaturgus as author of the farewell address. This multi-level structure of comparison will still allow for discussion of chronological change, but will also bring into view functional shifts (how does the religious role of the subjects being portrayed change) and discursive shifts (how does each author manifest scope for individualizing religious life in the act of writing).

The substantial chronological discrepancy between the two texts means that, even without assuming a sudden turn with the rise of a certain emperor at the beginning of the fourth century, we can reasonably expect some reflection of religious change as we turn from one text to the other and as we attend to all three levels of comparison. While causes of religious change will not be directly pursued in this essay, we can posit that a major aspect of religious change in this period was a shift in how much individual scope for determining the shape and substance of religious life there was. A standard rise-of Christianity model would make it appear that the imperial Christian church in the period of our later text, that of Gregory of Nyssa, is working towards an in-depth invasion of personal life, while at the same time universalising and regularising and centralising religion. This push for control could be seen, for example, in the intensification of doctrinal controversies, the popularisation of asceticism among non-monks and non-clerics, and the demand for assent to closely-defined doctrinal propositions, all of which increase dramatically in the latter half of the fourth century. On this model, one would similarly tend to see the third century as characterized by diversity in doctrine and praxis and a broad array of local cults and local norms, often based on the teachings or examples of individual religious ancestors, whether martyrs, apostles, or ascetic teachers. Taking these generalisations as given, however, assumes without argument that what we see the Cappadocians doing in the late fourth century and what we see Origen doing in the early third century are both manifestations of "Christianity", where Christianity is conceived of as a meta-historical constant. Such an uncritical conceptualisation of the relation in which these two texts stand to each other leads to plotting them quite innocently on the same, and the only, (Christian) trajectory. However, if scope for individualisation is a significant aspect of religion, and if there are significant differences between how it appears in the one text and the other, then it may be necessary to accept that despite the fact that both texts are traditionally categorised as Christian, what we have before us are manifestations of significantly different samples of religious life. Here the plain difference of the two must be defended strictly as difference, and not as greater or lesser purity, greater or lesser correctness, or a more or less complete unfolding of a reified Christian essence.

Texts and Procedure

In the first text under consideration here, Gregory thanks his teacher, Origen, with whom he has been studying while in Caesarea in Palestine. The *Address* was first delivered orally around 242.[1] It is a very rare example of a speech of departure and one of only two third-century accounts by students of their teachers.[2] The *Address* was passed down in the manuscript tradition as a preface to Origen's apologetic work, the *Contra Celsum*. Eusebius appears to know of this text which was presumably in the holdings of the library founded by Origen at Caesarea

---

1   In the following I am drawing on the Greek edition by GUYOT; KLEIN 1996 and on Michael Slusser's English translations SLUSSER 1998.
2   On the authenticity of Gregory's authorship see Klein in GUYOT; KLEIN 1996, 47–63 who concludes that the text is authentic after reviewing all of the relevant arguments.

and later accessible to Eusebius, who may be drawing on it in his mention of Gregory as an example of foreign students drawn to Caesarea to study with Origen.[3]

While Origen's excellence as a teacher is ostensibly the topic at hand, the genre and occasion both require that Gregory present himself in relation to Origen and portray his experience as a student. Given that it is a speech of departure, Gregory must form a trajectory through the last several years of his life to the present moment and establish what it is that he is departing from and lend the moment specific significance. As a result, his self-presentation plays a large role and reflects what he takes to be presentable, if not laudable, religious behavior. The curriculum at Origen's school involved a full course of religious and spiritual formation through an intellectualised medium, and that basic religious tasks, such as the orientation of the person to the divine and the articulation of moral ideals and the internalisation of ethical norms, were all included.[4]

In his panegyrical account, Gregory of Nyssa, the Cappadocian bishop, presents the works of Gregory Thaumaturgus when he had returned to his native Pontus where he was ordained and became 'bishop' of Neocaesarea.[5] This latter text has Gregory as its overt topic, but appears in the context of the emerging Cappadocian ecclesiastical theology and in the midst of growing consolidation, centralisation, and totalisation of spiritual authority. We can be fairly certain that it was delivered as a homily or a festal address in Neocaesarea in the year 380, and can even reasonably set the precise date as November 17, which was the regionally celebrated feast day of Gregory Thaumaturgus.[6] Not only the occasion of delivery but also the content of the oration suggest significant regional concerns: the Nyssan demonstrates no knowledge at all of the Thaumaturg's own writings, including the *Address to Origen*, and re-

---

3   SLUSSER 1998, 17 ff. Cf. Eusebius, Historia Ecclesiastica VI.30.
4   See also STEFANIW 2010a, 281–294 for more on Christian and Neoplatonist philosophical schools, also addressed in Chapter 5 of STEFANIW, BLOSSOM 2010.
5   The *Vita Gregorii Thaumaturgi* is accessible in Latin and Greek in PG 46.893–957 among the homilies of Gregory of Nyssa. English quotations here are from Slusser's 1998 translation as above. There are also traditions on Gregory's life preserved in Syriac which suggest his continuing popularity.
6   There is no way to firmly resolve debate on this point, as there are viable arguments, for example, for a date after 381, such that Gregory of Nyssa is writing in the context of pressure to live up to his role as defender of orthodoxy as foisted upon him by the emperor Theodosius ABRAMOWSKI 1976, 162.

lies solely on local traditions for his sources.[7] His account became popular and was received into other eastern languages in varying versions.
As a result, it is this late portrayal of Gregory, and not his own account
of his student years, which has formed the basis of the image of Gregory
as Gregory the Wonderworker passed down from the fourth and fifth
century. The dominance of the image of Gregory in the *Address* by
his portrayal in the *Panegyric* has been carried through in the historio-
graphical tradition, such that it is taken as read to this very day that,
as the Nyssan portrayed it, Gregory Thaumaturgus was a third-century
bishop of Cappadocia who did exactly what his biographer said he did.

   In addition to belonging to different epochs, these texts are also each
reflective of diverse social and geographical contexts. This may or may
not have direct bearing on the type and degree of individualisation
which each portrays as laudable and exceptional. Social and geographical
differences may be superficial, but may also have just as much explana-
tory force as do the respective epochs of each text. That is, Christian or
not, urban centres may have allowed for different types and degrees of
individualisation than did provincial towns, and life within a philosophical school brought with it different religious ideals than were relevant
or even feasible in the context of popularising and universalising church
efforts among a mainly uneducated rural population. Religious individualisation will inevitably be effected by the concerns of the people
involved, and even in the same period, will not be the same in a context
where people's main concerns are health, wealth, and family standing as
in a context where a small elite is ostentatiously distancing itself from
such concerns.

   Initially, (and from outside the text) the Gregory of the *Address*
would seem to have more space for individual religious practice. His account of his studies with Origen suggests no institutional controls on
what Origen taught or who studied with him, and philosophical schools
of this type were able to function more or less autonomously, depend-
ing primarily on the personality and charisma of the teacher for their status and drawing power. Gregory's decision to study with Origen, and
his portrayal of his education, may thus appear to be purely determined
by the person of the teacher and by Gregory's own personality, so that
Gregory-the-student could be seen to have a maximal degree of scope
for individualised religious action. He has all the privilege and leisure
necessary to engage in religious action on his own terms and without

---

7   Cf. SLUSSER 1998, 14 ff.

conforming to public or communal requirements. He can choose how and with whom to engage in a very particular elite form of religious life, and does so. Further, this decision leads him into religious activity which is intimately connected to the formation of the person, so that his own self is the forum for exercising and applying religious agency.

This surface assessment would pave the way to arguing for a large degree of individualisation among elites in the third century, flattening out into institutionalised conventions determined by church hierarchy in the late fourth century, when the biography of Gregory was written. The textual Gregory-the-bishop would then be seen as a puppet of Cappadocian episcopal ideology, performing religious actions which are formulaic and bounded to the interests of the consolidating project of the author, who is busy discouraging individualisation of any kind.[8] However, besides being generally simplistic and far too tidy, there are several problems with arguing along those lines. Firstly, such an argument would conform with the assumption that the time of Origen's school was part of a newly unfolded bud of Christianity, yet to fully blossom and then be sullied by imperial power. This is a narrative of late antique religious change which should be recognised as precisely that: an ideologically loaded narrative and not the result of critical study. Hypotheses put forward because they conform with it will thus lead to circular conclusions and merely serve to maintain the narrative. On the other hand, conclusions which incidentally do not contradict this narrative should not be rejected only for that reason.

The second, but equally grievous, problem with seeing the primary shift in our accounts of Gregory as one from greater to lesser scope for individualised religious action from the third to the fourth century is the fact that the basis for such a picture of the shift from Gregory-the-student to Gregory-the-bishop is located well outside of either text. In making that complaint, however, I am not leading up to a positivistic

8   This could be seen, for example, in the Cappadocian attitude toward asceticism, elsewhere an area of religious life which allowed for and encouraged a large degree of self-direction in choosing how, where and with whom to practice asceticism. As the *Historia Monachorum* and *Apophthegmata Patrum* reflect, freestyle forms of asceticism such as minding a cripple, pretending to be an idiot or selling oneself as a slave were especially admired, and monks could relocate or change their practice at will. The Cappadocians, on the other hand, especially Basil, worked to cultivate a regimented and regularised monasticism under the authority of the bishop and with a stable and specific set of rules valid for everyone.

read-the-text-and-see exhortation. Instead, the problem arises from a reification of individualization, as if it were an object which could be found in greater or lesser quantities at different times. Religious change happens in and through discourse, and one means by which people work away at shifting religion, or at comprehending shifts in religious life, is by constant and ungoverned production of discourse, including the production of texts intended for public consumption as ours both were. Thus, remaining in the text is also a means of wading into the disoriented perspective of the authors, who did not and could not know what was shifting (or would successfully shift), nor how, at the time that they wrote. The texts not only manifest shifts in religion but also contribute their particular bit of verbiage to the larger cascade of discourse which made religious change both happen and appear to happen (two different but equally important processes).

So in looking at each text in the following, I am asking what sort of scope for private and individual religious action is articulated (in the shift from the author-Gregory to the subject-Gregory, and in the portrayal of both subjects and the work of both authors), and which changes become apparent when the two texts are compared on multiple analytical levels. More broadly, I am interested in what becomes visible if we forego interpreting these changes along the lines of a rise-of-Christianity model. Instead, it may be that the constructive ends to which individualisation can be put within religious life itself are what changes. In other words, rather than finding more or less individualisation present in each text, we may find individualisation itself changing, being applied to different tasks and, accordingly, operating on different terms. This could also be stated as a hypothesis that it is more worthwhile, from the perspective of the historical study of religion, to look for qualitative than for quantitative changes in a complexly understood scope for individualization in religious life.

Shifts in Narrative Space: Gregory Thaumaturgus as Student and Bishop

Based on the evidence of the *Address,* Gregory was a student in Origen's school in Caesarea for about eight years. Like other up-and-coming young men from the provinces, Gregory and his brother had been given rhetorical training, and they harbored ambitions to study law at

the prestigious centre of Beirut. By happenstance, however, they trav-
elled via Caesarea when accompanying their sister to relocate to her
husband's new appointment with the governor of Palestine. There
they encountered Origen, possibly in the context of a public lecture
or by pursuing hearsay advice about a worthwhile teacher in the
city.[9] Gregory decided to stay on in Caesare rather than continue to
Beirut and his farewell address marks the end of his course of study
with Origen.

The *Address* is overtly about Origen, but for our purposes in doing
this first comparative task it must be read against the grain to see what it
says about Gregory. Gregory inscribes himself as part of the student-
teacher relationship and articulates the significance of his time with Origen. Because of the centrality not only of the teacher, but also of the
teacher-student bond, to this text and indeed to the type of education
practiced in Origen's school, Gregory is necessarily a key player in
the text as part of the pedagogical bond which was fundamental in similar philosophical schools of the third century. He cannot talk about his
gratitude to his teacher without talking about himself, since teaching is
based on teacher-student attachment rather than on the mere convey-
ance of information.

What becomes conspicuous as soon as one tries to get a look at
Gregory through this text is that, while there is high potential for individual religious action by a privileged young man in an urban centre,
Gregory goes out of his way to efface that potential. He persistently portrays himself as the object of larger spiritual and emotional processes
which are beyond his control. Gregory indeed refers to himself a
great deal, but always and insistently casting himself in a passive role.
In order to get as clear a view as possible of what is happening with
this ostentatious passivity, textual samples will be sorted into those
which serve to suggest and maintain his own passivity in in the period
up until Gregory's meeting with Origen, and those from his encounter
with Origen to the point of the delivery of the speech.

In his account of his upbringing, Gregory constructs himself as unable to resist the forces of providence that are operating upon him. It is
an account of mental development at the hands of various caretakers, be
it his mother or his earlier teachers of rhetoric.[10] Gregory is being passed
forward along an ever-improving line of agents, bucket-brigade fashion,

---

9 Oratio 5. 56–72, SLUSSER 1998, 100–102.
10 Oratio 5.48 ff. (SLUSSER 1998, 99).

until he is finally deposited with Origen. Origen himself is the person to whom Gregory's guardian spirit hands him over, a holy man appointed to 'govern and nurture' him.[11] The vocabulary Gregory uses to describe this process of development repeatedly casts everyone else as guides, protectors, and guardians, where as he himself is 'blind and ignorant', receiving reason 'more under compulsion than of my own accord'.[12] He claims that he 'neither intended nor even hoped for' the opportunity to meet Origen, but still, their meeting was divinely orchestrated.[13]

The account of this introductory phase of Gregory's life is veritably crowded with extra entities, such as Gregory's own divine guardian who makes sure that he reaches Caesarea shortly after Origen had moved there.[14] Here the personal circumstances of chaperoning his sister are occluded and replaced with a scheme in which he is the one being chaperoned and guided safely to the place and person he is intended for. What is more, constructing the meeting with Origen as the aim of this process makes the situation of departure all the more distressing and dramatic, as if he had already achieved the aim of his life, reached home, fulfilled his destiny, and is now being wrested away. Thus being with Origen, as such, is developed into a key part of Gregory's identity and his fate. Inasmuch as studying with a specific teacher is an elective and rare step to take, one may see it as the exercise of individualized religion. Gregory interprets it as a result of divine agency and providential

---

11 Oratio 4.40 (SLUSSER 1998, 97). Origen is designated *to andra to hiero tode*.
12 Oratio 7.70 (SLUSSER 1998, 102) and Oratio 5.48 (SLUSSER 1998, 99). It should also be noted that Gregory constantly uses passive verb forms when referring to himself, active only when referring to others: he was led, had been favored, was persuaded, etc.
13 Oratio 2.13 (SLUSSER 1998, 93).
14 Oratio 4.39 (SLUSSER 1998, 97). These include 'the boundless providence over all', 'the enduring Word' and 'the animate Word of the first Mind itself' in the space of one sentence. Previous extra entities included 'the God of the universe' (Oratio 3.31, SLUSSER 1998, 96), 'the Director and Cause (*hegemoni kai aitio*) of all things' (Oratio 3.32, SLUSSER 1998, 96), etc. While some or all of these terms may refer to more or less the same entity, what is significant for our purposes is that Gregory is gratuitously generating non-agency by constantly naming others as the causes of his experience. There are definitely at least four non-human entities involved, namely a highest god, a pilot/demiurge/champion type god, Gregory's own guardian spirit acting as personal pedagogue (Oratio 4.44, SLUSSER 1998, 98) and Origen's personal spirit who Gregory suggests could be the angel of the great council (as in Isaiah 9:6 or Jeremiah 32:19 LXX) or 'the common Savior of all' (*ton koinon panton sotera*) (Oratio 4.42, SLUSSER 1998, 98).

action in his life. This is the section of the text where we get the most personal information and the most expression of Gregory as an individual with a particular family, heritage, and private emotional reactions to circumstances and changes, but all of these individual details are pitched as factors providentially coordinated to lead him to the meeting with Origen.

Closely related to this belabored passivity and helplessness in the early autobiographical section of the text is the rhetoric of compulsion which characterizes the account of his actual encounter with Origen upon arriving in Caesarea. Gregory continues the pattern of constructing non-agency for himself by casting Origen in the role of a magical magnetic being whose words and whose person are so compelling that exposure to them necessarily results in submission to them. As he describes his decision to study with Origen, it is in terms of being more or less forced by Origen's charisma to join the school even against his will. Gregory waxes dramatic on this point, saying that Origen 'took him in hand'[15] although he struggled like a wild animal in a trap. Origen lauds the life of philosophy until Gregory was 'pierced as by a dart by his discourse... for he combined a kind of winsome grace with persuasiveness and compelling force' and was 'drawn toward him by his words as if under some greater constraints'.[16] Not to belabor the point, Gregory adds that Origen's arguments brought him and his brother 'to a complete standstill like men under a spell, he was supported in his words, I know not how by some divine power (*tini theia dunamei*)'.[17] He is then worked over by Origen's teaching without once asserting that he himself undertook anything. When Gregory describes the actual process of education, it is in terms of being drawn up and drawn in and always responsive to Origen's spiritual authority, but Gregory never casts himself as an agent. That is, Gregory is falling all over himself to efface any suggestion of individual autonomy and his own capacity to choose to attend the school or not, to stop in Caesarea or carry on to Beirut, to stop with Origen or with anyone else. The effacement of individualisation is energetically developed and constantly repeated throughout this sizable section of the address. Gregory is, when exposed to Origen and while being prepared for and delivered to him, at the mercy of forces larger than himself. He is being processed, so to

---

15 Oratio 6.73 (SLUSSER 1998, 102)
16 Oratio 6.78 (SLUSSER 1998, 103)
17 Oratio 6.80 (SLUSSER 1998, 103)

speak, by the divine *oikonomia* and by the privileged friend of the divine, Origen.[18] On the other hand, he is not fully opaque as a person, given the high emotional colour of this passage, and the individuality of his own religious path through attachment to this one divine teacher.

The question now is, why are we finding a deliberate and almost awkwardly repetitive effacement of individualisation in exactly the milieu where there is a high degree of potential for private religious? And why, despite all of the noise being made, does this effacement remain ambivalent and still fulfill a role of self-definition and the exercise of individual scope for determining what constitutes religious action? Gregory seems to be engaging in a certain appropriately thaumaturgical sleight of hand.

An explanation for both aspects of this paradox, as well as for the maintenance of the paradox itself, can be found in the type of education to which Gregory had committed himself. It is education which, as mentioned above, depends both on the relationship with the teacher and on the teacher's charisma and authority. Such a teacher is the next best thing to a god, so highly distilled as to hardly be human at all.[19] The efficacy of a divine man upon the persons engaged with him was a sort of natural law which constituted the basic mechanism through which education operated in philosophical schools of this type in the third century. In this sort of school, one is educated through attachment to an extraordinary individual and through identification with him. For Gregory, Origen's person has a magnetic effect arising out of his own special ontological status as nearly divine and because of his mediation of divine power through his teaching. A mechanism like that does not allow for the students to articulate themselves as individuals and take initiative. It does not invite them to obtrude their particular interests or talents or ideas into the proceedings. Once he has submitted to the compelling call exuding from the divine teacher, Gregory has cast himself into a dynamic which operates upon him, and

---

18 Origen is described as a 'friend and confidant' of the divine (Oratio 6.83, SLUSS-ER 1998, 104), such that his being so justifies the displacement of *eros* for the Word onto Origen. Gregory casts this irruption of desire in himself as being wounded by a spark in the middle of his soul and then, quite awkwardly, attempts to paper over his emotion by a not much less emotional analogy of Origen and himself to the biblical David and Jonathan.

19 Gregory says that while Origen might appear to be a human being, he has 'already completed most of the preparation for the reascent to the divine world.' (Oratio 2.10, SLUSSER 1998, 93).

which he accepts as a hermeneutic for his past life as well, interpreting everything that has happened to him since his birth as leading up to his encounter and engagement with Origen.

The individualisation manifest in the *Address* is the deliberate and energetic discursive effacement of the scope for individual religious action, even while engaged in a sophisticated and high-stakes realm of religious agency. Even in a social context which just begs for individualised religion, the actual social power to concentrate religious life on oneself is persistently and insistently surrendered to a sort of machine of development towards the divine which pulls Gregory in. The effacement of individualisation is a by-product of the particular religious context within which Gregory is operating in this text. It need not be typical of other religious milieus of the third century, but it certainly is typical of an intellectualised form of religious life as practiced in the schools. In other words, from within the text, from Gregory's perspective, the effacement of individualization is part and parcel of his religious life. From our perspective, however, the path he chooses which requires such an insistent degree of effaced individualization is defined by his individualized choice to engage with religious projects in this very particular way. He is exercising scope for individualized religious practice precisely by effacing his own individuality and taking that effacement as the definition of the high quality of his religious formation with Origen.

Gregory the Bishop

We can now turn to the account of Gregory Thaumaturgus given by his namesake, Gregory of Nyssa, in his panegyrical biography. In order to avoid undue repetition, this section will serve as the basis for discussion of both the Gregory-and-Gregory comparison leading to consideration of a narrative shift and the subject-to-subject comparison leading to consideration of a functional shift.

The Gregory portrayed in the *Vita* has the standard panegyrical childhood, growing in virtue, and choosing an exceptional path.[20] None of the particulars mentioned by Gregory himself about his family or his parentage in the *Address to Origen* are recounted. It may be that the Nyssan is concealing his ignorance of any such details by averring that

---

20 Vita 2.12–14, SLUSSER 1998, 46–47.

'the only kinship deserving of praise is kinship with God'.[21] The Nyssan also all but ignores Origen's role in Gregory's life and instead emphasizes a local notable, Firmilian, as his religious mentor.[22] With alarming abruptness, the entire period of study in Caesarea is elided, and Gregory is back in Cappadocia within one sentence.[23] On his return to his homeland, despite his potential for worldly success and the fact that, according to the author, everyone is clamouring to have Gregory stay in their city, he withdrew and '… lived in a remote place alone with himself, and through himself with God'.[24] Because of his incredible virtue, the bishop of a nearby town, Phaidimos of Amaseia, persists in trying to find Gregory so that he can ordain him. Gregory persists in avoiding him. In the end, the bishop solves the problem by ordaining Gregory *in absentia*, and eventually Gregory realises he must participate in public life when a vision of John the Apostle and the Virgin Mary tells him so.[25]

With these watertight orthodox credentials in hand, Gregory makes his entrance into public life by spending the night in a temple and displacing the 'demons' who had habitually made appearances there, thus enraging the local priest. This same priest, however, throws in his lot with Gregory when Gregory demonstrates that he is able to call the demon back if he wants to, while the priest had been unable to do so, and that he is able to move a very big rock by commanding it to move. The priest is thus convinced that 'Gregory possessed a divine power' and becomes his companion as he travels about the region.[26] The same principle applies to the other miracles and their audiences: Gregory's ability to perform miracles, such as drying up a lake which had become the cause for a family feud between two brothers, is interpreted by those who see it as clear evidence that he has divine power and is therefore representative of a winning ticket, so to speak: '… everyone was longing to share the faith corroborated by such deeds'.[27]

Here we should note that the decision to side with Gregory is perfectly consistent with the mores of local traditional religion: a god who

---

21 Vita 1.5, SLUSSER 1998, 43.
22 Vita 2.22, SLUSSER 1998, 50. This may be due to lack of information or a means of underscoring Gregory's regional identity. At the time of composition, the Origenist controversy had not yet broken out.
23 Vita 3.23, SLUSSER 1998, 50.
24 Vita 3.24, SLUSSER 1998, 51.
25 Vita 3.26–4.0, SLUSSER 1998, 51 ff.
26 Vita 5.36–40, SLUSSER 1998, 56–7.
27 Vita 9.62, SLUSSER 1998, 69.

can do things is obviously better than a god who can't. Also, in taking
on the role of judge and mediator, Gregory is not only applying his
semi-divine status, but also carrying forward the role of local religion
in being the focus for people's problems and needs in everyday life.
By keeping the peace and performing miracles, Gregory also continues
the role of local cults in serving as a foundation for hometown pride.[28]
The combination of these two continuities is what makes the winning
mix for Gregory's countrymen: he is someone who can not only deal
with everyday needs and concerns especially well and consistently because of the strength of his divine power, but people also have something to really be proud of if their local boy come home can dish up
spectacularly effective divine power. This is why one should only
speak of Gregory converting the people of Pontus with a Kierkegaardi-
an degree of methodological fear and trembling. Somehow, more or
less, everyone ends up Christian, but nothing fundamental has changed.

What sort of shift in the scope for religious individualization can be
found between Gregory the student and Gregory the bishop on the
level of narrative? What remains consistent is the paradoxical manuever
of simultaneously eliding and defining individual scope for religious
practice. On the one hand, Gregory seems to be a generic virtuous ascetic who has achieved extraordinary status and is able to apply the
power resulting from that to his community. We have seen this sort
of figure before in fourth-century literature and will see more of it in
the fifth century as well. On the other hand, despite the neutralization
of any significant personal identifiers, the Nyssan's Gregory is, in himself, the location of religious power. He is able to legitimately and ex-
cellently engage with religious life, and even shape and re-shape it,
thus exercising a very broad scope for individualized religious life.
Even this is ambivalent, however: what qualifies him to become a person who is the source of religious power is a standardized formation of
virtue and asceticism and identification with the divine, which the Nyssan has purged of any of the intellectualist aspects reflected in the *Address
to Origen*. Also, there is only one interpretation of his actions and his
person which Gregory of Nyssa accepts, and it is always the same: Gregory's miracles manifest divine power and are therefore a compelling reason to follow Gregory's God. This way of parsing the Thaumaturg's religious power has a sort of mechanic causality which neutralizes any individual scope for religious practice on the part of those who witness

28 See VAN DAM 1982, 297–299.

Gregory's miracles. They are just as compelled to react as they do as Gregory-the-student was compelled to react when exposed to Origen's divine power.

Functional Shifts: Individualisation in the Subjects of Laudatory Accounts

Gregory, when made the subject of a text about a model of religious excellence, most resembles the subject of his own text, Origen. That is, what seems to matter most is not who one is, but rather whether or not one is the subject of a laudatory account and a figure of religious authority to whom others should attach themselves. Thus the most significant shift to be traced is not from the young Gregory in Origen's school to the older Gregory working wonders in his home region later in life. The shift to watch is the one from how Gregory the student portrays his subject to how Gregory of Nyssa, the bishop, portrays his subject in turn. That shift is reflective of changes in the terms on which legitimate and exceptional religious authority is constructed. While we would justifiably expect both texts, due to their genre and subject matter, to be about certain people, in neither text do we learn anything really specific or particular about either Gregory or Origen. Neither text can be said to be about a recognisable person – they are both about religious life conceived of as the reception of and engagement with divine power. This requires a closer discussion of what exactly is shifting, while remembering that it is both the authors who are exercising scope for religious individualisation in engineering their accounts as they do, and their subjects who serve to define what is or is not possible and legitimate for the individual in relation to the divine.

Gregory in the *Vita* and Origen in the *Address* are given many of the same or similar attributes, and their common attributes cluster around the topic of their relationship to the divine. Both are credited with having divine power, and that phrase is repeated very often in the *Vita*[29],

---

29 The Greek of the PG edition of the Vita has the same terminology as used by Gregory of Origen to explain the compelling nature of his teaching. In the example passage here (5.39, SLUSSER 1998, 56, Migne 46, 917 A), the bested temple priest similarly recognises that Gregory must have divine power to explain the compelling nature of his miracles: *Touton de gegono ton, ennoian auton lasein*

while in Origen's case it is posited as the means by which his arguments
for taking up a life of virtue and philosophy are given compelling
force.[30] In contrast to this refined and elite application of divine
power, Gregory Thaumaturgus mediates divine power to more popular
(and possibly more obviously useful) ends by performing miracles which
conform with the needs and interests of ordinary local people in his
home region.

While both subjects become able to mediate divine power based on
their virtue and asceticism, Origen is also credited with constant intellectual effort towards this end, while any intellectual aspect of Gregory's
qualifications is elided. This is achieved not only by skipping over his
years of study, but also by making his perception of divine truth not
the noetic apprehension of the godhead, but the delivery of a doctrinally
'correct' creed in a dream. Apprehension of divine truth is no longer an
obscure and elevated achievement of a select few. The 'divine mysteries'
now appear in the form of doctrine, in a creed which everyone should
memorise.[31]

The basis for access to divine power and the ability to mediate divine power go along with an assertion of affinity to the divine. Origen
is described as some one who 'looks and seems like a human being but
… has already completed most of the preparation for the re-ascent to
the divine world'.[32] Gregory is similarly distanced from the realm of ordinary humanness on the occasion of his triumphant *adventus* into Neocaesarea, when all the people come out to see some one 'who, though a
human being, has power like an emperor over those whom they
deemed gods…'.[33] Again, the shift towards directly and practically manifested power is apparent. While Origen is busy ascending to the divine
world, Gregory can subdue demons and thus exercise an imperial degree
of dominance over this world.

Both subjects are also apply wisdom and discernment to those attached to them. Origen knows precisely how to dose out philosophical
arguments in order to encourage his students to think critically rather
than simply reacting to the eloquence or popularity of the argument.[34]

---

tou theian einai tina para to Gregorio ten dunamin, di' es ephane ton daimonon epikra-
testeros. Other instances of this attribution are, for example, Vita 7.49 and 8.59.
30 Oratio 6.80, SLUSSER 1998, 103.
31 Vita 4.32, SLUSSER 1998, 55.
32 Oratio 2.10, SLUSSER 1998, 93.
33 Vita 6.42, SLUSSER 1998, 59.
34 Oratio 7.100–108, SLUSSER 1998, 107–108.

Gregory is also praised for his judgment and discernment as he applies it to those who have given him their loyalty, but, although he is constantly referred to as 'the teacher', his judgment is mainly applied to solving disputes and instituting law and order.[35] Probably the most curious common attribute of each subject's relationship with those who are attached to them is the fact that they are both described on the metaphor of a good horseman. Origen is described as having sunk 'the spur of friendship' into the flanks of his student Gregory, who also says that Origen had to react when he saw his students 'fighting the reins like unbroken horses, veering off the road and running aimlessly every which way, until by persuasion and coercion, as by the bit which was the word from our own mouth, he made us stand quietly before him'.[36] Similarly, the Gregory of the *Vita* is praised for his wisdom because 'in re-educating his whole generation to a new life at one time, while taking charge of nature like a sort of charioteer and harnessing them safely by the reins of the knowledge of God, he allowed his subjects to cavort a little in the yoke of faith through merriment... he let them rejoice at the memories of the holy martyrs...'. While both subjects exercise this sort of pedagogical domination, Gregory's mastery is focused on the popular and non-intellectual. He realizes, through his great wisdom, that people enjoy parties, and allows conviviality on the occasion of martyr's festivals. Origen's handling of his students is more intensely domineering and more focused on intellectual formation.

While both Origen and Gregory have a special affinity with the divine, their exceptional status is declined in different ways and to different ends. Gregory the student, in relation to Origen, is not individualised. Any other student would do, and what the student should do is set. His role is like the result of a physical or chemical reaction, formulaic and necessary. Gregory the bishop, who has some of the same characteristics that he had previously attributed to Origen, manifests his divine status to different ends, but on a framework that produces an equally formulaic result in his audience: they see his miracles and feel compelled to believe in the legitimacy and efficacy of his god. So we are still coming up empty when looking for increasing or decreasing individualisation, but we do see a shift in the means and manner in which individual scope for religious action is effaced and elided but also subtly defined. Here the changed effacement of individualisation is what's telling, as

---

35   Vita 7.49, SLUSSER 1998, 62.
36   Oratio 6.81 (SLUSSER 1998, 104) and 7.97 (SLUSSER 1998, 107).

are the changed relationships within which the scope for individual religious action of one party is surrendered.

We can articulate the significance of the different forms of effacement in terms of several subtle but vital shifts. Firstly, the people who receive the effects of each divine man's special status shifts: Origen's quasi-divine status operates upon a limited group of privileged people and compels them to engage in philosophy with a view to developing virtue and the ability to engage noetically with divine truth. It improves them morally and mentally through prolonged contact and concentration on valuable intellectual undertakings under his leadership. Origen's special status functions as an embodiment of the ultimate goal of the educational project they have undertaken, for any student who commits to the life of philosophy can potentially also become a divine man. Thus those on the receiving end of the effects of divine status are limited in number and they are expected to make a substantial investment of time and attention, but the available payoff is extraordinary. They can reach the same heights that Origen has reached.

Gregory the bishop is granted the same ability to tap into divine power and the same status as some one on especially good terms with the divine, but his status operates upon the public in general (everybody), whether they have elected to pay attention to him or not. Indeed in most cases Gregory-the-bishop does not make the same sort of bid for attention that was the basis of Gregory-the-student's decision to stop with Origen. No one is invited to observe a miracle or not, but anyone and everyone is confronted with the fact of the miracle. The miraculous effects of Gregory-the-bishop's divine affinity is just as compelling as Origen's near-divinity, but those confronted with him do not feel compelled to commit to a life of philosophy and engage in the study of the virtues. Rather, Gregory's audience feels compelled to assent to the basic proposition that Gregory's god is stronger and more effective than other gods and to throw in their lot with Gregory's side.[37]

---

37 It should be noted that there is no reason to believe that people casting their loyalty onto Gregory Thaumaturgus and his God constitutes a conversion to Christianity in any recognisable sense. Even in the Nyssan's account, immediate decisions attached to the encounter with Gregory himself, with little or no instruction or knowledge of Christian doctrine, are more the norm than the exception on this scheme. People, even on Gregory's account, are converting to follow the Thaumaturg on the basis of his efficacy, and only incidentally to become Christians, inasmuch as this is part of the package which gets them the patronage of the miraculously worthwhile Thaumaturg.

While the breadth of audience is far greater for Gregory-the-bishop than it was for Origen, and what is being asked from those exposed to the effects of his near-divine status is much more manageable for ordinary people, the potential pay-off is correspondingly smaller: no one is, simply by witnessing miracles, going to obtain the same status as Gregory-the-bishop. This divine man is not only exceptional, but exclusively exceptional. The people have a digital rather than an exponential process to engage in when exposed to his semi-divinity: they can see that his god is real and behave accordingly. The magnet with which Origen slowly and indefinitely drew up his students towards spiritual truths has changed into a turnstile by means of which anyone and everyone can be sorted into the group of those who recognize that Gregory's god is the best one. So in the second text, individual scope for religious action is also effaced, but for different reasons. Although much of the same vocabulary is being used, massive changes have taken place in the type of relationship with a divine man that is available, the requirements placed on a person who engages in such a relationship, and the expected outcome of such a relationship. Attachment to a divine man remains a focal point of religious life, but how and to what ends that attachment works has been transformed.

Discursive Shifts: Individualisation in the Authorship of Laudatory Accounts

Each text also manifests the religious agency and individualization of the authors concerned. Their historical contexts and personal circumstances both place them in a distinct relationship with the religious life of their times. Authorship as such would seem a natural opportunity to indulge existing scope for religious individualization. Yet the manner in which that opportunity is engaged differs greatly between the two authors, and it is the shifting authorial exercise of scope for the individualization of religious life which represents the largest contradiction to the model of decreasing scope for individualization parallel to the rise of the imperial church.

Gregory Thaumaturgus is writing as one of many young men from the provincial well-to-do who were sent off to nearby centres like Beirut, Caesarea, or later Constantinople, in order to get the sort of education which would contribute to their own success and to the status of their families at home. His mother's initial guidance, and that of his teacher at home, were both reflective of standard strategies for the off-spring of provincial elites manuevering for a foothold in the context of an ever-changing imperial administration. Studying law, and learning the Latin which Gregory makes such a fuss about in the introduction to his speech, were both wise choices for those with a view to moving up the ranks when they returned home. It is unclear to what degree studying with Origen contributed to success for Gregory or to the status of his family, not least because it is also unclear whether he also com-pleted legal studies as originally planned. In the long term, however, Gregory does achieve success in his home region inasmuch as he is re-membered as a leader and patron of the welfare of his community, but on terms different than those aimed at by his mother or even pictured by himself originally.

The authorial exercise of individualized scope for religious practice has already been touched upon in the discussion of Gregory as he ap-pears in the *Address* in the first comparative section above. By writing himself into the farewell address to his teacher, Gregory is interpreting himself, and his position in religious life, in terms of his relationship with Origen and the fact of having studied with him. He does grant himself some personal contours and indeed includes more information on his own kinship ties and home region than on Origen's. But, as noted above, the content of this particular religious activity necessarily entails eliding individuality and crediting all agency to others, especially to divine others. So Gregory is using his individualized scope for reli-gious practice in order to define his religious practice in a way which requires the elision of individuality. This is what leads to the very noisy and very insistent self-effacement we see in this text.

Gregory of Nyssa, likewise from the local elite and similarly having already done his grand tour and come back to his home region, is writ-ing not a speech of departure but a piece of historiography, connecting Christianity in his region with a past founder. Like the Thaumaturg, he is addressing people who share knowledge of the subject at hand, as there were local traditions on Gregory Thaumaturgus just as there was common experience with the teacher Origen among the Caesarean audience. There is a certain continuity in Gregory's actions and the pri-orities of local religion, but the Nyssan is also disrupting and re-writing these traditions with a view to making the Thaumaturg his own, ortho-dox episcopal ancestor. He makes the most of the affection and author-ity already enjoyed by the Thaumaturg in oral tradition, which was the source for the vignettes presented in the panegyric. Gregory of Nyssa can hardly afford to downplay the status of a figure to whom a great deal of local sentiment seems to have been attached, but he can bow to that necessity while simultaneously hog-tying it by seizing the opportunity to define why and how the Thaumaturg was deserving of local fame. This heavy-handed, and single-handed, re-writing of local religious life is achieved by means of a number of revisions.

As we saw in the summary of the text above, the author of the *Vita* (and presumably also his audience) only really gets interested when Gregory emerges into public life and starts performing miracles and benefitting his home community. The main body of the text consists of recounting a series of miracles which are then interpreted, comparing Gregory favourably with biblical models like Moses. RAYMOND VAN DAM has also pointed out how the specific miracles portrayed, such as drying up a lake and constructively limiting the extent of fluvial flooding, serve to allow Gregory to outdo former kings of the region, who dammed the river or built mills to harness its power.[38] Gregory of Nyssa is thus realigning the heritage of power in his region so that it makes a Christian trajectory which leads down to himself. He also argues for the reliability of his knowledge of his subject based on family tradition, claiming that his own ancestors were converted by Gregory. Here Gregory Thaumaturgus is the man who can solve your problems, who has divine power, and who is responsible for law and order in the community, and Gregory of Nyssa is his descendent and hence also a figure of authority who can be depended on as a leader and protector. The author is thus using the available scope for individualizing religious life not only to articulate his own place in religious life, but also to disrupt and re-define that of an entire region.

The most blatant example of this revisionist project is the anachronistically Nicene creed which Gregory is portrayed as having received in a vision and then set up as a standard throughout the region. This serves both to make the Thaumaturg more orthodox than he could possibly have been before the definition and establishment of orthodoxy and to make Cappadocia consistently and traditionally orthodox rather than the scene of multiple contested theologies. It has been demonstrated, however, that Gregory Thaumaturgus could not possibly have writ-

---

38 VAN DAM 2003, 91.

ten that creed.[39] Here Gregory of Nyssa is, by fiat, retrospectively defining the content of the religion of the community in terms of contemporary ideology, while simultaneously identifying his revision with ancient local tradition.

Thirdly, the oddness of Gregory's ordination must give us pause. Gregory is supposed to be a lonely ascetic wandering in the wilderness who is avoiding ordination deliberately, but is finally ordained against his will and in absentia: 'For this reason Phaidimos ... disregarding the intervening distance by which he was separated from Gregory ... laid on Gregory his word in place of his hand, consecrating to God one who was not present in body...'. Here again, the Nyssan has to rush over the important part and mention in one sentence that Gregory received his visions (in which the creed mentioned above was delivered) when 'later all the proper ceremonies had been carried out on him'. This is indeed extraordinary. It would tend to suggest that Gregory was never ordained at all, and may have been recognized as a religious leader simply on the basis of his charisma and achievements. Such a marginalization of ecclesial procedure is not amenable to Gregory of Nyssa, but he may be prevented by local knowledge from claiming that the Thaumaturg was ordained normally. While any conclusions on this point must remain speculative, claiming that Gregory underwent distance ordination seems to be an act of rhetorical desperation. What is happening here? Is the individual, free and indeterminate exercise of religious agency being harnessed to the ecclesiastical machine? Or is a third-century ascetic misfit being harnessed by a fourth-century bishop to serve as a model for himself and for proper and acceptable forms of religious authority after the fact?

These revisionist factors in the *Vita*, along with the fact that the Nyssan's version of Gregory Thaumaturgus became the definitive story which was passed down even to us, suggests a much more far-reaching potential impact for individualized religious practice than that available to Gregory as the author of his own *Address*. A similar

---

39 Cf. ABRAMOWSKI 1976. I would tend to agree with the explanation offered by Michael Slusser, that Gregory of Nyssa, although he refers to an inscription of the creed on the church walls, is extrapolating on a more realistically brief inscription point by point, such that what could be pointed at on the walls read 'One God, One Lord, One Holy Spirit, Perfect Trinity'. The Nyssans definition of what each of these terms means serves to give Gregory Thaumaturgus impeccable Nicene credentials before he emerges as a religious leader. The creed is found at Vita 4.32, SLUSSER 1998, 54.

awkward tension and ambivalence to what we saw in Gregory's self-eli-
sion results from the Nyssan's strategies: he is disrupting and re-writing
local religious life while pretending very noisily not to be doing so, and
he is re-writing his own role in the religious life of Cappadocia while
also pretending only to be getting in line with his esteemed episcopal
ancestor, Gregory Thaumaturgus. This is indeed a spectacular application of an effaced individual religious practice, which is only effective
because it is effaced, in order to impose a new definition of what constitutes the legitimate content and structure of the religious life of a
whole community.

Conclusions: Authorship, Individualisation and Religious Change

Religious change is happening from one text to the next, but what's
happening is not on a single trajectory that could be described as the
rise of Christianity. We also find, in the above analysis, no reason to
confirm the hypothesis that the increasing coercive force of imperial religion corresponded with a decrease in the scope for individualized religious practice. In fact, as we have just seen in the final comparative
section, it is in this later phase that we can observe the most energetic,
far-reaching, and potent exercise of individual religious creativity.
Gregory of Nyssa is able to force religious change (at least in the rhetorical realm) in a way that was unthinkable for the young Gregory of
Thaumaturgus. Granted, the young Thaumaturg is not in a position
of leadership, but even where we see religious leadership in his context,
in the person of Origen, it is not used to these same energetically and
even violently creative ends.

On a discursive level, in comparing author with author, we see a
massive increase in the impact of individualization, a continuity of the
wonder-working sleight of hand involved in simultaneously effacing
and defining the role of the individual. We also see a shift in the
realm in which such projects can take effect. While Gregory-the-student is working upon himself or allowing Origen to work upon him,
Gregory of Nyssa is working upon a large community and re-shaping
their religious identity. On the level of narrative, what Origen is
doing and what Gregory of Nyssa is doing are two different things,
two separate projects which cannot be seen as naturally related to

each other or necessarily developing from Origen's school to Gregory of Nyssa's popular wonder-worker. Gregory of Nyssa *makes* a relationship between the two, from his late fourth century perspective.

On the functional level, we can also see a major shift in the role of the subject of each text. Clearly, a form of religious life like that experienced by Gregory as a student does not and cannot translate well onto a Cappadocian, late fourth-century agenda, nor does it translate well onto the requirements of (remembered) third-century popular religion in Pontus. The philosophical religion of Origen is a hard sell if you want to sell it to everyone, because it requires a high degree of investment but offers zero explicit tangible pay-off: possibly becoming divine in ten years is not attractive if what you want is for the children to stay healthy and the crops to come in well. However, Gregory's own history of himself engaging in a religious life of high commitment can be translated effectively if it is shoved into the background. His time of study is made to function as his credentials for being the representative of a better religion, where what is meant is a better religion in the sense of a better resource for dispensing divine power and coping with people's everyday needs and concerns. A religion like Origen's cannot supplant the traditional religion of Pontus. However, a religion which copes with people's needs and concerns and acts as an object of local pride can supplant traditional religion if it can make a plausible bid to achieve all of the tasks that traditional religion achieved, but better.

Bibliography

ABRAMOWSKI, LUISE 1976. "Das Bekenntnis des Gregor Thaumaturgus bei Gregor von Nyssa und das Problem seiner Echtheit", *Zeitschrift für Kirchengeschichte* 87. 145–166.

GUYOT, PETER; KLEIN, RICHARD (edd.) 1996. *Gregor der Wundertäter – Oratio Prosphonetica ac panegyrica in Origenem.* Fontes Christiani Bd. 24. Freiburg i. Br.; New York.

SLUSSER, MICHAEL (trans.) 1998. *St. Gregory Thaumaturgus – Life and Works.* The Fathers of the Church 98. Washington D.C.

STEFANIW, BLOSSOM 2010. *Mind, Text, and Commentary: Noetic Exegesis in Origen of Alexandria, Didymus the Blind, and Evagrius Ponticus.* Early Christianity in the Context of Antiquity Vol. 6. Frankfurt am Main.

—2010a. "Exegetical Curricula in Origen, Didymus and Evagrius- Pedagogical Agenda and the Case for Neoplatonist Influence. Procedings of the 15th International Conference on Patristic Studies held in Oxford 2007", *Studia Patristica* 44. 281–294.

Van Dam, Raymond 1982. "Hagiography and History: The Life of Gregory
Thaumaturgus", *Classical Antiquity* 1.2. 272–308.
—2003. *Becoming Christian: The Conversion of Roman Cappadocia*. Philadelphia.

The Father of Man: Abraham as the rabbinic Jesus

Ron Naiweld[°]

> *When the wicked Nimrod cast our father Abraham into the fiery furnace, Gabriel said to the Holy One, blessed be he: 'Master of the world, let me go down, cool [it], and deliver that righteous man from the fiery furnace.' Said the Holy One, blessed be he, to him: 'I am unique in my world, and he is unique in his world: it is fitting for him who is unique to deliver him who is unique' (b. Pesahim 118a).*[1]

0 Introduction: The Ethical Schism – Father and Son

In his book *Moses and Monotheism*, SIGMUND FREUD distinguishes between Judaism and Christianity by designating the former as a religion of the father and the latter as a religion of the son.[2] FREUD seems to see a very concrete significance in this assertion: for the Christians, 'The old God the Father fell behind Christ; Christ, the Son, took his place, just as every son had hoped to do in primeval times'.[3] What I would like to show in this article is that while FREUD's assertion appears in the context of a highly debatable historical thesis, to say the least, it does echo a discursive reality of rabbinic and Christian sources from the first centuries of our era. In that formative period, Christianity and rabbinic Judaism each articulated a moral and spiritual role model whose characteristics are closer to the biblical archetypal figures of the *Son* – Isaac – and of the *Father* – Abraham – respectively.

By arguing this point, I hope to show that the ethical dimension is as important as other dimensions such as doctrine, ritual or ethnicity when we come to discuss Christian-Rabbinic relationship. The growing liter-

---

[°]   I would like to thank JÖRG RÜPKE for the invitation to the conference. His remarks after the presentation of the paper, as well as those of TESSA RAJAK, DANIEL STÖKEL BEN EZRA and BLOSSOM STEFANIW, were extremely helpful. I would also like to thank KATELL BERTHELOT, JOSÉ COSTA, ILINCA DÖBLER-TANASEANU and SHARON WEISER who read and commented drafts of the article.
1   For two other versions of this story from the Cairo Geniza see MANN 1940, 43 (156 in the Hebrew part).
2   FREUD 2001, 88.
3   *Ibid.*

ature dealing with this relationship in the first centuries CE has focused for the main part on theological and doctrinal questions on the one hand, and on social-identity and political tensions on the other.[4] However, Christian-rabbinic polemic evolves also, and perhaps mainly, around ethical issues, i. e. around the modality in which each discourse constructs the ethical project of the individual. Both Christianity and rabbinic Judaism participate in what MICHEL FOUCAULT has called 'The Culture of the Self' of the Greco-Roman world.[5] Both use their rhetoric and their mythologies in order to set down for the individual a way to live a meaningful life, according to some transcendent, divine truth. More particularly, they offer to their adepts to live their lives in terms of an individual ethical project. By this, both distinguish themselves from archaic forms of religion, in which the individual use a rather fix set of actions to communicate with the divine. However, their demarcation from old conceptions of piety is not articulated similarly. Christian and rabbinic literature do not provide the same definition of virtue and of moral life, nor do they promote the same method to achieve it.

Whereas the archetype of the Christian moral individual[6] is without any doubt Jesus, can we speak of a rabbinic archetype, and if yes, how is it shaped by rabbinic discourse? I wish to claim that Palestinian sources

---

4 Obviously, it will not be possible to provide here a comprehensive bibliography of recent books and articles that discuss the question. The main works that I used in the preparation of this article are BOYARIN, 2004; BECKER AND YOSHIKO REED 2003, 1–33; YOSHIKO REED 2006, 323–346.

5 On Christianity in the context of ancient philosophy as a movement proposing a philosophical way of life and not only a doctrinal, theological dogma, see for example TROELTSCH, 1992, 65–82; HADOT 2002 and FOUCAULT 2005. As for rabbinic Judaism, almost no attempt has been made to put it in the context of the Greco-Roman 'Culture of the Self', in light of HADOT's and FOUCUAULT's works. An important exception is SCHOFER 2005, that reads 'Abot de Rabbi Nathan as a mode d'emploi for the rabbinic disciple.

6 I use the term 'moral individual' following the French Anthropologist LOUIS DUMONT. In his book Essays on Individualism (DUMONT 1986) he distinguishes between two types of individuals, or two senses we can give to the term individual. The first one, 'empiric individual', refers to the individual as the undivided unit of a larger group – of humans, of animals or of objects. The moral individual, on the other hand, exists only in some human societies. This individual, according to DUMONT, is every man or woman who individualizes his or her morality (makes it his or her own private law); who lives his or her life according to virtue, or some other term designating a transcendent, divine or natural superior good.

from the turn of the sixth century attribute to Abraham this archetypal function. They do so by appropriating Christian motives used in the description of Jesus as the archetype of the holy man. Abraham can thus be seen as the rabbinic Jesus, not so much in the eschatological sense as in the ethical sense: his life, as described and explained by the rabbis, offers an exemplary mythical model for the rabbinic Jew to follow.

In order to support this claim I will analyze texts from rabbinic compilations redacted in Palestine – the first around the end of the third century, and the second around the end of the fifth century. In other words, both are redacted in a time and a place in which the presence of Christians and Christian teachings in rabbinic environment is certain. When reading these rabbinic references to the Patriarch, one cannot ignore the existence of some similar elements between the rabbinic understanding of Abraham's historical role and the Christian description of Jesus Christ. Just as with Jesus, Abraham's coming to the world marks a crucial turning point in the history of humanity; just like Jesus, Abraham modifies radically the relationship between God and the world; and just like Jesus, Abraham is regarded as the person whose life should serve as a model for everyone who wishes to lead a moral life.

As we will see, along with the rabbinic articulation of Abraham's exemplarity, the Palestinian rabbis also diminish the role of Isaac, especially in the context of the Binding story. Whereas Christian and non-rabbinic Jewish accounts of the Aqedah attribute to Isaac a very clear and positive moral agency (he is willing to be sacrificed out of piety), rabbinic Palestinian elaborations of the same story are much more ambivalent on the issue of Isaac's agency while leaving that of Abraham intact. By reducing Isaac's role, the Palestinian rabbis emphasize that of Abraham, thus contributing to the reinforcement of his status as a role model.

In the first part of this article, I will discuss Isaac's agency in the story of the Binding, in both Jewish and Christian sources. In the second part, I will show how rabbinic Palestinian compilations depict the figure of Abraham in a way that corresponds to the Christian figure of Jesus, both on the cosmological and the ethical level. Then I will propose an explanation to the fact that most of the rabbinic material concerning Abraham as the ethical and spiritual role model is found in Genesis Rabbah, redacted in Palestine at the turn of the sixth century.

1 The Agency of Isaac as a Pivotal Element in Rabbinic-Christian Polemic

1.1 Christian and Non Rabbinic Jewish Sources

In very general terms one can argue that early Christian authors use Isaac's figure as a prefiguration of Jesus. Just as Abraham, the father, wanted to sacrifice his son, so did God, the father, sacrificed his – Jesus. Thus, most of the references to Isaac, or at least the most important ones, deal with the story of Genesis 22 – the sacrifice of Isaac.

The use of the Binding story in Jewish-Christian polemic has been the object of scholarly interest and dispute for many years. At the risk of simplifying, one can say that most, if not all, of the work done on the subject has dealt with the soteriological aspect of the story – Isaac's auto-sacrifice (or his sacrifice by Abraham) as a means to ensure Israel's (or humanity's) salvation. These works tried to determine whether the soteriological aspect, not present in the book of Genesis, is of post-biblical Jewish or Christian origin. I will refer to these works in the following, but the question I would like to ask is different; since my perspective is more ethical than theological, I deal only with the question of Isaac's moral agency as presented in the diverse interpretations of Genesis 22.

The use of Isaac as a precursor of Jesus, and of the Christian community in general, can be traced already to the New Testament.[7] Paul compares between Abraham's seed and Jesus in Galatiens 3:16. In Romans 9:7 he mentions specifically Isaac as Abraham's seed that is consecrated by God. Another possible New Testament reference is in *Mark*, in God's words to Jesus (1:11) 'You are my son, my beloved'; this can refer to God's words to Abraham when he commands him to bind his son.[8] As for the Gospel of Matthew, I am content to quote Leroy Huizenga's conclusion that 'the Matthean Jesus and the Isaac of ancient Jewish tradition resemble each other to a remarkable degree'.[9] To some extent, this conclusion can also apply to the other Gospels. The allusions to the sacrifice of Isaac become much more obvious and ex-

---

7   For a comprehensive list of NT references to Genesis 22 see Davies and Chilton 1978, 529–533. Davies and Chilton discuss the NT references pointed out by Daly 1977, claiming that there is no soteriological aspect in the NT references to Genesis 22.

8   Dowd and Struthers Malbon 2006, 273. See also Vermes 1961, 218–227.

9   Huizenga 2009.

plicit in early patristic literature. Thus, already in *the Epistle of Barnabas* we find the following comparison between the Crucifixion and the binding: '… because himself was going to offer the vessel of the spirit as a sacrifice of our sins, in order that the type established in Isaac, who was offered upon the altar, might be fulfilled'.[10]

In order to speak of Isaac as a precursor of Jesus or of Christ, one has to diverge from the biblical account in which Isaac shows no understanding of Abraham's intention, thus cannot accomplish any act of self-sacrifice as did Jesus. That is probably the reason why patristic sources from the end of the second century onwards continue to promote Barnabas' typology but, unlike him, they also insist on Isaac's agency. Thus, in his *Homily on Genesis* 22[11], Origen writes:

> After this the text says, 'Abraham took the wood for the holocaust and laid it on Isaac his son, and he took the fire in his own hands and a sword, and they went off together.'
> That Isaac himself carries on himself 'the wood for the holocaust' is a figure, because Christ also 'himself carried his own cross' and yet to carry 'the wood for the holocaust' is the duty of a priest. He himself, therefore, becomes both victim and priest. But what is added also is related to this: 'And they both went off together'. For when Abraham carries the fire and knife as if to sacrifice, Isaac does not go behind him, but with him[12], that he might be shown to contribute equally with the priesthood itself.

The mise-en-scène cannot be clearer – Isaac is going with his father; he does not follow him but actively participate in the project of the sacrifice. He is offering himself, and that is why he merits the title of a priest.[13] Tertullian follows the same line when he discusses the cross carried by Jesus: 'Accordingly, to begin with, Isaac, when led by his father as a victim, and himself bearing his own 'wood', was even at that early period pointing to Christ's death; conceded, as He was, as a victim by the Father; carrying, as He did, the 'wood' of His own passion'.[14]

We have to put this Christian emphasis on Isaac's agency in the context of a tradition, attested in several Jewish sources from the first centuries, according to which Isaac has willingly agreed to be sacrificed and even urged his father to tie him to the altar. For the purpose of this ar-

---

10 Barnabas, 7.3. I used the translation of *The Apostolic Fathers I* (1952), 365.
11 Homily on Genesis 8.6.
12 Compare to Genesis Rabbah 56:8.
13 Cf. KESSLER 2001, 405.
14 Tertullian, Answer to the Jews X (*ANF* 3:165). See also STROUMSA 2004.

ticle, I will name it 'the tradition of Isaac's agency'. The first testimony of this tradition is probably found in the Qumran text known as *Pseudo-Jubilees*[a] (4Q225) from the middle of the second century BCE.[15] The part relating the Binding was badly conserved but as was suggested by scholars[16] it contained Isaac's explicit demand to be tied to the altar (and not just put on it).[17]

This tradition is further developed by Josephus[18] who praises Isaac as being brave-hearted (*genaion fronema*)[19], and tells us that he was filled with joy in the prospect of his own sacrifice.[20] Pseudo-Philo's *Liber Antiquitatum Biblicarum* refers two times to Isaac consent. The first and most elaborated reference is in Deborah's song (32:2), where Isaac encourages his father to pursue the act so his (Isaac's) 'blessedness will be above that of all men'.[21] A second reference is made in the story of Seila (40:3), the daughter of Jephthah who encourages her father to sacrifice her by reminding him that Isaac gave consent to his father.[22] The Jewish–Hellenistic author of 4 Maccabees refers to Isaac as the first in a series of exemplary figures that went willingly to die out of piety.[23]

The tradition of Isaac's agency is found also in the early Palestinian Targum. Again, we find here an explicit demand of Isaac to be thor-

---

15 VERMES 1996; MARTÍNEZ 2002, 53.
16 See VERMES 1996, 142 n. 12.
17 4Q255 frg. 2 col. ii 4. See BERTHELOT 2006, 171.
18 Josephus, *Ant.* 1.232.
19 On Josephus' use of the adjective *genaios* in this text see BERTHELOT 2006, 171.
20 As was noted by L. H. Feldman, the importance of Abraham to Josephus is much greater than that of Isaac (FELDMAN 1998).
21 'The son said to his father, 'Hear me, father. If a lamb of the flock is accepted as an offering to the Lord as an odor of sweetness and if for the sins of men animals are appointed to be killed, but man is designed to inherit the world, how is it that you do not say to me 'Come and inherit a secure life and time without measure'? What if I had not been born into the world to be offered as a sacrifice to him who made me? Now my blessedness will be above that of all men, because there will be no other. Through me nations will be blessed and through me the peoples will understand that the Lord has deemed the soul of a man worthy to be a sacrifice'. Translation from JACOBSON 1996, 149. See *ibid.*, 864 for the commentary ('Isaac indirectly encourages Abraham to go through with the act: you should have told me that I am now going to inherit immortal life').
22 JACOBSON 1996, 160.
23 4 Maccabees 16: 16–21.

oughly tied to the alter. Here is the version of the Fragmentary Targum of Genesis 22:10:[24]

> Abraham stretched out his hand and took the knife to kill Isaac his son. Isaac answered and said to Abraham his father: Bind my hand properly that I may not struggle in the time of my pain and disturb you and render your offering unfit and be cast into the pit of destruction in the world to come". The eyes of Abraham were turned to the eyes of Isaac, but the eyes of Isaac were turned to the angels of heaven. Isaac saw them, but Abraham did not see them. In that hour the angels of heaven[25] went out and said to each other: let us go and see the only two just men in the world. The one slays, and the other is being slain. The slayer does not hesitate and the one being slain stretches out his neck.

In a certain sense this is the most radical transformation of the biblical story so far since it praises Isaac's spiritual greatness at the expense of Abraham's. The piety and righteousness of the two is praised by the end of the passage in a similar way to that of 4 Maccabees. But here the possibility to communicate with the divine sphere is at stake – it is Isaac who is considered more compatible with the spiritual realm than his father. Abraham hears God and follows His orders, but his eyes stay in this world. Only Isaac can elevate his gaze in order to see God's angels. It is the son who brings salvation not only to himself but also to his father.

1.2 Rabbinic sources

In general, scholars have considered rabbinic literature to also reflect in the tendency of attributing moral agency to Isaac. In the words of G. F. MOORE, whereas the biblical Isaac is 'purely passive', in rabbinic literature 'the voluntariness of the sacrifice on Isaac's part is strongly emphasized'.[26] This stance is shared by scholars like GEZA VERMES[27], who believe that the Christian traditions on Isaac borrow from and rely on Jewish sources, as well as by scholars like DAVIES AND CHILTON, who consider that the Jewish tradition on the Aqedah is a reaction to the Chris-

---

24   I used the translation of VERMES 1961, 194.
25   The Neofiti reads here 'a heavenly voice'.
26   MOORE 1932, 539, quoted in VERMES 1961, 196.
27   VERMES 1961.

tian teachings.[28] Without entering into the details of the discussion
whether the tradition of Isaac's auto-sacrifice is of Jewish or Christian
origin (the answer to which depends on how we understand this tradition), I would like to point out a problem that characterizes it. This
problem is well reflected in the conclusion of VERMES' 1996 article
about the Qumran text mentioned earlier. According to VERMES, the
discovery of 4Q225 has put a definite end to this quarrel for it revealed
'the pre-Christian skeleton of the targumic-midrashic representation of
the sacrifice of Isaac'.[29]

This last sentence of VERMES is emblematic to his and others' approach in the sense that it puts the Qumran scroll, the Targum, the Jew-
ish-Hellenistic texts and rabbinic sources in the same 'Jewish' basket,
opposing it to another basket – that of 'Christianity'.[30] The essentialist
vision of the two separate entities has proven in the last decades to be
problematic in many aspects, in both Christian and Jewish 'sides'. The
tensions among the Jewish groups that VERMES include on the same
side of the fence are sometimes greater than the tension between
some of the 'Jews' and 'Christians'. One of the themes around which
this tension is revealed is precisely Isaac's agency in the story of the
binding. If we look more closely at the Palestinian *rabbinic* sources
from before the sixth century, we see that the tradition of Isaac's agency
appears only in one very brief tannaitic source, and that the amoraic
sources that refer to it reflect a very pronounced ambivalence.

The only tannaitic source referring to Isaac's moral agency is in Sifre
Deuteronomy in an exegetical comment attributed to R. Meir on
Deut. 6:5. Meir interprets the command to love God 'with your entire
soul' by referring to Isaac 'who tied [עקד] himself on the altar'. Isaac's
agency is non-existent in another reference to the Binding story from
Sifre Deuteronomy 313.[31] It is an exegesis on the word 'only' in
God's command to Abraham 'Take your only son' from Gen. 22:1. Ig-
noring the existence of Ishmael, the *midrash* says that since we know that

---

28 DAVIES AND CHILTON 1978, 516. For a critical view of their theory see HAY-
    WARD 1990. For Geza Vermes' response to their critique see VERMES 1996, 144–
    145. For other critiques see: SWETNAM, 1982, 18–21; HAYWARD 1990, 306.
29 VERMES 1996,145.
30 Even when DAVIES and CHILTON (*op. cit.*) distinguish between rabbinic and
    non-rabbinic sources they are basing their argument on chronological criteria,
    as if from a certain point all Jewish sources has to be rabbinic.
31 Ed. Finkelstein, 355. All page numbers of Sifre Deut. refer to the Finkelstein
    edition.

Abraham had only one son, this word comes to designate Abraham *himself* as the sacrifice. We will read this exegesis more closely later.

There are no tannaitic compilations on Genesis, and one can claim that this is the reason for the scarce evidence of the tradition of Isaac's agency in these sources. However, that is not the case in the amoraic period when Genesis Rabbah, a Palestinian compilation of aggadic texts consecrated entirely to the book of Genesis, is produced. Indeed, Genesis Rabbah refers many times to the Binding story. Moreover, many of its texts attribute moral agency to Isaac. However, as we will see shortly, all of these texts are ambivalent in their portrayal of this agency, and sometimes even describe it in clear negative terms. This, I would suggest, reflects the uneasiness among rabbis in Palestine towards the tradition of Isaac's willingness to sacrifice himself. It is therefore possible that the scarceness of tannaitic evidence for Isaac's agency reflects the same discomfort.

The most obvious Genesis Rabbah reference to the tradition of Isaac's agency is in 56:8. It relies on the same tradition found in the Targum – Isaac asks his father to bind him tight. However, this part is found only in the print edition and in one manuscript witness (the Yemenite). It is noteworthy that in these two witnesses the Isaac's request is followed by a rhetorical question – 'can one bind a man thirty-seven (some say twenty-six) years old without his consent?' This question is intended to explain why Isaac's consent is so important. Contrary to the other, non-rabbinic, versions of the tradition mentioned before, Genesis Rabbah's text does not use Isaac's demand to praise his piety or to accentuate his spiritual capacities. For one reason or another the redactors of this version of the *midrash* chose to incorporate the tradition of Isaac's agency. However, they did not follow the author of 4 Maccabees or the Fragmentary Targum who compare Isaac's piety to his father's and suggest the spiritual inferiority of the latter. This is especially salient in another story from Genesis Rabbah (56:4), where Samel tries to convince Abraham and than Isaac not to proceed with the sacrifice. Abraham remains firm but Isaac allows doubt to enter his heart and asks his father for mercy.

Another interesting example is Genesis Rabbah 65:10 which provides an explanation of Isaac's blindness in his old age. Just like the targumic Isaac, also the rabbinic one looks at the angels in the moment of the Binding:

When our father Abraham bound his son Isaac, the ministering angels wept
…: tears dropped from their eyes into his, and left their mark upon them,
and so when he became old his eyes dimmed …[32]

Contrary to the targumic tradition, here no reference is made to Isaac's
spiritual superiority. The second explanation proposed by the Genesis
Rabbah paragraph to Isaac's blindness is even more striking when we
compare it to the non-rabbinic tradition of Isaac's agency:

When our father Abraham bound Isaac on the altar he [Isaac] lifted up his
eyes heavenwards and gazed at the *Deity*. This may be illustrated by the case
of a king who was taking a stroll by his palace gates, when looking up he
saw his friend's son peering at him through a window. Said he: 'If I exe-
cute him now, I will make my friend suffer; therefore I will rather order
that his windows be sealed up'. Thus, when our father Abraham bound
his son on the altar he looked up and gazed at the *Deity*. Said the Holy
One, blessed be He: 'If I slay him now, I will make Abraham, my friend,
suffer; therefore I rather decree that his eyes should be dimmed' …[33]

It is clear from this passage who is God's friend. It is Abraham, and not
Isaac. Of course, Isaac is an agent and not a mute object in the story. He
gazes at God actively. But not only does the text not praise him on that
account, it lets us understand that it is precisely this direct, insolent gaze
cast on the Deity itself that incited God to slaughter him!

The last example of the ambivalence of Genesis Rabbah's redactors
towards Isaac's agency can be found in their version of a story that we
find also in the later Targum Yerushlami on Genesis 22:1. According to
this story, Ishmael teases Isaac by telling him that he is more pious than
him because contrary to Isaac, he was willing to circumcise himself
when he was thirteen years old. Isaac, according to the Targumic version, answers by saying that he will not refuse God if He asks him
for all of his organs. Hearing this, God commands Abraham to sacrifice
his son. Again, the Genesis Rabbah version of the story[34] bears a small
but important difference. Isaac *hopes* to be called by God to sacrifice
himself. His use of the Hebrew word 'הלוואי' (I wish) leaves no

32 719 (585–586). For the English translations of Genesis Rabbah I relied on the
    Soncino edition – *Midrash Rabbah* I-II (1961) – but I took the liberty to modify
    it, when I found it was necessary. The page numbers for Genesis Rabbah refer
    to the scientific edition of Theodor-Albeck and to the Soncino edition in pa-
    rentheses.
33 719–720 (586).
34 54:4. p. 588.

doubt about it. Thus, it is not necessarily out of piety that he wants to be sacrificed, but perhaps also in order to prove a point.

In general, the Genesis Rabbah references to Isaac's agency are either negative, or neutral. Reading the relevant passages, one gets the impression that more emphasis is put on Abraham's moral agency and piety than on Isaac's. This is the case even in the well-known text of Genesis Rabbah 56:3, an exegesis on Gen. 22:6: "And Abraham took the wood of the burnt-offering and put it on Isaac his son" – Like the one who charges [טוען] his crucified [צלובו] on his shoulder'.[35] In fact, the subject of the verb 'carries [טוען]' is most probably Abraham and not Isaac. *He* is the one who charges *his* crucified. Maybe the most salient expression of this tendency to insist on Abraham's moral agency at the expense of Isaac's is to be found in 56:7, when God says to Abraham that He considers his willingness to sacrifice his son 'as if I had bidden you to sacrifice yourself and you had not hindered'.[36]

In summary, rabbinic Palestinian sources from the tannaitic and amoraic periods clearly display some ambivalence towards the tradition of Isaac's agency in the story of the Binding. Some of them even deny it completely, while placing agency entirely in Abraham. It is therefore difficult to speak of a rabbinic participation in a more general Jewish-Christian tendency to emphasize Isaac's role in the interpretation of Genesis 22. In fact, when putting these rabbinic sources in the context of this tradition, one has to ask oneself – what is the reason for this rabbinic exception?

The explanation which I will offer in the following is that the by distancing themselves from this tradition, and even criticizing and mocking it, the Palestinian rabbis react to the growing importance of Isaac in Christian discourses that used his figure as a prefiguration of Christ. The rabbis do not content themselves with reducing or criticizing Isaac's actions in the Binding story; they also propose an alternative model to Isaac. This is the rabbinic Abraham who, as I will claim, is shaped by Palestinian rabbinic literature as its own version of God's companion whose appearance in this world changes its course ultimately and definitively.

---

35 598 (493).
36 602 (497).

2 Abraham in rabbinic literature

2.1 End of tannaitic period

One of the several common motives that run through rabbinic literature is the exemplarity of Abraham. In fact, the exemplarity of Abraham is not unique to rabbinic culture, and is shared by many Jewish discourses prior to the Talmudic period.[37] As for the rabbinic corpus, there are almost no negative exegeses or stories related to him, whether the texts in question are from a tannaitic, amoraic, Babylonian or Palestinian origin. This is striking especially when we compare him to the figure of Moses. Unlike other Jewish post-biblical sources, the rabbis do not hesitate to criticize or even to ridicule the latter. But when it comes to Abraham, they seem to participate in a Jewish tendency of the first centuries to praise his figure and to use it as a role model on both ethical and spiritual level.

As was already argued by scholars, the figure of rabbinic Abraham is shaped in the context of the Jewish-Christian polemic, and is sometimes used to convey ideas and values of each side. Scholars who study the figure of Abraham in the context of Jewish-Christian polemics, usually tend to concentrate either on matters of identity (the True Israel)[38], or on the question of the validity of the biblical Law in general[39] and of the circumcision in particular.[40] I would like to focus on another dimension of the shaping of the rabbinic Abraham in the context of the rabbinic-Christian polemic. In fact, in both tannaitic and amoraic Palestinian compilations the rabbis describe the birth of Abraham or his acceptance of God as a critical turning point in the history of the world and of humanity. By doing so, they do not leave any place for any supplementary major transformation in the relationship between God and humanity, thus rendering the Catholic understanding of Jesus futile.

---

37   See YOSHIKO REED 2009. According to the author, Abraham is 'arguably the exemplary exemplar of Jewish culture' (188). She relies on SANDMEL 1954. Based on the Genesis *Apocryphon* from Qumran, it seems that Qumran's literature makes an exception to this Jewish and Christian tendency to set Abraham as the 'exemplary exemplar' (cf. 1QapGen col. 19). As far as I know, no serious study has been conducted on this matter. EVANS' Article (EVANS 2001) is by no means satisfying.
38   Cf. SIKER 1991; LEVENSON 2004, esp. 28–35.
39   Cf. CALVERT-KOYZIS 2004.
40   Cf. HIMELFARB 2008; NIEHOFF 2003; MIMOUNI 2007.

Abraham is God's new creation, a better one than the flawed first man. He is, to paraphrase a *midrash* from the tannaitic period, the first 'son of man'.[41]

The idea that Abraham's coming to the world is a crucial turning point in the history of humanity, in particular regarding its relationship with God, is expressed in the following *mishnah*:

> [There were] ten generations from Adam to Noah, to show you how great is his [=God's] longsuffering, for all the generations were provoking him until he brought upon them the Flood. [There were] ten generations from Noah to Abraham, to show you how great is his longsuffering, for all the generations were provoking him until Abraham came and received the reward of them all.[42]

To the best of my knowledge, the image of Abraham as taking on himself the 'reward' (שכר) of the rest of humanity is not found in non-rabbinical Jewish sources. In rabbinic literature, we find this idea mainly in relation to Israel – Abraham's right (זכות) still stands to expiate the sins of Israel and to plea before God on their behalf.[43] Again, by means of this depiction of Abraham the rabbis are probably replying to Christian assertion that the old covenant, between God and Abraham, was no longer valid. However, the main point for our purpose is the very concept of an individual whose appearance, just like Jesus', enables expiation, whether of the entire humanity or of Israel.

The Abot tractate was probably redacted after the rest of the Mishna, in the second half of the third century.[44] It is also around this time that the midrashic compilations of the tannaitic period were edited. In one of them, the Sifre on the book of Deuteronomy, we find two

---

41 '*When the Most High gave to the nations their inheritance, [when he separated the children of man]* (Deut. 32:8) – Before our father Abraham came to the world, the Holy One Blessed Be He judged the world with a strict measure, so to speak. The people of the flood sinned, He set them afloat like sparks in water; the people of the tower sinned, he scattered them from one end of the world to the other; the people of Sodom sinned, He bathed them with brimstone and fire. But, when our father Abraham came to the world, it merited receiving suffering, and they started to come gradually, according to the matter. As it is said, *there was a famine in the land, and Abram went down to Egypt*' (Sifre Deut. 311). p. 351–352 Finkelstein.

42 *m* 'Abot 5:2. The following *mishna* specifies Abraham's 'ten' tests.

43 Cf. Gensis Rabbah 49 on 'and YHWH left …' where Abraham is compared explicitly to a *sanegor*, or *b* Ber. 7b – 'Rav said: Also Daniel was heard only in the sake of Abraham'.

44 STERMBERGER 1996, 122.

very instructive passages for our purpose. I alluded to one of them before, when I mentioned the rabbinic description of Abraham as the first
'son of man'.[45] According to that *midrash*, Abraham's coming to the
world transforms radically the relationship between God and humanity
– from now on, people are judged 'according to the matter'; their relation to the moral code becomes subjective.

This thesis is even more salient in the following paragraph:

> **A.** *He found him in a land of desert [in a barren and howling state; He shielded*
> *him and watched him; He guarded him as the apple of his eyes]* (Deut. 32:10)
> – this is Abraham. [It is] like a king who went with his armies to the des-
> ert.[46] His armies left him in the midst of troubles, of [foreign] troops, of
> robbers, and went away. One hero appointed himself. He said to him:
> My master the king, do not be afraid [lit. do not let your heart fall], and
> do not let horror control you over nothing. I promise not to abandon
> you until you will get inside your palace and will sleep in your bed, as it
> is said: And He said unto him: I am YHWH that brought you out of
> Ur of the Chaldeans (Gen. 15:7). He shielded him – as it is said: And
> YHWH has said to Abram – go leave your country (Gen. 12:1).

> **B.** *[He] watched him* – before Abraham came to the world, the Holy one,
> blessed be He, was the king of Heaven alone, as it is said: *YHWH, God*
> *of Heaven who took me* (Gen. 24:7). But when Abraham came to the
> world, he crowned Him over heaven and earth, as it is said: *I want you*
> *to swear by YHWH, the God of heaven and the God of Earth* (Gen. 24:3).

> **C.** *He guarded him as the apple of his eyes* – had God asked him for his eye, he
> would have given it to him. And not only his eye, but also his own soul,
> that is precious to him more than anything. As it is said: *Take your son, your*
> *only [son], Isaac ...* (Gen. 22:2). We know that he is his only son, but the
> verse refers to the soul that is called 'one', as it is said: *Save my soul from*
> *the sword, my one from the dog* (Psa. 22:21).[47]

The first part of the text leaves its reader somewhat perplexed. Who is
the king? Who is the hero? Who found whom in the desert? Is it God
who have found Abraham in the desert and promised him to take him
to his palace (the land of Canaan) and to his bed? This is without any
doubt the more obvious reading of the verse *He found him in a land of*
desert in this context – 'he' refers to God, 'him' to Abraham. But is it
also the reading proposed by our exegete? Yes, God is the king, but

45 See note 41.
46 In the Midrash Hagadol – 'to the war'.
47 Sifre Deut. 313 (354–355). Cf. *b* Ber. 7b: 'Rabbi Yohanan said in the name of
    Rabbi Shim'on bar Yohai: From the day the Holy one, blessed be He, created
    the world, there was no one to call him Lord, until Abraham came...'

the king is the one who was left in the desert and it was him who was rescued by a hero who *appointed himself* – Abraham. The latter calms the king down and promises him to bring him (back?) to where he belongs.

This reading is confirmed by the second part of the *midrash*. Abraham is the one who makes God the king of the world. This is a remarkable expression of the rabbinic thesis mentioned above, according to which the coming of Abraham marks a radical change in the relationships between God and the world. This change is described now on the cosmological (rather than only ethical) level. According to our text, it is Abraham who actively provokes it. Note that in the previous part Abraham was the hero who 'appointed himself'. Abraham is described as a moral agent, whose agency can even affect God's bond to the world. The Sifre does not provide us with explanation of how the Patriarch could modify this bond. As we will see, an answer to this question is provided in Genesis Rabbah.

Finally, the last part of our *midrash* refers to the scene of the Aqedah discussed above. It rejects the common narrative – 'Abraham sacrifices his son' – and replaces it by this one – 'Abraham is willing to sacrifice himself'. We should understand this part as a rabbinic reaction to the tradition of Isaac's agency – the real model of piety in the story of the Binding, the rabbis seem to say, is Abraham and not Isaac. In the first two parts of our text Abraham was described as a moral agent – he appoints himself and crowns God to be the king of the earth. It is probably in order to enforce this idea that the last part was added here. Abraham's decisions are entirely his own and affect his own being; his actions are voluntarily pious, just as your actions, the one who listen to or read this text, should be.

2.2 Amoraic Period in Palestine

The two elements that we find in the Sifre – the radical change in the relationship between God and the world, and the description of Abraham as the first moral agent – are present in Genesis Rabbah. However, the redactors of Genesis Rabbah add two other dimensions to the relationship between God and Abraham. First, they describe Abraham as a new creation, a better version of Adam, that is an 'Adam' who can fight his desire to do evil. Second, they emphasize the interpersonal relationship between Abraham and God; the former is described as the counterpart of the latter. Doing this, the redactors allow us to think of Abraham as a man, the first man, whose moral agency equals to that of God.

Abraham Makes God the Leader of the World

In a *midrash* from Genesis Rabbah 39:1[48], Abraham is compared to a passer-by who sees a tenement house (*birah*)[49] on fire, and wonders whether this *birah* has no leader (*manhig*). The owner of the *birah* looks out at him and declares himself to be the owner. According to the *midrash*, it is in the same manner that Abraham asked himself whether the world has no leader, after which 'the Holy one, blessed be He, looked at him and said "I am the leader, the master of the entire world"'. According to PAUL MANDEL, God's statement is 'a cry of help', uttered once He realizes that Abraham thinks that the world is without a leader. The passer-by, or Abraham, is the one who helps God to put out the fire, to save or to bring order to the world.[50]

Another exegesis from Genesis Rabbah conveys a similar idea. In the context of the comparison between Abraham and Noah (to the benefit of the former, of course), Rabbi Nehamiah pronounces the following teaching:

> [The case of Noah might be compared] to a king's friend, who was plunging about in dark alleys.[51] When the king looked out and saw him plunging, he said to him: 'Instead of plunging about in dark alleys come walk with me'. But [the case of] Abraham [might be compared] to a king who plunged about in dark alleys. When his friend looked out [and saw him plunging], he casted light on [the dark alleys] through the window. [The king] told him: 'Instead of casting light through the window, come and cast light before me'. So said the Holy one, blessed be He, to Abraham our father: 'Instead of casting light for me from Mesopotamia and its environs, come and cast light before me, in the land of Israel'.[52]

The same principle found in the Sifre is expressed here – God is the king, but He is a king in need. Abraham helps him to get out of the mess He is in by casting light for Him from the outside. But God

---

48 p. 365.
49 In this interpretation of the word *birah* I am relying on MANDEL 1994, 274–276. According to MANDEL, 'The rabbinic *birah* is [...] a translation of the Latin *insula*' which is 'a large tenement house, containing a number of distinct and separate dwellings' (275).
50 Mandel, *op. cit.*, 276.
51 In some manuscripts – 'in clay' or 'clay of feces'.
52 Gensis Rabbah 30 (276–277).

wants Himself and Abraham to share the same destiny; He wants Abraham to get inside the 'dark alleys' instead of keeping himself apart. Again, Abraham's appearance changes radically the relationship between God and the world. Whereas until Abraham God was plunging about in the dark, now He can actually exercise His rule and become the master of the world.

What kind of light does God need Abraham to throw for Him? The answer to this question is not clear from the text. The following exegesis may provide us with the answer.

Abraham as God's Counterpart

According to the Sifre exegesis quoted above, Abraham is the first 'son of man' to be treated by God as an individual. Genesis Rabbah takes this idea further, designating the patriarch as God's counterpart:

> He [Abraham] asked: if circumcision is so precious, how come it was not given to the first man?
> The Holy one, blessed be He, told him: 'Let it be enough for you, Abraham, that only I and you are in the world. If you do not accept to undergo circumcision, it is enough for my world to have existed until now, and it is enough for the foreskin to have existed until now, and it is enough for the circumcision to have been forlorn until now.'
> He said: 'Before I circumcised myself, people came and married me. Would you say that once I am circumcised they will [still] come and marry me?'
> The Holy one, blessed be He, told him: 'Abraham, let it be enough for you that I am your God; let it be enough for you that I am your protector (*patronkha*). And not only for you – but it is enough for my world that I am its God, that I am its protector (*patrono*)'.[53]

Obviously, this *midrash* is a rabbinic reaction to Christian arguments against the validity of circumcision. Abraham's question in the first part can be found in Justin's Dialog with Trypho[54], while his interrogation in the second part is probably a rabbinic attempt to justify the price of the insistence on circumcision. However, besides their rhetoric val-

---

53 Gensis Rabbah 46 (460). See also chapter 47 (478): 'Abraham said: 'Before I circumcised myself, travelers used to visit me; now that I am circumcised, perhaps they will no longer visit me?' The Holy one, blessed be He, said to him: 'Before you were circumcised, uncircumcised men visited you, now I in my glory appear to you'. As it is written (Gen. 18:1) *And YHWH appeared unto him.*'

54 Cf. Dialogue with Trypho XIX. In another text from Genesis Rabbah 11, a *philosophos* asks R. Hosh'aya the same question.

ues, the answers to both of these questions provide us with a genuine rabbinic conception of the relationship between man and God.

According to the first part of the text, Abraham's reluctance to circumcise himself will lead to God's decision to put an end to the world. However, the *midrash* does not articulate this 'promise' to destroy the world as a threat. In fact, God is presented in our text in one of His most stoic moments – He seems to say to Abraham: 'do whatever you want, for Me that is all the same'. The abolition of the world is not a punishment. The liberty of Abraham to accept or reject God's authority stays absolute.

If Abraham's reluctance to circumcise will bring the end of the world, this is because it will provoke a major interruption in the divine program that includes the concretization of the circumcision (so it will not stay 'forlorn'). The realization of this program lies literally in the hands of Abraham. It is for him to decide whether God will modify his relationship to the world. Only if he accepts to circumcise himself, it will happen. Again, God declares himself to be the ultimate master of Abraham and of the world; He is the 'king' of the previous *midrash*. But at the same time, He also acknowledges His incapacity to accomplish His project without Abraham.

In the second part Abraham is worried about the implications the circumcision will have on his proselytizing efforts. God's answer distinguishes clearly between Abraham's responsibility towards himself and towards others. It is enough for Abraham to have God as his patron, even if he does not succeed in convincing others to join him. He should not worry about anyone else – if they want to join him, they will. It is *their* choice.

This is how I understand the somewhat opaque final sentence of the text. What God seems to say is that it is enough for the world, i. e. for other people than Abraham, to accept Him as their God. If they understand the significance of this choice, they will do what is necessary. If not – there is not much Abraham can do about it. Just as Abraham can decide to do the right thing (what is 'enough') and to accept God's authority, so can they.

Abraham is described as the first person to conform his will to that of God. In fact, this is the essence of the change in the relationship between God and humanity, announced by the Patriarch. From now on, God is not only a distant owner of the universe, a king who cannot practice his rule. Once Abraham came to the world, and accepted God's authority, the link that ties God to the world was established. The rest of the world can now take the path established by Abraham.

Abraham as a Turning Point

All these exegeses convey also the idea that Abraham's coming to the world is a decisive turning point. We have seen that this idea was already present in the Sifre and in the Mishnah Abot, but the redactors of Genesis Rabbah seem to elaborate on it much more:

> R. Abba b. Kahana said: In general practice, when a man joints a pair of beams [posed against each other in order to support the ceiling], where does he place them? Surely in the middle of the vestibule, so they will support the beams in front and behind. So the Holy one, blessed be he, created Abraham in the middle of the generations, so he might bear the generations before and behind.[55]

This intermediate position of Abraham in the history of humanity is also expressed by another *midrash* from the same compilation[56], according to which 'the real home of the divine presence was the nether sphere', with each sin, it ascended to a higher heaven. Thus, when Adam sinned it ascended from the first to the second; with Cain – from the second to the third, and so forth until the 'Egyptians in the days of Abraham' whose sins caused the divine presence to ascend to the seventh heaven. Abraham is the first among the seven biblical figures who brought the *shekhinah* back down to earth.[57]

Further on in Genesis Rabbah we find the following *midrash* on Song of Songs' 1:3 (*'We have a little sister …'*).[58] According to R. Bere-khiah, the word sister, *Ahot*, refers to Abraham, 'who united [אחה] the whole world for us'. And Bar Kapra adds: 'who sewed [אחה] the tear'.

According to some commentators, Abraham's action of uniting the world consists in bringing together the entire world under the rule of one God. In the same way, Bar Kapra's 'tear' is understood as the split between God and His people, repaired by Abraham.[59]

Be that as it may, we should notice that the *midrash* does not put forward any action or teaching of Abraham that can be accountable to this

---

55 Gensis Rabbah 14 (130).
56 Gensis Rabbah 19 1(76–177). See THEODOR ALBECK for parallels.
57 The number 14 can be regarded as referring to the genealogy in the beginning of Matthew.
58 Gensis Rabbah 39 (p. 366)
59 Cf. THEODOR ALBECK, 366

'sewing of the tear'. The main issue is that Abraham's presence unites the world with its creator; it is his being that repairs the tear.

Abraham as the Flawless Adam

After arriving at the conclusion that Abraham, and no other person, is essential to the realization of God's project to the world, we have to ask – why? What makes him so unique in the eyes of the Rabbis? The answer, according to the following *midrash*, is very simple – Abraham is a better version of Adam, the first man:

> [*Then YHWH God formed*] *the man*: for the sake of Abraham. R. Levi said: It is written (Josh. 14:15) *The greatest man among the 'Anaqim*. 'Man' means Abraham. And why is he called the greatest man? Because he was worthy of being created before Adam, but the Holy one, blessed be he, reasoned: 'He may sin and there will be no one to set it right. Hence I will create Adam first, so that if he sins, Abraham may come and set things right'.[60]

The *midrash* does not explain the nature of Adam's flaw and how exactly Abraham fixed it. However, in one of the passages discussing the concept of the *evil inclination* (יצר הרע), Abraham is considered as the first one to understand 'that it has no purpose' and to start 'fighting it'.[61] Another teaching, further on the same compilation[62], is attributed to R. Levi who tells us that God gave Abraham control over his evil inclination (שהשליטו ביצרו).

The tradition according to which Abraham is one of the rare persons who managed to perfectly control their evil inclination is attested in other Palestinian rabbinic sources as well. Thus, according to Numbers Rabbah 14, Abraham has bent (כפף) his inclination. The Palestinian Talmud, in two occasions[63], mentions Abraham as the 'perush of love'[64] who transformed his evil inclination into the good one.[65]

Once again the concept of Abraham as the first moral agent is expressed here, but this time, with more precision. Abraham is the first

---

60 Gensis Rabbah 14 (130). Gensis Rabbah 39 (373) brings a teaching of R. Berekhiah according to whom God creates Abraham as 'a new creature'.
61 Genesis Rabbah 22 (211).
62 Genesis Rabbah 59.
63 jBer. 9:5, 14b; Sot. 5:5, 20c.
64 For a discussion about the list of the seven types of 'perus' see DIAMOND 2004, 89.
65 See also bNed 32b for the teaching of Ami bar Aba (according to MS Munich) about Abraham who controls all 318 (רמח) parts of his body. A similar source if found in Tanhuma (Buber) חיי שרה 6.

to conceive of his life as an ethical project; he is the first to fight his passions in the name of moral duty. This is the point of him being a flawless version of Adam. This is the rabbinic essence of his exemplary status. The piety of Abraham consists in his ability to control his inclinations, to overcome his self-interest. This is how the scene of the Binding is understood, as well as that of the circumcision – obviously, circumcising oneself is to go way beyond the principle of pursuing immediate pleasure. Neither Adam nor Noah would have been able to postpone or to conquer their interest in themselves and in their pleasures. Only Abraham can sacrifice himself, i.e. his beloved son; only he can control all the parts of his body[66], in the name of God.[67]

2.3 A Rabbinic Model of the Holy Man

Most rabbinic sources that describe Abraham as a 'rabbinic Jesus', i.e. a historical figure whose coming to the world changes radically the link between God and humanity, come from Genesis Rabbah. The materials used by the Genesis Rabbah's redactors are based on traditions that we can find in other strata of rabbinic literature, anterior or posterior, as well as in Christian or Jewish non-rabbinic sources. However, it is only in Genesis Rabbah that they are articulated in this rather systematic and definitely provocative way.

This phenomenon, as I would like to propose, has to be understood in the context of rabbinic-Christian relationship in Palestine at the turn of the sixth century. Palestine is a spiritual center of Christianity, both for pilgrimage and what is more important for us, for the important monastic activity taking place in it.[68] This last point can explain why the Genesis Rabbah redactors gather earlier traditions and shape them so to design Abraham as the rabbinic model of the holy man.

The phenomenon of Christian monasticism has its roots before Constantine's conversion, but it flourishes after the consolidation (still relative) of Christian rule in the east. One of the reasons of its impressive expansion in the fourth and the fifth centuries is the fact that offer-

---

66 See note above.
67 This is also the way Philo describes Abraham – as a model of the *metriopathes* (cf. *De Abrahamo* XLIV 256 with regard to Abraham's reaction to the death of his wife).
68 Cf. RUBENSON 2007, 652–655.

ing one's life to God through martyrdom as a testimony to one's faith is no longer possible. Thus, new forms of extreme piety have to be developed. The monk does not offer his life to God by letting himself be killed by those who oppose his faith, but by renouncing on his bodily and social needs, consecrating his life entirely to God's Word.[69] The Christian monks can be hermits attached to a tree or to a pillar as the most famous Syrian monk Symon the Stylite. They can also live in a cell with a master or a disciple, as did 'the father' of Christian monasticism – Anthony, or in semi-cenobitism like Evagrius Ponticus in Egypt. Or they can be cenobites and live in a large monastery as that of Pachomius in Egypt.[70] Even if we leave aside the tensions between these forms of monasticism and their different levels of acceptance by other parts of the Christian establishment, we cannot ignore the fact that the Palestinian Rabbis from the fifth century onwards are surrounded by all sorts of Christian monasticism. It is not only the presence of actual monks that is at stake, but also, and maybe mainly, that of spiritual writings that explain, justify and charge with signification the monastic experience.

As was indicated by Pierre Hadot[71] in the course of the fourth century, Christian monasticism integrates philosophical values, directly or indirectly, and uses them in order to legitimize and to articulate the ethical project of the Christian monk.[72] It is especially during this period that we find more Platonist influence on Christian monasticism. The Platonist conception of the human being, with its morally charged dualism, was integrated in the Christian eschatological framework. The salvation became to be understood as the liberation of the soul from the body.

The objective towards which the Christian monk should aspire is *apatheia* – the eradication of passions. Christian as well as Neoplatonist[73]

---

69 Cf. Brakke 2006, 23–47.
70 For an exhaustive list of types of monk in the east see Rubenson 2007, 643–647.
71 Hadot 2004, 237–260.
72 In fact, as was indicated more recently by Samuel Rubenson (2007, 640) in general Christian monasticism re-interprets and transforms older spiritual and ethical notions and values. Thus, the strong dualistic conception of the human being, which is common to all the variants of Christian monasticism, is not only philosophical by origin but also Jewish and Gnostic.
73 For Neoplatonism see Hadot 2004.

schools use this originally Stoic value[74] to designate one of the final steps in the spiritual progress. The Gospel in general and the passion of Christ in particular are interpreted along these lines. The imitation of Christ passes by the conquest and eventual eradication of the passions, in order to accomplish the call of Evagrius 'to flee from the body' (*Praktikos* §52). There are several degrees in which this flight can be concretized, but obviously the monastic way is the most efficient one as it combines celibacy, abstinence and obedience to a spiritual master. The monk becomes thus a living example of the holy man, that is to say – the man whose communication with God is the most genuine, close and spiritually authentic.

This status of the monk, as the one who can eventually communicate personally with God, could displease the church authorities since it seems to create a spiritual hierarchy which is parallel to the one of the clergy. These tensions still exist in the fifth century and afterwards, but they also seem to begin to go towards some sort of appeasement. Christian monasticism gains more legitimacy and power inside Christian establishment. 'During the fifth century, a tradition rapidly developed in the East that all bishops ought to be monks'.[75] Thus, the monastic model of the holy man becomes almost an official model, and the ideals and values that his figure promotes are officially consecrated.

I think that we should understand Genesis Rabbah's references to Abraham in the light of these developments. Not only Christianity has established itself as the official religion of the Eastern Empire, but also it proposes a spiritual model that in many ways opposes the one promoted by the rabbis. We have to bear in mind that it is during the second half of the fifth century, i.e. shortly before (or contemporary to) the redaction of Genesis Rabbah, that the redaction of the *Apophthegmata patrum*, a collection of stories and saying of the fathers of Egyptian monasticism, takes place in Palestine.[76] This, together with the relative consolidation of the status of the monk within the Christian establishment, or the institutionalization of the figure of the holy man, might have served the Palestinian rabbis as a "cue" to fully articulate their own version of the holy man. One of the ways to do it was to choose a historical figure and describe it as the archetype of the holy man, as the model that he who wishes to lead a good, spiritual life, should aspire

74 Cf. DILLON 1983, 508–517.
75 RUBENSON 2007, 642.
76 Cf. REGNAULT 1987, 65–83.

to. Because of its already established exemplarity, and the existence of early traditions that can be found in late Tannaitic literature, it is the figure of Abraham that was chosen to fulfill a role equivalent to that of Jesus in Christian spirituality.

Thus, by the description of Abraham as the person who actually brings the kingdom of God to earth (by making God the king of the world), the rabbis propose an ethical role model that has to be followed by all those who wish to lead their life according to the Law of God.[77]

Conclusion

According to the synoptic Gospels, on the moment Jesus died on the cross, the curtain of the Temple was torn in two. It is one of the most concrete expressions of the idea that the coming of Jesus modifies radically the relationship between God and the world. God's presence is no longer confined to the Holy of Holies, but is accessible anywhere. Jesus' death is the moment in which he achieves his initial project – to have himself killed in order to expiate the sins of humanity. Hence, his death enables a new form of communication with the divine, qualitatively different than what was possible before.

The 'tear' repaired by Abraham in the *midrash* cited above may be regarded as a rabbinic reference to this moment in the Gospels. Whereas Jesus' death provokes a tear in the curtain that separates God from the world, the birth of Abraham repairs it; it repairs the tear caused by what the rabbis might have understood as a dangerous conception of the relationship between God and the world. The rabbinic Abraham cleans after Jesus; the father mends the horrible mistake of his son.

Rabbinic Abraham is God's counterpart, a 'new creature', a better version of Adam, because of his ability to bend his will in order to act according to God's Law. He is the first to fight his evil inclination; he agrees to circumcise himself in order to help God's divine program – that is how he takes on himself the sins of past and future generations.

---

77 This argument can also explain another interesting point concerning the rabbinic ideological (and not halakhic) position towards *nazir*. Whereas tannaitic sources treat mainly the halakhic aspects of the *neziruth*, some amoraic sources are very critical towards the phenomenon itself and the people who practice it. The text from the Palestinian Talmud from the beginning of the Nazir treatise (1, 5, 51ac) is particularly revealing from this point of view.

Through the shaping of the figure of the first patriarch the Palestinian rabbis propose to the individual their understanding of moral life – fighting against personal desires in order to accomplish God's Law. This is the new life brought to the world with Abraham; here lies the originality of his message; this is how he makes possible the (re)union between human beings and the ultimate source of truth and authority.

Bibliography

BECKER, ADAM H. and YOSHIKO REED, ANNETTE 2003. "Introduction: Traditional Models and New Directions", in: *idem*. (ed.). *The Ways that Never Parted: Jews and Christians in Late Antiquity and the Early Middle Ages*. Tübingen. 1–30.

BERTHELOT, KATELL 2006. "Jewish Views of Human Sacrifice in the Hellenistic and Roman Period", in: FINSTERBUSCH et al. (ed.). *Human Sacrifice in Ancient Mediterranean Religion and Later Recurrences*. Leiden. 151–173.

BOYARIN, DANIEL 2004. *Border Lines: The Partition of Judaeo-Christianity*. Philadelphia.

BRAKKE, DAVID 2006. *Demons and the Making of the Monk: Spiritual Combat in Early Christianity*. Cambridge.

CALVERT-KOYZIS, NANCY 2004. *Paul, Monotheism and the People of God: The Significance of Abraham Traditions for Early Judaism and Christianity*. London.

DALY, R. J. 1977. "The Soteriological Significance of the Sacrifice of Isaac", *Catholic Quarterly Review* 39. 45–75.

DAVIES, P. R. and CHILTON, B.D. 1978. "The Akedah: A Revised Tradition History", *Catholic Quarterly Review* 40. 514–546.

DIAMOND, ELIEZER 2004. *Holy Men and Hunger Artists: Fasting and Asceticism in Rabbinic Culture*. Oxford.

DILLON, JOHN 1983. "Metriopatheia and Apatheia: Some Reflections on a Controversy in Later Greek Ethics", in: *idem*. *Essays in Ancient Greek Philosophy II*. Albany. 508–517.

DOWD, SHARYN and STRUTHERS MALBON, ELIZABETH 2006. "The Significance of Jesus' Death in Mark: Narrative Context and Authorial Audience", *Journal of Biblical Literature* 125/2. 271–297.

DUMONT, LOUIS 1986. *Essays on Individualism: Modern Ideology in Anthropological Perspective*. Chicago.

EVANS, CRAIG A. 2001. "Abraham in the Dead Sea Scrolls", in: FLINT, PETER W. (ed.). *The Bible at Qumran*. Grand Rapids. 149–158.

FELDMAN, LOUISE H. 1998. "Isaac", in: *idem*. *Josephus' Interpretation of the Bible*. Berkeley. 290–303.

FOUCAULT, MICHEL 2005. *The Hermeneutics of the Subject: Lectures at the Collège de France*. New York.

FREUD, SIGMUND 2001. "Moses and Montheism", in: *The Standard Edition of the Complete Psychological Works of Sigmund Freud* v. XXIII (1937–1939). London.

GARCÍA MARTÍNEZ, F. 2002. "The Sacrifice of Isaac in 4Q225", in: E. NOORT and E. TIGCHELAAR (edd.). *The Sacrifice of Isaac: The Aqedah (Gen 22) and its Interpretations*. Leiden. 44–57.

HADOT, ILSETRAUT ET PIERRE 2004. *Apprendre à philosopher dans l'Antiquité : l'enseignement du Manuel d'Epicète et son commentaire néoplatonicien*. Paris.

HADOT, PIERRE 2002. *What is Ancient Philosophy*. Cambridge.

HAYWARD, C.T.R. 1990. "The Sacrifice of Isaac and Jewish Polemic against Christianity", *Catholic Quarterly Review* 52. 292–306.

HIMELFARB, MARTHA 2008. "The Ordeals of Abraham: Circumcision and the Aqedah in Origen, the *Mekhilta* and *Genesis Rabbah*", *Henoch* 30. 289–310.

HUIZENGA, LEROY A. 2009. "Obedience to Death: The Matthean Gethsemane and Arrest Sequence and the Aqedah", *The Catholic Biblical Quarterly* 71. 507–526.

KESSLER, EDWARD 2001. "The Exegetical Encounter between the Greek Church Fathers and the Palestinian Rabbis", *Studia Patristica* 34. 395–412.

LEVENSON, JON D. 2004. "The Conversion of Abraham to Judaism, Christianity, and Islam", in: NAJMAN, HINDY and NEWMAN, JUDITH H. (edd.). *The Idea of Biblical Interpretation. Essays in Honor of James L. Kugel*. Leiden. 3–40.

MANDEL, PAUL 1994. "The Call of Abraham: A Midrash Revisited", *Prooftext* 14. 267–284.

MANN, JACOB 1940. *The Bible as Read and Preached in the Old Synagogue. Volume I: The Palestinian Triennial Cycle: Genesis and Exodus*. Cincinnati.

MIMOUNI, SIMON C. 2007. *La circoncision dans le monde judéen aux époques grecque et romaine. Histoire d'un coflit interne au judaïsme*. Paris-Louvain.

MOORE, GEORGE. F. 1932. *Judaism in the First Centuries of the Christian Era*, I. Cambridge.

NIEHOFF, MAREN R. 2003. "Circumcision as a Marker of Identity: Philo, Origen and the Rabbis on Gen 17:1–14", *JSQ* 10. 89–123.

REGNAULT, LUCIEN 1987. *Les pères du désert: à travers leurs Apophtegmes*. Solesmes.

RUBENSON, SAMUEL 2007. "Asceticism and monasticism, I: Eastern", in: CASIDY, AUGUSTINE and NORRIS, FREDERICK W. (edd). *The Cambrdige History of Chrisitanity* 2. *Constantine to c. 600*. Cambridge. 637–668.

SANDMEL, SAMUEL 1954. "Philo's Place in Judaism: A Study of Conceptions of Abraham in Jewish Literature, Part I", *HUCA* 25. 209–237.

SCHOFER, JONATHAN WYN 2005. *The Making of a Sage: A Study in Rabbinic Ethics*. Wisconsin.

SIKER, JEFREY S. 1991. *Disinheriting the Jews: Abraham in Early Christian Controversy*. Louisville.

STEMBERGER, GÜNTER 1996. *Introduction to the Talmud and Midrash*. Minneapolis.

STROUMSA, GUY G. 2004. "Christ's Laughter: Docetics Origins Reconsidered", *Journal of Early Christian Studies* 12. 267–288.

SWETNAM, JAMES 1982. *Jesus and Isaac: A Study of the Epistle to the Hebrews in the Light of the Aqedah.* Rome.
TROELTSCH ERENST 1992. *The Social Teachings of the Christian Churches* (trans. Olive Wyon). Louisville.
VERMES, GEZA 1961. *Scripture and Tradition in Judaism. Haggadic Studies.* Leiden.
—1996. "New Light on the Sacrifice of Isaac from 4Q255", *Journal of Jewish Studies* 47. 140–146.
YOSHIKO REED, ANETTE 2006. "Rabbis, Jewish Christians, and Other Late Antique Jews: Reflections on the Fate of Judaism(s) after 70 C.E.", in: I.H HENDERSON and G. S. OEGEMA (edd.). *The Changing Face of Judaism, Christianity and Other Greco-Roman Religion in Antiquity*, Gütersloh. 323–346.
—2009. "The Construction and Subversion of Patriarchal Perfection: Abraham and Exemplarity in Philo, Josephus, and the Testament of Abraham", *Journal for the Study of Judaism* 40. 185–212.

Sources

The Apostolic Fathers I (trans. KIRSOPP LAKE; Cambridge: Harvard University Press, 1952).
A Commentary on Pseudo-Philo's Liber Antiquitatum Biblicarum *with Latin text and English Translation* (trans. H. JACOBSON), Leiden: Brill, 1996.
Midrash Rabbah I-II (trans. and ed. H. FREEDMAN and MAURICE SIMON; London: Soncino Press, 1961).
Tertullian, Answer to the Jews X (*ANF* 3:165).

Reading and Writing

Reading Practices in Early Christianity and the Individualisation Process

Guy G. Stroumsa

I

On September 12, 2008, Pope Benedict XVI. gave an important speech, in French, at the Collège des Bernardins in Paris. He sought in this speech to explain how Christian monasteries became at once the locus where the treasuries of ancient culture were preserved and where a new, Christian culture was slowly elaborated.[1] Benedict underlined the fact that the monks had intended neither of these two major developments. The monks' much simpler motivation, insisted the Pope, was only to search for God, *quaerere Deum*, as Martin Luther, who had once been a monk in the *Augustinerkloster*, knew well. Here as on other occasions, Benedict makes an important theological point, while treating history in rather cavalier fashion. For him, it is in the monasteries of the Medieval West that this great cultural transfer and creation took place. I shall argue here that it is, rather, in the monastic movement of late antiquity that one must search for the roots of the cultural transformation of Western society. More precisely, I shall seek to ask how in early Christianity, and in particular among the Eastern monks, the new *Kulturträger* in a world where civil society was fast disappearing, a new attitude to books emerged, that had much to do with the individualisation process, and which would eventually permit and even embody the late antique cultural and religious transformation.

Under the Roman Empire, Mediterranean and Near Eastern societies underwent a series of deep cultural and religious transformations, which amount to nothing less than a revolution, the impact of which cannot be underestimated.[2] Christianization processes reflect and incor-

---

1 Benedict's speech can be read (and heard) on the internet site of the French Catholic newspaper La Croix.
2 On this religious revolution, see STROUMSA 1999b and STROUMSA 2009.

porate these transformations more than anything else, as JÖRG RÜPKE reminds us in his programmatic papers. I have argued elsewhere that the end of sacrifices, perhaps the clearest and most widely partaken expression of public religion, can be seen as the epitome of this revolution. The Christian ascetic movement, culminating in the birth and fast growth of monasticism in the Near East, and from there to other parts of the Empire, represents one of the most striking aspects of this religious revolution. In Weberian parlance, one can speak of ascetic and marginal communities of religious virtuosi – and this is no oxymoron. Such communities had previously existed in ancient societies, from the Pythagoreans to the Essenes. In a sense, the early Christian monks were following an old tradition of liminal, elitist communities of wisdom. But nothing as dramatic, it seems, had ever occurred previously: in great numbers, young Christian men and women were now freely rejecting a fundamental social imperative: marriage and reproduction. In rejecting, consciously and forcefully, what was expected from them, and in asserting so loud and clear that their bodies belonged only to themselves, they were sapping the very foundations of traditional societies, a fact underlined by PETER BROWN.[3] Although *monachos*, etymologically, points to the monk living *alone*, anachoretes in the Egyptian or Syrian desert were soon outnumbered by monks living together in *coenobia*, communities of ascetics. To be sure, the monks themselves were quite aware of the linguistic paradox, and monastic literature, both in Greek and in Syriac, retains a traditional etymology of *monachos* (Syriac *ihidaya*), according to which the term refers to the monk having learned, through his ascetic practices, to *unify* his own self, to have become, in the terms of our enterprise, a new, fully integrated individual. During his last years, MICHEL FOUCAULT became fascinated by the phenomenon of early Christian monasticism, whose revolutionary character he sought to interpret. In the footsteps of PIERRE HADOT, FOUCAULT focused upon the spiritual exercises, a Greek philosophical tradition involving the 'care of the self (*epimeleia heautou*)' which the monks transformed. FOUCAULT argued that this transformation brought to the suppression of the self.[4] Rather, it seems to me that the Christianized spiritual exercises must be understood within a religious context where the self was not seeking to define and refine his own self within, and in contradistinction to the cosmos at large. For the Christian, the

---

3   BROWN 1988.
4   FOUCAULT 2001. Cf. HADOT 2002.

cosmic drama is epitomized in the life, death and resurrection of one single individual, Jesus Christ, both human and divine, while it is through the constant reflection upon the Holy Books of divine revelation that the Christian could find his own self: text and self would now be deciphered through one another. The self-presentation of early Christianity as a 'school' of philosophy was not only meant for apologetical purposes: it also reflected the deep conviction of a self-perception.

Following ERNST TROELTSCH, or rather broadening the framework of his analysis of the steps of individualisation in different societies, and giving them a clear anthropological formulation, MARCEL MAUSS, who was both EMILE DURKHEIM's nephew and his most significant follower, offered a succinct, yet global vision of the transformations of the concept of the person in traditional societies and religious systems. MAUSS's essay, entitled 'Une catégorie de l'esprit humain: la notion de personne, celle de 'moi',' moved from the juridical to the theological sphere, and from the latter to anthropology. To some extent, the gist of his seminal paper remains, more than seventy years after it was first published, at the core of comparative anthropological history. Even CHARLES TAYLOR's *Sources of the Self* (1989) can be traced back to the impact of MAUSS's article.

From the first to the fifth century, a new conception of the individual would progressively take shape in Christian literature.[5] This new conception would permit the transformation of attitudes to the body, in particular in the ascetic movement, and the emergence of a newly reflexive self. 'Reflexive self', and 'person', although not identical, belong to the same nexus, and describe the late antique sensitivity to the individual. The Augustinian synthesis, which insisted upon the radical reflexivity of the self – a reflexivity lacking in the ancient world – would then be bequeathed to the West, and would remain the leading thread of anthropological perceptions, at least until the end of the Middle-Ages. More than a new anthropology, it is a new attitude to the self that emerges in early Christian literature. This new attitude is grounded in a few fundamental points of Christian theology, and highlights the relationship between the reflection upon God's nature and conceptions of man. From a methodological perspective, these reflections on the emergence and crystallization, in late antiquity, of new attitudes to the individual are predicated upon the fact that pivotal concepts around

---

5   STROUMSA 2009, chapter 1.

which religions or civilizations are organized appear very early in their development.

The first theological conception informing Christian (as well as Jewish) conceptions of man is of course the Biblical idea of man having been created in God's image, *homo imago Dei* (*Gen* 1.26). This entailed a dignity given to the human body which had been unheard of in Greek thought, and a new unity given to the human person as a whole, soul and body, and hence a broadening of the self, not restricted any more to the intellect or the soul. The new status of the body was highlighted by the idea of divine incarnation. Hence Tertullian could coin his famous lapidary expression: *Caro salutis cardo*, the flesh is the axis of redemption (*De ressurectione mortuorum*, 2), a sentence incomprehensible for a pagan.[6] The broadening of the individual was synchronic with another movement: the growing and dominant importance of sin (and in particular of the original sin, with its ineluctable consequences). These two movements, together, would form the backbone of Augustinian anthropology, and would thus become a major chapter in the history of Western consciousness. The capital importance of original sin, however, would be mitigated by the concept of *metanoia*, repentance, and the cleansing of the individual from the blemish of his or her past sins. *Metanoia* (Hebrew *teshuva*; in contradistinction to Greek *epistrophè*) entails moral progress, a concept remarkably analyzed by Gerhard Ladner, who underlined its leading role in the constant dynamism of Christian anthropology.[7]

The new parameters of personal identity emphasized the integration of soul and body into the definition of the human person as a composite. In the emerging conception, however, the person was not quite a harmonious one. Instead of the divide between soul and body typical of Platonism, the idea of an original sin brought with it a new break, this time within the soul itself. This break was due to a sense of guilt, inescapable because sin was inherited and ever present. This state of affairs strengthened the need for a salvation which went far beyond the individual and his behavior. Repentance for one's sins, indeed, expressed this need of salvation only in part. Christian salvation entailed ridding oneself of the consequences of a sin which went far beyond the individual. Such an attitude was bound to enhance a tension within the soul unknown among Greek philosophers. In this framework, faith became

---

6   See STROUMSA 1990.
7   See STROUMSA 1999a.

not only the condition *sine qua non* of salvation, but also almost equivalent to it. Faith in Jesus Christ and His redemptive sacrifice, in itself, saved.

Identity, however, is social as much as it is personal. Social identity, too, was submitted in early Christianity to a radical reinterpretation. For the first time in the ancient world, identity became defined essentially in religious terms, rather than in mainly ethnic or cultural-linguistic ones, as was the case in the Hellenistic and Roman worlds. This new approach to social identity is perhaps best reflected in the new corpus of laws established from Constantine to Theodosius II., in the first decades of the fifth century, and collected in the Theodosian Codex. These laws reflect the crucial importance of defining the Church and the centers of authority within it. This implied a constant effort at defining the boundaries of the Christian community. Since the traditional Jewish criteria, such as ethnicity, language and *halakha*, were not available any more, only dogma (i. e., the proper way to understand Jesus Christ, His nature and His mission) could provide the definition of the new social identity. Hence, for the first time, collective identity was defined in terms directly rooted in internalization, in belief. True belief, or orthodoxy, was itself defined by its negation, and reflected the many faces of error: schism and heresy, from within, Judaism and paganism from without.

The social definition of Church boundaries, however, did not only reflect opposition to error, but also the desire, inherent to Christianity from its very beginnings, to broaden its appeal; in other words, the church boundaries reflect Christianity's very catholicity, its strong and successful urge to convert. Conversion is the other side of the essentially dogmatic definition of the new religion: it implies a choice between truth and error.

The consequences of this state of affairs for our present purpose are as follows:

Both individual and collective identities are redefined in early Christianity in direct relation to the internalization process. As pointed out above, both also reflect the limitations of this process. The fight between faith and sin within the individual and the fight between truth and error at the collective level seem to follow parallel patterns. Since truth comes from Jesus Christ, error comes from the Antichrist, of Satan. A choice of belief stands at the basis of the formation of both individual and collective identity, and establishes a strong element of intolerance in the very definition of Christian identity: while truth is uni-

---

valent, the hydra of heresy has numerous heads, which must all be cut out.

II

Among the many facets of the religious revolution of late antiquity, which eventually led to the Christianization of the Empire, one of the most striking ones is what one can call the 'scriptural turn' of religion. From early Christianity to early Islam, through the various Gnostic trends, Mandaeism, Manichaeism, and even the Neo-Platonists, many religious movements offer a central place to holy books, prophetic or otherwise revelatory, to their hermeneutics and to their ritual roles.[8] The concept of 'religions of the book' might well be a modern one (it was invented by MAX MÜLLER), reflecting a Qur'anic term (*ahl al-kitab*, 'people of the book'), it can be applied to a broader spectrum of movements than the canonical three monotheistic religions, today increasingly dubbed 'Abrahamic'.[9] It is doubtless to its Jewish roots that Christianity owes the central role it attributes to the collection of revealed books which became the *Biblia*. To be sure, early Christianity shares many characteristics with other religious movements of the ancient world. None of them, however, can be claimed to be more specific to it than its attitude to the revealed book. JAN ASSMANN has spoken of the passage, in our period, of the passage from *Kultreligion* to *Buchreligion*.[10] ASSMANN's pregnant expression seems to imply the disappearance of ritual at the core of the new 'religions of the book'. I would prefer to argue that for Christianity (as earlier for Judaism, and later for Islam), the revealed book has become the focus, the center, of the ritual: *Buch als Kult*. In Christian communities, or at least within the Christian elites, i.e., both the religious hierarchy and the ascetic virtuosi, bishops and monks, reading and writing were at the core of the new religion, a phenomenon quite unknown in the Roman world, with the exception of the Jews. One could say that the Logos was not only incarnated in the *Corpus Christi*, but also in the corpus of the *Biblia*. To be sure, such radically new attitudes do not percolate very fast, and it is possible that literacy rates remained rather low within the Christian communities, al-

---

8 See in particular SMITH 1993.
9 MÜLLER 1870. On the concept of Abrahamic religions, see STROUMSA 2011.
10 ASSMANN 2003.

though, as GILLIAN CLARK reminds us, 'Christianity uniquely offered increased access to book-based education'.[11] I shall not deal here with the complex case of late antique Judaism, where reverence for the Holy Book was so high that it seems to have prevented for a long time, or at least strongly impeded, the writing of books, with the consequence that much of the hermeneutical involvement of the elites with the Torah remained oral for a very long time.

The newly acquired central role of books in the religious world of late antiquity cannot be disconnected from the transformations in the production and form of books in the Roman Empire: from the second century on, more and more books are written as codices rather than in the traditional form of rolls; by the end of the fourth century, the codex has definitively won the battle.[12] This revolution in the form of the book is paralleled in the early centuries by the new development of silent reading, which would not really become common practice for centuries. Much attention has been granted recently to reading and writing practices in the ancient world, and more precisely to the status of books in the Empire. Early Christian books have also been the focus of some excellent studies in recent years, up to the papyrologist ROGER BAGNALL, who argues in his newly published monograph on Early Christian books in Egypt that the place of books in ancient society and the role of the Christians in the history of the codex has been misrepresented, mainly because much of the scholarship retains a self-enclosed character.[13] Some of these studies have put a new stress on the sociological dimensions of ancient literacy. WILLIAM JOHNSON, in particular, has studied elite reading communities in the high empire, in a very recently published collection of articles on the culture of reading in Greece and Rome.[14] Such studies, however, have more often than not been authored by classical scholars with relatively little interest in the history of religions in late antiquity. It seems that there is room for fresh efforts seeking to better understand the *religious* dimensions of book culture in late antiquity. We still need a historical anthropology of book writing and reading in antiquity. From a methodological point of view, it makes sense to focus on the monastic communities, which provide the clearest example of the new 'textual communities' (to use a concept

---

11 CLARK 2004, Chapter 5, 78-92.
12 CAVALLO 1997.
13 BAGNALL 2009.
14 JOHNSON, PARKER 2009.

forged by BRIAN STOCK for medieval monasteries; cf. 'interpretive communities', a term coined by the specialist of English literature STANLEY
FISH).[15]

A paradox seems to shroud the status of books in early Christianity.
On the one hand, there is nothing to indicate clearly that the literacy
rate among Christians was higher from that in Roman society at
large. According to KEITH HOPKINS, 'many or most Christian communities … simply did not have among them a single sophisticated reader or
writer'.[16] On the other hand, it is obvious that early Christians wrote
many books and that Christianity was a movement connected and
maintained by the written word. In other words, early Christianity, following Judaism in this, can clearly be identified as a 'religion of the
book'.

Now this transformation was completed much faster among Christians than outside the community. Indeed, the Christians clearly seem to
have played a pioneering role in using the codex. While the passage
from roll to codex was slow and gradual, papyrologists have noted
that almost all Christian papyri belonged to codices, while very few
were written on rolls. At the end of the second century, the codex
had become a Christian innovation. For a *religio illicita* that was both
outlawed and strongly missionary, the easy circulation of books of
small dimensions was particularly significant. In a sense, early Christianity might be described, rather than a religion of the book, a religion of
the paperback.[17] In fact, various testimonies reflect the deep interest in
books on the side of Christians. They seem to write so much that WIL-
LIAM HARRIS, the author of an important study on ancient literacy, has
been able to speak of the 'acute logorrhea of Christian authors'.[18]

The reasons for the clear Christian preference for the codex have
been sought in various directions. Some of the complex reasons for
this fact seem to have been of a practical order. The codex was a
new, modern, kind of book, cheaper to produce (as it could be written
on both sides of the page) and easier to manipulate (as there was no need
to unroll it). The codex, moreover, had a dramatic impact upon both
attitudes to and roles of books – to start with the books of the Bible.
The codex permitted to read the Bible (in translation) and carry it

15 STOCK 1990.
16 HOPKINS 1991, 213.
17 STROUMSA 2003.
18 HARRIS 1989.

around easily, to quote and move from text to text with relative freedom. The new form of the book entailed a new, lower, more popular
status, and this new status brought new roles to books. Books, including
the Scriptures had become, literally, handy, more easily kept, carried,
opened and read.

But it stands to reason that side by side with such practical reasons
for the Christian preference to the codex, this preference must also
have been of an inherent or religious nature, and stemmed from the
self-perception of Christianity. The codex did not possess the hieratic
but frozen cultural character discernable in the roll. Christianity, indeed,
perceived itself as a new religion, free from the inhibitions and cultural
habits of past traditions. I have analyzed elsewhere the ambivalent attitudes of early Christian intellectuals to the idea of the book, and sought
to explain the rise of the Christian codex through the marginal position
of the Christians in society, which permitted and encouraged disengage-
ment from hallowed patterns and accept new, more popular forms of
cultural transmission. The multiple and powerful roles of the Bible in
Christian missions and education, as well as in the creation of a Christian
culture, have been duly noted by scholars. Yet, various aspects of these
roles remain to be studied in depth, from the global approach of the
new status and roles of books in religions of the book.

It would then seem that Christian literacy was a literacy of a new,
revolutionary kind, an oral form of literacy, as it were. MARY BEARD
points out that Roman paganism, far from being a 'text-free' religion,
devotes a considerable significance to writing, in numerous ways.[19]
On his side, KEITH HOPKINS insists on what he calls the 'sub-elite' literacy among late antique Christians, and on the essential part this played
in the Christian 'conquest' of the Roman Empire.[20] As a major instance,
he refers to Coptic, a language which originated as a 'script of protest', a
fact reflected in many of the preserved manuscripts, which stem from
Gnostic, Manichaean, or monastic circles, all of them, in different
ways and varying degrees, marginal movements. Stressing the dynamic
interaction between the written and the oral, HOPKINS concludes that
its peculiar attitude to the body of its scriptures and other, connected
texts permitted Christianity to develop the religious coherence essential
for any understanding of its eventual victory over traditional religion
and culture in the Roman Empire. Words indeed have much power, es-

---

19   BEARD 1991 b.
20   HOPKINS 1991.

pecially when they are holy, but this power is reflected in a number of ways, orally as well as in their 'original' written form. Words are spoken, sometimes hurled at, like in polemics, which played such an important role in inter-religious contacts in late antiquity.

In the ancient world, and far beyond, all cultures remained highly oral, and literacy remained, even in the best of times, the privilege of very few. In such cultures, books were often used as instruments for the authentication of texts, rather than as the means for their communication. This fact helps to explain why in the conversion movement launched by Christianity, the role of books must have remained modest. As most Christians could not read, they heard the holy texts, or rather small parts of them, some of the most expressive or powerful stories, figures, and words, through 'preaching, catechesis, apologetic debates, intramural theological disputes, and personal edification'. The strong warning against too much free access to the scriptures, as reflected in Cyril of Jerusalem's *caveat* in his *Catechetical Homilies*, may not necessarily reflect an insatiable interest in scripture on the part of most individuals.

In his synthetic work, *Books and Readers in the Early Church*, HARRY GAMBLE JR. adopts a broad perspective, integrating the Christian attitude toward the canonical books with the more general question of the status of literacy among Christians in the early centuries.[21] GAMBLE analyses the various uses of books among Christians during the first centuries, both in church, i. e., in public cult, and in private: up to the fourth century, there was a clear distinction between public and private reading of canonical books. Cyril of Jerusalem, for one, insists on the fact that 'what is read in church should not be read privately'. GAMBLE also calls due attention to other, perhaps not less important, uses of the Scriptures. Scriptures are used, for instance, as magical protection, or in magical incantations. GAMBLE's working hypothesis, according to which the use and status of books and reading among Christians was similar to what obtained in the society at large. Such a method has the obvious advantage of permitting the use of large scale arguments, where evidence is scarce. But it is also seriously flawed and deeply misleading, since much of this evidence may not be applicable to the Christian case. The early Christians, even before the end of the second century, and despite some quite peculiar behavioral patterns, remained a rather porous society, never isolated from the world at large, and rather

---

21 GAMBLE 2000.

different from what sociologists call an 'enclave society'. None the less, there is no good reason to believe that their attitudes to texts in general, and to their holy books in particular, was no different from that of surrounding society. It stands to reason to assume that here as elsewhere the early Christians showed a great sense of independence and originality. The very fact that they did not feel bound by cultural and religious traditions permitted them, in many ways, to be innovative. The early development of Christianity can be characterized as nothing less than a religious revolution, not only *vis-à-vis* Judaism, but, more generally, in relation to all previous perceptions of religion. Radically new, too, was the Christian conception of scripture, as well as the status and use of books altogether in the early Church.

ROBIN LANE FOX has argued that Christianity offered 'a less reverential attitude to the written word' than that extant in both Judaism and in traditional culture in the Roman Empire.[22] This is certainly true, but falls short of adequately characterizing the attitude of early Christianity to the written word. The matter is more complex. The scriptural origin of Christianity certainly prevented it from developing into an oral religion, deprived of sacred texts; hence the Christian ambivalent attitude to books. More precisely, one can argue that Christianity soon developed an attitude to literacy and the written word which was quite new, or even revolutionary. Popular, spoken language was a central character of earliest Christianity. Thus, one may sum up the quarrel of the Church with the Empire, to a great extent, as that between two opposed attitudes toward language, traditional and 'high', or new and 'low'. This background entailed the development in Christian civilization of conflicting systems of literacy. The popular, 'low' level of early Christian teachings meant that the literary ideals current in Greco-Roman culture were not applicable to Christianity. On all counts, then, books, at least as they had been perceived in the upper classes of pagan society, do not seem to have occupied a major place in the early Christian mind.

Despite the limited place of books in Roman society, they certainly 'made a statement', as notes PHILIP ROUSSEAU.[23] Recent studies have dealt with the question of the specificity of the Christian book culture in the Roman world. One must first insist on the fact that the evidence is painfully lacking, and that any suggestion must remain hypothetical.

22 LANE FOX 1994.
23 ROUSSEAU 2007.

Against GAMBLE and IAN H. HENDERSON, I argue that books must have
had a characteristic status in early Christianity, an enclave society which
was to a great extent established upon a divinely revealed book (or corpus of writings).[24] In that society, the holy book was not only held in
great honor, but also played a central role in ritual, as well as in religious
education. It stands to reason that such a status of the Bible had a significant impact upon the ritualizing of reading and on the complex relationship between reading and ritual. In any case, the relationship between texts and rituals in Early Christianity is a highly complex one.
The early Christians, indeed, may be defined as 'reading communities',
whose cultural and religious capital was, to a great extent, represented
by its books. Moreover, while early Christian literature sometimes follows known patterns (such as the Clementine 'novel', both in the Greek
Homilies and in the Latin *Recognitions*), it represents usually rather original genres, such as Gospels and theological treatises and commentaries,
quite different from anything in Latin *Belles Lettres* or philosophical literature. Reading, which had been an essentially recreational activity,
now became a mainly normative one.

Recently, ANTONY GRAFTON and MEGAN WILLIAMS have argued
quite cogently, focusing on the case-study of Caesarea Maritima and
the figures of Origen and Eusebius, that early Christian intellectuals
were able to leave a clear mark upon the transformation of the book
in the Roman Empire.[25] Incidentally, while we know that Origen
maintained close contacts with Rabbis in Caesarea, we know very little
about Jewish books in late antiquity. In Judaism of the Second Temple
period, in the Hellenistic world, a rich literature was written. Most of
these texts, however, would be identified as marginal, dangerous, or
simply heretical by the Rabbis (probably under the impact of Christianity), and the Rabbis sought to ignore them. To be sure, Rabbinic Judaism functioned as an almost only oral system, in which oral texts could
be fixed, and even canonized, such as the Mishna. Yet, as Jewish and
Christian intellectuals could meet and discuss Biblical hermeneutics,
some of the Rabbis, at least, must have expressed intellectual curiosity
about books such as Biblical commentaries and homiletics. It is a matter
of frustration that we do not know more about it.

In Antiquity, books were mostly available in public and private libraries, and the establishment of ecclesiastical libraries, even before the

---

24   See HENDERSON 2006.
25   GRAFTON, WILLIAMS 2006.

development of monastic libraries, entailed new attitudes to, and uses of books.[26] In the East, the Christian community became often built and organized around the library. While the Alexandria library remains the archetype of all libraries in late antiquity, Christian libraries and schools function around the community's library. This is true not only of Cassiodorus's Vivarium in the West – which is not a monastic library in the limited sense, and of Nisibis in the East – but also of Augustine's own library, around which his disciples live, pray and study.

Another major transformation of the attitude to books took place in the reading system, rather than in the writing methods. Side by side with the passage from roll to codex, our period saw the development of silent reading, a development (rather than a discovery) for which Augustine offers our best testimony, in a famous passage of the *Confessions* (VIII.12). To be sure, the development of silent reading, which would take a very long time, as it is not before the thirteenth century that it is well established, did not entail the disappearance of reading aloud. In parallel, the public reading of Scriptures, aloud, had become a major aspect of Christian ritual. The kind of recitative reading (*Sprechgesang*) that the monks were commonly using for the Biblical texts highlights their close relationship with these texts, which they often knew by heart. In both cases, to be sure, the Christians were following the Jews, who had for centuries developed such a dual, private and public, pattern of reading the Bible.[27]

The Christian adoption of silent reading seems to be directly linked to the private reading of the Bible in the monastic milieus (in particular of the Psalms, a corpus also central to public worship), in meditation and oration. The ability to read the holy text in silence and to memorize it brought to its internalization. In other words, it permitted the conception of an interior book, written not on parchment, but in the heart of the believer. This metaphor of the 'Book of the Heart', indeed, will have a long and rich future in the history of Christian spirituality. In other words, the development of silent reading among early Christian elites reflected the transformed status of the individual in the new religious system, and it must have been as closely related to it as was the use of the codex.

More than in any other milieu, indeed, it is in the monastic movement that new roles of the book took shape, and that a new culture of

---

26 On ancient libraries, see CASSON 2001.
27 STROUMSA 2012.

the book was born. Such a proposition might at first seem odd, almost paradoxical. For all we know, the first monks, either in Egypt or in Syria and Palestine, were far from being the obvious carriers of traditional literate culture. Peter Brown, among others, has highlighted the deep differences between the attitude to books and learning, reading and writing, among early Christian urban intellectuals, such as the Alexandrian Fathers, Clement and Origen, and that which developed among the early monks in the Egyptian deserts.[28] BROWN has insisted upon the fact that the new *cultura Dei* that the monks sought to create, and which represented nothing less than an alternative cultural model, remained usually oral, and was expressed in vernacular (Coptic, Syriac, Armenian, etc.). It was quite alien to the traditional high brow 'system of reading' of the urban Christian elites. Referring to the *Life of Anthony*, PETER BROWN speaks of an alternative cultural model, often oral and on the margins of literacy, propounded by the monks. There is no denying the major differences in cultural attitudes between monks and urban elites. Yet it would be misleading to conceive the new culture of the monasteries as radically different from a book culture. Despite the centrality of the oral relationship between spiritual master and disciple, the new monastic culture did not give up on the dimension of writing and reading, and certainly that of *listening* to the book being read or recited. It soon became identified as a culture of the book. More precisely, this was a culture based almost exclusively upon one book, or one set of books, the Bible, the revealed Scripture, as DOUGLAS BURTON-CHRISTIE has shown so well.[29] From extensive, reading became intensive, as it were. In this sense, one can argue for some similitude between the attitude of the monks and that of the Rabbis. Like in the Jewish *Beit hamidrash*, the Bible was not only read, copied, and recited in the monasteries. Some parts, at least, (in particular the Psalms) were learned by heart and used in prayer, others were deemed particularly fit for commenting upon.

For the monks, then, the 'religion of the book' often meant the community of religious virtuosi, centered on the holy Scriptures. While their new culture remained to a great extent oral, focusing upon the dialogical relationship between the monk and his spiritual master, the written word (in particular the Word of God) played a major role in it. Like the medieval monastic communities, although

28 BROWN 1992.
29 BURTON-CHRISTIE 1993.

in a different way, the early monastic groups can also be called, to use an expression coined by BRIAN STOCK for a different milieu, and in a later period, 'textual communities'.[30] The monks, indeed, read, and their intellectual activity focused around this reading. As STOCK has duly noted, the same could not be said of philosophers. Neither Epictetus nor Marcus Aurelius tell us much about reading and writing. Plotinus, whose teaching was oral, cannot be said to have related to the text of either Plato or Aristotle in the sense that the monks related to that of the Bible. The Christian monks, then, can truly be said to have developed a new system of reading, a system based upon the constant and central presence of a book whose contents were almost known by heart (to be sure, this is true only in theory; in practice, it is doubtful that the knowledge of many monks went much beyond the Psalms and the New Testament).

In the monastic communities, however, reading the Scriptures had a purpose entirely different from that ordinarily attributed to reading: the transmission of knowledge. The constant repetition of a text known by heart – and the Pachomian monks, for instance, were expected by their rule to know by heart at least the Psalms and the New Testament – was not meant to inculcate or assimilate any new knowledge. This activity, which would be known in Medieval monasticism as *lectio divina* (or *sacra pagina*), was soteriological in essence: it was meant as a technical method of concentration of the mind, a way of praying the Scriptures, so that the Word of God may enter the mind or heart and expulse or repulse evil thoughts, sent by Satan. One may quote here Abba Hilarion, the father of the monastic movement in Palestine:

> He also said: 'The acquisition of Christian books is necessary for those who can use them. For the mere sight of these books renders us less inclined to sin, and incites us to believe more firmly in righteousness.'
> He also said: 'Reading the Scriptures is a great safeguard against sin.'
> He also said: 'It is a great treachery to salvation to know nothing of the divine law.'
> He also said: 'Ignorance of the Scriptures is a precipice and a deep abyss.'[31]

A constant prayer, as demanded by Cassian, this peculiar form of silent reading of the Scriptures is meditative in essence (*meletē, meditatio, ruminatio*). The *lectio divina* developed in the early phases of Egyptian monasticism would play a major role throughout the Middle Ages, both in By-

---

30   STOCK 1990, 157; see further STOCK 2005.
31   WARD 1975, 49.

zantium and in the West, as well as in later forms of Christian spirituality, for instance in the *devotio moderna* or among the first Jesuits.

In the preceding pages, then, we have seen the emergence of a new, reflexive self, who is at once, by nature, a sinner and strung toward constant moral and spiritual progress. Under such conditions, the individual, or at least the ascetic virtuoso, is not interested anymore, as was the Greek philosopher, in *cultivating* his own self. Rather, it is *transforming* his own self that he seeks. This inner transformation of the individual culminates in the *imitatio Christi* or, in the mystical Eastern tradition, in divinization (*theosis*) through the beatific vision. In his path towards inner transformation, the monk follows, as it were, the traces left by God's incarnation. It is through a constant reading of the Holy Scriptures and a constant meditation upon them that such traces can[32] be made visible.

Bibliography

ASSMANN, JAN 2003. *Die Mosaische Unterscheidung, oder der Preis des Monotheismus.* München, Wien.

BAGNALL, ROGER 2009. *Early Christian Books in Egypt.* Princeton.

BEARD, MARY et al. (edd.) 1991a. *Literacy in the Roman World.* Journal of Roman Archaeology Supplementary Series 3. Ann Arbor, Mi.

BEARD, MARY 1991b. "Writing and Religion: Ancient Literacy and the Function of the Written Word in Roman Religion", in: BEARD, MARY et al. (edd.) 1991a. 35–58.

BOWMAN, ALAN K.; WOOLF, GREG (edd.) 1994. *Literacy and Power in the Ancient World.* Cambridge, New York.

BROWN, PETER 1988. *The Body and Society: Men, Women, and Sexual Renunciation in Early Christianity.* New York.

—1992. *Power and Persuasion in Late Antiquity: Towards a Christian Empire.* Madison.

BURTON-CHRISTIE, DAVID 1993. *The Word in the Desert: Scripture and the Quest for Holiness in Early Christian Monasticism.* Oxford, New York.

CASSON, LIONEL 2001. *Libraries in the Ancient World.* New Haven, London.

CAVALLO, GUILLELMO 1997. "Du volumen au codex: la lecture dans le monde romain", in: CAVALLO, GUILLELMO; CHARTIER, ROGER (edd.). *Histoire de la lecture dans le monde occidental.* Paris. 85–114.

CLARK, GILLIAN 2004. *Christianity and Roman Society.* Cambridge.

FOUCAULT, MICHEL 2001. *L'herméneutique du sujet: Cours au Collège de France. 1981–1982.* Paris.

HADOT, PIERRE 2002. *Exercices spirituels et philosophie antique.* Paris.

---

32 STROUMSA 1999a.

KENNEY, EDWARD J. 1982. "Books and Readers in the Roman World", in: KENNEY, EDWARD J. (ed.). *Cambridge History of Classical Literature*, vol. II. Cambridge. 3–32.

GAMBLE, HARRY Y. JR. 2000. *Books and Readers in the Early Church: A History of Early Christian Texts*. New Haven, London.

GRAFTON, ANTHONY; WILLAMS, MEGAN 2006. *Christianity and the Transformation of the Book: Origen, Eusebius, and the Library of Caesarea*. Cambridge, Mass., London.

HARRIS, WILLIAM 1989. *Ancient Literacy*. Cambridge, Mass.

HENDERSON, IAN H. 2006. "Early Christianity, Textual Representation and Ritual Extension", in: ELM VON DER OSTEN, DOROTHEE; RÜPKE, JÖRG; WALDNER, KATHARINA (edd.). *Texte als Medium und Reflexion von Religion im römischen Reich*. Heidelberg. 81–100.

HOPKINS, KEITH 1991. "Conquest by Book", in: BEARD, MARY et al. (edd.) 1991a. 133–158.

JOHNSHON, WILLIAM A.; PARKER, HOLT N. (edd.) 2009. *Ancient Literacies: the Culture of Reading in Greece and Rome*. Oxford.

KLINGSHIRN, WILLIAM E.; SAFRAN, LINDA (edd.) 2007. *The Early Christian Book*. Washington D.C.

LANE FOX, ROBIN 1994. "Literacy and Power in Early Christianity", in: BOWMAN, ALAN K.; WOOLF, GREG (edd.) 1994. 126–147.

MAUSS, MARCEL 1950. "Une catégorie de l'esprit humain: la notion de personne, celle de 'moi'", in: MAUSS, Marcel. *Sociologie et anthropologie*. Paris. 331–362.

MÜLLER, MAX 1870. *Introduction to the Science of Religion*. London.

ROUSSEAU, PHILIP 2007. "Introduction: From Binding to Burning", in: KLINGSHIRN, WILLIAM E.; SAFRAN, Linda (edd.) 2007. *The Early Christian Book*. Washington D.C. 1–9.

SMITH, WILFRED CANTWELL 1993. *What is Scripture? A Comparative Approach*. Minneapolis.

STOCK, BRIAN 1990. "Textual Communities: Judaism, Christianity, and the Definitional Problem", in: STOCK, BRIAN. *Listening for the Text: On the Uses of the Past*. Baltimore. 140–158.

—2005. "L'histoire de la lecture: Thérapies de l'âme dans l'Antiquité et au Moyen-Age", in: STOCK, BRIAN. *Bibliothèques intérieures*. Grenoble. 107–126.

—2011. "From Abraham's Religion to the Abrahamic Religions" Historia Religionum 3 (2011), 11–22.

STROUMSA, GUY G. 1990. "*Caro salutis cardo*: Shaping the Person in Early Christian Thought", *History of Religions* 30. 25–50.

—1999a. "From Repentance to Penance in Early Christianity: Tertullian's *De paenitentia* in Context", in: ASSMANN, JAN; STROUMSA, GUY G. (edd.). *Transformations of the Inner Self in Ancient Religions*. Leiden. 167–178.

—1999b. *Barbarian Philosophy: the Religious Revolution of Late Antiquity*. Tübingen.

—2003. "Early Christianity: a Religion of the Book?", in: FINKELBERG, MARGALIT; STROUMSA, GUY G. (edd.). *Homer, The Bible and Beyond: Literary and*

Religious Canons in the Ancient World. Jerusalem Studies in Religion and Culture 2. Brill, Leiden. 153–173.

—2003. "The Scriptural Movement of Late Antiquity and Christian Monasticism", *JECS* 16. 61–76.

—2009. *The End of Sacrifice: Religious Transformations of Late Antiquity*. Chicago.

—2012. "Augustine and the Book", in: VESSEY, MARK (ed.). *The Routledge Companion to Augustine*. London.

WARD, BENEDICTA (transl.) 1975. *The Sayings of the Desert Fathers: The Alphabetical Collection*. London.

Reading and Religion in Rome

Greg Woolf

1 A life in books

Augustine's spiritual crisis ended in a garden. His intellectual journey
was done, the way forward had been pointed out by Ambrose, he
had the support of his mother and his closest friends, and the encouragement of powerful sponsors in church and at court. He was certain what
course he should follow. Yet he still could not bring himself to make the
final break with his old life and commit wholly. In the midst of his mis-
ery, he heard a voice calling out, again and again, *'tolle lege'*, 'take up and
read'. Accepting this as a sign from God, he went back into the house
and opened a book of Paul's *Letters*. The first lines he read spoke directly
to his dilemma.

> I wished to read no more, nor was there any need to do so. For at the very
> moment when I reached the end of that sentence it was as if my heart was
> filled with the light of confidence, and the shadows of doubt fled away.[1]

It is very appropriate that the moment of Augustine's ultimate phase of
conversion should be presented as a response to a text. For books provide every landmark in Augustine's spiritual journey, at least as it is related in the *Confessions*.[2] His love of the *Aeneid* encouraged his passions
and he indulged in the study of rhetoric, but an encounter with Cicero's
Hortensius set him on the path to philosophy.[3] The books of the Manichees ensnared him for a while, but God contrived it that Augustine
should come across some books of Platonic philosophy.[4] The study of
Neoplatonist texts brought him within sight of Scripture.[5] The reading

---

1   Aug. *conf.* 8.12. The passage he came across was from *Romans* 13.13.
2   Among many studies that have discussed this I have found especially suggestive
    MACCORMACK 1998; STOCK 1996.
3   Aug. *conf.* 3.4.
4   Aug. *conf.* 7.9.
5   Aug. *conf.* 7.20−21.

experiences of others, related by his friends, prepared the way. Simplicianus told Augustine how Victorinus, the translator of the Platonic books in question, had finally been converted to Christianity as a result of reading Holy Scripture. Ponticianus, the African courtier, tells Augustine of how two of his acquaintances had been converted to a monastic life by reading the *Life of St Anthony*. It was an anecdote from Anthony's life that came back to Augustine in the garden when he heard the voice. Anthony too had heard God's command in a line of a scripture. Rejoicing in his conversion, Augustine went to Ambrose for guidance ... and received a reading list.

Augustine was no ordinary Christian, and the *Confessions* is a densely allusive text, the reading of which at times feels like undergoing a course of bibliotherapy. Is it possible, in the face of these anecdotes, not to wonder what effects reading *The Confessions* might have on one's own spiritual journey? Yet there is something intensely familiar to any Christian, in an autobiography constructed as a sequence of commentaries on formative books, accompanied by memories of the teachers who had guided him through them. Certain varieties of Christianity have made reading so central to their practice that they generated what, by early modern standards, were phenomenally high levels of literacy. Christian reading is not necessarily a solitary pursuit. BRIAN STOCK coined the term 'textual communities' to describe those monastic groups whose communal lives came to centre on the reading and copying and exegesis of sacred texts.[6] There is no conflict here. Participation in communal reading, like learning to read together or reading the same things while apart, are all modes through which our subjectivities are formed, in parallel and in communion.[7]

But if Augustine's life in books seems familiar today, it cannot have done so at the time. Reading figures hardly at all in accounts, real or imaginary, of the lives of earlier spiritual figures, Pythagoras and Orpheus, Abraham, Christ, Paul and Apollonius of Tyana. Porphyry's *Life of Plotinus* describes his subject's intellectual evolutions as marked by the influence of particular teachers, not of books. Although Porphyry takes care to list all of Plotinus' works, his influence is presented as personal. This also applies to his role as a teacher, although again the *Life*

---

6   STOCK 1983. This idea was developed for antiquity by LANE FOX 1994.
7   On the socializing effects of education see, with different emphases, FOUCAULT 1975, 3.2; LEVI-STRAUSS 1955, ch. 28. On the formation of collective identities through common reading see ANDERSON 1991.

makes clear the central role accorded to the collective study of key books in the activities of his school and the controversies in which he came to be involved. Plotinus at points is represented as actually concealing his learning, and on one occasion criticized Longinus as *philologos* but not *philosophos*. This emphasis on teacher-pupil relationships above book-reader relationships had become conventional by at least the second century AD. Gellius' anecdotes about Favorinus conform to this and the pattern was evidently established in the various biographical collections consulted by Diogenes Laertius for his *Philosophic History*. Lucian's *Peregrinus* arguably responds to this tradition. Philostratus' *Lives of the Sophists,* Eunapius' *Lives of the Philosophers* and Iamblichus' *On the Pythagorean Life* offer other examples.[8] Books were clearly central to the activities of all these figures, as influences and as modes of influencing others, but it was their exemplary lives and teaching that was celebrated. The tendency among late antique pagans 'to associate holiness with philosophical learning' (in the phrase of GARTH FOWDEN[9]) converted discipleship into a kind of spiritual mentoring. It is all the more remarkable that Augustine departs from this model in writing his life around a series of readings.[10]

My aim in this chapter is not to pursue Augustine's revolution in reading practices any further, but instead to ask why reading figures so little as a ritualized form of self-fashioning in Roman religious practices of earlier ages. The textual communities of late antiquity, pagan and Christian, grew by gradual stages out of similar reading communities in the early imperial period.[11] Those communities provided, for one tiny sector of society, one means of creating and presenting complex and multi-layered personal identities. Yet the importance of reading in the *religious* history of the period seems minimal. The ubiquity of writing and of texts in Roman religion, on the other hand, is now appreciated better than ever. This paper sets out to offer a more precise account of where the difference between traditional Roman and Christian uses of reading lay, and to offer some suggestions on how to explain the new use of writing as a means with which to fashion religious selves.

---

8 On Iamblichus and Pythagoras see Gordon, this volume.

9 FOWDEN 1982.

10 On the revolutionary nature of Augustine's approach to reading see STOCK 1996.

11 For the complexity and variability of these elite groups see now JOHNSON 2010. This chapter owes a great deal to this book and the studies that preceded it. See also JOHNSON / PARKER 2009.

2 Reading, Writing, Ritual

A useful way of posing the problem is in the following terms. How unusual were Christian reading practices and uses of texts? Augustine's
world was full of sacred texts.[12] Alongside the growing number of
Christian texts were those books of the Manichees, and in some contexts Augustine obviously considered some Neoplatonic works as comparable to scripture. He was not alone. The same Marius Victorinus
who had translated a group of Neoplatonic texts into Latin had, following his conversion to Christianity, become in the middle of the fourth
century AD the first Latin commentator on the Pauline *Letters*.[13] A near
contemporary was Firmicus Maternus whose treatise *On the Error of Profane Religions* is a Christian polemic but who also wrote, perhaps before
or perhaps after his conversion, an account of astrology. These Latin sacred literatures may be thought of as the western fringe of an astonishingly complex body of written material including Christian, Jewish and
Manichean texts in Greek and other languages, magical papyri, the so-
called Hermetic corpus, Chaldean oracles and much more.[14] These texts
varied enormously in terms of how esoteric they were, in how far they
offered ethical or cosmological insights, and in how widely they circu-
lated. But if we consider the western, Latin, fringe alone, it does seem
that during the fourth century a number of educated individuals were
applying to texts emanating from different origins relatively similar
methods of reading and exegesis. With caution, it makes sense to
write of *convergent reading practices*. Equally cautiously, we can observe
that this phenomenon appears around roughly the same time as something like our notion of a plurality of religions.

It is much more difficult to conduct an archaeology of these reading
practices. In the eastern Mediterranean that investigation would have to
include a comparison between the exegetical practices of different styles
of Jewish intellectual – Philo and the Rabbis most obviously – with the
work of Paul and his successors and rivals.[15] It might also track Platonism back through Christian, Jewish and Hellenic versions. Perhaps it

---

12 This new feature of the religious landscape is what Guy Stroumsa, this volume,
    refers to as 'the scriptural turn of religion'. See also chapter 2 of STROUMSA
    2009.
13 For a recent account of his life, see the introductory material to COOPER 2005.
14 For a dazzling overview of the Greek language material see BOWERSOCK 1990.
15 An investigation along the lines of BOYARIN 2004.

would even be possible, somewhere between Plato and Plotinus, to spot the moment at which texts about religion become sacred texts. Plutarch's *Roman Questions* seem to stand in a tradition of dialogic antiquarianism[16], yet might *On Isis and Osiris* or *On the Decline of Oracles* already offer a revelatory experience to the reader? Egyptian sacred texts lie, in a slightly mysterious way, behind Plutarch's account of the Osiris myth. What about the Sibylline oracles? When was the first Greek text written the reading of which was a primarily religious experience?

Things are much simpler in the Latin tradition. There is a huge gap between non-Christian writing in Latin on religious matters, and the work of the first Latin apologists.[17] That gap was both chronological and conceptual. The *City of God* turns its fire on Varro and Cicero, on Seneca and on Apuleius. The Latin classics were naturally important because of their accumulated authority. But it is striking that Augustine finds no more recent opponents. That Latin tradition is also almost wholly a philosophical tradition, with a small admixture of historical or perhaps exemplary anecdotes. Varro and Cicero produced books about religion, but not sacred texts. Their works were scholarly and respected as such.[18] But the views within them remained those of individual scholars, presented as open to challenge, not least in the use of the dialogue form and in displays of scholarship that took the form of offering a range of answers to each controversy. It is true enough, as several studies have insisted, that these texts were not exterior to the religious life of the Romans in the sense that they do not imply a philosophical (let alone a rationalist and atheistic) rejection of traditional religious activity.[19] Yet there is little sign that they had much influence on the practice of Roman religion, and their readership must always have been small. This was an erudite game played *with* religion, not a theological controversy at the heart of the establishment, even when some participants, real or imagined, were priests. We are a long way distant from riots in Byzantium over theological controversies, or from the involvement of entire mediaeval communities in heresies and their suppression. The key difference concerns the authority of Roman texts about religion.

---

16 PRESTON 2001.
17 One recent mapping of the gap, see GOLDHILL 2008.
18 For Roman scholarship on ritual, and its literary uses see RAWSON 1973. On literary appropriations of the ritual system BARCHIESI / RÜPKE / STEPHENS 2004.
19 BEARD 1986; BEARD 1987; FEENEY 1998; FOWDEN 1982.

Something similar applied to the appropriations of myth and ritual
made by historians and poets.[20] No Latin authors had been accorded
the same status that Homer and Hesiod enjoyed among Greeks as
spokesmen for traditional religion. Virgil was often treated as the foundation stone of both poetic and rhetorical culture, not least because of
the central place given to the *Aeneid* in the educational syllabuses of
the Latin empire. But his presentation of the gods was never treated
as authoritative, in the way that Homer's was by presocratic critics
and Alexandrine scholars alike. The first Christians to write in Latin understood this. Tertullian and Minucius Felix engaged with the Latin
classics as rhetorical models, not as pagan counterparts to their own
scriptures and exegetical works. Firmicus Maternus and Prudentius
drew for their polemic against pagan rituals and supposed beliefs not
on pagan religious writing, but on a set of stereotyped images of exotic
cult practices derived from to satire as well as philosophical criticism of a
Euhemerist type. There were no pagan Latin sacred texts.

This line of approach might suggest that, at least in the Latin writing
parts of the empire, reading did not become a ritualized activity simply
because there were no sacred texts to read. But this only serves to defer
that question, so that we ask Why were sacred texts not created in Latin
prior to those (largely translations) that became central to religious conflict in late antiquity? One plausible answer might be Why should Romans have created sacred texts? Why indeed? Sacred texts in the sense I
have been using it are hardly a human universal. Yet there are two considerations that make this line of argument slightly unsatisfactory.

The first is the very widespread use of texts and especially ritualized
acts of writing in Roman religious activity. This is one area in which
recent research really has changed our awareness of the bookishness
of Roman cult. It is now appreciated how far the management of
Roman cults generated and depended on texts of various kinds.[21]
There were no prior normative texts, recipe books providing liturgical
models for future rituals. The various collections of oracular utterances
that at different times constituted the Sibylline Books were aids to exegetical performance rather than lucid books of instructions, and the exegeses we know of concerned ritual action rather than theological
knowledge. Most of the texts produced by priests were presumably
ephemeral, and of use and interest only to themselves. We should imag-

---

20 LEVENE 1993; DAVIES 2004.
21 See the papers collected by JOHN SCHEID within MOATTI 1998.

ine mundane lists of temple property and contracts, letters and perhaps documents for court cases. But there were also publically displayed documents such as calendars and notices displayed on wooden boards[22], and it seems to have been easy enough to obtain the *commentarii* of senior priests and also prodigy lists. Historians occasionally seem to have had access to quite detailed accounts of major public ceremonies, such as *consecrationes* and the dedication of temples.[23]

More relevant for present purposes are the many cases where the *act* of writing formed an integral part of the performance of a ritual. Examples include temporary displays of vows in temples, and permanent monuments to their fulfillment.[24] Then there are those rituals, such as cursing, in which performing the act of writing seems a vital component.[25] Ritual dimensions of epigraphic writing have also become more apparent.[26] It has been suggested that the monumentalization of names played a key role in asserting identities of various kinds; the great majority of Latin inscriptions are either funerary or votive.[27] More generally, there is an increased appreciation of how even apparently mundane Roman uses of writing played with different modes of ordering the world.[28] The conclusions are clear. Many texts were created in the course of ritual action, and the very act of writing was often ritualized. So why was reading not?

The second consideration is one about reading rather than ritual, and here the case can be made more simply. At the end of a long debate it has become clear that many literate Romans regularly practiced silent reading.[29] Not only was it possible, and common, for documentary texts to be consulted and understood without verbalizing them. There are also many cases of Roman writers referring to their own literary reading practices, practices that seem very similar to those of Augustine, with the exception that the texts in question are not religious ones. Just a few examples make this point more clearly. Epistolography often employs the device of explaining a letter as a response to an act of reading – sometimes of a previous letter, sometimes of an enclosure sent by a

---

22 RÜPKE 1995.
23 See, for example, the accounts of consecrationes compared in PRICE 1987.
24 VEYNE 1983 B; DERKS 1995.
25 GAGER 1992; GRAF 1997.
26 BEARD 1985.
27 WOOLF 1996; CORBIER 2006.
28 HABINEK 2009; PURCELL 1995.
29 JOHNSON 2000.

correspondent, but sometimes a re-reading of a classic, or the discovery of a chance find on a book-stall. This is true of Horace's *Letters* and those of Pliny, as well as more overtly philosophical texts such as Seneca's *Letters*.[30] The device constructs an imagined textual community into which the reader is invited as a spectator or guest, and offers the author the opportunity to characterize himself as a critic. A few texts even describe the impact on the authors of reading particular texts, usually in an educational context. Horace's *Letter to Augustus* provides autobiographical vignettes, as does Cicero's *In Defence of Archias*. We have then an apparent paradox. Writing was on occasion ritualized at Rome, and reading was widely accepted as a mode of individualization. Yet the reading was not ritualized, and the selves created by reading had no appreciable religious dimensions.

3 Texts and Authorities

To say there were no pagan Latin sacred texts is to make a statement about the authority of texts. Questions of authority and knowledge have recently been put at the centre of debates on Roman culture and Roman religion.[31] But these discussions have mostly concerned the location of authority. The invention of sacred texts concerns, rather, a transformation in the nature of the *kinds* of authority that might be vested in the written word.

Roman theological writing took several forms, but the two most important were philosophical (largely but not exclusively in prose) and poetry in a range of genres. Varro and Cicero both refer to a distinction of obscure origin between the theology of the philosophers, that of the poets and that of the statesmen.[32] The last kind was that manifested in ritual action and speech, and not in texts. Authority was built in each sphere slightly differently. Christian models of authority contrasted with each of these and stood opposed to the distinction between them.

Let me begin with philosophy. Augustine challenged Varro's *Antiquities* precisely because of the author's reputation for learning.[33] Augustine cites Cicero's much quoted praise of Varro, as if to add his authority

---

30 For example Hor. *epist.* 1.2 and 19, Plin. *epist.* 1.8, 2.5, 3.5, 4.20, Sen. *epist.* 100.

31 MOATTI 1997; HABINEK 1998; WALLACE-HADRILL 2008; ANDO 2008.

32 On this see RÜPKE 2005, and most recently ANDO 2010.

33 Quint. *inst.* 10.93 calls Varro *vir Romanorum eruditissimus*.

to that of Varro.[34] Elsewhere in *The City of God* Augustine lavishes similar praise on Cicero. His own argument needs formidable opponents and the status of these late Republican *érudits* remained very high in the late antique West. More subtly, Augustine fashioned out of them a sort of pagan orthodoxy, one which he might then demonstrate to be inconsistent and inadequate, rather as he might treat a Christian heresy.

Neither Varro nor Cicero would have seen things in this way. Menippean satire and the dialogue form each dramatized philosophy as a practice, not as an accumulating body of knowledge. Staged debates between proponents of different positions raised the reputation of all participants, rather than operating as a zero-sum game.[35] Readers were involved in an ongoing discussion, not simply instructed in its outcome. Philosophy offered a way of life, not its end. Philosophy about the gods – theology that is – was no different to other kinds. A corollary is that dialogue – actual or textualized – was not the same thing as a public debate between a Manichee and a Catholic Christian of the kind which Augustine attended in his youth. The stakes were different. So was the tacit frame. Stoics did not dream (so far as we can tell) of eliminating Epicureanism, nor of convincing auditors to abandon one affiliation for another. Indeed many texts required and encouraged readers to acquire a broad knowledge of different positions. In this sense the philosophical schools were mutually dependent and supportive. Catholics, on the other hand, could very well manage without Manichees. Theology thus had radically different significances for Christians and for philosophers. For the latter, it constituted simply an application of philosophical techniques to a particular subject matter. For Christians, the truth claims involved were more serious.

None of this is controversial but it points to fundamental differences in the manner in which books about the gods were deemed authoritative in classical and Christian traditions. The authority of Roman theological texts (or texts about religion) was *relative* rather than absolute. Varro might have produced the best account of the gods so far, but even he was open to challenge. Nigidius Figulus and Cicero might take slightly different views. *Auctoritas* was first gained and then tested agonistically. Nor were issues closed off by authoritative works. When Verrius Flaccus in the first century and Gellius in the second re-

---

34 Aug. *civ* 6.2 citing Cic. *ac.1*, 1.3.
35 BEARD 1986.

turned to some of the same issues, it was a legitimate activity, not a disruptive challenge to knowledge. Christian scripture by contrast was susceptible to exegesis, but it was not so open to amendment or correction. The formation of the Christian canon took centuries, but in general, once books had come to be widely treated as scripture they were difficult, if not impossible, to remove. Much of today's New Testament seems to have had this status by the end of the second century, and the rest before the end of the fourth century. It is striking that even with the rise of first episcopal authority and then church councils, more effort was invested in preventing additions to scripture than in removing works, like the Revelation of St John, that no longer cohered well with Christian teaching and practice. In short, Christian canon-formation followed different conventions than its classical counterpart, and required different cultures of reading.

Reading as a mode of self-fashioning does not, of course, require texts of unassailable authority. But the *kind* of authority that central philosophical texts were accorded was one that encouraged a critical mode of reading, and invited competitive responses, oral or in writing. Reading Varro or Cicero or Seneca was a contest between reader and author, one in which the persuasive rhetoric of the text encountered a potential resistance. That style of reading was, to be sure, the way Augustine approached his pagan adversaries. But he read sacred texts differently.

What about the religious authority accorded Roman poets? Poetry was not treated in most respects as like philosophical prose. Yet here too we find authority and status construed as both open and relative. Latin poetics notoriously emerged fully formed. Despite the claims of the critics of the late Republic and Augustan age, it is clear that even the earliest literary works composed in Latin were sophisticated compositions that stand comparison with contemporary Hellenistic Greek works, both in their consciousness of themselves as post-classical, and in the wide range of their intellectual and allusive reference.[36] If the poets of archaic Greece regarded themselves as religious authorities, their Roman counterparts deployed their Muses more knowingly. Roman poets had their places in religious festivals, in the Temple of Hercules Musarum and in the *collega poetarum*. Hymns and drama were originally composed in Latin, as in Greek, for performance at religious festivals. But Roman poets never plausibly claimed the inspired authority of primitive

---

36 Among many other studies, HINDS 1998; HUNTER 2006; HABINEK 1998; HABINEK 2005.

bards, an authority in other words that might be opposed to the established power of the priests. Ennius' theology already looked to Euhemerus' rationalizing approach to myth.

The dynamics of competition for status have been particularly well explored for epic, among the oldest of Latin genres. Epic poetry had authority, but it too was that kind of authority that invited challenge. Homer offered a target for every subsequent epicist, whether writing in Greek or Latin. Latin epicists happily conformed to this generic convention. Their contests for primacy have been mapped from Ennius' and Virgil's treatment of their predecessors to the coronation of Virgil as a Latin Homer, and the responses made to this in the first century AD. That agonistic intertexuality did not exclude the treatment of the gods.[37] But even variations as extreme as the godless epics of Lucretius and Lucan, or the sometimes comic gods of Ovid were not understood as theologically contentious. As new genres were created at Rome, poets took the opportunity to find new ways to play with the gods, but there is no real sign that this generated any religious anxiety. Readers and auditors of Latin poetry were, after all, sensitized to these discursive practices. Gods, when they appeared, came with a good deal of intertextual baggage which the cunning reader would recognize and appreciate. Readers would be alert to assess the success of each variation on a traditional theme. There was little danger of anyone losing, or enriching, their faith by reading Ovid's *Metamorphoses*. Even public ritual might on occasion be mobilized to such ends.[38] Among the consumers of textualized ritual there were certainly members of the priestly colleges, but this seems to have caused little more concern than when Cicero as an augur rehearsed Greek philosophical theology. Poetic appropriations of state cult and of philosophical ideas of religion are in fact common in Latin literature. The *Apocolocyntosis* achieves much of its humour through staging incongruous collisions between these discursive spheres.

It is possible, of course, that the differentiation of religious discourses in Rome was not always as clear cut. The educated aristocracy of the late Republic were already familiar, through their consumption of Greek cultural products and through the intellectual and professional specialization of their day, with a cultural landscape already marked out into distinct provinces. One possible origin for the triple theology

---

37 On the evolution of the portrayal of deities in the epic tradition after Homer see FEENEY 1991.
38 RÜPKE 2004.

– but it is difficult to be sure given the uncertainty over when the idea first appears – is precisely as a device to deal with the threat of cognitive dissonance for individuals and crises of authority within the élite. For Varro each theology related to a different kind of authority, each applied within a circumscribed sphere viz. epic and drama, *sacra publica* and philosophical debate. Statements in one could not disturb action or statements in another sphere. Poets, priests and politicians were not competitors since the discourses in which they participated did not intersect. This boundary demarcation had not always prevented conflict. Philosophers, from Socrates, were occasionally felt to be threats to ancestral religion, and attacks on the poets are present in some of the earliest surviving philosophical texts of the Greek world. By the late Republic, however, peace had been made or at least boundaries agreed. Varro's taxonomy corresponds to the cognitive move which FEENEY, following VEYNE, has called 'brain-balkanization'.[39]

In fact, the kinds of authority enjoyed by the most successful works of prose and poetry were broadly similar. Mundanely, these classics were copied in increasing numbers and became common reference points for intertextual reference. A few were enshrined in educational syllabuses. Admired, imitated, commented upon they were also subjected to that kind of competition the Romans termed *aemulatio* meaning an imitation that seeks to outdo its object of attention. Readers of both kinds of texts were expected to engage critically, to participate in the generation of meaning, and potentially to produce texts of their own. Poetic and philosophical competition, in other words, and came to be governed by the agonistic culture of the classical city-state. Reading and writing cultures were profoundly influenced by those wider social *mores*. Not all the ancient classics played central parts in discourses of theology, but many did. The separation of these discourses from each other and from the rituals of the state was pragmatic and, apparently, largely unproblematic.

The real contrast comes between the kinds of authority accorded theological *writing* of all kinds, and the authority of Roman priests. That authority was certainly not organized so as to invite challenges, least of all when it came to ritual expertise. The prerogative of priests were definitely resented at times. A set of historical traditions recall struggles to force the pontiffs to publish the calendar rather than simply to declare which days were *fas* or *nefas* for public and private business.[40]

39 FEENEY 1998, 14–21; VEYNE 1983a, 41–58.
40 PURCELL 2001.

Legislation moved by *popularis* politicians in the late Republic briefly introduced election to the major priesthoods rather than co-option. Later
Augustus took control of appointments, sat in all the major colleges and
appropriated the iconography of priesthood for his own presentation.
But at no point was the aristocratic monopoly of the priesthood challenged, nor were rival authorities on ritual established, neither charismatic prophets nor sacred books. The authority of books, it seemed,
might be challenged but not the authority of men.

4 Reading and Religious Individualization in classical Antiquity

I began with the question of why reading was not ritualized in Rome,
despite the ubiquity of theological texts and the prominence of the act
of writing in many rituals. The broad outlines of my answer are now
clear. Reading in Rome consisted of a set of discourse-specific practices
that had been formed alongside models of textual authority quite different to those accorded sacred texts by the religions of late antiquity. Poetic and philosophical texts that dealt with the gods embodied notions of
authority, according to which texts might become respected and emu-
lated, yet always remained open to criticism and (potentially at least) to
replacement. Conversely, readers were expected to be active critics and
to participate in modes of literary and philosophical life that were
open.[41] Reading practices, in other words, were a part of the pervasive
agonistic culture of ancient élites. As a result, there were no sacred texts.

The only religious discourse in Rome in which challenges to authority were discouraged was that implicit in the public cults performed
by magistrates and controlled by the priestly colleges. That discourse was
expressed through ritualized action, including speech acts; through the
organization of sacred space; and in the images of the gods: but not in
books. It follows that although reading more generally was a medium of
self-fashioning, it was one without a religious component. Elite readers
might hope to become better people, better educated and more sensitive
readers through their reading, but they neither sought nor achieved religious transformation.

---

41   A central theme of JOHNSON 2010.

The new kind of authority accorded sacred writing in many late antique religions was certainly inherited from Jewish attitudes.[42] But sacred texts, as they became more and more widespread, were not used in the same way in all the competing religions of the period. A full account of the differences between Zoroastrian, Mandaean, Manichean and Hellenic used of sacred texts is beyond the scope of this paper. But it is worth noticing the divergence in the reading cultures of Christians and Jews. The first generation of Christians wrote almost nothing, but the second created a new and rival set of scriptures. From there the paths diverge. There is – sadly – no Jewish Augustine to illuminate the strange history of the Jewish people between Roman and Persian Empires. Yet well before the conversion of Constantine, the production and circulation of texts, their appraisal, discussion, condemnation and canonization had become characteristic features of Christianity.

One reason for the distinctiveness of the reading practices of Roman Christians in late antiquity is likely to be their inheritance from the reading cultures of the early empire. That inheritance increased in importance as the social recruitment of Christians began to draw in members of those very select social classes which had had reading cultures during the early empire. Self-fashioning through reflective reading had been a prominent part of Roman imperial intellectual life. Perhaps, when combined with a new sense of the sacredness of certain texts, those practices contributed to the formation of the introspective life in books with which I, and Augustine, began.

Bibliography

ANDERSON, BENEDICT 1991. *Imagined Communities. Reflections on the origin and spread of nationalism*. Revised second edition. ed. London & New York.
ANDO, CLIFFORD 2008. *The Matter of the Gods. Religion and the Roman Empire*. Berkeley, Los Angeles, Oxford.
—2010. "The Ontology of Religious Institutions", *History of Religions* 50, no. 1. 54–79.
BARCHIESI, ALESSANDRO; RÜPKE, JÖRG; STEPHENS, SUSAN (edd.) 2004. *Rituals in Ink. A Conference on Religion and Literary Production in Ancient Rome held at Stanford University in February 2002*, Potsdamer Altertumswissenschaftlicher Beiträge. Stuttgart.
BEARD, MARY 1987. "A complex of times: no more sheep on Romulus' birthday", *Proceedings of the Cambridge Philological Society*, no. 33. 1–15.

---

42 STROUMSA, p. 180, this volume.

—1986. "Cicero and divination: the formation of a Latin discourse", *Journal of Roman Studies* 76. 33–46.

—1985. "Writing and ritual. A study of diversity and expansion in the Arval Acta", *Papers of the British School at Rome* 40. 114–162.

BOWERSOCK, GLEN 1990. *Hellenism in late antiquity*. Thomas Spenser Jerome Lectures. Cambridge.

BOYARIN, DANIEL 2004. *Border Lines. The partition of Judaeo-Christianity*. Divinations. Rereading late antique religion. Philadelphia.

COOPER, STEPHEN ANDREW 2005. *Marius Victorinus' Commentary on Galatians*. Early Christian Studies. Oxford.

CORBIER, MIREILLE 2006. *Donner à voir, Donner à lire: Mémoire et communication dans la Rome ancienne*. Paris.

DAVIES, JASON P. 2004. *Rome's Religious History. Livy, Tacitus, Ammianus on their gods*. Cambridge.

DERKS, TON 1995. "The ritual of the vow in Gallo-Roman religion", in: METZLER, JEANNOT et al. (edd.). *Integration in the early Roman west. The role of culture and ideology*. Luxembourg. 111–127.

FEENEY, DENIS 1991. *The Gods in Epic: Poets and critics of the classical tradition*. Oxford.

—1998. *Literature and religion at Rome. Culture, contexts and beliefs*. Latin Literature in Context. Cambridge.

FOUCAULT, MICHEL 1975. *Surveiller et Punir: Naissance de la prison*. Paris.

FOWDEN, GARTH 1982. "The Pagan Holy Man in Late Antique Society", *Journal of Hellenic Studies* 102. 33–59.

GAGER, JOHN G. 1992. *Curse tablets and binding spells from the Ancient World*. Oxford.

GOLDHILL, SIMON (ed.) 2008. *The End of Dialogue in Antiquity*. Cambridge.

GRAF, FRITZ 1997. *Magic in the Ancient World*. Cambridge, MA.

HABINEK, THOMAS (ed.) 1998. *The Politics of Latin Literature. Writing, Identity and Empire in Ancient Rome*. Cambridge.

—2005. *The World of Roman Song from ritualised speech to social order*. Baltimore.

—2009. "Situating Literacy at Rome", in: JOHNSON, WILLIAM A.; PARKER, HOLT N. (edd.). *Ancient Literacies. The culture of reading in Greece and Rome*. New York & Oxford. 114–140.

HINDS, STEPHEN 1998. *Allusion and Intertext: Dynamics of appropriation in Roman poetry*. Latin Literature in Context. Cambridge.

HUNTER, RICHARD 2006. *The Shadow of Callimachus. Studies in the reception of Hellenistic poetry at Rome*. Roman Literature and its Contexts. Cambridge.

JOHNSON, WILLIAM A. 2000. "Towards a sociology of reading in classical antiquity", *American Journal of Philology* 121. 593–627.

—2010. *Readers and Reading Culture in the High Roman Empire. A study of elite communities*. Oxford.

JOHNSON, WILLIAM A.; PARKER, HOLT N. (edd.) 2009. *Ancient Literacies. The culture of reading in Greece and Rome*. New York.

LANE FOX, ROBIN 1994. "Literacy and power in early Christianity", in: BOWMAN, ALAN; WOOLF, GREG (edd.). *Literacy and Power in the Ancient World*. Cambridge. 126–148.

LEVENE, D.S. 1993. *Religion in Livy*. Mnemosyne, Supplements #127. Leiden.

LEVI-STRAUSS, CLAUDE 1955. *Tristes Tropiques*. Paris.

MacCORMACK, SABINE 1998. *The Shadows of Poetry. Vergil in the Mind of Augustine*. The Transformation of the Classical Heritage. Berkeley.

MOATTI, CLAUDIA 1997. *La raison de Rome : naissance de l'esprit critique à la fin de la République (IIe-Ier siècle avant Jésus-Christ)*. Paris.

— (ed.) 1998. *La mémoire perdue: recherches sur l'administration romaine*. Collection de l'École Française de Rome 243. Rome.

PRESTON, REBECCA 2001. "Roman questions, Greek answers: Plutarch and the construction of identity", in: GOLDHILL, SIMON (ed.). *Being Greek under Rome. Cultural identity, the second sophistic and the development of empire*. Cambridge. 86–119.

PRICE, SIMON 1987. "From noble funerals to divine cult: the consecration of Roman emperors", in: CANNADINE, DAVID; PRICE, SIMON (edd.). *Rituals of Royalty. Power and ceremonial in traditional societies*. Cambridge. 56–105.

PURCELL, NICHOLAS 1995. "Literate Games. Roman urban society and the game of alea", *Past and Present* 147. 3–37.

—2001. "The ordo scribarum. A study in the loss of memory", *Melanges de l'École française à Rome* 113 no. 2. 633–674.

RAWSON, ELIZABETH 1973. "Scipio, Laelius, Furius and the ancestral religion", *Journal of Roman Studies* 63. 161–174.

RÜPKE, JÖRG 1995. *Kalender und Öffentlichkeit: Die Geschichte der Repräsentation und religiösen Qualifikationen von Zeit im Rom*, Religionsgeschichtliche Versuche und Vorarbeiten 40. Berlin.

—2004. "Acta aut agenda. Relations of script and performance", in: BARCHIESI, ALESSANDRO; RÜPKE, JÖRG; STEPHENS, SUSAN (edd.). *Rituals in Ink. A Conference on Religion and Literary Production in Ancient Rome held at Stanford University in February 2002*. Stuttgart. 23–43.

—2005. "Varro's *Tria Genera Theologiae*. Religious thinking in the late Republic", *Ordia Prima* 4. 107–124.

STOCK, BRIAN 1996. *Augustine the Reader. Meditation, self-knowledge, and the ethics of interpretation*. Cambridge, MA. 1996.

—1983. *The Implications of Literacy: Written language and models of interpretation in the eleventh and twelfth centuries*. Princeton N.J.

STROUMSA, GUY G. 2009. *The End of Sacrifice: Religious Transformations in Late Antiquity*. Trsl. by Susan Emanuel. Chicago.

VEYNE, PAUL 1983 a. *Les grecs ont-ils cru à leurs mythes? Essai sur l'imagination constituante*. Paris.

—1983 b. "Titulus Praelatus': offrande, solemnisation et publicité dans les ex-voto greco-romains", *Revue Archéologique*. 281–300.

WALLACE-HADRILL, ANDREW 2008. *Rome's Cultural Revolution*. New York.

WOOLF, GREG 1996. "Monumental writing and the expansion of Roman society", *Journal of Roman Studies* 86. 22–39.

„Einer jeden Gottheit ihren eigenen Kult": Verbriefte Individualreligion am *Clitumnus fons* (Plinius *epist.* 8,8)

Ulrike Egelhaaf-Gaiser

1 Einleitung[1]

In der Werbebranche wäre Plinius heute wohl ein gemachter Mann: Seine Befähigung zum eloquenten Reiseführer stellt er in einer Beschreibung des umbrischen *Clitumnus fons* unter Beweis, die mit jedem modernen Touristikprospekt konkurrieren könnte. Die Anziehungskraft des Quellheiligtums mit heiligem Hain erschöpft sich demnach nicht in seiner landschaftlich attraktiven Lage. Denn hinzukommen diverse Sport-, Kultur- und Freizeitangebote: Ob Bootsfahren oder Schwimmen, ein Besichtigungsrundgang zum Kultbild und zu den umliegenden Kapellen, eine optionale Befragung des Losorakels oder die erbauliche Lektüre zahlloser Wandgraffiti – der *Clitumnus fons* hat für jeden Besuchergeschmack etwas zu bieten. Wer das Flair altitalischer Ländlichkeit länger genießen und doch hauptstädtischen Komfort nicht missen will, findet direkt vor Ort ein Bad und eine Herberge – ein kostenloses Serviceangebot der Gemeinde. Dass es sich hier auch langfristig gut leben lässt, beweisen die Villen, die entlang dem Flussufer wie Perlen aufgereiht sind und ihren Besitzern als Sommerfrische dienen.

Der *Clitumnus fons* ist – so der spontane Eindruck – ein zauberhaftes Ausflugsziel mit umbrischem Lokalkolorit, das anders als die mondänen Villenorte am Golf von Neapel noch nicht hoffnungslos überlaufen ist, sondern als ein Geheimtipp unter echten Italienkennern und -liebhabern der Kaiserzeit gehandelt wird. Dem landschaftlichen Charme, der in dem einschlägigen Pliniusbrief mit allen Mitteln der rhetorischen Beschreibungskunst vermittelt wird, verdankt der

---

1   Herzlich gedankt sei Helmut Krasser und Meike Rühl für die eingehende Diskussion der Vortragsfassung sowie Alexander Germann für die sorgfältige Gegenlektüre und konstruktive Kritik des Manuskripts.

Clitumnus fons denn auch eine bemerkenswerte Wirkmacht: Die literarischen Reflexe namhafter Besucher an den Quellen des Clitumnus führen von Sueton und Claudians Preisgedicht auf den Kaiser Honorius über Goethe, Gibbon und Lord Byron bis zu Giosuè Carducci.[2]

Umso überraschender ist vor diesem Hintergrund, dass die Epistel 8,8 in der neueren Pliniusforschung kaum beachtet wurde. Neben einer ikonographischen Studie zum Kultbild des Clitumnus (GALLI 1941) und einer von LEFÈVRE 1988 vorgelegten Textinterpretation, die sich auf den Aspekt der Naturästhetik konzentriert, sind lediglich zwei religionsgeschichtliche Studien zu nennen: SCHEID 1996 bietet mit einer vergleichenden Analyse von Rechtsstatus und Verwaltung, Kultformen und räumlicher Gestaltung einen religionsgeschichtlichen Kommentar zu drei ländlichen Heiligtümern, die von Plinius beschrieben werden.[3] Dagegen nimmt BEARD 1991 im Rahmen einer survey-artigen Materialerschließung zur Wechselwirkung von ,Schriftlichkeit und Religion' nur ein Segment der Beschreibung, nämlich die im Brief erwähnten Wandgraffiti, in den Blick. Mein Beitrag setzt sich von diesen bereits vorliegenden Studien sowohl inhaltlich als auch methodisch ab: Er ist durch das spezifische Interesse an der Literarisierung einer typischen Form von Individualreligion – konkret des Votivkults – geleitet. Diese Fragestellung bedingt eine konsequente Zusammenführung von literaturwissenschaftlichen und religionsgeschichtlichen Perspektiven.

Mein Ziel ist es, die kommunikative Wirkungsabsicht der *epist.* 8,8 herauszuarbeiten. Ich möchte insbesondere danach fragen, in welcher Weise sich die religiöse Kommunikation in der Votivpraxis und die literarische Kommunikation im stilisierten Freundschaftsbrief aufeinander beziehen und reflektieren. Anknüpfen kann eine solche Fragestellung an RÜPKES religionswissenschaftliche Forschungsarbeiten, in denen Kommunikationsmodelle zur dichten Beschreibung religiöser Handlungen herangezogen werden.[4]

Auf den ersten Blick wirkt freilich der gewählte Text für solche Fragen denkbar unergiebig. Denn die Ekphrasis, die den Brief zu

---

2 Suet. *Cal.* 43,1; Claud. *Pan. de VI. cons. hon. Aug.* 506–514; Zusammenstellung der Zeugnisse zur Rezeptionsgeschichte bei LEFÈVRE 1988, 251–258, erweitert in LEFÈVRE 2009.
3 Neben *epist.* 8,8 werden *epist.*4,1 und 9,39 behandelt.
4 RÜPKE 2001, 2001 a, 2001 b.

großen Teilen vereinnahmt, drängt die Dialogstruktur auf den äußeren Rahmen zurück. Demzufolge scheint auch die individualisierende Darstellung von Autor und Adressat auf die einleitende Motivation des Briefs und den resümierenden Schlussabschnitt beschränkt.

Ich möchte diesen ersten Negativbefund in meinem Beitrag widerlegen: Nach meiner Meinung hat Plinius den Brief vom *Clitumnus fons* als ein gattungsgebundenes Schaustück gestaltet, durch dessen kunstfertige Gestaltung sich die Persönlichkeit und die Kompetenz des Briefliteraten profilierten. In welcher Weise dabei die Inszenierung von Individualreligon in den Dienst der brieflichen Selbstdarstellung tritt, soll in einer vierschrittigen Textinterpretation dargelegt werden. Dabei gilt es zu fragen,

- welche Rolle die religiöse Pluralität für die Individualreligion im Quellheiligtum spielt,
- mit welchen Gründen der Briefliterat für sich eine besondere Disposition für die altitalische Religion und Landschaft in Anspruch nimmt,
- durch welche spezifische Leistung sich die briefliche Kommunikation im konkurrierenden Vergleich zu verschiedenen Formen religiöser Kommunikation auszeichnet und
- warum gerade der Briefadressat Romanus als ein Modell-Leser der plinianischen Briefsammlung inszeniert und mit einem literarischen Freundschaftsvotiv geehrt wird.

Der textnahen Diskussion der genannten Aspekte sind zwei Grundlagenkapitel vorangestellt: Dort gilt es zunächst zu präzisieren, was der gewählte Pliniusbrief mit dem übergeordneten Thema der „Individualreligion" zu tun hat. Anschließend soll der Text vorgestellt und in seiner Struktur erläutert werden.

2 Individualreligion und (briefliches) Votiv

Für die „Individualreligion" in hohem Maße einschlägig ist die plinianische Beschreibung des *Clitumnus fons* dadurch, dass dort die Votivreligion eine ganz zentrale Rolle spielt. Der Votivkult gilt in der religionswissenschaftlichen Forschung als das klassische Fallbeispiel, anhand dessen sich individuelles religiöses Handeln rekonstruieren lässt.[5] Persönlich motiviert ist dabei nicht nur der Anlass für das Gelübde (z.B. Reisen, Krankheiten, Kinderwünsche). Vielmehr steht dem jeweiligen Adressanten auch – innerhalb eines situationsgebundenen Spektrums zuständiger Götter (bei Krankheitsfällen etwa Aesculap, Bona Dea und Isis; bei Reisen vorzugsweise Fortuna, Neptun, Mercur oder Isis) – die Wahl des von ihm bevorzugten Adressaten frei.

Die mediale Dokumentation des eingelösten Gelübdes ist an Vorgaben gebunden: Dazu zählen das vorgegebene Inschriftenformular, die Geldmittel des Stifters, das orts- oder kultspezifische Standardformat der Stiftung (Inschrift, Votivaltar, Weihrelief, bemaltes/beschriftetes Weihtäfelchen, Terrakotten, Nachbildungen von Körpergliedern) und schließlich auch das Repertoire des ausführenden Steinmetzes vor Ort. Obwohl die archäologisch ergrabenen Votivdepots und Kultanlagen ebenso wie die literarischen Textbelege den Eindruck von „religiöser Massenware" erzeugen,[6] sind andererseits doch auch Tendenzen der gesuchten Individualisierung festzustellen: Üblicherweise lassen die Stifter nicht nur ihre eigenen Namen, sondern auch die Namen der Gottheiten inschriftlich bezeugen.[7] Bei nicht beschrifteten Votivgaben erfolgt die Zuweisung an eine bestimmte Gottheit durch die Aufstellung bzw. Deponierung im jeweiligen Heiligtum.

Durch ihre öffentliche Präsentation im Heiligtum erhalten die Votivgaben neben den geehrten Gottheiten einen sekundären Adressaten: Gegenüber späteren Besuchern bezeugen die Votive den Erfolg des adressierten Gottes. Gerade durch die im Votivkult häufig feststellbare Massierung uniformer Weihegaben wird eine effiziente Verstärkung der religiösen Werbung erzielt.[8] Da zudem in den meisten Votivheiligtümern nicht nur Weihgeschenke für den göttlichen Haupteigentümer des Orts, sondern auch für andere Gottheiten aufgestellt werden, verbindet sich das chorische Gotteslob mit dem Aspekt der religiösen Konkurrenz, die sich aus der Kultpluralität und dem Wahlangebot für die Stifter ergibt.

---

5   Veyne 1983; Rüpke 2001, 154–165.
6   Tib. 1,3,27: *nunc, dea, nunc succurre mihi – nam posse mederi / picta docet templis multa tabella tuis;* Ov. *fast.* 3,267: *et posita est meritae multa tabella deae;* Ov. *met.* 8,744– 746: *stabat in his ingens annoso robore quercus, / una nemus; vittae mediam memoresque tabellae / sertaque cingebant, voti argumenta potentum;* Iuv. 12,102: *legitime fixis vestitur tota libellis porticus;* Beard 1991, 39–44; Rüpke 2001, 155; Rüpke 2012.
7   Veyne 1983, 288–292.
8   Rüpke 2001, 163; Rüpke 2012.

Gegenüber den reichen archäologischen Befunden stellt der Pliniusbrief einen bemerkenswerten Sonderfall dar: Sind doch literarische Texte für gewöhnlich durch die Perspektive der urbanen, finanzkräftigen Bildungselite bestimmt und thematisieren daher allenfalls beiläufig Aspekte der „billigen" Religionspraxis, die auch für ärmere Schichten der Stadt- und Landbevölkerung zugänglich und verfügbar ist.

Der Pliniusbrief beschränkt sich jedoch nicht auf eine distanzierte Beschreibung der zeitgenössischen Votivpraxis in einem ländlichen Heiligtum. Vielmehr macht er sich – dies meine These – die kommunikativen Strategien der religiösen Werbung zu Eigen und sucht die vor Ort aufgestellten Weihungen mit seinem eigenen, rhetorisch ungleich raffinierter ausgearbeiteten Briefvotiv zu überbieten. Die am *Clitumnus fons* exemplifizierte Votivpraxis wird somit zum interpretatorischen Schlüssel für den Brief 8,8; sie kann, über den Einzeltext hinausgreifend, als Demonstrationsbeispiel für Plinius' Selbstverständnis als Briefliterat dienen, der ausgewählte Freunde mit einem persönlich adressierten Freundschaftsvotiv ehrt.[9]

Dass der Brief in der Tat als eine ganz besondere Kostbarkeit präsentiert wird, lässt sich bereits aus der Wahl der beschriebenen Örtlichkeit vermuten. Denn Heiligtümer und Tempel sind nicht nur aufgrund ihres materiellen und dekorativen Schauwerts, sondern auch dank ihrer religiösen Symbolkraft zu einer Stilisierung als literarischer Sinn- und Bedeutungsträger geradezu prädestiniert: Insbesondere auf repräsentative Tempelfassaden lassen sich komplexe Bildprogramme projizieren. In großformatigen Textgattungen wie Epos und Roman können daher eingelegte Tempelbeschreibungen sowohl Leitlinien der vorausgehenden Erzählung rekapitulierend zusammenführen als auch auf bevorstehende Ereignisse vorausdeuten.[10]

---

9 Zur Bedeutung des Freundschaftsmotivs in Plinius' Briefen Mratschek 2003; Kählau 2010.
10 So werden Tempel häufig in Epen, aber auch in Romanen in Szene gesetzt: vgl. die Trojagemälde im Iunotempel von Karthago (*Aen.* 1,441–493) oder die bebilderten Tempeltüren des Orakelheiligtums im süditalischen Cumae (*Aen.* 6,14–41); zu poetologisch „aufgeladenen" Tempelbildern im Roman siehe insbesondere Longos *praef.* und Longos 4,2–3. Ein Pendant im elegischen Kleinformat bietet Properz' Beschreibung des neu geweihten Apollheiligtums auf dem Palatin (2,31). Zur Programmatik und Semantik poetischer Beschreibungen von Tempeltürbildern Wedeniwski 2005, bes. 8–18.

Ein heiliger Hain wie das Quellheiligtum des Clitumnus bietet naturgemäß keine vergleichbare Monumentalarchitektur; hier ist es vielmehr die numinose Aura, die das Naturheiligtum in Abgrenzung vom menschlich kultivierten Raum als genuines Eigentum der Götter kennzeichnet.[11] Die religiöse Qualität spiegelt sich in literarischen Beschreibungen heiliger Haine, denen sie ein besonderes Gewicht und einen hohen, gegebenenfalls auch poetologisch nutzbaren Verweischarakter verleiht: Insbesondere in Texten epischer Tradition ist der Begriff des unberührten „Waldes" mit einer komplexen poetischen Semantik belegt.[12]

Die Vermutung, dass Plinius mit seiner Schilderung des *Clitumnus fons* den literarischen Anspruch seiner Briefe als kostbares Freundschaftsvotiv beispielhaft vor Augen führt, lässt sich auch aus der dafür gewählten literarischen Form der Ekphrasis begründen: Stellt doch die Überführung eines Bilds in einen Text stets eine besondere Herausforderung an die rhetorische Technik und den virtuosen Einsatz der Wortkunst dar.[13] Eine Ortsbeschreibung wie die des *Clitumnus fons* ist demnach geradezu unvermeidlich durch einen hohen literarischen Wert und Selbstbezug gekennzeichnet.

Ein letztes Argument für die postulierte Engführung von Votivpraxis und Brief lässt sich aus den strukturellen Parallelen zwischen beiden Kommunikationsformen gewinnen, dank derer sich die Textgattung „Brief" in ganz besonderer Weise für einen konkurrierenden Vergleich mit der Weihepraxis empfiehlt.[14] Im intermedialen Wettstreit variiert oder intensiviert der Brief konstitutive Elemente des Votivs freilich so stark, dass neben den strukturellen Ähnlichkeiten stets auch die kontext- und gattungsbedingten Unterschiede Konturen gewinnen. Dabei kann es nicht überraschen, dass entsprechend den Usancen der „Konkurrenz der Künste" der literarische Text gegenüber der Votivinschrift respektive dem Bildvotiv regelmäßig die Vorrangstellung beansprucht.

---

11 SCHEID 1993, 18 f.; zum Schutz heiliger Haine vor wirtschaftlicher Nutzung
     RÜPKE 2009, 254 f.
12 Exemplarisch Verg. *Aen.* 1,441–452; 7,81–91; 8,347–354; Lucan. 3,399–425;
     Ov. *fast.* 3,9–20. Zur poetologischen und intertextuellen Qualität HINDS 1998,
     10–16, FANTHAM 1996; PANOUSSI 2003.
13 BOEHM 1995, 23; zur Ekphrasis in der rhetorischen Tradition ebenda 31–36.
14 Zum Folgenden grundlegend MÜLLER 1985; SCHMID 1988; RÜHL 2009, 15–73;
     speziell zu den Pliniusbriefen RADICKE 2003.

Wie die Votivhandlung, so ist der Brief durch die Persönlichkeit des Adressanten und Adressaten vordefiniert. Allerdings zeichnet sich der Brief durch einen informativen Mehrwert aus, da beide Kommunikationspartner nicht nur namentlich, sondern auch durch eine individuelle Figurenzeichnung und Wahrnehmungsperspektive dem literarischen Text eingeschrieben werden. Falls der Einzelbrief wie in unserem Fall zusätzlich im Rahmen einer Publikation in einen größeren, derselben Person gewidmeten „Briefzyklus" integriert wird, können die literarisch imaginierten Porträts von Sender und Empfänger im Zuge einer fortschreitenden Lektüre mit immer neuen Facetten angereichert werden.[15] Mit seinen vielfältigen sprachlichen und stilistischen Gestaltungsoptionen und seiner thematischen Offenheit eröffnet der Brief somit weit größere Freiräume als die an eine einmalige Situation gebundene und sprachlich standardisierte Weihinschrift.

Votivkult und Brief verbindet weiterhin der Gestus der persönlichen Zueignung und Mitteilung. Dieser wird vom Briefschreiber auch, ja gerade dann beibehalten und sogar noch gezielt intensiviert, wenn sich der Autor über den Primäradressaten hinaus an eine erweiterte, sekundäre Leserschaft richtet und diese im Schreibakt einbezieht.[16] Das für den publizierten Brief konstitutive Zweitpublikum ist auch für das Votiv vorauszusetzen, das sich seinerseits durch den Ausstellungsort sowohl an die Götter als auch an die Öffentlichkeit der Heiligtumsbesucher richtet.[17]

Zwei wichtige Spezifika der religiösen und brieflichen Kommunikation leiten sich schließlich aus den besonderen Kommunikationsbedingungen ab, die Form und Verlauf der Mitteilung beeinflussen: Erstens ist der Adressant in beiden Fällen aufgrund der Abwesenheit des Adressaten auf den Einsatz von unterstützenden Medien verwiesen. Während allerdings der Brief die Verwendung der Schrift und eines materiellen Schriftträgers (Papyrus, Pergament) notwendig voraussetzt, legt bei einem idealtypischen *votum* der Adressant sein Versprechen zunächst nur mündlich ab (wobei er durch den zusätzlichen Einsatz von Opfergaben die Erfolgswahrscheinlichkeit seiner Bitte erhöhen kann); erst mit Einlösung des Gelübdes

---

15 Zu den formalen und funktionalen Spezifika plinianischer Briefzyklen Kählau 2010, bes. 3–11 und 57–60.

16 Exemplarisch ausgeleuchtet durch Radicke 2003.

17 Rüpke 2001, 163; vgl. Rüpke 2001 b, 29.

werden der Erhalt der von den Göttern erbetenen Leistung und die
dafür erbrachte Gegengabe im bildlichen oder inschriftlichen Votiv
dokumentiert und verstetigt.

Ergänzend zur räumlichen Ferne sind zweitens *votum* und Brief
durch eine Zeitverschiebung bzw. einen Phasenverzug zwischen der
Äußerung und deren Aufnahme seitens des Adressaten bestimmt.[18]
Antike Briefliteraten und Rhetorikhandbücher definieren daher den
Brief als einen „halbierten Dialog": Obwohl der Briefschreiber seinen
Zustand des Alleinseins zu überwinden sucht, indem er sich den fernen
Adressaten durch verschiedene literarische Techniken – z. B. durch
fiktive Einwürfe, die Vorwegnahme der erwünschten Leserreaktion
oder die literarische Imagination des Rezipienten – als persönlich
anwesend vorstellt, bleibt er letztlich immer auf die monologische
Einzeläußerung begrenzt.

Eine Zeitverschiebung ist auch genuiner Bestandteil des *votum*,[19]
wobei freilich diese Form der „Zerdehnung" strukturell anders begründet ist. Denn während sich die kleinste Einheit einer freundschaftlichen Briefkommunikation aus zwei Kommunikationsakten,
dem initiativen Brief und einem (nicht immer notwendigen, aber
jedenfalls erwünschten) Antwortschreiben, zusammensetzt, besteht
das Ritual des Gelübdes in seiner idealtypischen Grundstruktur aus
drei Kommunikationsphasen. Am Anfang steht das Versprechen, das
vom Adressanten im Zuge eines Bittgebets um eine bestimmte Leistung formuliert wird; auf den zweiten Schritt – die positive Antwort
seitens der Gottheit – reagiert im erneuten Gegenzug das Dankgebet,
das dem Erhalt der göttlichen Hilfeleistung durch Einlösung des Gelübdes Rechnung trägt. Angesichts dieser eher technischen Beschreibung sollte allerdings die ausgeprägt persönliche Komponente
der Kommunikation nicht in Vergessenheit geraten: Für ein *votum* ist
eine existenzielle Krisensituation und womöglich eine lange, ver-
zweifelte Suche nach einer Rettungsmöglichkeit vorauszusetzen.
Gegebenenfalls offenbart die Gottheit dem Rettung Suchenden eine
bestimmte Lösung in einer nächtlichen Traumerscheinung. In Votivinschriften wird durch entsprechende Formulierungen wie *ex visu*
diese persönliche Gottesnähe eigens akzentuiert.

Erneut lassen die beiden letztgenannten Merkmale der räumlichen
Distanz und der zeitlichen Zerdehnung neben den genannten Ge-

---

18 Zum Phasenverzug im Brief MÜLLER 1985, 70–73.
19 Zur idealtypischen Grundstruktur des *votum* RÜPKE 2001, 161 f.

meinsamkeiten signifikante Unterschiede zwischen der religiösen Votivpraxis und der brieflichen Kommunikation und damit die Grenzen ihrer Vergleichbarkeit erkennen: Votiv und Freundschaftsbrief sind aus unterschiedlichen Bedürfnissen motiviert. Folgerichtig ist die Konstellation von Sender und Empfänger anders definiert: Dem Ideal eines brieflichen Freundschaftsgesprächs unter Gleichgesinnten steht die unstrittige Hierarchie zwischen Menschen und Göttern gegenüber. Auch die beim Gabentausch gepflegten Kommunikationsformen unterliegen anderen Gesetzmäßigkeiten: Während für das Gelingen des *votum* im Sinne der Orthopraxie die formkorrekte Einlösung einer exakt vordefinierten Leistung entscheidend ist, liegt umgekehrt eine ganz besondere Attraktivität der brieflichen Ehrengabe in deren inhaltlicher und sprachlicher Gestaltungsfreiheit.

Meiner Meinung nach bieten gerade die Abweichungen dem Briefliteraten Anlass, nicht nur vereinfachende Parallelen zu konstruieren, sondern vielmehr auf der Folie der normierten Votivpraxis die Einzigartigkeit und die spezifische Eigenleistung des adressatenbezogenen Freundschaftsbriefs zu akzentuieren. Die vom Briefliteraten postulierte Vorrangigkeit des literarischen Freundschaftsvotivs werde ich in den Kapiteln 6 und 7 erneut in den Blick nehmen. Bevor wir aber in die Diskussion verschiedener Aspekte der Individualreligon eintreten, sei zunächst der Brief selbst vorgestellt.

3 Literarische Imagination und Leserappell im Brief 8,8

Im Dienste einer ersten Erschließung sollen zunächst die argumentative Struktur und sprachliche Gestaltung des Briefs analysiert werden. Zunächst der Text:

C. PLINIVS ROMANO SVO S. C. Plinius grüßt seinen Romanus

Vidistine aliquando Clitumnum fontem? Si nondum – et puto nondum: alioqui narrasses mihi –, vide; quem ego (paenitet tarditatis) proxime vidi.

Hast Du schon einmal die Clitumnus-Quelle gesehen? Wenn noch nicht – und ich glaube nicht, denn sonst hättest Du es mir erzählt –, so sieh sie Dir an! Ich habe sie erst kürzlich (die Verspätung reut mich) gesehen!

EXPOSITION UND SEHAPPELL

Modicus collis adsurgit, antiqua cupressu nemorosus et opacus. Hunc subter exit fons et exprimitur pluribus venis sed imparibus, eluctatusque quem facit gurgitem lato gremio patescit, purus et vitreus, ut numerare iactas stipes et relucentes calculos possis. Inde non loci devexitate, sed ipsa sui copia et quasi pondere impellitur, fons adhuc et iam amplissimum flumen, atque etiam navium patiens; quas obvias quoque et contrario nisu in diversa tendentes transmittit et perfert, adeo validus ut illa qua properat ipse, quamquam per solum planum, remis non adiuvetur, idem aegerrime remis contisque superetur adversus. Iucundum utrumque per iocum ludumque fluitantibus, ut flexerint cursum, laborem otio, otium labore variare. Ripae fraxino multa, multa populo vestiuntur, quas perspicuus amnis velut mersas viridi imagine adnumerat. Rigor aquae certaverit nivibus, nec color cedit.

Ein sanfter Hügel erhebt sich, dicht bewachsen und beschattet von alten Zypressen. An seinem Fuss entspringt eine Quelle und sprudelt in mehreren, aber ungleichen Adern hervor; und wenn sie sich aus dem Strudel, den sie bildet, herausgearbeitet hat, öffnet sie sich zu einem breiten Becken, glasklar und durchsichtig, so dass man die hineingeworfenen Münzen und reflektierenden Steinchen zählen kann. Von dort wird sie nicht durch die Abschüssigkeit des Bodens, sondern durch ihre eigene Wassermenge und sozusagen durch ihr Eigengewicht weitergetrieben. Eben noch eine Quelle, ist sie nun schon ein sehr breiter und sogar schiffbarer Fluss, der auch Schiffe, die sich begegnen und mit unterschiedlichem Kurs nach verschiedenen Richtungen fahren, aneinander vorbeilässt und ans Ziel bringt; seine Strömung ist so stark, dass man stromabwärts, obgleich das Gelände eben ist, keine Ruder braucht; aber gegen den Strom kann man kaum mit Rudern und Ruderstangen vorwärts kommen. Beides ist für die angenehm, die nur zum Spaß und Zeitvertreib auf dem Fluss fahren, so dass sie, je nachdem, wie sie die Fahrtrichtung ändern, Anstrengung mit Ruhe und Ruhe mit Anstrengung abwechseln lassen. Die Ufer sind reichlich mit Eschen, reichlich mit Pappeln bewachsen, die der klare Fluß, gleichsam als wären sie versenkt, als grünes Abbild widerspiegelt. Das Wasser dürfte so kalt wie Schnee sein und hat auch die gleiche Farbe.

BILD-
BESCHREI-
BUNG
NATUR

Adiacet templum priscum et religiosum. Stat Clitumnus ipse
amictus ornatusque praetexta;
praesens numen atque etiam fat-
idicum indicant sortes. Sparsa sunt
circa sacella complura, totidemque
di. Sua cuique veneratio suum
nomen, quibusdam vero etiam
fontes. Nam praeter illum quasi
parentem ceterorum sunt minores
capite discreti; sed flumini mi-
scentur, quod ponte transmittitur.
Is terminus sacri profanique: in
superiore parte navigare tantum,
infra etiam natare concessum.
Balineum Hispellates, quibus illum locum divus Augustus dono
dedit, publice praebent, praebent
et hospitium. Nec desunt villae
quae secutae fluminis amoenitatem margini insistunt.

In der Nähe liegt ein uralter, BILD-
ehrwürdiger Tempel. Darin steht BESCHREI-
Clitumnus selbst, bekleidet und BUNG
geschmückt mit der Toga prae- ARCHI-
texta; Orakeltäfelchen weisen TEKTUR
darauf hin, dass eine Gottheit
anwesend ist und auch weissagt.
Ringsum liegen mehrere Kapellen verstreut, jede für einen Gott.
Jeder hat seine eigene Verehrung,
seinen eigenen Namen, manche
auch ihre eigenen Quellen. Denn
außer jener Quelle, gleichsam der
Mutter der übrigen, gibt es noch
kleinere, die von der Hauptquelle
getrennt sind; aber sie ergießen
sich in den Fluß, den man auf
einer Brücke überquert. Sie bildet
die Grenze zwischen dem heiligen und weltlichen Bereich. Im
oberen Bereich darf man nur mit
dem Boot fahren, in dem unteren
auch schwimmen. Die Einwohner von Hispellum, denen der
göttliche Augustus diesen Ort
zum Geschenk gemacht hat,
bieten Bad und Unterkunft auf
Kosten der Gemeinde an. Auch
fehlt es nicht an Landhäusern, die
wegen der anmutigen Lage des
Flusses an seinem Ufer stehen.

In summa nihil erit, ex quo non
capias voluptatem. Nam studebis
quoque: leges multa multorum
omnibus columnis omnibus parietibus inscripta, quibus fons ille
deusque celebratur. Plura laudabis,
non nulla ridebis; quamquam tu
vero, quae tua humanitas, nulla
ridebis. Vale.

Insgesamt wird es nichts geben, SUMME
woran Du nicht Vergnügen fin- UND LESER-
dest. Denn Du wirst auch Studien APPELL
betreiben können; an allen Säulen, an allen Wänden wirst du
zahlreiche   Inschriften   vieler
Menschen lesen, durch die jene
Quelle und ihr Gott gepriesen
werden. Mehrere wirst Du loben,
über einige wirst Du lächeln; aber
freilich, in Anbetracht Deiner
Menschlichkeit wirst Du über
nichts lächeln. Lebe wohl!

Die Makrostruktur des Briefs weist die gattungstypische Dreiteilung auf:
Auf eine adressatenbezogene Eröffnung und Motivation des Schreibens

folgt die erzählende oder beschreibende Entfaltung des Gegenstands, bevor sich der Briefliterat im apellativen Schluss erneut an den Adressaten wendet und – häufig in Verbindung mit einem demonstrativen Freundschaftskompliment – nochmals auf die Eröffnung seines Schreibens zurückgreift.

Einleitung und Ende der *epist.* 8,8 sind nach den Regeln der Brieftopik, laut denen ein Brief den urbanen *sermo* literarisch abbilden soll, durch eine sekundäre Mündlichkeit geprägt: Ablesbar ist die gesuchte Nähe zum literarischen Gespräch am Imperativ *vide* (§ 1) oder an dem zusammenfassenden *in summa* (§ 7). Einleitung und Ende verbindet zudem, dass beide eine spontane Reaktion auf die Wahrnehmung eines bestimmten Gegenstands postulieren: Nach Aussage des Briefschreibers ist der optische Eindruck des Quellheiligtums (§ 1 *vidisti aliquando*) dergestalt, dass jedem Besucher – und wie viel mehr einem versierten Redner wie Romanus! – wie von selbst eine wortreiche Erzählung von den Lippen strömt (§ 1 *alioqui narrasses*). Dabei sollte das umgangssprachliche *narrare* nicht darüber hinwegtäuschen, dass hier ein rhetorischer Topos aufgerufen wird: Ein kompetenter Betrachter – und als einen solchen lanciert Plinius sich und seinen Briefpartner – reagiert auf den inspirierenden Anblick eines Kunstwerks angemessen, indem er dessen herausragende Schönheit in einer nicht minder kunstvollen Beschreibung würdigt.[20]

Der dreifachen Aufforderung zur Imagination am Kopf des Briefs (§ 1 *vidisti – vide – vidi*) entspricht im Schlussabschnitt eine zweifache Aufforderung zur Lektüre (§ 7 *studebis – leges*). Während also die Brieferöffnung mit aller Emphase an die visuelle Vorstellung des Lesers appelliert, wird diesem am Ende erneut ins Bewusstsein gerufen, dass dieses Bild allein mittels des soeben gelesenen Textes erzeugt wurde. In der Tat ist die plinianische Ortsbeschreibung so anschaulich, dass der Adressat Romanus dabei wie von einem Reiseführer im virtuellen Spaziergang durch das umbrische Quellheiligtum geführt wird. Die erfolgreiche Animation zu einem tatsächlichen Besuch des *Clitumnus fons*, die der Brief einleitend als Zielsetzung suggeriert, ist damit zwar nicht ausgeschlossen. Doch ist andererseits die persönliche Ortsansicht für den Leser nicht mehr notwendig: Dank der Imaginationskraft des brieflichen Reisepräsens kann nun Romanus seinerseits die umbrische Quelle besuchen, ohne dass er dafür die Unbequemlichkeiten des Reisens auf sich nehmen muss.

---

20 *De domo* 1 und *Imagines* 1.

Die eingelagerte Ortsbeschreibung erfolgt ihrerseits in zwei Teilen, die konsequent aufeinander bezogen sind. Indem nahezu alle zentralen Landschaftselemente im zweiten Teil jeweils erneut variierend aufgenommen und durch funktional entsprechende Bauformen ergänzt werden, wandelt sich die Flusslandschaft Schritt für Schritt und wird zur architektonisch geformten Sakrallandschaft überhöht. Dadurch wird nicht nur das Landschaftsbild optisch stetig angereichert, sondern auch die sakrale Aura sukzessive aufgebaut und intensiviert.

Der sanften Erhebung des Hügels (§ 2 *collis adsurgit*) wird auf diese Weise der Tempel zugeordnet (§ 5 *adiacet templum),* dessen ehrwürdiges Alter (§ 5 *priscum et religiosum*) den alten Baumbestand (§ 2 *antiqua cupressu*) modifizierend aufnimmt. Die natürliche Quelle (§ 2 *fons*) gewinnt ihrerseits im Kultbild des Clitumnus (§ 5 *Clitumnus ipse*) körperliche Gestalt. Den mehrfachen Wasseradern, die dem Boden entspringen (§ 2 *pluribus venis),* werden dementsprechend mehrere Kapellen (§ 5 *sacella complura*) zugeordnet.

Zu diesen architektonischen Ergänzungen treten verschiedene Formen der Präzisierung und Ausdifferenzierung: Das im ersten Teil breit entfaltete Motiv des mit Kähnen befahrbaren Flusses (§ 3 *iam amplissimum flumen, atque etiam navium patiens*) wird in einer Wortassonanz wieder aufgenommen (§ 6 *in superiore parte navigare tantum, infra etiam natare concessum)* und durch eine Brücke ergänzt (§ 6 *quod ponte transmittitur).* Da durch diese die Grenze des heiligen Bezirks markiert wird (§ 6 *is terminus sacri profanique),* erhält die Beschreibung nun zusätzlich eine sakralrechtliche Komponente. Eingerahmt wird die Sakrallandschaft abschließend durch die Villen, die den optischen Charme des natürlichen Flusslaufs unterstreichen (§ 6 *nec desunt villae quae secutae fluminis amoenitatem margini insistunt*) und damit die dekorative Funktion der im Heiligtum wachsenden Eschen und Pappeln (§ 4 *ripae fraxino multa, multa populo vestiuntur)* auf einer profan-architektonischen Ebene imitieren.

Ungeachtet aller landschaftlichen und architektonischen Details ist und bleibt der *Clitumnus fons* das eigentliche Leitmotiv, das den gesamten Brief durchzieht: Programmatisch eröffnet Plinius seine Beschreibung mit der namentlichen Benennung seines Reiseziels (§ 1 *vidisti aliquando Clitumnum fontem?*). Die beiden beschreibenden Mittelteile würdigen getrennt zunächst die natürlichen (§ 2 *fons*), dann die religiösen (§ 5 *Clitumnus ipse*) und weltlich-artifiziellen Qualitäten der Quelle. Erst der Schlusspassus verklammert Landschaft und Sakralarchitektur mit Hilfe der rühmenden Wandinschriften erneut zu einer genuinen Einheit (§ 7 *in-*

scripta, quibus fons ille deusque celebratur), die der Besucher des Heiligtums ebenso wie der Leser des Briefs als solche wahrnehmen und würdigen soll.

Vor dem Hintergrund dieser sorgfältigen Textkomposition wollen wir uns nun unserer Leitfrage, der argumentativen Funktionalisierung verschiedener Aspekte der Individualreligion, zuwenden. Ausgehend von der Beobachtung, dass der Brief gerade im zentralen Mittelteil des Briefs (§ 5) den Blick auf die religiöse Pluralität im beschriebenen Quellheiligtum lenkt, soll zunächst untersucht werden, welche Stroßrichtung dieser Verweis auf die Kultvielfalt hat, und inwiefern sich das optionale Angebot göttlicher Adressaten als ein genuiner Bestandteil der Individualreligon deuten lässt.

4 „Einer jeden Gottheit ihren eigenen Kult": Religiöse Pluralität im Quellheiligtum

Insbesondere der zweite Hauptteil der Beschreibung fokussiert gleich einleitend auf die Vielfalt von Lokalgottheiten, die im Quellheiligtum verehrt werden. Dabei lässt Plinius den Leser nicht darüber im Zweifel, dass innerhalb der zahlreichen Kapellen und Quellen, die für den Besucher im heiligen Hain ein breites Kultspektrum anbieten, Clitumnus die unstrittige Vorrangstellung gebührt. Dementsprechend wird sein ehrwürdiger Tempel auch kompositorisch in das Zentrum des Briefes gerückt. Ein zusätzliches Alleinstellungsmerkmal erhält Clitumnus dadurch, dass ungeachtet der Vielzahl der im Heiligtum verehrten Lokalgötter allein sein Kultbild nochmals eigens durch eine knappe Beschreibung ausgezeichnet wird. Von diesem literarisch wie religiös markierten Mittelpunkt wird der Blick des Lesers auf die anderen, ringsum verstreuten Kultorte gelenkt, die dem zentralen Tempelbau in einem erweiterten Radius zu- und untergeordnet werden (§ 3 *sparsa sunt circa sacella complura, totidemque di*).

Wenn Plinius dabei ausdrücklich auf die individuelle Verehrung der namentlich anrufbaren Gottheiten sowie auf die Existenz jeweils eigener Kultbauten verweist (§ 3 *sua cuique veneratio suum nomen, quibusdam vero etiam fontes*), so greift er damit ein Grundprinzip der religiösen Kommunikation auf: Gebete, Anfragen und Danksagungen müssen eindeutig adressiert werden. Um die Übermittlung an den richtigen Adressaten zu garantieren, werden in der Gebetssprache die Namen der angerufenen Götter durch zusätzliche Angaben erweitert, die Ort und erwartetes

Erscheinungsbild sowie Funktion, Wirkung und Zuständigkeit der Adressaten näher bestimmen.[21] Dem Rangunterschied zwischen den „Mitbewohnern" des heiligen Hains und dem eigentlichen Ortsbesitzer Clitumnus entspricht, dass Plinius zwar auf die namentliche Anrufbarkeit der in das Heiligtum integrierten Quellgottheiten ausdrücklich verweist, aber diese zugleich hinter dem Hauptgott Clitumnus in einer undifferenzierten Anonymität zurücktreten lässt.

Auch aus der Landschaftsbeschreibung lassen sich nuancierte Hierarchien ablesen: So gibt es nicht nur einen qualitativen Abstand zwischen Clitumnus und den Nebengottheiten, sondern auch zwischen eben diesen, insofern zwar alle eine individuelle Verehrung genießen, aber nur einige über eine eigene Quelle verfügen. In einem dritten Schritt wird diese religiöse Pluralität, deren fein skalierte Unterschiede sich erst sukzessive enthüllen, nochmals in einem Vergleich umschrieben: Gegenüber den kleineren Seitenquellen nimmt der namengebende Clitumnus quasi eine Vaterrolle (§ 5 *parens*) ein. Umgekehrt kann er freilich nur deshalb zum machtvollen Strom anschwellen, weil ihm alle Seitenarme ihr Wasser zuleiten.

Religiöse Individualität und lokale Kultvielfalt sind nun aber nicht nur auf der Ebene der göttlichen Adressaten, sondern auch bei den Adressanten im Text nachweisbar: So weist Plinius an exponierter Stelle, nämlich im Resümee seines Briefs, auf „die vielen Inschriften vieler Menschen" hin, die der Besucher „an allen Säulen, allen Wänden" lesen könne. Die Zahl und Dichte der Graffiti, von deren schierer Masse der Leser vor Ort zutiefst beeindruckt wird, sind im Brief durch nicht minder kumulative Wortwiederholungen auf engstem Raum reprojiziert (§ 7 *leges multa multorum omnibus columnis, omnibus parietibus inscripta*).

Die stilistisch so auffällig markierte Polyphonie der persönlich motivierten Lob- und Danksagungen wird allerdings sofort wieder relativiert. Denn überraschenderweise zielt die Vielzahl verschriftlichter Besucherstimmen – jedenfalls in der literarischen Konstruktion des Briefs – gerade nicht auf das optionale Lob aller im Heiligtum verehrten Gottheiten, sondern vielmehr auf das gemeinsame Preis ein und desselben Gottes und Ortes: Letztlich scheinen also alle Lokalgottheiten im Dienst des Heiligtumsbesitzers Clitumnus zu stehen. Die Zusammenführung des von den Besuchern intonierten Stimmenchors wird im Brief durch die Überführung der bisher dominanten Pluralformen in den Singular (§ 7 *quibus fons ille deusque celebratur*) angezeigt. Das solchermaßen „polyphon

---

21 SCHEER 2001; RÜPKE 2001a, 76.

verstärkte" Finale des Briefs übermittelt zugleich einen impliziten Appell an den Leser: Dieser kann und soll durch die Brieflektüre die Lob- und Dankinschriften der Heiligtumsbesucher erneut aktivieren und in ihr polyphones Lob auf Clitumnus einstimmen.

Die Beobachtung, dass die individuelle religiöse Handlung letztlich doch ungeachtet aller situations-, personen- und zweckbedingter Diversifikationen in eine einheitliche, stabile Form gebracht wird, findet in der auffälligen Anonymität der Besucher ihre Entsprechung. Denn wie die neben Clitumnus verehrten Gottheiten, so bleiben auch die Verfasser der Wandgraffiti unspezifiziert. Da keine einzige der Inschriften im Wortlaut zitiert oder zumindest paraphrasiert wird, bleibt es dem Leser überlassen, diese Leerstelle aus seiner eigenen Kenntnis der Votivpraxis und ihrer typischen Inschriftenformen aufzufüllen, ohne über die persönlichen Motivationen der Verfasser und etwaige (orts-/ kult)spezischen Konventionen näher informiert zu sein.

Von der namenlosen Menge der Heiligtumsbesucher setzt sich nun umso markanter der Briefliterat ab, der sich selbst in der Eröffnung als ein begeisterter Besucher des Heiligtums einführt. Abgesehen davon, dass Plinius eine ganz unmittelbare Vermittlung seiner Reiseeindrücke verheißt, verfügt er als literarisch Vorgebildeter, als Einwohner der Transpadana und als renommiertes Mitglied der norditalischen Lokalelite über besondere Qualitäten, aufgrund derer er für eine adäquate Beschreibung dieses Heiligtums geradezu prädestiniert ist. Im Folgenden soll näher erläutert werden, wie Plinius seine persönliche Disposition für den sakralen Ort in Szene setzt und sich damit literarisch in die norditalische Erinnerungslandschaft des *Clitumnus fons* einschreibt.

5 Die individuelle Perspektive des Heiligtumsbesuchers

Bereits die Einleitung des Briefs impliziert, dass das Quellheiligtum des Clitumnus – anders als etwa die intermittierende Quelle am Comer See (*epist.* 4,30) – einem gebildeten Briefliteraten wie Plinius nicht unbekannt war und ihn daher eigentlich schon längst zu einer Reise in das nahe Umbrien hätte veranlassen müssen. Umso mehr reut ihn nun der Zeitverzug: Hat doch der persönliche Ortseindruck alle Vorerwartungen übertroffen, die – so darf man unterstellen – auf der Lektüre einschlägiger Texte beruhten.

Die Eröffnung deutet indirekt an, dass das Ortslob auf den Fluss Clitumnus geradezu den Rang eines literarischen Topos beanspruchen kann und der Brief daher im konkurrierenden Vergleich mit älteren *laudes Italiae* sein eigenes Profil gewinnen wird.[22] Der schwach markierte, nicht näher präzisierte Intertextualitätsverweis ist mit einem versteckten Kompliment an den Adressaten verknüpft: Gerade weil der literaturkundige Romanus die Quelle längst aus Büchern kennt, wird er alle im Brief enthaltenen Varianten und Zusätze anerkennend vermerken. In der Tat hatten frühere Dichter – die Palette reicht von Vergil über Properz und Statius bis zu Silius Italicus – die Quelle des Clitumnus stets nur summarisch als „schattig" und „eiskalt", als „heilig" und „schön" charakterisiert.[23] Für seine auf Autopsie beruhende Beschreibung beansprucht Plinius demgegenüber eine größere Bildlichkeit, einen inhaltlichen Mehrwert und eine neue Perspektive auf den bekannten Gegenstand.

Wie uns die Prätexte einhellig lehren, ist der *Clitumnus fons* vor allem mit einem Markenzeichen belegt, das jeder literarisch gebildete Römer sofort mit dem Ortsnamen in Verbindung bringen wird: Die üppigen Weiden am Fluss bringen besonders prächtige Rinder hervor, die dank ihrer Farbe vorzugsweise für die stadtrömischen Triumphe verwendet wurden. Der literarische Topos der „schneeweißen Opferrinder vom Clitumnus" legt nahe, dass die Rinder womöglich das Produkt einer speziell auf den religiösen Absatzmarkt ausgerichteten Zucht waren.

Ausgerechnet dieses bekannteste Markenzeichen der Örtlichkeit bleibt nun freilich im Pliniusbrief unerwähnt – eine Beobachtung, die die ältere Pliniusforschung zutiefst irritiert und zur Suche nach Erklärungen genötigt hat: Will man etwa ECKARD LEFÈVRE folgen, so hat der Briefliterat den Geschichtsbezug bewusst unterdrückt, um die Ästhetik der Naturschilderung nicht zu stören. Nach seiner Auffassung „gehören Landschaft und Religion zusammen. Das Thema ‚Geschichte' hätte das Genos gesprengt."[24] Ich möchte dieser Behauptung aus zwei Gründen

---

22 Zu den *laudes Italiae*: GÄRTNER; HARTMANN 2003.
23 Verg. *georg.* 2,147–149: *hinc albi, Clitumne, greges et maxima taurus / victima, saepe tuo perfusi flumine sacro, / Romanos ad templa deum duxere triumphos*; Prop. 2,19,25 f.: *qua formosa suo Clitumnus flumina luco / integit*; Prop. 3,22,23 f.: *Clitumnus ab Umbro / tramite*; Stat. *silv.* 1,4,128–131: *nec si vacuet Mevania valles, / aut praestent niveos Clitumna novalia tauros, / sufficiam*; Sil. 4,544–546: *Mevanas Varenus, arat cui divitis uber / campi Fulginia et patulis Clitumnus in arvis / candentis gelido perfundit flumine tauros*; Iuv. 12,13–17: *laeta sed ostendens Clitumni pascua sanguis / et grandi cervix iret ferienda ministro / ob reditum trepidantis adhuc horrendaque passi / nuper et incolumem sese mirantis amici*.
24 LEFÈVRE 1988, 247 und 262.

widersprechen: Zum einen gehören die Opferrinder zunächst und vor
allem zur religiösen Sphäre – ein Rückgriff auf das Themenfeld „Geschichte" ist dafür, wie die Mehrzahl der poetischen Erwähnungen be-
stätigen, nicht unbedingt nötig bzw. erfolgt erst sekundär. Zum anderen
hat Plinius den Aspekt der Geschichte aus seiner Ortsbeschreibung ja gar
nicht ausgeblendet, sondern vielmehr neue Akzente gesetzt, indem er
seine erklärte Bewunderung für die norditalische Vergangenheit im de-
monstrativ „privaten" Gestus des literarischen Briefs konsequent persönlich perspektiviert.

Die summarischen Erwähnungen des Clitumnus werden nun durch
eine „dichte Beschreibung" des Quellheiligtums abgelöst, die bislang
unerwähnte und unbekannte Qualitäten ans Licht treten lässt: Das ver-
gilische Italienlob[25] hatte den umbrischen Clitumnus aus einer römisch-
imperialen Perspektive als einen erstrangigen Zulieferanten von Opfer-
rindern ausgewiesen, die im hauptstädtischen Triumphzug die kontinuierliche Ausdehnung und Wehrhaftigkeit des augusteischen Weltreichs
visualisieren. Auch in den Elegien des Properz dominiert eine erklärt
stadtrömische Sicht: Hier wird der Clitumnus zu einer bukolischen
Gegenwelt stilisiert, in der sich das elegische Ich die harmlose Jagd auf
Vögel und Hasen – und vor allem die Erfüllung seiner Liebe zu Cynthia –
als Wunschbild ausmalt.

Plinius nimmt dagegen eine neue Haltung ein, wenn er den *Clitumnus
fons* als ideales Reiseziel für die urbane Bildungselite empfiehlt: Zwar
behält er eine stadtrömische Perspektive bei, doch fokussiert er zugleich
den Blick auf die lokalen Kulttraditionen. Der *Clitumnus fons*, der vormals
nur als Dienstleister für die Bedürfnisse der Hauptstadt – sei es als Baustein
der Katalogdichtung oder als Kulisse für elegische Liebesträume – diente,
avanciert damit erstmals zu einem eigenständigen Beschreibungsgegen-
stand. Der schattige Hain wird aufgewertet zu einem sakralen Ort, an dem
die altitalische Religion in besonderer Intensität bewahrt und gegenwärtig ist. Die Briefbeschreibung des umbrischen Heiligtums schließt
damit an themenverwandte Briefe an, in denen Plinius emphatisch die
norditalischen Regionen zum Inbegriff der tradierten altrömischen
Wertewelt – der Bescheidenheit, der Sittenstrenge und alten Ländlichkeit

---

25 Hierzu McKay 1972; Cramer 1998, 70–114; Jenkins 1998, 350–371; Gale
    2000, 214–219; zu Vergil und der Transpadana Goodfellow 1977; Gasser
    1999, 62–73; Mratschek 1984, 160–171; Mratschek 2003.

– stilisiert,[26] ja sogar zur utopischen Ideallandschaft einer *aurea aetas* verklärt.[27]

Insbesondere im zweiten Teil der Ekphrasis wird deutlich, dass der Briefliterat entgegen der naturästhetischen Interpretation von ECKARD LEFÈVRE keine „zeitlos-schwebende" Sakrallandschaft, wie sie die pompejanischen Wandmalereien erzeugen, sondern vielmehr einen persönlichen Erinnerungsort beschreibt. Im Dienst einer konsequenten Fokalisierung setzt Plinius die norditalische Landschaft, den Quellgott und seine eigene Person in einen engen Bezug: Wenn er als erste Qualität das hohe Alter des ehrwürdigen Tempels nennt, so macht er damit sich und dem Leser bewusst, dass er – ähnlich wie beim Besuch seiner tuscischen Villa – in das „Land der Vorfahren" gereist ist.[28] Als geschichtskundiger Besucher, der sich aufgrund seiner Heimatbindung an die Transpadana auch und gerade der norditalischen Landschaft und ihren Werttraditionen eng verbunden fühlt, ist Plinius besonders empfänglich für die Dignität und Bodenständigkeit des Clitumnus. Daher schenkt er auch der Gestalt des Kultbilds besondere Aufmerksamkeit: Der ehrwürdige Gott war bezeichnenderweise nicht im üblichen Bildtypus des liegenden Flussgotts,[29] sondern stehend dargestellt und mit der purpurverbrämten Toga bekleidet, die die stadtrömischen Beamten und Priester mit altrömischer *auctoritas* auszeichnet.[30]

Die enge Ortsbindung des umbrischen Quellgotts dokumentiert sich zudem in der Existenz eines Losorakels *(sortes)*.[31] Denn damit ist eine typisch italische Kultpraxis bezeichnet: In Griechenland und Kleinasien überwiegt die Inspiration eines Mediums, etwa der Pythia in Delphi. Dagegen werden in den italischen Heiligtümern die Bescheide üblicherweise durch das Ziehen und Deuten von beschrifteten Lostäfelchen eingeholt. Im Unterschied zu den Orakeln in der östlichen Reichshälfte

---

26 Z.B. in *epist.* 1,14,4: *patria est ei Brixia ex illa nostra Italia, quae multum adhuc verecundiae, frugalitatis atque etiam rusticitatis antiquae retinet ac servat.* Dazu MRATSCHEK 1984, 171 f.; GASSER 1999, 186–216.

27 *Epist.* 5,6,4–13.

28 Vgl. *epist.* 5,6,6: *hinc senes multi; videas avos proavosque iam iuvenum, audias fabulas veteres sermonesque maiorum, cumque veneris illo, putes alio te saeculo natum.*

29 OSTROWSKI 1991; KLEMENTA 1992.

30 So bereits beobachtet von LEFÈVRE 1988, 261; SCHEID 1996, 255. GALLI 1941 vermutet die Ausführung des Kultbilds in Form einer mit Gewändern bekleideten Akrolithstatue, die sowohl dem archaisierenden Charakter als auch den ländlich-altitalischen Bildtraditionen entspräche.

31 Zur italischen Orakelpraxis CHAMPEAUX 1990, 1990a, 1990b.

ist weiterhin der Einzugsbereich der auskunftsgebenden Götter in Italien lokal begrenzt. Nicht einmal das imposante Terrassenheiligtum von Praeneste, das sich rühmen kann, die größte Kultanlage auf italischem Boden zu sein, erreicht eine überregionale Bedeutung.[32] Ein Pendant zum griechischen Apoll, der in den überregionalen Orakelorten Delphi, Didyma und Klaros amtiert, gibt es demnach in Italien nicht. Statt den (begrenzten) Einzugskreis des Losorakels am *Clitumnus fons* zu thematisieren, hebt daher Plinius im Gegenzug die individualisierende Kultvielfalt im umbrischen Heiligtum hervor.

Im sukzessiven Abschreiten der Kapellen, die sich dem Clitumnus-Tempel angelagert haben, macht sich der Besucher Plinius das Spektrum und die individuelle Persönlichkeit der norditalischen Götter gegenwärtig. Seine temporäre Anwesenheit als pietätvoller Verehrer des Clitumnus verstetigt freilich der Briefliterat im signifikanten Unterschied zu allen anderen Besuchern gerade nicht vor Ort durch die Aufstellung eines Dankvotivs oder die Abfassung eines Graffito. Vielmehr schreibt er sich im Medium des transportablen Briefs literarisch der umbrischen Sakrallandschaft ein, indem er der Beschreibung des Heiligtums seine persönliche Perspektive einprägt.

Wenn bereits die ehrwürdige Kultstatue des Quellgotts und die bodenständige Praxis des Losorakels dem Heiligtum und seinem Besitzer ein betont altitalisches Flair verleihen, so wird diese wertekonservative Aura nochmals durch den expliziten Bezug auf Augustus verstärkt. Denn nach Plinius verdankt die Clitumnus-Quelle ihre aktuelle Bedeutung der einstigen Würdigung durch den Princeps: Dieser hatte die Vorrangstellung der iulischen Kolonie Hispellum im umbrischen Gebiet dadurch sanktioniert, dass er den Hispellaten die Verwaltung des Heiligtums übertrug. Die Stadteinwohner dankten ihm im Gegenzug für dieses Ehrengeschenk, indem sie seitdem den Heiligtumsbesuchern kostenfrei Bad und Herberge bereitstellten.[33]

Mit dem exemplarischen Kultrestaurator Augustus erhält der Pliniusbrief nun aber nicht nur historische Tiefe. Denn verbunden wird dieser Verweis mit einem verdeckten Appell zur Aktualisierung: Bezeichnenderweise hebt Plinius gerade nicht die militärische Sieghaftigkeit des Princeps hervor, sondern seine vorbildliche Städteverwaltung und Re-

---

32 Mit guten Argumenten herausgearbeitet durch FRATEANTONIO 2011.
33 Zur Verwaltung des *Clitumnus fons* und zum Rechtsstatus der augusteischen Koloniestadt Hispellum SCHEID 1996, 246 f., der hier ein typisches Grenzheiligtum vermutet.

ligionspolitik, also zwei Bereiche, in denen die trajanischen Eliten – und namentlich der Briefschreiber selbst – vorrangig tätig sind.[34] Augustus kann daher zu Plinius' persönlicher Identifikationsfigur stilisiert werden: Hat der Princeps doch schon damals dem altitalischen Quellheiligtum seine besondere Aufmerksamkeit geschenkt und zugleich die Hispellaten durch den Gestus des Gebens zum freiwilligen Gewähren von Leistungen motiviert.

Durch Augustus' großzügiges Geschenk und die entsprechende Reaktion der Führungsschicht von Hispellum kann sich Plinius nicht nur in seiner Zugehörigkeit zur norditalischen Elite und in seinen Leistungen für das Gemeinwohl und für den Kaiser bestärkt, sondern vor allem in seinen privat finanzierten Tempel- und Statuenstiftungen zur Imitation des kaiserlichen Vorbilds motiviert sehen.[35] Darüber hinaus sind die Leser der Pliniusbriefe gehalten, sich ihrerseits an Plinius ein Beispiel zu nehmen und sich im Konsens mit dem Kaiser Trajan für die Prestigesteigerung der eigenen Heimatstadt und für den Erhalt regionaler Heiligtümer einzusetzen.

Insgesamt vermittelt das Landschaftsbild vom *Clitumnus fons* in seiner Akzentuierung und demonstrativen Bewahrung norditalischer Werttraditionen (*verecundia, pietas, rusticitas*) dem Leser ein beispielhaftes Selbstporträt des Adressanten Plinius. Dabei wird der praktizierten Religion eine wichtige Stellung im Bildungs- und Vergangenheitsdiskurs der Briefe zugeschrieben. Ihre Bedeutung bestätigt sich in einer beträchtlichen Zahl von Briefen, die religiöse Themen zur Sprache bringen und vorzugsweise an prominenter Stelle in den Briefbüchern platziert sind.[36] Darüber hinaus sind im Brief 8,8 die persönliche Kommunikation im literarisierten Privatbrief und die religiöse Kommunikation im Votivkult für Clitumnus konsequent aufeinander bezogen. Dieser Aspekt wird im nächsten Kapitel im Zentrum stehen, wobei insbesondere die zur Kommunikation eingesetzten Medien ausgeleuchtet werden sollen.

---

34 Zum Verhältnis von Selbstdarstellung, Personenporträt und Inszenierung eines sozialen Netzwerks PAUSCH 2004, 71–78.
35 Siehe *epist.* 3,6 (Statuenstiftung für den Iuppitertempel in Como); 4,1 (Tempelstiftung); 9,39 (Tempelrestauration); 10,8 (Tempel- und Statuenstiftung für den Kaiserkult).
36 Mit der *laudatio funebris* auf Verginius Rufus wird das 2. Briefbuch eröffnet, mit der Tempelstiftung von Tifernum Tibertinum wird das vierte Buch; die Statuenstiftung für den Iuppitertempel (*epist.* 3,6) ist ihrerseits zwischen zwei Literatenporträts (3,5 Plinius d.Ä., 3,7 Silius Italicus) gesetzt.

6 Religiöse und literarische Kommunikation an der Quelle

Ausgangspunkt ist meine in der Einleitung formulierte Annahme, dass der Brief vom *Clitumnus fons* einen hohen Selbstbezug besitzt: Indem die Ekphrasis die Funktionen und Techniken religiöser und brieflicher Kommunikation abbildet und miteinander verschränkt, impliziert sie zugleich einen Wettbewerb zwischen den persönlichen Votiven an der Quelle und dem literarischen Freundschaftspräsent.

Die Charakteristika brieflicher Kommunikation lassen sich am Anfang der Epistel 8,8 noch gut greifen. So kann Plinius aufgrund der Distanz nur vermuten, dass sein Freund die Clitumnus-Quelle noch nicht mit eigenen Augen gesehen hat. Anstelle einer Reiseerzählung soll daher ein Bild die persönlichen Ortseindrücke übermitteln. Innerhalb der Ekphrasis tritt folgerichtig die Anrede des Adressaten zugunsten der Imagination zurück. Erst am Ende wird Romanus als virtueller Clitumnus-Besucher nachträglich in das Gemälde eingeblendet.

Die eigentliche Raffinesse des Briefs liegt nun darin, dass er sich mit dieser Leerstelle gewissermaßen einen Durchblick auf die Sakrallandschaft eröffnet. Auf diese Weise wird die briefliche Kommunikation im beschreibenden Mittelteil auf eine andere Ebene verlagert, nämlich auf die der religiösen Kommunikation in Form ritueller Handlungen. Als signalverstärkende Medien erwähnt Plinius

- erstens Münzen, die frühere Besucher in die Quelle geworfen haben,
- zweitens beschriftete Losstäbchen des Orakels, das Besucher konsultieren können,
- drittens Graffiti an Wänden und Säulen, die von Clitumnus' Wirkkraft zeugen.

Indem der Heiligtumsbesucher Plinius die Aufmerksamkeit des Lesers auf diese visuellen Indizien praktizierter Religion lenkt, eröffnet er sich neue Möglichkeiten zur literarischen Selbstpositionierung: Kann doch nun seine transportable Briefmitteilung die religiösen Kommunikationstechniken und -medien vor Ort erfolgreich überbieten.

Nehmen wir zunächst die einzelnen Medien religiöser Kommunikation näher in den Blick.[37] Da die Gemeinsamkeiten und Unterschiede zwischen Votiv und Brief bereits oben auf einer allgemeinen Ebene erörtert wurden, lassen sich nun auf dieser Grundlage die Spezifika, Vorzüge und Grenzen der Münzen, Losstäbchen und Graffiti näher bestimmen.

---

37   Unter anderer Akzentsetzung bereits durch SCHEID 1996, 250 f. besprochen.

Unter den drei im Brief erwähnten Medien sind die Münzen am wenigsten auf einen Kommunikationskontext festgelegt: Im Gegensatz zu den Orakelstäbchen und Graffiti waren sie ursprünglich für andere, profane Kontexte gefertigt und an ein offenes, nicht näher definiertes Publikum gerichtet. Erst durch ihre rituelle Deponierung in der Quelle werden sie an Clitumnus als neuen Primäradressaten umgewidmet. Bei dem Münzopfer handelt es sich somit um einen Kommunikationsakt, dessen Initiative stets von den Menschen ausgeht. Anders als die Orakellose und die Graffiti nimmt der Betrachter die Münzen vor allem in ihrer Bildlichkeit wahr: Ausdrücklich weist der Brief darauf hin, dass das glasklare Wasser der Quelle den Blick auf die Münzen und Kieselsteine am Flussgrund ermögliche. Vor allen späteren Heiligtumsbesuchern, die sekundär angesprochen werden, dokumentieren die Münzen den Vollzug des Opfers, die *pietas* der anonymen Spender und die Wirkmacht des Quellgotts. Offen bleibt dabei nicht nur, ob das Münzopfer von einem verbalen Kommunikationsakt begleitet wurde; auch der situations- und personengebundene Anlass – sei es Wunsch oder Dank –, der Zeitpunkt sowie der Stifter der Gabe lassen sich von den späteren Besucher nicht mehr rekonstruierend erschließen.

Gegenüber den Münzgaben ist die Kommunikation zwischen Menschen und Gottheit im Medium des Losorakels an besondere formale Vorgaben gebunden:[38] Im Gegensatz zum inspirierten Seher, dessen mündliche Aussage im Trancezustand keiner Vorkontrolle unterliegt und erst nachträglich in eine gebundene Sprache übertragen wird, ist der schriftliche Orakelbescheid bereits im Vorfeld fixiert. Gestaltung und Umfang der Texte sind zusätzlich durch die Form und Größe des Schriftträgers präterminiert. Verstärkt wird die Reglementierung durch den Einsatz eines *sortilegus*, der als Kontroll- und Vermittlungsinstanz fungiert.

Die Existenz eines Orakels stellt demnach ein adressatenunspezifisches Kommunikationsangebot der Quellgottheit dar; erst durch die Formulierung einer individuellen Anfrage an Clitumnus wird die Kommunikation in Gang gesetzt. Während dabei der Besucher den Gott Clitumnus als Adressaten eindeutig und namentlich spezifiziert, werden dessen optionale Antworten erst durch die Auswahl eines Loses auf eine einzige Botschaft reduziert und dem Anfragenden persönlich zugeordnet. Dieser verfügt seinerseits bei der präzisierenden Auslegung der Botschaft über gewisse Freiräume. Der schriftlichen Festlegung der Texte steht also

---

38 Grundlegend hierzu CHAMPEAUX 1990; 1990a, bes. 816–828; 1990b.

eine prinzipielle Deutungsoffenheit gegenüber. Die Möglichkeit des
kommunikativen Missverständnisses wird in Einzelfällen den Orakel-
texten selbst eingeschrieben: Auf einem in die späte Republik datie-
renden Orakelstäbchen aus Bahareno wird der Vorwurf einer Fehlaus-
kunft ausdrücklich zurückgewiesen. Das Scheitern der Kommunikation
wird damit in die Verantwortlichkeit des Anfragenden überstellt, der das
Orakel falsch konsultiert habe.[39]

Im Gegensatz zum *votum*, für das die Zeitverschiebung zwischen
Gelübde, Antwort und Erfüllung des Gelübdes konstitutiv ist, antwortet
der Gott bei Einholung eines Losorakels sofort. Allerdings dürfte am
Clitumnus fons die Konsultation des Orakels, wie JOHN SCHEID im Verweis
auf Praeneste plausibel gemacht hat,[40] nur in enger zeitlicher Beschrän-
kung, d. h. wahrscheinlich nur zu bestimmten Tagen im Jahr möglich
gewesen sein: Nach Aussage der *Fasti Praenestini* stand das Orakel in
Praeneste an zwei Festtagen im April zur Befragung offen.[41] Im Quellheiligtum des Clitumnus weisen laut Plinius „Orakeltäfelchen darauf hin,
dass eine Gottheit anwesend ist und auch weissagt". Dies lässt vermuten,
dass ein am Tempel angebrachtes Reliefbild – sei es im Tempelgiebel, auf
den Tempeltüren oder den Wänden – auf die Kompetenzen des
Clitumnus als Orakelgottheit verwies.[42] Die im Brief erwähnten *sortes*
signalisieren dem Tempelbesucher somit optisch die prinzipielle An-
sprechbarkeit, die Gegenwart und die weissagende Kraft der Quellgottheit, ohne dass damit ein kontinuierlicher Orakelbetrieb notwendig
vorauszusetzen wäre.

Gegenüber den Münzgaben und den Orakellosen, die erst im rituellen Kommunikationsakt eindeutig adressiert werden, zeichnen sich die
Graffiti an den Tempelwänden, die als drittes Kommunikationsmedium
erwähnt werden, durch einen deutlich höheren Grad der Individualisierung aus: Die namentliche Bezeichnung von Adressat und Adressant ist
ein genuiner Bestandteil aller im Votivkult gebräuchlichen Inschriften-
formulare.

---

39 CIL 1², 2184: *non sum mendacis quas dixti consulis stulte.* Abbildung bei CHAM-
    PEAUX 1990, 298, Fig. 15.
40 SCHEID 1996, 250–252.
41 *F. Praen.: [biduo sacrific]ium maximu[m] / [fit] Fortunae Prim[i]g(eniae). Utro eorum
    die / [eius] oraclum patet.*
42 Wie man sich dies vorzustellen hat, kann ein Blick auf den Apolltempel auf dem
    Palatin illustrieren: Dort fungierten die mit Dreifüßen gezierten Eingangstüren
    als Bildchiffre für die Sehergabe des Tempelbesitzers: BALENSIEFEN 2002, 100
    Abb. 132.

Allerdings ist dabei in Rechnung zu stellen, dass sich reguläre Votivinschriften und Graffiti ungeachtet gewisser Schnittmengen in ihren sprachlichen Kommunikationsformen und ihrer visuellen Darstellung ebenso wie in ihren Produktions- und Rezeptionsmechanismen unterscheiden: Votivinschriften sind üblicherweise auf einem eigenen, möglichst repräsentativen Schriftträger – sei es eine Tafel, ein gemaltes Votivbild oder ein Votivaltar – angebracht und durch relativ enge Sprach- und Gestaltungskonventionen normiert, ja geradezu stereotypisiert. „Individualreligion" führt hier offenkundig nicht zu einer eigenständigen oder gar kreativen Text- und Bildgestaltung, sondern artikuliert sich lediglich in der Nennung des Namens und gegebenenfalls des Stiftungsanlasses. Im Unterschied zu den standardisierten Votivinschriften und -geschenken, die zumindest mit Einwilligung, wenn nicht auf die ausdrückliche Aufforderung seitens der Gottheit bzw. des verantwortlichen Kultpersonals hin gestiftet und aufgestellt werden, sind die Graffiti informell und unregelmentiert, ja zu großen Teilen sogar illegal platziert: Mehrere überlieferte Sakralvorschriften enthalten explizite Verbote, Wände und Säulen in Kultanlagen mit Graffiti zu bekritzeln.[43]

Gerade dadurch, dass solche persönlichen Zeugnisse „billiger Individualreligion" die gesetzten Regeln und Konventionen unterlaufen und optisch eher unscheinbar sind, eröffnen sie dem jeweiligen Verfasser maximale Freiheiten.[44] Ein vergleichender Blick auf die fragmentarisch erhaltenen Graffiti im Heiligtum des Hercules Curinus in Sulmo lässt die Palette von Gestaltungsmöglichkeiten zumindest erahnen:[45] Das Spektrum reicht dort von mehr oder minder konventionellen Votivformeln, die sich im konkret-pragmatischen Ziel der schriftlich fixierten Danksagung erschöpfen,[46] über die namentliche Verewigung vor Ort *(hic fuit ...)*[47] bis zu ambitionierten Produkten, die den Anspruch einer ästhetischen Formung, ja einer bewussten Literarisierung erkennen lassen.[48]

---

43 ILS 4335: *C. Iulius Anicetus / ex imperio Solis / rogat, ne quis velit / parietes aut triclias / inscribere aut / scariphare;* SOKOLOWSKI 1962, Nr. 123.
44 Zu Graffiti als Kommunikationsmedien VOEGTLE 2012.
45 BUONOCORE 1989; zusammenfassend SCHEID 1996, 250 f.
46 BUONOCORE 1989, Nr. 13: *C(aius) Nonius L(uci) f(ilius) Serg(ia) [---] / e munici[p]io Sulmone p[romisit], / miles, Herc[ul]i curino sei salv[us e] / castris redis(s)et, vot[a ferre?] / ver(r)em et vitulu[m]; / et votis dam[natus, / a]dest.*
47 BUONOCORE 1989, Nr. 17:—/ [h]abes / [---] hic fuit / [—Hercul]ei Corino.
48 BUONOCORE 1989, Nr. 11: *Augustis, te sancte Curin[e], / digna paramus; spectat / nam debita solvere vota, / numenque sacratum / ecce venit felixque pat[et]; / pristina vota*

Eine Kombination von Bild und Text ist unter den in Sulmo überlieferten Wandgraffiti zwar nicht bezeugt, aber prinzipiell denkbar – auch wenn statistisch bei den Graffiti die reinen Texte eindeutig dominieren.

Primäradressat aller Graffiti ist, wie Plinius ausdrücklich hervorhebt, der Quellgott Clitumnus. Zugleich konstituieren die Wandkritzeleien jedoch eine Öffentlichkeit für die religiöse Handlung. Die Existenz von späteren Lesern ist bereits bei der Abfassung einberechnet und schlägt sich im inschriftlichen Habitus nieder: Ein Spezifikum der unerlaubt verschriftlichten Graffiti ist ihre hohe Appellkraft. So kann ein Graffito eine ganze Sequenz von kommentierenden Antworten und Gegenmeinungen provozieren. Offenkundig bieten gerade die Gestaltungsfreiheit, die geringe Normiertheit und die unkontrollierte Fixierung der Graffiti hohe Anreize, die den Leser zur spontanen Fortsetzung der Texte animieren.

Gerade dieser letzte Aspekt, die appellative Gestaltung der persönlichen Mitteilung im Blick auf eine spätere Öffentlichkeit, bildet ein Bindeglied zwischen den anspruchslosen Graffiti und dem stilisierten Brief: Da die briefliche Erzählung vom *Clitumnus fons* auf das Lob des Heiligtums zielt, leistet sie letztlich ganz ähnliches wie die im Schlussabschnitt erwähnten Wandgraffiti, die ihrerseits die Wirkmacht des Clitumnus preisen und ihren Leser zu einem ebensolchen Lob zu motivieren suchen.

Die anschauliche Ekphrasis lädt ihrerseits den Leser ein, über das Verhältnis von Bild und Text nachzudenken. Unter ästhetischen Kriterien ist das literarische Landschaftsgemälde unstrittig höher einzustufen als die unscheinbaren Schriftzeichen am Tempelgebäude. Dennoch enthalten ausgerechnet die Graffiti den Schlüssel zur literarischen Bilddeutung: Eine Sonderstellung der Säulen- und Wandkritzeleien ist dadurch implizit markiert, dass sie nicht in ihrem ursprünglichen Ortskontext, das heißt zusammen mit dem Tempel und Kultbild in der Briefmitte, erwähnt werden. Stattdessen sind sie funktional dem Resümee zugeordnet. Ihre gründliche Lektüre bleibt einem idealen Besucher wie Plinius vorbehalten, der sie nicht nur als „billige Massenware" in einem summarischen Gesamteindruck der vollgeschriebenen Säulen und Tempelwände zur Kenntnis nimmt, sondern vielmehr ihrem individuellen Anliegen und ihrer jeweiligen sprachlichen Ausgestaltung Rechnung trägt, indem er sie geradezu durchstudiert. Derselbe Anspruch ist für den Adressaten Romanus vorauszusetzen, den Plinius zur vertieften Textlektüre auffordert.

---

feren[tes / veni]mus, scimus qui fuerint; ipse[met] / isdem ces voves H(erculi) C(urino) V (ictori?) / si mis omnia ex sen[tentia].

Indem nun die literarische Beschreibung an rhetorischer Feile die Wandkritzeleien zweifellos weit übertrifft und das Bild einer Sakrallandschaft im Text erzeugt, kombiniert sie den appellativen Habitus der Graffiti mit der werbenden Repräsentationskraft der Votivpraxis: Inspiriert von der sakralen Landschaft und motiviert von der Graffitilektüre, errichtet Plinius mit dem Brief ein literarisches Votiv, das dem ideellen Wert und der Schönheit des Ortes entspricht. Dabei feiert sein eigenes Weihgeschenk nicht nur die Wirkkraft des Clitumnus, sondern auch die Sprachkunst des Stifters.

Abschließend ist zu bedenken, dass Plinius dieses Votiv als Freundschaftsgeschenk dem Briefadressaten weiht. Das Reisepräsent würdigt Romanus als idealen Bildbetrachter und Leser des Briefs. Dadurch erhält der Schlusspassus, der vordergründig nur die angemessene Rezeptionshaltung gegenüber den Wandgraffiti vorschreibt, eine neue Vielschichtigkeit: Obwohl sich der Lektüreappell streng genommen nur auf die Graffiti im Heiligtum bezieht, lässt er sich doch aufgrund seiner exponierten Endstellung im Rückblick auch auf den Brief übertragen. Eine solche Deutung legen auch die Werturteile nahe, die laut Plinius aus der künftigen Lektüre der Wandkritzeleien entspringen könnten und im Brief bereits antizipiert sind: Die persönliche Religiosität altitalischer Färbung, die der Besucher Plinius von den Graffiti auf sein literarisches Votiv überträgt, mag dem Briefempfänger Romanus vielleicht ein leises Lächeln entlocken. Andererseits kann die kunstvolle Ekphrasis des heiligen Hains zu Recht beanspruchen, ein geeigneter Gegenstand für das Studium in Mußestunden zu sein. Vor allem aber darf der Briefschreiber voraussetzen, dass der gebildete Freund ungeachtet aller sprachlichen Qualitätsunterschiede an den Wandritzungen und am stilisierten Brief den Gestus der ehrenden Zueignung wertschätzen und nicht belächeln wird.

7 Ein briefliches Freundschaftsvotiv

Wie stehen nun aber die Aussichten, dass der Briefadressat den ins Bild eingeschriebenen Leserappell auch realisiert? Nehmen wir die literarische Inszenierung von Adressant und Adressat näher in den Blick: Wie zu zeigen sein wird, ist Romanus in der Briefsammlung wie kein anderer Freund als Plinius' *alter ego* gezeichnet. Daher liegt die Vermutung nahe, dass er für die Leserschaft Modellfunktion hat. Ein Streifzug durch die für

unsere Fragestellung besonders einschlägigen Romanus-Briefe kann diese
These erhärten.[49]

Ich setze bei der Überlegung an, dass die Epistel 8,8 nicht ausschließlich als privates Reisepräsent für Romanus abgefasst ist. Denn
Plinius hat bekanntlich seine Briefe selbst publiziert; mit diesem erlesenen
Corpus wendet er sich an eine größere Öffentlichkeit, der nun eine
kontinuierliche Lektüre der Einzelbriefe ermöglicht wird.[50] Diese neue
Rezeptionsebene ermöglicht einerseits eine differenziertere Figurenzeichnung der Adressaten und eine facettenreiche Selbstdarstellung des
einen Adressanten Plinius. Namentlich „Mehrfachadressaten" wie Romanus, die im Netzwerk des Plinius einen besonderen Ehrenplatz haben,
gewinnen nun über mehrere Briefe hinweg immer wieder neue Konturen. Andererseits etablieren und unterstützen wiederkehrende Leit-
motive ebenso wie Mehrfachadressaten ergänzend zur Ganzlektüre aller
Briefe eine alternative Wahrnehmungsmöglichkeit des Briefcorpus,
nämlich die der selektiven, themen- oder motivorientierten Querlektüre.

Als Empfänger von acht Briefen gehört Romanus – neben dem
Historiker Tacitus und dem Dichter Caninius – zu den drei am häufigsten
genannten Briefadressaten. Die quantitative Nachrangigkeit gegenüber
Tacitus wird durch eine besondere Intensität der Gemeinschaft ausge-
glichen. Plinius' Beziehung zu Tacitus ist als eine Freundschaft unter
Ungleichen zu bezeichnen: Der hochverehrte Geschichtsschreiber ist für
Plinius ein leuchtendes und kaum erreichbares Vorbild.[51] Romanus ist
dagegen dem Briefautor nicht nur fast gleichrangig und gleichaltrig,
sondern in nahezu jeder Hinsicht geistesverwandt.

Dies macht insbesondere die Epistel 2,13 deutlich. Es handelt sich um
ein Empfehlungsschreiben, mit dem Plinius den Legaten Priscus um
einen Militärposten für Romanus bittet. Nach knappen Angaben zu
Romanus' Stand, Familie und Amtserfahrung als Sonderpriester der
spanischen Provinz begründet Plinius sein eigenes Engagement für den
Freund. Romanus wird als enger Gefährte (contubernalis), als treuer Freund
(fidelis amicus) und angenehmer Gesellschafter (sodalis iucundus) gepriesen.
Die enge Gemeinschaft führt zu einem nahezu deckungsgleichen Lebens-
und Bildungskonzept: Wie Plinius selbst, so hat sich auch Romanus in der
Öffentlichkeit als verantwortungsvoller Beamter, als hochrangiger
Priester und als erfahrener Gerichtsredner bewährt. Darüber hinaus, oder

---

49 Zum Romanus-Zyklus ausführlich KÄHLAU 2010, 12–27.
50 Zur „kommunizierten Kommunikation" der Pliniusbriefe RADICKE 2003.
51 Zu Plinius und Tacitus MARCHESI 2008, 97–143; KÄHLAU 2010, 28–42.

besser: vor allem schreibt er so elegante Briefe, dass man „glauben könnte, die Musen selbst redeten Latein" (§ 7 *epistulas quidem scribit, ut Musas ipsas Latine loqui credas*). Mit diesem besonderen Qualitätsprofil, das zugleich Plinius' eigenes Engagement im Metier des sorgfältig literarisierten Freundschaftsbriefs (und in dessen kompetenter Beurteilung) reflektiert, erweist sich Romanus als ein echter Gesinnungsverwandter, den es in jeder Weise zu unterstützen gilt – umso mehr, als er sich für jede Gefälligkeit so dankbar zeigt, dass er mit diesem Dank den gebenden Freund wiederum zu neuen Gefälligkeiten anspornt: Das religiöse Leitprinzip des *do, ut des* findet damit in der freundschaftlichen Briefkorrespondenz eine literarische Entsprechung.

Mit dem zweckgebundenen Empfehlungsschreiben gibt Plinius dem Sekundärleser eine Handreichung, worauf er in den Romanus zugeeigneten Briefen zu achten hat. In der Tat beleuchten deren jeweilige Inhalte stets auch den Adressaten. Im Fall von Romanus treten dabei vor allem zwei Aspekte in den Vordergrund: zum einen seine rhetorische Bildung und seine herausragenden Rednertalente, und zum anderen die private Interessensgemeinschaft mit dem Briefliteraten Plinius, deren Intensität und inhaltliche Breite den Großteil der im Briefcorpus bedachten Adressaten weit übertrifft.

So sprechen die ersten beide Briefe (*epist.* 1,5 und 2,1) vor allem die besonderen Kompetenzen und Interessen des Redners Romanus an. Dieser wird dann in der Epistel 3,13 gebeten, Plinius' eigene Preisrede auf Kaiser Trajan kritisch zu prüfen. Die amüsante Anekdote in *epist.* 6,15, die von einer verpatzten Gedichtrezitation berichtet, lanciert Romanus' literarische Bildung und Vortragserfahrung, wogegen der Brief 6,33 erneut eine Prozessrede zur Korrektur überstellt.

Der anschließende Brief zum *Clitumnus fons* ist dann seinerseits mit dem in Zyklus nächstfolgenden Brief 9,7 durch das typische Briefmotiv einer gefühlten Gemeinsamkeit trotz räumlicher und zeitlicher Trennung verbunden[52]: Die Ekphrasis im Brief 8,8 erlaubt dem ortsfernen Adressaten Romanus durch eine imaginierende Lektüre den zeitversetzten Besuch im Quellheiligtum, an dem er zweifellos ebenso großen Gefallen finden wird wie sein Briefpartner Plinius. Auch der folgende Brief, *epist.* 9,7, inszeniert eine gemeinsame Leidenschaft beider Freunde: In diesem Fall geht es um den Ausbau von landschaftlich besonders attraktiven Villen, dem beide frönen. Allerdings tun sie dies an unterschiedlichem Ort: Während Plinius vorzugsweise am Comer See in-

---

52 KÄHLAU 2010, 21–23.

vestiert, baut Romanus seinerseits am Meer. Wie in der *epist.* 8,8, so überwindet auch hier die Gesinnungsverwandtschaft die räumliche und zeitliche Distanz.

Den Briefzyklus beschließt ein letzter Brief, der geradezu eine poetologische Dimension erhält und zugleich auf den Porträtbrief 2,13 zurückverweist: In der Epistel 9,28 bestätigt Plinius den Eingang von drei „höchst eleganten, liebenswürdigen und sehnsüchtig erwarteten" Briefen des Romanus (§ 1 *omnes elegantissimas, amantissimas et quales a te venire, praesertim desideratas, oportebat*); zugleich wird dem Freund dessen kompetenter Kommentar zu einer Pliniusrede in intimer Vertrautheit halb scherz-, halb ernsthaft heimgezahlt.

In der Zusammenschau aller Romanusbriefe bestätigt sich, dass dieser Adressat geradezu als Spiegelbild des Plinius gezeichnet ist. Romanus wird damit nicht nur zum perfekten Korrekturleser der plinianischen Reden, sondern auch zum idealen Empfänger seiner ausgearbeiteten Briefe.[53] Auch im Fall des Clitumnus-Briefs wird Romanus als ein geschulter Redner und Verfasser stilistisch hoch gefeilter Episteln zweifellos die rhetorische Gestaltung des Clitumnus-Briefs würdigen: Ist doch das Orts- und Städtelob auch ein prominentes Thema der Schuldeklamation und Festrede.

Insbesondere kann der geistesverwandte Adressat aber das erlesene Reisepräsent als ein Zeugnis von Plinius' engagierter Freundschaft verstehen: Mit seinem literarisierten Bildvotiv erweist Plinius in vorbildhafter Weise dem kundigen Redner, dem musischen Briefautoren, dem provinzialen Priester und namentlich dem gleichgesinnten Freund die Ehre. Dieser wird seinerseits den sakral überhöhten Gestus der persönlichen Widmung als ein besonders elegantes Freundschaftskompliment wertschätzen. Die persönliche Würdigung strahlt selbstredend auf den Autor zurück: Immerhin gereicht ein idealer Leser, der selbst wie die Musen Briefe schreibt, auch einem Plinius zur Ehre.

---

53 Zur Strategie des Plinius, der im Medium der Briefe gezielt seinen Ruhm als Redner lanciert, MAYER 2003.

8 Medienkonkurrenzen in der brieflichen und religiösen Kommunikation

Welche allgemeinen Folgerungen lassen sich nun aus der Analyse des Pliniusbriefs ziehen? Inwiefern eröffnet das Fallbeispiel des *Clitumnus fons* neue, über den Einzeltext hinausweisende Perspektiven? Als ein interpretatorischer Hebel für die rhetorisch sorgfältig durchstilisierte Briefbeschreibung haben sich – einigermaßen überraschend – ausgerechnet die unscheinbaren Graffiti erwiesen; daher sollen abschließend nochmals die spezifischen Qualitäten und die Konkurrenzfähigkeit dieses Kommunikationsmediums innerhalb des plinianischen Briefcorpus und des Votivkults reflektiert werden.

Dass sich der Briefliterat Plinius im Dienste einer vorteilhaften Selbstdarstellung verschiedener Schrift- und Bildmedien bedient, ist in der Pliniusforschung längst erkannt: Neuere Arbeiten haben sich eingehend mit der intermedialen Wechselwirkung von Porträtbriefen und Porträtstatuen bzw. gemalten Bildnissen,[54] mit den ausführlichen Villenbeschreibungen, die den Charakter ihres Besitzer reflektieren,[55] und mit Plinius' großzügigen Stiftungen (Bibliothek und Schule, Tempel, Weihestatue im Iuppitertempel von Como)[56] auseinandergesetzt. Wie sind nun in diesem medialen Spektrum die Graffiti einzuordnen, zu deren aufmerksamer Lektüre der Leser explizit aufgefordert wird? Können diese anspruchlosen Kritzeleien auch nur annähernd mit den hochgradig repräsentativen und publikumswirksamen Monumenten konkurrieren?

Die argumentative Pointe des Briefs 8,8 liegt darin, dass sie gerade aus den produktionsästhetischen Defiziten des Kommunikationsmediums „Graffito" eine umso höhere Tugend des literarisch gebildeten Lesers macht: Eben weil die Graffiti optisch so unscheinbar sind und stilistisch zweifellos weit unter den Ansprüchen des befreundeten Briefadressaten liegen, fordern sie in besonderer Weise dessen wohlwollende Bereitschaft und Fähigkeit, eben nicht nur im sorgfältig literarisierten Freundschaftsbrief, sondern auch in der weit ungefeilteren Textform der Graffiti die persönliche Orts- und Gotteserfahrung wahrzunehmen. Wenn Plinius

---

54 Henderson 2002; Radicke 2003.
55 *Epist.* 2,17; 5,6 und andere; dazu Lefèvre 1977 und 1987; Ludolph 1997, 121–141; Hoffer 1999, 29–44.
56 *Epist.* 1,8 (Bibliothek): Krasser 1996, Kapitel 4.3.1; *epist.* 4,13 (Schule): Manuwald 2003; *epist.* 4,1; 9,39; 10,8 (Tempel): Scheid 1996; *epist.* 3,6 (Weihestatue für Iuppitertempel): Krasser 1996, Kapitel 4.2.3.

dabei voller Zuversicht konstatiert, dass der adressierte Romanus bei
seinem Werturteil – ungeachtet eines leisen Lächelns über die ungelenken
Formulierungen – die dahinter stehende Intention der ehrenden Zueignung lobend anerkennen wird, so ist dieses Kompliment umso größer,
als es sich nicht in den literarischen Kenntnissen des Freundes erschöpft,
sondern primär auf dessen sozialen Kompetenzen, d. h. seine *humanitas,*
zielt.

Gerade der informelle Charakter der Wandkritzeleien, die großenteils
von literarisch ungeübten Besuchern verfasst wurden, plausibilisiert diese
Form der subliterarischen Textproduktion als spontanen Ausdruck eines
persönlichen Bedürfnisses. Was also den Graffiti an formaler Ästhetik
fehlt, das gewinnen sie umgekehrt an individueller Authentizität: Ihr
minimaler materieller Wert wird durch einen beachtlichen ideellen
Aussagewert kompensiert.

Aus diesem Grund sind die Graffiti als ein optionales Medium religiöser Kommunikation für die Heiligtumsbesucher nicht weniger at-
traktiv als repräsentative Votive. Neben der Medienkonkurrenz ist dabei
aber auch der Aspekt des Komplements mitzudenken: PAUL VEYNE hat
darauf hingewiesen, dass im Votivkult üblicherweise Votiv und Inschrift
eine Handlungseinheit bilden.[57] Für die Kommunikationsmedien
„Graffito" und „Votivinschrift" sind nun allerdings zwei verschiedene
Handlungen vorauszusetzen; dies heißt aber noch nicht notwendig, dass
sie einander ausschließende Alternativen darstellen, zumal sie ja durchaus
verschiedene Kommunikationsformen ermöglichen und insofern auch
unterschiedliche Bedürfnisse der Heiligtumsbesucher befriedigen. Gegenüber den stereotypisierten Inschriften der Votive verfügen die
Wandkritzeleien dank ihrer ausgeprägten Kreativität, ihrer appellativen
Experimentierfreude und unreglementierten Gestaltungsfreiheiten über
ein ganz anderes Aussagepotential.

Wie der Pliniusbrief erahnen lässt, wirken sich diese Freiräume auch
auf der rezeptionsästhetischen Seite, d. h. auf das intendierte Sekundär-
publikum der Heiligtumsbesucher, vorteilhaft aus: Während die Votivinschriften auch einen geneigten Leser aufgrund der stetigen Wieder-
holungen normierter Formeln zwangsläufig schnell ermüden müssen,
tragen die Graffiti eine ganz persönliche Handschrift: Der hohe Inno-
vationsgrad und die Spontanität der Äußerung, die sich aus der offenen
Textform ergeben, werden durch das Phänomen der seriellen Kom-
mentierung noch gesteigert und laden damit jeden Leser nicht nur zu

---

57 VEYNE 1983, 290–292.

intensiven Lektüre, sondern auch zur kreativ-variierenden Fortschreibung der Texte ein.

Dagegen handelt es sich beim Votiv zunächst und vor allem um die korrekte Erfüllung einer vertraglich vereinbarten, klar vordefinierten Leistung. Zwar darf man angesichts der existentiellen Krisensituation eine hohe emotionale Engagiertheit voraussetzen, weshalb denn auch kaum eine Votivinschrift darauf verzichtet, die „freudige und verdienstvolle" Einlösung des Gelübdes zu dokumentieren. Dennoch erlaubt das Medium des Votivs nichts weniger als eine spontane Äußerung: Setzt doch seine Einlösung eine längere Planung und gegebenenfalls einen beachtlichen Geldaufwand voraus.

Da umgekehrt die Graffiti zumeist eilig und behelfsmäßig auf dem vergänglichen Schriftträger des Säulen- und Wandverputzes eingekratzt sind, können sie mit dem Schauwert einer sorgfältig gesetzten Inschrift oder einem Votivaltar *a priori* nicht konkurrieren und aufgrund ihres minimalen materiellen Aufwands die spezifische Leistung eines Dankvotivs nicht ersetzen. Sie scheinen vielmehr durch den Wunsch motiviert, sich in größtmöglicher Gottesnähe persönlich zu verewigen: Der Stifter eines Votivs kann sich aufgrund der schieren Masse früher gesetzter Weihegaben leicht auf die zweite oder dritte Reihe – fernab von Kultbild und Tempel – verwiesen sehen. Dagegen kann er sich im Medium des illegalen Graffiti über formelle Normen und Regeln hinwegsetzen und sich eigenmächtig und kompetitiv eine persönliche Nahbeziehung zu Kultbild und Gott erschreiben.[58]

Es dürften eben diese individuellen Freiräume gewesen sein, die den unscheinbaren Graffiti zu ihrer literarischen Nobilitierung im Pliniusbrief verholfen hat: Stehen sie doch in ihrer inhaltlichen und formalen Offenheit sowie in ihrer impliziten Einladung zur respondierenden, ja seriellen Fortsetzung dem Kommunikationsmodus des literarischen Briefs ähnlich nahe wie das Medium des ehrenden Votivs.

Angesichts der sich stetig mehrenden Befunde zur „sakralen Graffitiszene"[59] wäre zweifellos auch die moderne Forschung gut beraten, Plinius' Aufforderung zum intensiven Studium religiös motivierter

---

58 In eine ähnliche Richtung könnte Iuv. *sat.* 10,54–55 weisen, der die Befestigung von Wachstäfelchen mit Gebeten an den Knien der Kultbilder erwähnt: *ergo superuacua aut quae perniciosa petuntur? / propter quae fas est genua incerare deorum?*
59 Graffiti wurden nachgewiesen z.B. im Iseum und im „Komplex der magischen Riten" in Pompeji; einen beachtlichen Fundkomplex stellen die Graffiti im christlichen Tricliakomplex innerhalb der Nekropole von San Sebastiano dar.

Graffiti nachzukommen – in der Gewissheit, dass sie dabei nicht nur leise lächeln, sondern vor allem loben – und neue Erkenntnisse gewinnen könnte. Um mit Plinius zu sprechen: *In summa nihil erit, ex quo non capias voluptatem!*

Bibliographie

BALENSIEFEN, LILIAN 2002. „Die Macht der Literatur. Über die Büchersammlung des Augustus auf dem Palatin", in: HÖPFNER, WOLFRAM (Hrsg.). *Antike Bibliotheken*. Mainz. 97–116.

BEARD, MARY 1991. „Writing and Religion. Ancient Literacy and the Function of the Written Word in Roman Religion", in: dies. *Literacy in the Roman World*. Ann Arbor. 35–58.

BOEHM, GOTTFRIED 1995. „Bildbeschreibung. Über die Grenzen von Bild und Sprache", in: BOEHM, GOTTFRIED; PFOTENHAUER, HELMUT (Hrsg.). *Beschreibungskunst – Kunstbeschreibung*. München. 23–40.

BRODERSEN, KAI (Hrsg.) 2001. *Gebet und Fluch, Zeichen und Traum. Aspekte religiöser Kommunikation in antiken Staatswesen*. Antike Kultur und Geschichte 1. Münster.

BUONOCORE, MARCO 1989. „La Tradizione epigrafica del culto di Ercole tra i Peligni", in: MATTIOCCO, EZIO (Hrsg.). *Dalla Villa di Ovidio al santuario di Ercole*. Sulmona. 193–206.

CASTAGNA, LUIGI; LEFÈVRE, ECKARD (Hrsg.) 2003. *Plinius der Jüngere und seine Zeit*. Beiträge zur Altertumskunde 187. München; Leipzig.

CHAMPEAUX, JACQUELINE 1990. „*Sors Oraculi*. Les oracles en Italie sous la république et l'empire", *Mélanges de l'École française de Rome 102*. 271–302.

—1990a. „,Sorts' et divination inspirée. Pour une préhistoire des oracles Italiques", *Mélanges de l'École française de Rome 102*. 801–828.

—1990b. „Les oracles de l'Italie antique. Hellénisme et italicité", in: *Oracles et mantique en Grèce ancienne*. Colloque de Liège 1989. Kernos 3. 103–111.

—1997. „De la parole à l'écriture. Essai sur le Langage des oracles", in: HEINTZ, JEAN-GEORGE (Hrsg.). *Oracles et prophéties dans l'antiquité*. Actes du Colloque de Strasbourg 15–17 juin 1995. Paris. 405–438.

CRAMER, ROBERT 1998. *Vergils Weltsicht. Optimismus und Pessimismus in Vergils Georgica*. Untersuchungen zur antiken Literatur und Geschichte 51. Berlin; New York.

FANTHAM, ELAINE 1996. „*Religio ... dira loci*. Two Passages in Lucan de Bello Civili 3 and Their Relation to Virgil's Rome and Latium", *Materiali e discussioni per l'analisi dei testi classici 37*. 137–153.

FRATEANTONIO, CHRISTA 2011. „Heiligtum und Orakel der Fortuna Primigenia in Praeneste (Italien)", in: EGELHAAF-GAISER, ULRIKE; PAUSCH, DENNIS; RÜHL, MEIKE (Hrsg.). *Kultur der Antike. Transdisziplinäres Arbeiten in den Altertumswissenschaften*. Berlin. 174–199.

GÄRTNER, URSULA; HARTMANN, ANJA V. 2003. *Zum Lob Italiens in der griechischen Literatur*. Stuttgart.

GALE, MONICA R. 2000. *Virgil on the Nature of Things. The* Georgics, *Lucretius and the Didactic Tradition*. Cambridge.

GALLI, E. 1941. „Clitumnus", *Studi Etruschi 15*. 9–26.

GASSER, FRANZISKA 1999. Germana patria. *Die Geburtsheimat in den Werken römischer Autoren der späten Republik und der frühen Kaiserzeit*. Beiträge zur Altertumskunde 118. Stuttgart; Leipzig.

GOODFELLOW, MARIANNE S. 1977. *Vergil and Transpadane Italy*. Fredericton.

HENDERSON, JOHN 2002. *Pliny's statue. The letters, Self-portraiture and Classical Art*. Exeter.

HINDS, STEPHEN 1998. *Allusion and Intertext. Dynamics of Appropriation in Roman Poetry*. Cambridge.

HOFFER, STANLEY E. 1999. *The Anxieties of Pliny the Younger*. Atlanta.

JENKINS, RICHARD 1998. *Virgil's Experience. Nature and History. Times, Names, and Places*. Oxford.

KÄHLAU, FLORIAN 2010. Quid enim illo aut fidelius amico aut sodale iucundius? *Plinianische Briefzyklen als inszeniertes Freundschaftspräsent*. MA-Arbeit Göttingen.

KLEMENTA, SYLVIA 1992. *Gelagerte Flußgötter des Späthellenismus und der römischen Kaiserzeit*. Bonn.

KRASSER, HELMUT 1996. 'Sine fine lecturias'. *Zu Leseszenen und literarischen Wahrnehmungsgewohnheiten zwischen Cicero und Gellius*. Habilitationsschrift Tübingen.

LEFÈVRE, ECKARD 1977. „Plinius-Studien I. Römische Baugesinnung und Landschaftsauffassung in den Villenbriefen (2,17; 5,6)", *Gymnasium 84*. 519–541.

—1987. „Plinius-Studien. III. Die Villa als geistiger Lebensraum (1,3; 1,24; 2,8; 6,31; 9,36)", *Gymnasium 94*. 247–262.

—1988. „Plinius-Studien IV. Die Naturauffassung in den Beschreibungen der Quelle am *Lacus Larius* (4,30), des Clitumnus (8,8) und des *Lacus Vadimo* (8,20)", *Gymnasium 95*. 236–269.

—2009. *Vom Römertum zum Ästhetizismus. Studien zu den Briefen des jüngeren Plinius*. Berlin.

LUDOLPH, MATTHIAS 1997. *Epistolographie und Selbstdarstellung. Untersuchung zu den ‚Paradebriefen' Plinius' des Jüngeren*. Classica Monacensia 17. Tübingen.

MANUWALD, GESINE 2003. „Eine ‚Schule' für Novum Comum (*epist.* 4,13)", in: CASTAGNA; LEFÈVRE 2003. 203–217.

MARCHESI, ILARIA 2008. *The Art of Pliny's Letters. A Poetics of Allusion in the Private Correspondence*. Cambridge.

MAYER, ROLAND 2003. „Pliny and *gloria dicendi*", *Arethusa 36*. 227–234.

MCKAY, ALEXANDER G. 1972. „Vergil's Glorification of Italy (Georgics II.136–74)", in: MARTYN, JOHN R.C. (Hrsg.). *Cicero and Virgil. Studies in Honour of Harold Hunt*. Amsterdam. 159–161.

MRATSCHEK, SIGRID 1984. „*Est enim ille flos Italiae*. Literatur und Gesellschaft in der Transpadana", *Athenaeum N.S. 62*. 154–189.

—2003. „*Illa nostra Italia*. Plinius und die Wiedergeburt der Literatur in der Transpadana", in: CASTAGNA; LEFÈVRE 2003. 219–241.

MÜLLER, WOLFGANG G. 1985. „Der Brief", in: WEISSENBERGER, KLAUS (Hrsg.), *Prosakunst ohne Erzählen. Die Gattungen der nicht-fiktionalen Kunstprosa.* Tübingen. 67–87.

OSTROWSKI, JANUSZ A. 1991. *Personifications of Rivers in Greek and Roman Art.* Warschau; Krakau.

PANOUSSI, VASSILIKI 2003. „Virgil and Epic topoi in Lucan's Massilia", in: THIBODEAU, PHILIP; HASKELL, HARRY (Hrsg.). *Being There Together. Essays in Honor of Michael C.J. Putnam on the Occasion of his Seventieth Birthday.* Afton, Minnesota. 222–239.

PAUSCH, DENNIS 2004. *Biographie und Bildungskultur. Form und Funktion von Personendarstellungen bei Plinius dem Jüngeren, Gellius und Sueton.* Berlin; New York.

RADICKE, JAN 2003. „Der öffentliche Privatbrief als ‚Kommunizierte Kommunikation' (Plin. *epist.* 4,28)", in: CASTAGNA; LEFÈVRE 2003. 23–34.

RÜHL, MEIKE 2009. *Ciceros Korrespondenz als Medium literarischen und gesellschaftlichen Handelns.* Habilitationsschrift Göttingen.

RÜPKE, JÖRG 2001. *Die Religion der Römer. Eine Einführung.* München.

—2001 a. „Religiöse Kommunikation im provinzialen Raum", in: SPICKERMANN, WOLFGANG (Hrsg.). *Religion in den germanischen Provinzen Roms.* Tübingen. 71–88.

—2001 b. „Antike Religionen als Kommunikationssysteme", in: BRODERSEN 2001. 13–30.

—2009. „Kult auf dem Land. Antik-juristische und modern-religionswissenschaftliche Konzepte und Wahrnehmungen", in: AUFFARTH, CHRISTOPH (Hrsg.). *Religion auf dem Lande. Entstehung und Veränderung von Sakrallandschaften unter römischer Herrschaft.* Potsdamer Altertumswissenschaftliche Beiträge 28. Stuttgart. 247–261.

—2012. „Rituelle Uniformität und individuelle Distinktion. Eine ritualtheoretische Perspektive auf Altarweihungen", in: BUSCH, ALEXANDRA; SCHÄFER, ALFRED (Hrsg.). *Römische Weihealtäre in Tempeln und Heiligtümern.* Frankfurt (im Druck).

SCHEER, TANJA 2001. „Die Götter anrufen. Die Kontaktaufnahme zwischen Mensch und Gottheit in der griechischen Antike", in: BRODERSEN 2001. 31–56.

SCHEID, JOHN 1993. „*Lucus, nemus.* Qu'est-ce qu'un bois sacré?", in: BROISE, HENRI; SCHEID, JOHN (Hrsg.). *Les bois sacrés. Actes du Colloque International organisé par le Centre Jean Bérard et l'École Pratique des Hautes Etudes (Ve section). Naples 23–25 Novembre 1989.* Bonn, Collection de Centre Jean-Bérard 10. 13–20.

—1996. „Pline le Jeune et les sanctuaires d'Italie. Observations sur les lettres IV.1, VIII.8 et IX.39", in: CHASTAGNOL, ANDRÉ; DEMOUGIN, SÉGOLÈNE; LEPELLEY, CLAUDE (Hrsg.). *Splendissima civitas. Études d'histoire Romaine en Hommage à Francois Jacques.* Paris. 241–258.

SCHMID, IRMTRAUD 1988. „Was ist ein Brief? Zur Begriffsbestimmung des Terminus ‚Brief' als Bezeichnung einer quellenkundlichen Gattung", in: WOESLER, WINFRIED (Hrsg.). *Editio. Internationales Jahrbuch für Editionswissenschaft Bd. 2.* Tübingen. 1–7.

SHERWIN-WHITE, ADRIAN N. 1966. *The Letters of Pliny*. Oxford.

SOKOLOWSKI, FRANCISZEK 1962. *Lois sacrées des cités Grecques. Supplement*. École Francaise d' Athènes. Travaux et mémoires des anciens membres étrangers de l'école et de divers savants 11. Paris.

VEYNE, PAUL 1983. „,*Titulus praelatus*'. Offrande, solennisation et publicité dans les ex-voto Gréco-Romains", *Revue archéologique 18, 7. Ser.* 281–300.

VOEGTLE, SIMONE 2011. „'*Admiror, paries, te non cecidisse ruinis*'. Karikaturen und Graffiti als Medium der Kommunikation im städtischen Raum", in: MUNDT, FELIX (Hrsg.). *Kommunikationsräume im kaiserzeitlichen Rom. Internationale Tagung 24. bis 28. Februar 2010*. Berlin; New York (im Druck).

WEDENIWSKI, ESTHER 2006. *Antike Beschreibung von Tempeltüren. Vergil Georgica 3, Properz 2,31, Vergil Aeneis 6, Ovid met. 2, Valerius Flaccus 5 und Silius Italicus 3*. Marburg.

Four Letter-writers: Religion in Pliny, Trajan, Libanius, and Julian

Veit Rosenberger

Ancient authors considered letters as 'mirrors of the soul'.[1] Therefore, letters might be helpful evidence in the search for traces of 'individualization' or 'individuation' in antiquity.[2] This paper focuses on the letters of Pliny, Trajan, Libanius, and Julian. It needs no explanation that such an approach involves serious methodological questions, if not insurmountable problems. i. Quantity and quality: in the case of Pliny and Trajan, we have a set of 121 letters; the correspondence between Julian and Libanius is much smaller; Libanius produced more than 1500 surviving letters. In some cases, it is doubtful whether a letter was actually written by its supposed author, letters might be regarded as genuine or as forgery.[3] The corpus of the letters of Julian or of Libanius differs in every edition; it can be a difficult task to find a letter from the *Loeb* edition in the *Tusculum* series or in the respective volume of the *Collection Budé*. ii. Letters mirror highly various communicative situations: a letter to a friend is quite different from a letter to the emperor, which might go through many hands until finally read aloud to the ruler; some of the texts in the editions of Julian's letters are edicts sent to his subjects. Pliny wrote to the emperor as *legatus Augusti* in a Roman province, Libanius as a professor of rhetoric. Furthermore, one has to be aware of the thorny field of 'private' and 'public' in ancient letters, of letters originally written or later revised to be published to a wider audience, of posthumous publications of letters. iii. Letters are only a fraction of the literary production of our authors. It might seem unbalanced to ignore Pliny's *Panegyricus*, Libanius's speeches, Trajan's rescripts, Julian's Misopogon,

---

1 Demetrios, *Peri hermeneias* 227. On the ancient epistolographic tradition cf. DICKEY 1996; THRAEDE 1970; WHITE 1986; STOWERS 1986; EDWARDS 2005, 270–283; DRECOLL 2006; LAURENCE 2006; CORBINELLI 2008.

2 GRAF 2009, critizises that 'individualization' is too vague, because it describes everything and nothing. Since Graf writes about the modern world, we might feel safe from Graf's verdict for the moment.

3 E.G. VAN NUFFELEN 2001, 131–150.

imperial coins and inscriptions, to name but a few. By confining my research to the genre of letters, I hope to shed unusual and fresh light on
the views of the four authors. To some degree, all four writers belong to
the Second Sophistic or its aftermath: the knowledge of Greek, the importance of paideia is paramount to them – with the exception of Trajan: his letters to Pliny are short and technical; but as a member of the
elite, Trajan knew his Greek, too.

Taking into account all these methodological problems, there are
quite a number of utterances about religion in the letters of Pliny, Trajan, Libanius and Julian. Writing about a quarter of a millennium after
Pliny and Trajan, Libanius and Julian witnessed a changed religious
world. While Pliny and Trajan still lived in the heydays of the pagan
cults, Libanius and Julian had to defend their paganism – *hellenismos*,
as Julian would say – against the omnipresent Christians. Because
'changes' can indicate the phenomenon of 'individualization', the analysis of the four authors promises to be fruitful. This paper attempts to
show an intensification of 'individuality' in the letters of Julian compared to the other three writers. The first chapter shall deal with
Pliny and Trajan; the second chapter examines religion in the letters
of Libanius and Julian.

1 Pliny and Trajan

It is hard to trace 'individuation' or 'individuality' in the letters of the
Younger Pliny. Although Pliny has strong opinions about Domitian,
about the heroes of the elite opposition against the tyrant, or about
the importance of *Bildung*, he hardly ever leaves the mainstream of
the senatorial and philosophical discourse about how to lead a proper
life. Pliny's letters underline the importance of their author, they
show him as part of a network of educated men including Suetonius,
Tacitus and Trajan. There is no space to mark a difference between
Pliny and his correspondents. And yet, some aspects of religion are rather telling. Pliny's letters are, as JOHN HENDERSON remarked, 'oceanic' in
scope – and can therefore be interpreted in various ways[4]. In the Early
Modern period, Pliny's confession became an issue: The edition of *C.
Plinii Caecilii Secundi Epistolae et Panegyricus*, by CHRISTOPH CELLARIUS,
Leipzig 1700, contains a *iudicium, quo Christianum eum non fuisse, ut vol-*

---

4   On Pliny's letters in general: LUDOLPH 1997; RADICKE 1997, 447–469.

unt alii, ostenditur. For early modern authors, it was an important question whether Pliny was a Christian or not. In the eyes of G. Boissier Pliny treated the gods with the greatest respect: 'Pline ne parle jamais des dieux qu'avec le plus grand respect, et il ne paraît pas qu'autour de lui il y eût beaucoup d'incrédules.'[5] Contrary to this, we find in the Zürich dissertation of Hans-Peter Bütler, that the gods were hardly important in Pliny's letters: 'Die Bedeutung der Götter innerhalb der thematisch so umfassenden und vielfältigen plinianischen Briefsammlung ist... ziemlich gering'.[6]

Although Pliny gives no advice about orthopraxy, he clearly announces that superstition is wrong. His personal enemy, M. Aquilius Regulus, worked also as advocate. Regulus was Quaestor under Nero and passed the *cursus* up to the praetorship.[7] Regulus is described as extremely superstitious and greedy. Once he visited a wealthy and sick widow, made her horoscope and concluded that she would live on; to be on the safe side, he also consulted a haruspex (of the cheap sort), who came to the same conclusion. The widow died soon after, not without having granted Regulus a part of her money (2,20,6). At another time, Regulus asked a haruspex how fast he could make a fortune of 60 million sesterces (2,20,13 f.). In the town of Hippo in North Africa, a dolphin befriended some boys. It swam with them and even came to the shore to rest in the sand for some time. The animal became an attraction; people gathered to see and touch it. Octavius Avitus, the legate of the governor of Africa, anointed the dolphin, because he regarded it as a god. Pliny denounces this as performed *religione prava*. Funnily enough, the poor fish fled from the unknown smell of the oil.[8]

In some letters Pliny writes about dreams. He refers to the deceased Gaius Fannius, who was engaged in writing the lives of those who were put to death or banished by Nero. Fannius had already finished three books, in an unadorned and accurate Latin, when he had a strange dream: He was dressed for study and had his writing desk before him, when Nero came, sat down and took the first book which Fannius had written. Nero rolled up the whole volume, then he did the same with Fannius' other two books. After that Nero left. Fannius interpreted the dream that he would only live to write the first three books of his

---

5   Boissier 1878, 171.
6   Bütler 1970, 10.
7   Syme 1958, 101 f.; Sherwin-White 1966, 93.
8   Plin. *ep.* 9,33,9.

project. And so it proved.[9] Pliny does not criticise this story as superstitious. He comments it with an almost epicurean remark: 'Let us do our
best, therefore, while life lasts, that death may find as few works of ours
as possible for him to destroy'. There seems to be a connection between
dreams or visions and literary production: Pliny the Elder wrote 20
books about wars with the Germans, because the deceased Drusus
told him to do so in a dream.[10] In the famous letter to Suetonius
about the meaning of dreams, Pliny quotes a warning dream he once
had; he ignored the warning and was successful.[11] There is a method behind this ambiguity: others may believe in their dreams, but an educated
man will not allow a dream the power to change his plans. History offered enough examples of successful men who interpreted a dream to
their advantage.

In a letter to Fabatus, the grandfather of his wife, Pliny announces
his visit. On the way to Fabatus, there will be only a short delay in Tifernum Tiberinum. The citizens of that town had selected Pliny as their
patronus when he was still very young. Pliny wanted to give back some
of the respect he had earned at Tifernum Tiberinum, and decided to
build a temple at his own expense. He explains to Fabatus: 'Now that
it is completed it would be hardly respectful to the gods to put off its
dedication any longer. So we shall be present on the dedication day,
which I have arranged to celebrate with a banquet.'[12] The point of
this story is that Pliny does not waste a single word on the god for
whom he had built the temple. From the letter it is clear that Fabatus
did not know about the temple before. Two conclusions are possible.
First, Pliny had no religious feelings at least in this case. He paid for
the temple and received the proper honours in the delicate game of a
patronus and his *clientes*. Second, applying the concept of individuality,
new aspects turn up. Being a member of the elite competing for social
capital Pliny was extremely eager to have an inscription at the temple
mentioning his name – and quite probably also the name of the deity.

9 Plin. *ep.* 5,5.
10 Plin. *ep.* 3,5,4. One example of the reception of this topos might be sufficient:
    FREUD 1942, 13 mentions that the elder Scaliger, while writing a poem about
    the famous men of Verona, dreamt of one person named Brugnolus who com-
    plained to be forgotten; the poet inserted some verses about him. When Sca-
    liger's son came to Verona many years later, he learnt that Brugnolus really
    had existed.
11 Plin. *ep.* 1,18.
12 Plin. *ep.* 4,1.

In another letter he plans to donate the statue of an old man to the temple of Iuppiter in Comum: Pliny takes care that the statue gets the appropriate base of noble marble containing *nomen meum honoresque*.[13] The box-shrubs in his villa were cut so that they would spell his name.[14] Such a *titulus* can be understood in the terms of competitive individuality and of representative individuality. The name of Pliny was eternally connected to the name of the god.[15] Opting for a special deity was a way to display a choice and therefore a sort of individuality. What Pliny certainly did in Tifernum Tiberium by setting up an inscription was not worth to be mentioned in the rather private medium of a letter. Names and inscriptions play a significant role in the grave monuments. Pliny muses about a tomb and the proper inscription: 'Everyone who has done some great and memorable deed should, I think, not only be excused but even praised if he wishes to ensure the immortality he has earned, and by the very words of his epitaph seeks to perpetuate the undying glory of his name.'[16] Although we might doubt whether this belongs to the field of 'individualization', it is worth mentioning because a significant number of Cicero's letters bring to light his efforts to find the proper place for a grave-monument.

In another case, Pliny actually names the god. There was an old temple of Ceres on his property. He was admonished by the *haruspices* to rebuild it, 'for it is certainly very old and too small considering how crowded it is on its special anniversary, when great crowds gather there from the whole district on 13 September and many ceremonies are performed and vows made and discharged.'[17] Again, there is no word about a special relation to the god, but this time he gives us the name of the god. He acts not *sua sponte*, but *haruspicum monitu*. This resembles an old religious term, often to be found in the context of the expiation of prodigies in republican times.[18] Therefore, it is likely that Pliny had

---

13   Plin. *ep.* 3,6; cf. 5,11; 6,10; 8,6; 8,10; 9,23.
14   Plin. *ep.* 5,6,35.
15   Cf. Plin. *ep.* 2,7
16   Plin. *ep.* 9,19,3: Omnes ego, qui magnum aliquid memorandumque fecerunt, non modo venia, verum etiam laude dignissimos iudico, si immortalitatem, quam meruere, sectantur victurique nominis famam supremis etiam titulis prorogare nituntur.
17   Plin. *ep.* 9,39; cf. SCHEID 1995, 424–432; BRACONI/UROZ SÁEZ 2007, 129–144.
18   Livy 1,31,4; 25,16,3; *haruspicum iussu*: Obsequens 3; 25; 56; 70; *haruspicum responso*: Obsequens 29; 43.

asked proper haruspices, not just some wandering priests. A man of Pliny's rank – senator, consul, even augur – would deal with the legitimate religious authorities. Pliny shows his *pietas*, he regards the temple and the precinct as a gathering place, and he seizes the opportunity to demonstrate that he is a good *patronus*: he wants to build porticoes in order to keep people sheltered from rain and sun. In the famous letter about the sanctuary of Clitumnus, Pliny offers an ekphrasis of the temenos: there is clear water, the temple and the image of the god, beautiful trees etc.[19] Of special interest are the numerous inscriptions honouring the spring and the god. Every pillar and every wall is inscribed by the clients of the god. Pliny comments the inscriptions: 'Most of them you will admire, but some will make you laugh – though I know you are really too charitable to laugh at any of them.' The educated visitor, as eager to read the inscriptions as a modern antiquarian, might be tempted to laugh at the texts – probably epigraphical documents recording the healing of a sickness. But his *humanitas* will refrain him from laughing at the naïvety of the texts. In all, if Pliny describes a sanctuary, he is the educated man of culture interested in what the others do there. He shows no religious feelings – and he has no interest in the motivations of the clients to come to the sanctuary.[20] Probably the most personal uttering about religion is in a letter to Valerius Maximus. When a person is sick 'it is then that he remembers the gods and realizes that he is mortal'.[21] That is the time when a man starts to behave like a real philosopher. If deliberate deviance indicates individuality, this case works upside down: sickness, the deviance in health, so to speak, leads to reflections about the gods.

More than once, Pliny prays for the emperor: 'I pray that all success worthy of your reign may accrue to you, and through you to the human race'. 'I beg the immortal gods that so happy an outcome may attend all your projects'.[22] In general, Pliny displays his *pietas* and loyalty towards the emperor.[23] He petitions Trajan to award him the augurate or the status of septemvir, *ut iure sacerdotii precari deos pro te publice possim, quos nunc precor pietate privata*.[24] When Pliny finally was awarded with the augu-

---

19 Plin. *ep.* 8,8: See Egelhaaf-Gaiser, this volume.
20 Scheid 1996, 241–258; Beard 1991, 39–48.
21 Plin. *ep.* 7,26.
22 Plin. *ep.* 10,1 and 10,14; cf. Moralee 2004, 27–30.
23 Plin. *ep.* 10,9.
24 Plin. *ep.* 10,13; cf. 10,17a,2; 10,35; 10, 100 and 102. Cf. Eck 1992, 151–160.

rate, he used the priesthood for his self-fashioning, since his great idol Cicero had also been augur. Another aspect is by far more interesting: Pliny explains that he revers Trajan with his *pietas privata*; the priesthood offers him the possibility to pray for the emperor *pietate publica* – this line of thought seems to be the opposite of 'individualization': Pliny's approach to the imperial cult can be described as 'popularization' of religion – and is thus according to the concept of the 'civic cult'.[25] We know Trajan's letters only through the tradition edited after the death of Pliny. What we have is the tip of an iceberg. In reality, an enormous mass of letters was issued from the imperial offices during the 19-year-reign of Trajan. The emperor answers twice on questions concerning sacred space in Pliny's province Bithynia. In both cases, the ruler gives the subjects, in whose name Pliny had asked, green light to carry out their building activities.[26] In the letter about the Christians, Trajan backs Pliny's strategy, too. For Pliny, the Christian belief was nothing but *superstitio prava, immodica*. There is no utterance of personal religion, no trace of an 'individualization' of religion. This is due not only to the nature of the correspondence between Pliny and the emperor, but also to the pagan world Trajan lived in.

2 Libanius and Julian

Libanius was probably the most prolific letter-writer in antiquity. More than 1500 letters still survive.[27] Although he strongly favoured Julian's religious politics, Libanius does not differ significantly from Pliny when it comes to religion. In the letter to the *praeses Arabiae* Belaios, who persecuted a Christian, Libanius presents the case of Marcus, the bishop of Arethusa in Syria. He had been responsible for the destruction of a temple and was severely punished. He was racked and flogged, his beard was plucked out. Marcus endured the punishment and gained enormous prestige; Libanius warns Belaios to produce another Christian martyr.[28] In a letter to Quintus Aurelius Symmachus, Libanius remembers how he and Symmachus' father made vows for young Symma-

---

25   Cf. Noreña 2007, 239–277.
26   Plin. *ep.* 10,50; 10,72; cf. 10,76.
27   Wiemer 1995; Wöhrle 1995, 71–89; Fatouros 1996, 114–122.
28   819 F = Loeb 103 = Tusculum 51; Rosen 2006, 309.

chus.[29] As professor of rhetoric, Libanius had many students, some of them Christians. His most famous pupil was John Chrysostomos. When Amphilochios, another student of Libanius, became bishop of Iconium the teacher congratulated in a polite letter. It is worth mentioning that Libanius does not use the word 'bishop/episkopos'; he describes Amphilochios simply as a good orator with the ability to move his audience. For Libanius, it seems to make no difference if one moves people as a pagan rhetorician or as bishop. He certainly regards Amphilochios not as a dissident.[30]

Quite a dissident – Apostata – was the emperor Julian in the eyes of the Christians, because he gave up the Christian faith. His deviance from the course of his predecessors was substantial and therefore needed explanation. In his letters, Julian reaches a discursive level about religion and about his decisions far beyond everything we have from Pliny, Trajan, and Libanius.[31] The debate about the exact moment of Julian's apostacy, when he gained sole power or long before, shall be of no interest for us. As emperor, Julian confessed to be a pagan, or in his words, a 'Hellenist'.[32] He was the first to use the ethnicon 'Hellenist, Hellenismos' in a strictly religious sense, to distinct the worshippers of the pagan gods from the Christians, some of which also maintained to be good Greeks with a decent *paideia*.[33] In inscriptions, Julian was hailed as *restitutor libertatis et religionis Romanae*.[34] It is probably too harsh to judge that his efforts 'were largely divisive and served to fuel the rising tide of intolerance'.[35] Some of the letters are not private letters, but rather laws or decisions sent to a particular city in order to solve a specific problem. Since religion is omnipresent in the letters of Julian, we are in the comfortable situation to make a selection, to look for hints of changes in the traditional religious patterns. The utterings of the emperor regarding religion belong to the field of representative individuality. Julian fulfilled his religious role by taking seriously the gods which had made Romans and Greeks the masters of the world; furthermore, the

29 1004 F = Loeb 177 = Tusculum 63.
30 1543 F=Loeb 144=Tusculum 74. Some editors regarded the letter as forged, see FATOUROS/KRISCHER 1980, 467 f.
31 Cf. MASTROCINQUE 2007, 391 f.
32 On Julian, cf. ROSEN 2006; SCHÄFER 2008.
33 In the New Testament, 'Hellenes' is a synonym for 'gentiles'. ATHANASSIADI 1992, 122–131; BOUFFARTIGUE 1992, 658–661; ROSEN 2006, 242 f. and 301 f.
34 CIL 8,4326=ILS 752.
35 So SALZMAN 2007, 118. Cf. CANCIK 2009, 372.

ruler tried to live an exemplary life by breaking the usual pagan silence and writing about his religious practices.

Again and again, Julian claims that the gods order him to act. Julian was proclaimed Augustus by his troops in Gaul in 360. Seemingly reluctant, he accepted the honour. In the next year he was ready to fight Constantius, but the emperor died, leaving Julian as the sole ruler. In a letter to his uncle, he invokes Helios and Zeus as witnesses that he never wanted to kill Constantius. 'Why then did I come? Because *the gods expressly ordered me*, and promised me safety if I obeyed them, but if I stayed, what I pray no god may do to me!' (9; 5,382). The dream which Julian describes in his letter to Oribasius of Pergamon is perfectly within the usual set of dreams prophesying the throne.[36] In a letter to the philosopher Maximus, Julian explains again how the gods urge him to act:

> Above all, it is right that you should learn how I became all at once conscious of the very presence of the gods ... I worship the gods openly, and the whole mass of the troops who are returning with me worship the gods. I sacrifice oxen in public. I have offered to the gods many hecatombs as thank-offerings. The gods command me to restore their worship in its utmost purity, and I obey them, yes, and with a good will. For they promise me great rewards for my labours, if only I am not remiss.

In another letter, Julian pronounces: 'the gods told to keep everything sacred as good as I can (κελεύουσιν οἱ θεοὶ τὰ πάντα ἁγνεύειν εἰς δύναμιν) – and I obey them on my own accord'.[37] Julian offers insights into his religious feelings.

At Beroia, he sacrificed to Zeus and then discussed with the members of the city-council about the worship of the gods. Although they applauded his arguments, only very few of them were convinced by the emperor. And they had the same views about religion as Julian anyway (24 = 399D–400 A). When Julian came to Batnae, he smelled frankincense and saw the victims ready for sacrifice. Nevertheless, he was not content with the situation:

> But though this gave me very great pleasure, nevertheless it looked to me like overheated zeal, and alien to proper reverence for the gods. For things

---

36 WEBER 2000, 215–222.
37 21,415 C. For quotes from Julian, I use the translation by WILMER CAVE WRIGHT in the Loeb edition. Julian writes to the philosopher Eusthatius that their friendship is strong because 'it is inspired by the best education attainable and by our pious devotion to the gods' (44 = 9,416).

that are sacred to the gods and holy ought to be away from the beaten track
and performed in peace and quiet, so that men may resort thither to that
end alone and not on the way to some other business.

This very personal assessment demonstrates the dilemma of the pagan
cults. On the one hand, most rituals gained their power and attraction
because they were publicly performed. On the other hand, Julian prop-
agates a very private religion. It ought to be not in the centres of public
life, but in some place reserved only for the cults. In the same letter, we
learn that Julian sacrificed every day in the evening and again at early
dawn (401B). Again, Julian is probably the first pagan to write about
his sacrificial habits. In a letter to his uncle Julian, the emperor exclaims
that wishes he had more time to pray (29 = 12). Cicero or Pliny would
never mention such a thing in their letters.[38]

Endowed with a good contact to the gods and legitimized by his
own religiousness, Julian wants to introduce some changes in the
pagan world. It is needless to say that many of his ideas derive from
the Christians. Much has been written about this emperor's religious
programme; a few aspects of his ambitious plans shall be sufficient. In
the 'letter to a priest', one of the emperor's longest letters, Julian explains his thoughts about the proper priest. A priest should lead a life
more holy than the political life. 'You must above all exercise philanthropia, for from it result many other blessings, and moreover that
choicest and greatest blessing of all, the good will of the gods'
(289 A). Philanthropia means charity, e.g. to help former prisoners or
to feed the poor. Philanthropia was already for the Neoplatonist Porphyry the foundation of piety.[39] For this aspect, Julian evokes the nature
of Zeus Hetaireios: how can it be that someone worships Zeus Hetaireios – and refuses to give some money to a poor neighbour? According
to Julian, it is necessary to take the epikleses of the gods seriously:
'When I observe this I am wholly amazed, since I see that these titles
(sc. the epikleses) of the gods are from the beginning of the world
their express images, yet in our practice we pay no attention to anything
of the sort' (291 C). Since all people descent from the first humans created by the gods, all people are kindred. Thus, it is only natural to help
others. Julian plans to revive the prestige of the pagan priests, 'because

---

38 Christians talk pagans into conversion (24 = 401C). There are pagans so stead-
    fast that the Christians do not succeed in infecting their sickness (nosos); Julian
    manages to convert a bishop to Hellenismos (35).
39 Porphyry, *Letter to Marcella* 35.

they minister to us what concerns the gods, and they lend strength to the gods' gift of good things to us; for they sacrifice and pray on behalf of all men' (296 B/C). Priests are so important, Julian proceeds, that they should be well-paid and should receive the same honours as the magistrates of the state. Then, the emperor defines a good priest: a priest must be respected, unless he is guilty of a crime. But as long as he 'sacrifices for us and makes offerings and stands in the presence of the gods, we must regard him with respect and reverence as the most highly honoured chattel of the gods' (297 A/B). The letter offers further prescriptions regarding the purity of the priests. Although laws concerning the purity of a priest were not unknown in the ancient world, Julian reaches a new level by defining a canon of writings appropriate for a priest. A priest ought not to read the works of Archilochos or Hipponax, nor should he read works of the Old Comedy. Good authors are Pythagoras, Plato, Aristotle, the school of Chrysippus and Zeno.[40] Parallels to the canonization of the Bible are obvious.

In all, we know much more about the religious beliefs and practices of Julian than of any other pagan.[41] He wrote letters to the Athenians[42] and Antiochians just as Paul wrote letters to the Corinthians and the Ephesians. As the evidence of the papyri shows, it was not unusual to invoke a god in a letter.[43] Formulae like 'I greet you and I pray to all gods for you'[44], or 'first of all, I pray to all gods that everything in your life shall go as you wish'[45], 'if the gods help us'[46] are numerous. Cicero, Pliny or Libanius often use similar phrases, like 'by the gods', 'by Hercules' etc. Julian differs from the other letter-writers by the sheer number of invocations. In almost every letter, we find sayings like 'the gods know' (ἴσασιν οἱ θεοὶ 20=384D), 'the gods bear me witness', 'by the gods'. He uses invocations to corroborate his agenda. By this change in quantity, Julian displays his deviance from his predecessors

---

40 ROSEN 2006, 297 f.
41 The letter to Basileios, by some editors regarded as a letter to Basileios the Great, contains not a word on religion (27 = 381).
42 STENGER 2006, 153–179.
43 Cf. EXLER 1923; DÖLLSTÄT 1934; TIBILETTI 1979; BUZÓN, 1984; CHAPA 1998; NALDINI 1998.
44 PAPATHOMAS 2006, n.1 (2nd/3rd century); cf. P. Brem. 58,4–6 (113–120); BGU I 38, recto 4–6 (2nd/3rd century).; in extenso PAPATHOMAS 2006, 5.
45 P.Oxy. 26,2783 = TIBILETTI 1979, 145; P.Oxy. 42 = TIBILETTI 1979, 147; almost garrulous: P.Oxy. 7,1070 = TIBILETTI 1979, 158.
46 P.Oxy. 42,3069,20 = TIBILETTI 1979, 167.

by his use of the seemingly insignificant phrases: representative individuality in the trifles of epistolography.

Summary

In the ancient world, wealthy individuals could dedicate temples to their favourite gods. One of the earliest examples is Xenophon – he built a temple for Artemis in Skillous because the Artemis of Ephesus had helped him. Pliny the younger paid for a temple as well, but did not mention the god to dwell in it. Although Julian had a favourite god, Helios,[47] he wanted to strengthen all 'Hellenic' cults. While Pliny, Trajan and Libanius do not offer insights into their religious experience, Julian is different: he talks about how the gods ordered him to act and about his religious practices; he gives us some insights about his concept of religion on the discursive level. His philosophical influences, e. g. Iamblichus and Libanios, do not show such decided individualization, because they lacked the ambitious plans of the emperor. We have strong reasons to believe that individualization gained enormous momentum with the rise of Christianity. The numerous martyrs who decided to give up their lives in order to win a better life after their death were powerful role models. In his reaction on the Christians, Julian introduced a part of this religious intensity and representative individuality to the pagan discourse.

Bibliographie

ATHANASSIADI, POLYMNIA 1992. *Julian: An Intellectual Biography*, 2nd ed. London/New York.
BEARD, MARY 1991. "Ancient Literacy and the function of the written word in Roman religion", in: BEARD, MARY et al. (ed.). *Literacy in the Roman World*. Ann Arbor. 35–58.
BOISSIER, GASTON 1878. *La religion romaine d'Auguste aux Antonins*, 2ieme éd. Paris.
BOUFFARTIGUE, JEAN 1992. *L'empereur Julien et la culture de son temps*. Paris.
BRACONI, PAOLO; UROZ SÁEZ, JOSÉ 2007. "Il tempio della tenuta di Plinio il Giovane in Tuscis", in: CIARDIELLO, ROSARIA (ed.). *La villa romana*. Naples. 129–144.

---

47 Julian, *Hel.* 130C-131 A; ROSEN 2006, 54–63.

BÜTLER, HANS-PETER 1970. *Die geistige Welt des jüngeren Plinius: Studien zur Thematik seiner Briefe.* Heidelberg.

BUZÓN, RODOLFO 1984. *Die Briefe der Ptolemäerzeit: Ihre Struktur und ihre Formeln.* Diss. Heidelberg.

CANCIK, HUBERT 2009. "Religionsfreiheit und Toleranz in der späteren römischen Religionsgeschichte (zweites bis viertes Jahrhundert n. Chr.)", in: CANCIK, HUBERT; RÜPKE, JÖRG (edd.). *Die Religion des Imperium Romanum.* Tübingen.

CHAPA, JUAN 1998. *Letters of Condolence in Greek Papyri,* Pap.Flor. 29, Florence.

CORBINELLI, SILVIA 2008. *Amicorum colloquia absentium: La scrittura epistolare a Roma tra comunicazione quotidiana e genere letterario.* Naples.

DICKEY, ELEANOR 1996. *Greek Forms of Address: From Herodotus to Lucian.* Oxford.

DÖLLSTÄT, WALTER 1934. *Griechische Papyrusprivatbriefe in gebildeter Sprache aus den ersten vier Jahrhunderten nach Christus.* Diss. Jena.

DRECOLL, CARSTEN 2006. *Nachrichten in der römischen Kaiserzeit: Untersuchungen zu den Nachrichteninhalten in Briefen.* Freiburg.

ECK, WERNER 1992. "Die religiösen und kultischen Aufgaben der römischen Statthalter in der hohen Kaiserzeit", in: MAYER, MARC; GOMEZ PALLARÈS, J. (edd.). *Religio Deorum. Actas del colloquio internacional de epigrafia. Culto y sociedades en occidente.* Sabadell. 151–160.

EDWARDS, CATHERINE 2005. "Epistolography", in: HARRISON, STEPHEN (ed.). *A Companion to Latin Literature.* Oxford. 270–283.

EXLER, FRANCIS 1923. *The Form of the Ancient Greek Letter of the Epistolary Papyri (3ʳᵈ c. B.C.–3ʳᵈ c. A.D.). A Study in Greek Epistolography.* Diss. Washington D.C.

FATOUROS, GEORGIOS; KRISCHER, TILMAN 1980. *Libanios, Briefe.* Munich.

FATOUROS, GEORGIOS 1996. "Julian und Christus: Gegenapologetik bei Libanios?", *Historia* 45. 114–122.

FREUD, SIGMUND 1942. *Die Traumdeutung.* Gesammelte Werke vol. II, London; reprint Frankfurt 1999.

GRAF, FRIEDRICH WILHELM 2009. *Missbrauchte Götter: Zum Menschenbilderstreit in der Moderne.* Munich.

LAURENCE, PATRICK 2006 (ed.). *Epistulae antiquae IV. Actes du IVe Colloque International "L'Épistolaire Antique et ses Prolongements Européens".* Louvain.

LUDOLPH, MATTHIAS 1997. *Epistolographie und Selbstdarstellung: Untersuchungen zu den "Paradebriefen" Plinius des Jüngeren.* Tübingen.

MASTROCINQUE, ATTILIO 2007. "Creating One's Own Religion: Intellectual Choices", in: RÜPKE, JÖRG (ed.). *A Companion to Roman Religion.* Oxford. 378–391.

MORALEE, JASON 2004. *"For Salvation's Sake": Provincial Loyalty, Personal Religion, and Epigraphic Production in the Roman and Late Antique Near East.* New York/London.

NALDINI, MARIO 1998. *Il Cristianesimo in Egitto: Lettere private nei papiri dei secoli II-IV.* 2nd ed. Fiesol.

NOREÑA, CARLOS F. 2007. "The social economy of Pliny's correspondence with Trajan", *American Journal of Philology* 128. 239–277.

PAPATHOMAS, AMPHILOCHIOS 2006. *Fünfunddreißig griechische Papyrusbriefe aus der Spätantike*, Corpus Papyrorum Raineri, Band 25. Munich/Leipzig.

RADICKE, JAN 1997. "Die Selbstdarstellung des Plinius in seinen Briefen", *Hermes* 125. 447–469.

ROSEN, KLAUS 2006. *Julian: Kaiser, Gott und Christenhasser*. Stuttgart.

SALZMAN, MICHELE RENEE 2007. "Religious Koine and Religious Dissent in the Fourth Century", in: RÜPKE, JÖRG (ed.). *A Companion to Roman Religion*. Oxford. 109–125.

SCHÄFER, CHRISTIAN 2008. (ed.). *Kaiser Julian "Apostata" und die philosophische Reaktion gegen das Christentum*. Berlin et al.

SCHEID, JOHN 1995. "Les espaces cultuels et leur interpretation", *Klio* 77. 424–432.

—1996. "Pline le jeune et les sanctuaires d'Italie", in: CHASTAGNOL, ANDRÉ; LEPELLEY, CLAUDE. *Splendidissima civitas: Études d'histoire romaine en hommage à François Jacques*. Paris. 241–258.

SHERWIN-WHITE, ADRIAN 1966. *The Letters of Pliny 1966*. Oxford.

STENGER, JAN 2006. "Gattungsmischung, Gattungsevokation und Gattungszitat: Julians Brief an die Athener als Beispiel", *Würzburger Jahrbücher für die Altertumswissenschaft* 30. 153–179.

STOWERS, STANLEY K. 1986. *Letter Writing in Greco-Roman Antiquity*. Philadelphia.

SYME, RONALD 1958. *Tacitus*. Oxford.

THRAEDE, KLAUS 1970. *Grundzüge griechisch-römischer Brieftopik*. Munich.

TIBILETTI, GIUSEPPE 1979. *Le lettere private nei papiri greci del III e IV secolo d.C.* Milan.

VAN NUFFELEN, PETER 2001. "Deux fausses lettres de Julien l'Apostat (La lettre aux Juifs, ep. 51 [Wright], et la lettre à Arsacius, ep. 84 [Bidez]", *Vigiliae Christianae* 55. 131–150.

WEBER, GREGOR 2000. *Kaiser, Träume und Visionen in Prinzipat und Spätantike*. Stuttgart.

WHITE, JOHN L. 1986. *Light from Ancient Letters*. Philadelphia.

WIEMER, HANS-ULRICH 1995. *Libanius und Julian*. Munich.

WÖHRLE, GEORG 1995. "Libanios' Religion", *Études Classiques* 7. 71–89.

Index*

Abaris   *82,* 83, 86, *100*
Abba Hilarion (father of monastic
    movement in Palestine)   189
Ablabius   110
Abot   *146,* tractate of   157, *157,*
    163
Abraham   6, 145–171, 180, 194
Acheloos   30
Acousmatics   78
Adam   157, 159, 163–165, 168
Aedesius   *100,* 107–108, 110
aemulatio   204; *see also* imitation
Aesculapius   14
agency   138, 153, 155, 159; divine
    127; moral   147–148, 151–
    153, 155, 160; religious   120,
    124, 130, 137, 140
agent   14, 57, 126, 128, 154; indi-
    vidual   3; moral   159, 164
Alexandrian Fathers   188
Ambrose (bishop of Milan)   193–
    194
Ammonius   90
Amphilochios (student of Libanius)
    254
Anthony (of Egypt, Father of All
    monks)   166, 188, 194
Antoninus (son of Sosipatra)   *100,*
    107, *110,* 112
Apamea   76,90
Apollo   13, 16, 20, 22, 28–29; Hy-
    perborean   82, 83; Stephane-
    phoros   22
Apollonius of Perga   21
Apollonius of Tyana (Life of)   90,
    93, 106, 110, 194
Appollonios of Delos   29
Apollonos   *20,* 55

Apuleius   105, 197
aqedah   147, 151, 159, 170, 171
Aquilius Regulus, M. (Quaestor under
    Nero)   249
Archedamos at Vari   4, 16–19, 21,
    28–29, 31
archetypal figures   145; function
    147
Archilochos   257
Aristeas of Proconnesus   86
Aristotle   75, 82, 189, 257
Aristoxenus of Tarentum   75, *75*
Artemidoros of Thera   4, 21–22, 24
    fig. 3–4, 25 fig. 5–6, 26 fig. 7, 26,
    29, 31, 37, 40
Artemis Aristobule   28, 33; of
    Ephesus   4, 11–15, 19, 28, 258;
    Lecho   30; Pergaia   26; at
    Skillous   258
asceticism   6, *50,* 77, 121, *124,* 132,
    134, 140, 176, 177, 180, 190
Asclepius   14, 20, 28, 29, *34,* 38, 40
Athen   11–14, 19, 28, 31–36, 38,
    40, 76
Athena   103; Hygieia   34; Nike
    34
Attica   16–18, 28, 29, 31, 32, 38
audience   44, 46–48, 50, 51, 53, 54,
    56, 60, 62, 100, 131, 135–139,
    160, 247, 254
Augustine   187, 192–197, 199–
    202, 206, 208
authority   48, 49, 51, 169, 203, 204,
    206; apostolic   55; bishop
    124; church   179; episcopal
    202; epic   203; poetry   204;
    God's   162–163; of Gregory,
    bishop of Nyssa   139; of Gre-

---

*   Compiled by Elisa Groff. Italics refer to notes only.

gory Thaumaturgus, bishop of
Neocaesarea   129, 138; in a Jesus-community   63; religious
133, 140; spiritual   122; textual   197, 201–205
authorship   109, 137, 141; of Gregory Thaumaturgus   *121;* of
laudatory accounts   137; Pauline   *44,* 46
autobiography   194

Bahareno   232
Bar Kapra   163
Barnabas (apostle to Antioch and Cyprus)   102, 149
Batnae   255
behaviour   62; de-traditionalized
2; deviant   2, *81;* devotional
50; identify   2; ethical   64, 77;
individual   74; religious   84,
85, 119; ritual   87
Beirut   126, 128, 137
Belaios   253
Bendis   14, 35, *35*
Beroia   255
biography   77, 80, 101, 119, 124;
panegyrical   5, 130
Bithynia   253
body   5, 52, 54, 57–60, 62–63, 113,
115, 139, 140, *164,* 165–167,
177–178, 183, 196, 201; association body-church   57–58; of
Christ   44, 53, 60–63; cult of
90
Bona Dea   212
Book, new attitude to   6, 175, 177,
180–189, 194–198, 201–202,
205–206; religion of   180, 182,
188; Sybilline   198; *see also* text;
writing
Byblos   84

Caesarea   121–122, 125–128, 131,
137–138, 191
Caesarea Maritima   186
Cappadocia   120–124, 131, 139,
141–143
Carmel Mt.   89

Cassian   189
Cassiodorus   187
Cephissus (Greek river god)   28, 30
Chaldean   104, 105, *110, 115,* 158,
196
Charites   20
Cholleidai   30
Christians   6, *136,* 145, 147, 152,
181–187, 198, 201, 206, 248,
253–258
Christianity   6, 7, *80,* 81, 88–89,
120–121, 124–125, *136,* 138,
141, 145–146, 152, 165, 167,
175, 177, 179–186, 194, 196,
206, 258
Christology   56
Chrysanthius (teacher of Emperor Julian)   107, 112
Chrysippus (Greek Stoic philosopher)   *76,* 257
Cicero, M. Tullius   193, 197, 200–
203, 251, 253, 256–257
Cimon (Athenian statesman)   32–33
Circe   113
Claros, oracle of   115, 228
Clement of Alexandria   *56,* 188
clerics   121
Clitumnus (in Umbria)   6, 7, 209–
214, 217, 219–239, 252
coenobia (communities of ascetics)
176 *see also* community
Colossians letter to the   4, 43–64
communication   7, 184, 210, 214–
217, 230–233, *236,* 239–241; by
letter   211, 215–217, 229–230;
personal   56, 229; religious
210–211, 222, 229–230, 239–
240; with the divine   85, 167–
168
community   47–49, 58, 63, 85, 90,
132, 138–141, 176, 182, 187–
188, 195, 197; ascetics   176, *see
also coenobia;* Christian   49, 148,
179–182, 187; interpretive
182; Jesus   48, 63; monastic   6,
181, 188, 189; Pythagorean   75,
87; reading   181, 186, 195; re-

ligious   176, 187; textual   181, 189, 194–195, 200
concentration of the mind   6, 189
Constantine Emperor   76, 89, 110, 165, 179, 206
Corinthians letter to the   47, 52, 59, 61, 257
corpus Hermeticum   196
crisis as reason for a *votum* or cult foundation   36, 216, 241; spiritual   193 *see also votum* and cult foundation
Croton   78–82, 88
cult   12, 14–16, 18, 30–37, 227; civic   253; foundation of   4, 11–38, 132, 175, *see also* crisis; individual   4; democratisation of cult to help paganism's transformation   91–92; funerary   15; Hellenic   258; imperial   253; local   121, 132, 223, 226, *see also* local; mystery   105; pagan   248, 256; places   11, 13–21, 27–33, 35–37, 222, 228, 233; private   184, 256; public   184, 295; religion   180; specificity   224; traditions   14, 226
Cybele   20
Cyril bishop of Jerusalem   184
Cyprus   20, 29, 31

Deborah, song of   150
dedication of temples   199; day   250
de-individualization   1
Delos   28, 29, 32
Delphi   13, 22, 27, 82, *87, 106,* 115, 227–228 *see also* Apollo
Democritus (pre-Socratic philosopher)   75, *75,* 84
de-traditionalization   1, 2
deviance   252, 254, 257; religious   2
*devotio moderna*190
Dicaearchus (Greek philosopher)   75, *75*
Didyma   115, 228

Diogenes Laertius (biographer of the Greek philosophers)   *75,* 195
Dioscuri   22, *27, 29*
divination   86, 106, *111,* 114; power of   115, *see also* power
Divinity   7, 83, 106, 108, 111, 136–137, *see also enthousiasmos*
Domitian Emperor   106, 248

Egypt   84, 89, *112, 157,* 163, 166, 167, 176, 181, 188, 189, 197
Eileithyia   30
Eleusis   35, 84, 105
Elijah   89
embodiment   47
Empedocles (Greek pre-Socratic philosopher)   84
Ennius, Quintus (Latin writer)   203
Enthousiasmos („filled with divinity")   106, 107, 110, 114, 115 *see also* divinity
Epaphras   48, 56
Ephesians letter to   47–49, 53, 61, 257
Ephesus   49, 101, 258
epic 203
Epictetus (Stoic philosopher)   189
Epicureanism   201
eschatology Pauline   4, 44, 47, 51, 52, 64
Essenes   176
Euhemerus (Greek mythographer)   203
Eunapius   5, 76, *76,* 99–116, 195
eusebeia   80, 85, 112, *see also pietas* and piety
Eusebius (bishop of Caesarea)   107, 121–122, 186
Eustathius (Sosipatra's husband)   *100,* 101, 104, 107–108, 110
Evagrius Ponticus (Christian monk and ascetic)   166
experience authorial   54; of Christ   62; of individuality   54; monastic   166; personal   47; reading of   194; revelatory   197; religious   3, 4, 7, , 43, 54, 55, 197, 258; of the Spirit   47

family   4, 77, 85, 101, 108, 123, 128,
   130–131, 138–139
Fannius, C. 249
Favorinus (Roman sophist)   195
Firmicus Maternus   196, 198
Fortuna   212, *232*
Foucault Michel   146, 176, *194*
Galatiens letter to the   51, 59, 62, 148
Gellius, A. *76,* 195, 201
gender   2, 113
Genesis   147, 148, *148,* 149, *149,*
   151–167, *see also* Rabbah
Gnostic   79, *166,* 180, 183
Graffiti   7, 18, 209, 210, 223, 224,
   230–235, 239–242
Gregory of Nyssa   5, 119–120, 122,
   130, 132–133, 138–142
Gregory Thaumaturgus   5, 119–
   123, 125, 130, 134, 136–141
Hecate   107, 112
Heliodorus   113
Helios   255, 258
Heracleides Ponticus   75
Hercules   257; Curinus   233;
   temple of Hercules Musarum
   202
Hermes   18, 20
Hesiod   198
Hestia   30
Hippo   249
Hipponax (Greek iambic poet)   257
Homer   90, 102–104, 198, 203, *203*
Homonoia   4, 22, 29
Honorius Emperor   210
Horace   200
Hymettos Mt. 16
Hypatia   99, *113*
Iamblichus   5, 7, 71–92, 100–101,
   107–108, 112–115, 195, 258
identity   44, 48, 71, 81, 127, 156,
   179; Christian   179; collecti-
   ve   44, 179; personal   2, 71,
   178; regional   141; religious
   141; social   146, 179
image   11, 209–210, 221–222,
   227–228, 234
Imbros   84

imitation   45, 51, 52, 54, 82, 100,
   204, 229; of Christ   167 *see also*
   aemulatio
individual   54; process   2; religiosity   2; religion   7
individualisation   5, 7, 43, 60, 71, *74,*
   119, 121, 123–125, 128–130,
   133, 135, 137, 141, 200, 247–
   248, 251, 253, 258; process   6,
   71–74, 175–189; religious   1,
   7, 71, 119, 123, 132–133, 137,
   205, 253
individuality   1–5, 43, 46, 48, 52,
   57–58, 64, 71, 74, 77, 80, 83, 91,
   114, 129–130, 138, 248, 250,
   252; competitive   4–5, 74, 91,
   251; moral   4, 74, 92; practical   4; pragmatic   74; reflective   4, 43–45, 48, 55, 64, 71, 74,
   91; religious   2–3, 43, 114;
   representative   4, 44, 74–75, 83,
   89, 92, 251, 254, 258; self-conscious   52; self-reflective   43
individuation   1–2, 56, 58, 71, 247–
   248
initiation   89, 104, 105, 110
innovation   37–38, 240; Christian   182; religious   4; ritual
   3, *see also* tradition
Isis   14, 28, 197, 212
Ithaka   13

John Chrysostomos (Archbishop of
   Constantinople)   254
Josephus   150
Julian emperor   7, 100, *104,* 107,
   112, 116, 247–258
Jupiter   102

Kafizin (Cyprus)   20, 29

Lampon (Greek seer)   35
language   47, 56, 58, 61, 63, 88, 123,
   179, 183, 185, 196, *196,*222, 231;
   conflictual   50; cultic use of
   56; distinctive   56; impersonal   58; kinship   63 *passim;* of

body   63; of self-examination
    80; spoken   185
Laodicea   48
Laurium (Attica)   31
lectio divina   189
Lemnos   84
letter as element of a *votum*   209–242
    passim; as medium to express in-
    dividual religious experience   3,
    43, 209–242, 247–258; of Hor-
    ace   200; Paulinian   4, 43–62
    passim, 193, 196; of Pliny   6, 7,
    200, 209, 213–215, *225,* 228,
    236, 239–241, 247–258 *passim;*
    of priests   199; as response to an
    act of reading   199, 200; of Se-
    neca   200; *see also* writing
Lex sacra / Leges sacrae   13, *13,* 21, 28–
    30
Libanius (Greek teacher of rethoric,
    Sophist)   7, 116, 247–249, 251,
    253–255, 257–258
Licinius Emperor   88
liturgy, spiritualisation of   91
local cults   121, 132, 223, 226; gods/
    relation with the divine   7, 87;
    specificity   48–50; tradition
    3, 14, 123, 131, 138, 140, 226
Logos   83, 180, 195
Longinus (Hellenistic philosophert)
    195
Lucan (Latin poet   113, 203, *214*
Lucian (Greek authort)   *76,* 195
Lucretius (Latin authort)   203
Lycurgus (Lawgiver of Spartat)   36
Lystra (Phrygiat)   102

Maccabees   150, *150,* 151, 153
Mandaeism   180, 206
Manichaeism   180, 196, 206
manuscript copying   121, 153, *160,*
    183, *see also* tradition and writing
Marathon   32
Marcus (bishop of Arethusa, Syria)
    253
Marcus Aurelius Emperor   189
Mater Magna   14
mathematics   778, *79*

Maximus of Ephesus (Neo-platonist
    philosopher)   100, *104,* 106–
    107, 110–112, 115–116, 255
Maximus I 107
Medea   113
Melite   28, 33, *33*
Menippean satire   201
Mercury   102, 212
Midrash   152–153, *154,* 159–164,
    168, 188
Miletus   84
Minucius Felix   198
Mishnah   157, 163
Mnesarchus/Mnemarchus (Pythago-
    ras' father)   82, *82,*
model: Abraham   147; Christian/
    monastic   120–121, 125, 133,
    137, 140, 145, 167, 188, 195, 200,
    258; biblical   133; for moral
    individuality   5, 6, 74, 91, 100,
    101, 114, 116, 205; liturgical
    198; Pauline   51, 55; philoso-
    phical   75, *78,* 81, 84, 90–91;
    Rabbinic-Judaism   145, 147,
    155–156, 159, 165, 168
monks   6, 89, 121, *124,* 166–167,
    175–176, 180, 187–190

Neocaesarea   122, 134
Neocles (Themistocles' father)   31
Neo-Platonists   76–78, *80,* 90, 180
Neo-Pythagoreans   78, 83–85, 88–
    89
Neptune   212
Nero Emperor   249
Nicomachus of Gerasa   *79, 82,* 88
Nigidius Figulus   201
Nisibis (Syria)   187
Numenius of Apamea (Neo-pytha-
    gorean)   78
Nymphaea   16–21, 28; genethlia
    30

Octavius Avitus (Legate of the gover-
    nor of Africa)   249
Olympius of Alexandria   111
Onesagora of Cyprus   29, 31
Oribasius of Pergamon   255

Origen 5, *89,* 90, 119–138, 141–142,
    149, 186, 188
Orpheus   194
Ovid   102, 203

Pachomius (Egypt)   166
Paian   82
Pan god   4, 14, 16–18, 20, *22,* 28,
    32–33
Parthenis (Pythagoras' mother)   82
passivity of body and soul   5, 115,
    126–128; ritual   112–114
Paul 4, 43–64, 102, 148, 193–194,
    196, 257
Pelargikon   35
Pergamon   107, 255
Perga (Anatolia)   21, 26, 29
Phaidimos (bishop of Amaseia)   131,
    140
Pharsalos   16, *18,* 20, 21, *21,* 28, 32
Philemon (addressee of Paul)   45, 48
Philemon and Baucis (married couple
    of Tyana, character of Ovid's
    Metamorphoses)   102
Philippians letter to   45, 46, 52, 56
Philo of Alexandria (Hellenistic Jewish
    philosopher)   165, 196
Philometer (A relative of Sosipatra
    who was in love with her)   107,
    111–112
Philostratus Lucius Flavius (Greek so-
    phist)   90, 195; see also Apol-
    lonios of Tyana
Phoenicia   84
piety   85, 89, 146–147, 150–151,
    153, 155, 159, 165–166, 229,
    231, 252–253, 256, *see also euse-
    beia*
pious   44, 111–112, 154, 159, *255*
    see also *eusebes*
Plato   11, 34–36, 75, *75,* 78, *81,* 84,
    106, 189, 197, 257
Pliny the Younger   6–7, 72, 200,
    247–258
Plotinus (Philosopher)   77, 78, *86,*
    90, 111, 114, 189, 194–195, 197
Plutarch 31, 33–34, *76,* 197

Ponticianus (friend of Augustine)
    194
Porphyry *75,* 77, 78, *86,* 88, 90, 110–
    111, 114, 194, 256
Poseidon   22
power, divine   56, 128–129, 131–
    133, *133,* 134, 136, 139, 142;
    religious   132; ritual   112–113
Praeneste   228, 232
praeparatio philosophica   79
presence, divine   163; of Christ
    62; of God   53, 168; of the
    gods   255, 257
Priscus (Roman diplomat and Greek
    historian)   107, 236
Propertius   *213,* 225, 226
Prudentius   198
pseudepigraphy   4, 43–46, 52, 58–
    59, 64
Pseudo-Philo (author of the *Liber An-
    tiquitatem Biblicarum*)   150
Pythagoras   5, 75–92, *106,* 113,
    194–195, 257
Pythagoreans   75–91, 176, 195
Pythia   82, 110, 227

Qumran   150, 152, *156*

Rabbah Genesis   147, *149,* 153–
    155, *157,* 159–165, 167
Rabbah Numbers   164
reading practices   6, 175–190, 195–
    196, 199, 205–206; silent   181,
    187, 189, 199
religio illicita   182; *prava*   249
religion, traditional form   131–132,
    138–139, 141
religious change   1, 5, 90, 119–120,
    124–125, 141; discourse   203,
    205; personality   3, 19; plurali-
    ty   211, 222–223; practice   6,
    7, 60, 83–84, 88, 123, 130, 132,
    138, 140–141, 195, 255, 258
resurrection   47
Romans letter to   148, *193*

sacrifice   77, 85, *87,* 91–92, 147–
   155, 159, 165, 179, 255, 257; end
   of   6, 91, 176
Salamis   31, 33
Samian   82
Samothrace   84
Serapis (Graeco-Egyptian god)   14,
   28, 32
Selbstcharakterisierung   55, 58
Serapeum   107, 112
Sidon   84
Silius Italicus   225, *229*
Simplicianus (Archbishop of Milan)
   194
Skillous   4, 11–13, 28, 32, 258
Skyron   17, 19
Socrates   75, 105, 204
Sopator   108, 110
Sosipatra   5, *82,* 99–116
Space, sacred   205, 253
Statius, Papinius 225
statue *see* image
student   89–91, 100–101, 107–
   108, 112, 120–126, 129, 132–
   137, 141–142, 254, *see also* teacher
Sulmo   233, *233,* 234
superstition   77, 84, 86, 249–250,
   253
Symmachus, Q. Aurelius   253
Symon (Syrian monk   166

Talmud   164, *168*
Targum   150–154
teacher   49, 79, *82, 83,* 89–91, 103–
   104, 107–108, 119–123, 126–
   127, 129, 135, 138, 194–195,
   254, *see also* student
Telemachus (Odysseus's son)   103
Tertullian   149, 178, 198
text, Latin classics   197, 200; Roman
   theological texts   201; *see also*
   community, textual
Themistocles (Athenian politician and
   general)   28–29, 31–33
Thera   6, 16, 21–23, 26–32, 37
Thessalonians letter to   53, 55
Theurgists   5, *79,* 99, 104, 106, 113–
   115

Tifernum Tiberinum   250
Titus letter to   44
Torah   60–61, 181
tradition   2–7, 37–38, 71, 74, 87,
   89, *89,* 90–91, 108, 121, *122,*
   123, 138, 140, 149, 159, 164–
   165, 167–168, 177, 185, 197,
   201, *203,* 204, 214, 227, 229, 253;
   Christian   151–155, 159, 176,
   183, 185, 201; cult   220; family   135; Jewish   148, 151–
   155, 159, 175; monks   176, 188;
   mystical   190; Paulinian   43–
   62 *passim*; religious   1, 131, 142,
   183, 197–198, 254; Pythagorean   75, *75, 76, 78,* 80, *82;*
   reading   188, 195, *see also* innovation, local and monks
Trajan Emperor   7, 229, 237, 247–
   249, 251–255, 257, 258
Tychicus   49
Tyre (Phoenicia)   84

Umbria   6, 224

Valerius Maximus 252
Vari (Attica)   4, 16–17, 21, 28, 31
Varro, M. Terentius   197, 200–204
Venus Erycina   14
Vergil   225, 226, *226*
Verrius Flaccus (Roman grammari-
   an)   201
Victorinus (translator of Platonic
   books)   194, 196
votum 13, 15, 17–21, 30, 36, 212,
   214–217, 228, 230, 232, 235,
   240–241; altar   212, 233, 241;
   cult   210–212, 215, 229, 232,
   239–240; forms   215, 233;
   image   214, 233, 238, 240; inscription   199, 214, 216, 233,
   240–241; practice   210, 213–
   214, 217, 224, 235; religion   85,
   211; temples   212; texts   17,
   19, 30
vow of friendship   211, 213–214,
   217, 235

writing   6, 248–250; about religious
    practice   255, 257; as explanati-
    on of the religious experience
    166; as core of the new religion
    180, 181, 183, 186–189, 195–
    197; as medium to interpret reli-
    gious life   122, 137–138, 141; as
    part of religious and ritual activi-
    ty   198–206 *passim;* as scope to
    individualize religious life   120,
    122; Jewish sacred   *80;* new
    modality of Pauline   48, 53–54,
    64, *see also* letter; text

Xanthos (slave of Gaius Orbius)   29,
    31
Xenokrateia   28, 29, 30, 31, *31*
Xenophon (Greek historian)   4, 11,
    12, 13, 16, 19, 28–29, 31, 258

Zeno (of Citium, Stoic philosopher)
    257
Zeus   22, 29, 81, 255; Hetaireios
    256; Olympus   22
Zoroastrian   206